THE REAL PEOPLE AND THE
CHILDREN OF THUNDER

Yup'ik, from *yuk*, human being, plus *-pik*, "genuine, real"; literally, "a genuine person"; plural, *Yupiit*, "real people."

There was an old shaman at Napaskiak, who strongly preached against adopting the white man's teaching. His strong point was that the white people were the children of thunder—therefore were not really human. He said—"Everything they do and everything they have is accompanied with noise."—John Henry Kilbuck, Box 7:5, Kilbuck Collection, Moravian Archives.

THE REAL PEOPLE AND THE CHILDREN OF THUNDER

The Yup'ik Eskimo Encounter with Moravian
Missionaries John and Edith Kilbuck

by
Ann Fienup-Riordan

University of Oklahoma Press : Norman and London

Library of Congress Cataloging-in-Publication Data

Fienup-Riordan, Ann.
    The real people and the children of thunder : the Yup'ik Eskimo
encounter with Moravian missionaries John and Edith Kilbuck / by Ann
Fienup-Riordan. — 1st ed.
        p.   cm.
    Includes bibliographical references and index.
    ISBN 0-8061-2329-X
    1. Kilbuck, John, 1861–1922.   2. Kilbuck, Edith, 1865–1933.
3. Yupik, Eskimos—Missions. 4. Moravians—Alaska—Kuskokwim
River Valley—Biography. 5. Alaska Moravian Church. 6. Moravians—
Missions—Alaska—Kuskokwim River Valley. 7. Yupik Eskimos—
Social life and customs. 8. Kuskokwim River Valley (Alaska)—Social life
and customs. I. Title.
E99.E7K4424   1991
266'.46'0922—dc20
[B]   90-50687
                                                                          CIP

Published with the assistance of the National Endowment for the Humanities, a federal agency which supports the study of such fields as history,
philosophy, literature, and languages.

The paper in this book meets the guidelines for permanence and durability of the
Committee on Production Guidelines for Book Longevity of the Council on
Library Resources, Inc. ∞

TO MY THREE THUNDEROUS CHILDREN,
FRANCES, JIMMY, AND NICK

CONTENTS

ACKNOWLEDGMENTS

THIS BOOK COULD not have been written without the help and encouragement of many people. Just when I thought I had finished my work in western Alaska, a research grant from the National Endowment for the Humanities combined with support provided by the Alaska Humanities Forum made me realize I had just begun.

An earlier draft, both individual chapters and the manuscript as a whole, profited immensely from the comments and criticisms of a number of friends and colleagues, including Lydia Black, Tiger Burch, John Bockstoce, Rick Condon, Dick Dauenhauer, Jim Ducker, Robert Fortuine, Sergei Kan, Gary Holthaus, Margaret Lantis, Harry Luden, Susan McKinnon, Elsie Mather, Phyllis Morrow, Terry Mousalimas, Michael Oleksa, Wendell Oswalt, Irene Reed, Louis Renner, Marshall Sahlins, David Schneider, Barbara Smith, Edie Turner, and Jim VanStone. Half the fun of writing is handing your thoughts to good readers and listening to what they have to say. I consider myself very fortunate to have had their help.

A number of institutions and organizations have also contributed to this book. Thanks to the staffs of the Library of Congress, the University of Oregon Archives, and the University of Alaska Anchorage Archives for opening collections to me. Thanks especially to Katherine Arndt for the detailed translations of Russian Orthodox Church records she provided from the Library of Congress microfilms at the University of Alaska Fairbanks Archives. Thanks also to the Alaska Anthropological Association for the many helpful comments members made on versions of chapters 6 and 8 read at annual meetings, and to the editorial staff of the Alaska Historical Society journal, *Alaska History* (especially Jim Ducker) who tirelessly preached the virtues of the active voice in revising chapter 8 for publication.

I also wish to thank Reverend Vernon Nelson of the Moravian Archives in Bethlehem, Pennsylvania, and Reverend Kurt Vitt of the Moravian Seminary in Bethel, Alaska, for comments, encouragement, and advice. I am especially indebted to Reverend Nelson, who answered my first inquiry concerning use of the Kilbuck collection with the name and address of the Kilbucks' granddaughter, Dr. Edith Kilbuck. Dr. Kilbuck subsequently introduced me to the rest of the Kilbuck family and was instrumental in fielding queries throughout the period of writing and research. As a result, what began as a two-week visit to the Moravian Archives to scout out their Kuskokwim collections evolved into one of the most personally engaging projects of my life. The months I spent absorbed in the Kilbucks' journals and letters gave me my first taste of what an archive can communicate about a particular time and place. I hope the small pieces of that archive contained here convey a part of that excitement.

When I began to work with the Kilbuck material, I did not intend to write anything approaching biography. At present, a growing literature calls into question the ethnographic authority of the biographer, whose inevitable selection and "lies of exclusion" are held to be as insidious as those of any ethnographer. The "fiction of realism" is certainly employed when the history of a time and place is framed within the story of a life. Though I agree that objective biography is logically and artistically impossible, I think the conclusion of some that biography should be rejected out of hand is unnecessarily dim. Rather than presenting undigested material as "facts," critical biography can heighten the reader's awareness of the ambiguity of the actions described. Robert Gittings's comment in *The Nature of Biography* best describes my sense of what I was about: "What is perhaps the highest necessity in a biographer . . . is enthusiasm: not necessarily enthusiasm blindly following the person written about, but enthusiasm for the whole daunting pursuit of trying to revive his or her life. It is a task that only the most extreme or even foolhardy enthusiasm can hope to accomplish."

The photographs contained in this book come primarily from the Moravian Archives, with additional prints generously supplied by the Kilbuck family. I would also like to thank James Barker for providing copies of prints from the Moravian Archives and presently in the collection of the Yugtarvik Regional Museum in Bethel. Marion Rioth of Ottawa University in Ottawa, Kansas, kindly engaged West Wilson to photograph a selection of the John and Edith Kilbuck artifact collection, which is at present housed in the university library. Diane Brenner, of the Anchorage Museum of History and Art, also supplied copies of several prints from their Romig collection.

The detailed maps of western Alaska that accompany the text were prepared by Karl Johansen, the great-grandson of John and Edith Kilbuck and a cartographer by profession. His generosity and attention to detail are very much appreciated. Thanks also to Ayse Gilbert for additional line drawings.

For help in the preparation of this book, I am indebted to the word-

processing and editorial skills of Dawn Scott and Judith Brogan, in Anchorage, as well as John Drayton and the editorial staff at the University of
Oklahoma Press. I appreciate both their personal encouragement and attention to technical detail.

Special thanks go the descendants of John and Edith Kilbuck, especially
Ruth Kilbuck Patterson, Margaret Patterson Wade, and Dr. Edith Henry
Kilbuck. Had it not been for their enthusiasm for family history, and their
willingness to share it, mine would have been nipped in the bud. Also
thanks to my Yup'ik friends here in Alaska. Insofar as I have succeeded in
interpreting the interaction between their ancestors and the missionaries who
came to convert them, it is thanks to what they have taught me. Last but not
least, thanks to my parents, my husband, and our three thunderous children,
who also accompany everything with noise.

ANN FIENUP-RIORDAN

THE REAL PEOPLE AND THE CHILDREN OF THUNDER

And this proves that the politics of conversion is no simple expression of conviction.

—Marshall Sahlins, *Islands of History*, p. 37

CHAPTER 1

ANTHROPOLOGISTS, MISSIONARIES, AND NATIVES

ANTHROPOLOGISTS AND MISSIONARIES

> *The Roman Catholics are going to establish on this river, too, and the Russian Priest would rather make friends with us, in preference to standing between two fires.*
>
> —*John Henry Kilbuck, 1892* [1]

Until recently, the position of the anthropologist who chose to study missionaries was comparable to that of the priest "standing between two fires." On the one side, the researcher's anthropological cohorts tended to judge a positive evaluation of the missionaries' role as either unscientific or indefensibly subjective. On the other side stood the missionaries, who feared, perhaps justifiably, that the objectivity of science was not always fairly applied in their case.

The rift between anthropologists and missionaries is long standing. Within anthropological literature, missionaries are a much-maligned group subject to both ambivalence and outright antipathy, as they have come to represent the "quintessential colonial figure" and "an essential part of empire." [2] They are alternately presented as ineffectual blunderers and all-too-effective destroyers of the cultural integrity of the native populations they set out to convert.

As one of the most obvious manifestations of the Western presence, missionaries are an easy target for criticism in the postcolonial era. Of all the parties in the colonial enterprise, missionaries are alternately the most revered and the most condemned. As a result, the question of their role has often been reduced to a value-laden argument as to whether they were self-sacrificing humanitarians or agents of imperialism. Because missionaries are simultaneously "emissaries of Christ and associates of Caesar,"[3] their position is necessarily ambiguous, which often results in blanket condemnation. Anthropologists, dispensing with their usual relativism, simultaneously have presented missionary activity as paving the way for Western civilization and undermining the basis of native society. Whereas anthropologists normally are sympathetic to the native point of view, when their subject is missionaries they are not.

Anthropologists do not stand alone in blaming past missionaries for not having practiced modern missiology. Native peoples lately have joined the fray, lumping missionaries with the atom bomb, air pollution, venereal disease, and other "questionable blessings" of Western civilization.[4] Natives' indictments of past missionary conduct tend to be as polemical as earlier condemnations of "savage" society by non-natives. The past pattern has been reversed, and the present tendency is to exaggerate missionary insensitivity while idealizing traditional native society. The myth of the noble missionary bent on saving savage souls has given way to the myth of the noble native ruined by "meddlesome missionaries."[5]

Until quite recently, the problematic relationship between anthropologists and missionaries was taken for granted and subjected neither to extended public debate nor published comment. During the last decade anthropologists have become increasingly aware that their presuppositions color "facts" observed in the field. From Marshall Sahlins' dictum "there is no ethnography without ethnology," through the more recent "crisis of representation" in anthropology and social science in general,[6] anthropologists have increasingly subjected their attitudes and expectations to self-reflective scrutiny. As part of this process, anthropologists have begun to evaluate how their views of missionaries have affected the ways in which they have described, or more often failed to describe, them.[7] Serious consideration is now given to the ambiguities and contradictions of the missionary persona and why it has taken anthropologists so long to recognize these factors.

A number of reasons has been proposed for the sometimes unstated and sometimes all too clearly articulated hostility between missionaries and anthropologists. One point of contention concerns differences between the anthropological and missionary evaluation of native culture.[8] Missionaries were, by definition, intent on changing, improving, or even eradicating all or part of the "primitive" native culture with which they came into contact. The anthropologists (specifically those of the British structural-functionalist school) saw tradition and society as an organic unity, integrated yet fragile, and thus prone to destruction by aggressive missionaries. This view dominated in the days when anthropologists studied societies as passive victims to the process of Westernization. The "practical reason" of British structural-functionalism now has given way to concern about cultural meaning and to recognition that change can involve a creative exchange, not merely a destructive imposition; nevertheless, it has left a legacy of distrust for the missionaries' *a priori* condemnation of the native point of view.

The hostility that missionaries evoke in anthropologists has also been attributed to the latter's negative view of Christianity, which they have had a "conversion experience" against: "The antipathy of anthropologists toward missionaries lies in the fact that missionaries take seriously and teach other people religious beliefs which the anthropologists have personally rejected."[9] Equally, the unenthusiastic reception anthropologists have sometimes received from missionaries in the field has contributed to a negative evaluation of missionaries in general. Differences in lifestyle, as well as different attitudes toward the relevance and value of the "scientific endeavour," may elicit negative stereotypes on both sides. The result is aptly described by Roger M. Keesing: "The caricatured missionary is a strait-laced, repressed, and narrow-minded Bible thumper trying to get native women to cover their bosoms decently; the anthropologist is a bearded degenerate given to taking his clothes off and sampling wild rites."[10]

Ironically, while these negative stereotypes revolve around real or supposed differences, anthropologists and missionaries actually have a great deal in common. They are both outsiders looking in, and, strictly speaking, they are both in the field to remake themselves as either doctor of philosophy or saved soul. Also, compared to their peers, both anthropologists and missionaries take a "high view" of natives and can be seen to act, according to their time and place, in their defense. The two missionaries with whom this book is primarily concerned endured the derogatory label "Indian lover" in their day: John Kilbuck for being an Indian, Edith Kilbuck for marrying one, and both for their defense of Alaska natives against non-native interests, commercial and political. Even as the anthropologist typically values natives for what they are (or were), John and Edith valued them primarily for what they could become.

Frank A. Salamone also suggests a similarity between anthropologists and missionaries in that both believe they have the truth, are protective of "their natives," and oppose that which they define as evil.[11] Mary T. Huber notes that both work with "fictions" that simultaneously make their practice possible and ironic.[12] Last but not least, twentieth-century missionaries and anthropologists share the dubious distinction of having recently replaced a superiority complex with a guilt complex in relation to the subject of their endeavors. In some respects the current crisis of representation in ethnology can be viewed as the anthropologists' equivalent of Vatican II.

Given these similarities, it is not surprising that at a time when anthropologists are reevaluating their encounters with natives, they also are reanalyzing missionary-native interaction. At a time when the connection between missionary activity and European expansion has remained undeni-

Fig. 1.1. John and Edith Kilbuck, circa 1910. (Moravian Archives)

able, it is also being acknowledged as subtle and full of nuance. Moreover, just as the anthropologists' preconceptions are increasingly recognized as coloring their representation of the native, so missionary preconceptions are understood to preordain their views.

In this self-critical atmosphere, anthropologists for the first time are giving serious consideration to the ambiguities and contradictions of the missionary enterprise. Scholars are calling for a reevaluation of the missionary-native encounter as cross-cultural hermeneutics;[13] cross-cultural communication;[14] the ironic disjunction between ideology and practice in the field, where circumstances require action that contradicts missionary ideals;[15] and the interplay between power and meaning.[16]

Along with this new appraisal of missionaries, new reasons to study them are also emerging. In part because of their position as the vanguard of Western civilization, missionaries often have been among the first to document native cultures and have written many classic accounts of native peoples. John Kilbuck himself made a substantial contribution to Yup'ik ethnography during his career, and the assiduity of his ethnographic descriptions of the Yup'ik people provided the original motivation for my own interest in the journals on which this book is based. Typical of the bias of my time and place, I had to come face to face with the drama of the native-missionary encounter before I let it take pride of place over gathering "facts" about "my natives." In the end the Kilbucks became natives interesting in their own right.

Studying the Kilbuck journals can tell us a great deal about the Yup'ik Eskimos at the turn of the century and about the character of native–non-native interaction. Missionary accounts are also an important contribution to our understanding of the culture of mission groups themselves; such documents possess their own concepts of space, time, personhood, and power. Mission studies not only address the issues of cross-cultural communication and the process of cultural transformation, they also pose questions of "how people encounter the exotic, how they tolerate ambiguity in the different regions of their lives, and how they manage the contradictions that arise from living and working in an unfamiliar world."[17]

The most persuasive reason for carefully scrutinizing our sometimes sworn enemy is the fact that while missionaries employ different means and seek different ends than anthropologists, both travel the same road. I predict that in this age of reevaluation, the missionary encounter will prove as attractive to scholars in the future as it has been neglected in the past. Although anthropologists may initially be drawn to missionary letters and journals for what they can tell us about "our people," what we end up seeing is ourselves in ways the analysis of few native peoples can provide.

MISSIONARIES AND NATIVES

> *From the moment there is contact . . . it is not a question of seeing only a*
> *continual series of cultural "rapes"; there are as many legitimate, fruitful*
> *"consenting unions."*
>
> —R. Lechat, "Evangelism and Colonialism"[18]

As reflexivity in anthropology has made possible a reconsideration of the anthropologists' role vis à vis the missionary, so it has also made possible a reconsideration of the missionary vis à vis the native. Missionaries often have been criticized for imposing themselves on native peoples, but the history of native-missionary interaction can more accurately be seen as an encounter between different systems of meaning. This encounter has resulted neither in total commitment nor in total rejection of one by the other. Instead, a subtle internalization of selected cultural categories takes place. This negotiation, sometimes intentional and deliberate and sometimes not, characterizes the relationship between natives and Westerners in Alaska.

The Far North is an attractive arena in which to study the relationship between native culture and mission history. In many parts of the world the missionary was an active but relatively ineffectual player in the encounter between native and Western culture; however, in Alaska in general, and western Alaska in particular, missionaries played a central role. The Eskimos of western Alaska were never conquered by military action or dispossessed of their lands by treaty or brute force. Furthermore, although traders were present in the region from the 1840s, they were neither influential nor numerous. For better or worse, western Alaska lacked significant amounts of any of the commercially valuable resources that first drew non-natives to other parts of the state. The region lagged behind other parts of the Arctic and sub-Arctic in sustained contact with the outside world. As a result, missionaries were among the first outsiders to interact with the scattered and isolated peoples of the Yukon-Kuskokwim delta.

The first to arrive were Russian Orthodox priests. Father Ioann Veniaminov visited Alexandrovski Redoubt on the Nushagak River in 1829 and again in 1832. Father Iakov Netsvetov subsequently worked out of Ikogmiut (Russian Mission) on the Yukon River from 1845. From that time forward a handful of Russian and Creole[19] priests claimed the entire region as their pasture and its scattered population as their flocks. Although the Russians were few in number and limited in resources, their influence was far more significant than might be supposed.

Orthodox hegemony was challenged by the establishment of a Moravian mission at Bethel[20] along the Kuskokwim River in 1885 and three years later by the founding of a Catholic mission on Nelson Island, relocated to the mouth of the Yukon a year later. These two missions made a much more sustained bid to convert the "baptized heathen" and to alter the natives' way of life. During the next four decades the region endured a struggle over

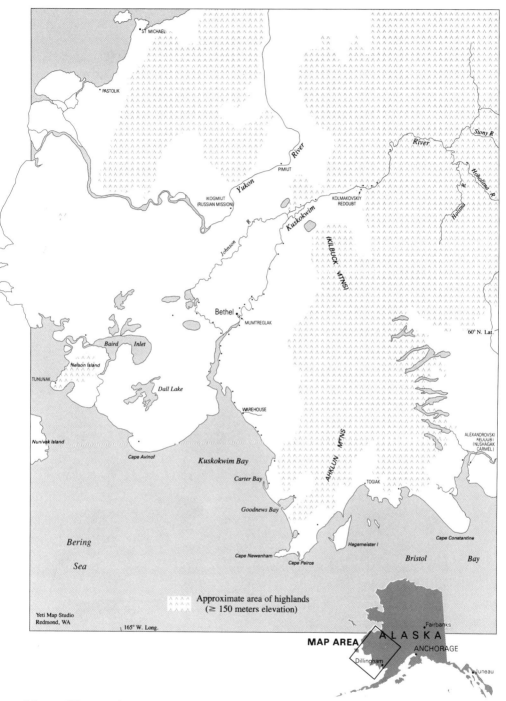

ST MICHAEL

PASTOLIK

^ Approximate area of highlands
^ ^ (≥ 150 meters elevation)

Yeti Map Studio
Redmond, WA

165° W. Long.

Bering

Sea

Cape Newenham

Cape Peirce

Kuskokwim Bay

Carter Bay

Goodnews Bay

Hagemeister I

Bristol   *Bay*

Cape Constantine

TOGIAK

ALEXANDROVSKI
REDOUBT
(NUSHAGAK
CARMEL)

Nunivak Island

Cape Avinof

Dall Lake

Nelson Island

TUNUNAK

Baird   Inlet

WAREHOUSE

Bethel

MUMTREGLAK

Johnson   *R.*

Yukon   *River*

PIMIUT

IKOGMIUT
(RUSSIAN MISSION)

Kuskokwim

KOLMAKOVSKIY
REDOUBT

IKILBUCK MTNS

ARKLUN MTNS

River

Stony R

Holitna R.

Holitna   *R.*

60° N. Lat.

MAP AREA

ALASKA

ANCHORAGE

Fairbanks

Dillingham

Juneau

Map 1. Western Alaska, 1885

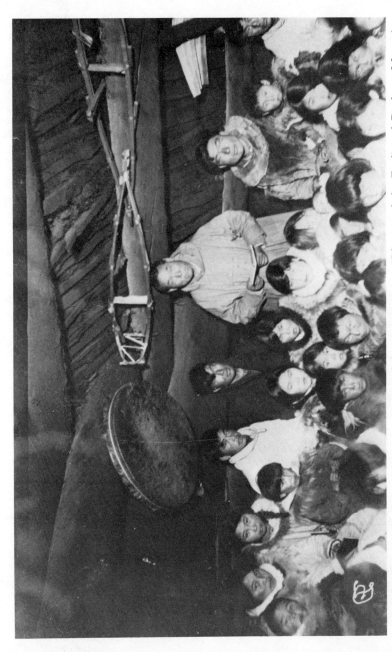

Fig. 1.2. Native Moravian helper preaching to his contemporaries. (Photograph by Ferdinand Drebert, Moravian Archives)

both the meaning and the mode of existence the likes of which it had never known.

K. S. Latourette has called the nineteenth century the "great century" of Christian missions,[21] and certainly the 1800s comprise the era of the missionary in western Alaska. During those years missionaries earnestly worked to restructure the natives' conceptual universe and, in so doing, laid the foundation for their integration into capitalist industrial society. Although Alaska Eskimos, unlike natives in other colonial situations, did not experience material dispossession, missionaries and, later, government agents did engender effective colonization of indigenous modes of perception and practice.

Ironically, though missionary efforts were decisive in the imposition of a new mode of being in the Arctic in general and in western Alaska in particular, anthropologists have all but ignored missionaries and have written few detailed studies of particular missions.[22] Although the exceptions make it clear how rich and varied were both the circumstances and results of the native-missionary encounter, no one followed their lead. The sub-Arctic has fared somewhat better in this regard; however, even where it has been considered, the missionary-native encounter is not presented as a dialogue but in terms of relative failure or success.[23]

Mission historiography also tends to gloss over this complex enterprise, which usually is presented as an account of the progress from mission to church, focusing on particular strategies of particular denominations.[24] Just as it may be unfair to blame missionaries for failing where they have not tried, it may be unfair to criticize mission history for its lack of coherent analysis of the missionary encounter. The fact remains that while historians have established the general patterns of mission history, they have given scant consideration to native and missionary motives as expressed in particular mission situations.[25] At present in Alaska and much of the Arctic and sub-Arctic, we know only in the most general terms the role played by missionaries' personalities, knowledge of the native language, and sensitivity to native values. At the same time we are just beginning to understand the ways in which native Americans comprehended their encounter with Christianity in traditional religious terms.[26] One could fairly say that no aspect of Eskimo experience has been analyzed with less objectivity than the Christian missionary effort to transform them.

In setting out to correct this situation, one could find no better starting place than a detailed consideration of John and Edith Kilbuck and their work among the Yup'ik Eskimos of western Alaska. John Kilbuck was arguably the most influential missionary along the Kuskokwim River prior to 1900 and the most important federal agent in all of western Alaska between 1911 and 1921. Moreover, the Kilbucks were perhaps unique in the degree to which they both represented and embodied the eternal triangle between missionary, government, and native interests.[27] John's native origin (he was full-blooded Delaware Indian) at the very least made him aware that other cultures existed. Even though he had more sympathy for the Yup'ik people than other nineteenth-century missionaries, still he strove for conversion in the broadest sense, preaching not only religion but the moral superiority of herding and gardening, the nuclear family, private property, and Western concepts of personal hygiene. As a government agent he had a "mission" of paternal guardianship and preached a nation's vision of society to an alien people.[28]

In the final analysis the Kilbucks represented a "greedy institution" seeking to totally transform the social landscape.[29] Their religious ideals shaped their work, but the ways in which these ideals were played out in particular situations shaped its contradictions. Though the Kilbucks saw themselves as bringers of light, the Yup'ik people originally viewed them as representing the proverbial powers of darkness. Their message may have been spiritual, but it relied on practical skills to make its delivery effective. The Kilbucks also were ambivalent toward Western society. Their goal was to establish a native church, yet this required "civilizing" the natives. Moreover, while the Kilbucks identified Western values with Christianity, they viewed Western society as corrupted by sin.

The Kilbuck history embodies the irony of colonialism—humanitarian goals embedded in a Western regime.[30] Whites valued the Kilbucks because of their ability to communicate with and control the "shiftless" natives, while the Kilbucks viewed their role as protecting the natives from no-account whites. Critics of missionaries have sometimes used ironies such as these to show how missionaries failed on their own terms;[31] but the Kilbucks were ultimately successful in their Christian mission. Unlike many missionaries, John Kilbuck's personal charisma and political power went hand in hand.[32] As a missionary he introduced the Yup'ik people to the politics of the spirit; later as government agent he exerted the power to produce the world to go with it. The result was a golden age.

The Kilbucks' success provides a counter-example to conversion understood as colonial domination. While missionaries in other parts of the world prepared natives to become part of an urban or rural proletariat, the Kilbucks made only limited progress in their efforts to transform the Yup'ik people into laborers in industrial society. Though their mission of change had an undeniable impact, Yup'ik culture ultimately dictated the terms of their success.

ANTHROPOLOGISTS AND NATIVES

Anthropologists increasingly are aware that in choosing the manner in which any encounter with natives or between natives is textualized they are at the same time determining the degree to which it will be fairly represented. Where choices are made, they need to be laid out in the beginning to qualify both the direction and conclusions of analysis.

In the case of the Kilbucks and the Yup'ik Eskimos, the framework I have chosen to display their dialogue is biography, largely constructed from thousands of pages of journal entries that in themselves marked a dialogue between John and Edith Kilbuck. Here the chronology of life history is not employed to underscore the relation between cause and effect, missionary effort and native response. Rather, event history provides the material from which structured change emerges. Biography constructed out of the Kilbucks' daily journals provides an ideal place to test Sahlins's suggestion that culture is both reproduced and changed in the course of everyday life.[33] If it is in practical projects, informed by received meanings of people and things, that men and women submit their cultural categories to empirical risks, then the Kilbucks' descriptive record of their reaction to the Yup'ik people and the Yup'ik reaction to the Kilbucks' "gospel of service" provide a rich field for investigation.

Christianity always is delivered by particular missionaries of particular denominations in a particular time and place. Many studies of missionaries never rise above this specificity. Others ignore it and consider all missionaries to be essentially the same, content to frame Christianity in universal terms. The biography of this particular missionary couple can provide a corrective on both counts. In historically specific situations, as the Kilbucks lived them, we can read the efficacy of the white man's mission, not so much placed in question as called to account. Any general model of missionary-native encounter will necessarily be grounded in such specificity.

Following T. O. Beidelman, my concern is with "prosaic, everyday activities, views, and reactions of individual missionaries and the native peoples with whom they worked."[34] While Beidelman's *Colonial Evangelism* reveals the history of subjugation and uses irony to show how the missionaries ultimately failed in their mission, the Yup'ik-Kilbuck dialogue recalls a more open-ended, ironic conversation. This difference is represented in the evaluation each made of the other. While the missionaries viewed their Eskimo converts as overgrown children with the missionary functioning as their father, the Yup'ik people bestowed the same epithet on their missionaries, whom they described as "children of thunder."

This reference to mutual evaluation brings to the fore a second analytical choice. As stated above, I have chosen to present the missionary-native encounter as a dialogue concerning different systems of meaning. Throughout that conversation, value words have been employed for both sides. Thus, what is involved is not only a study of missionary encounter, but a study in dialogics insofar as the impact of the text relies on the representation of different voices in the writing of the narrative account.[35] The text employs dialogue as a literary device in its use of alternating quotes from the journals of John and Edith Kilbuck. More important, it is dialogic in its attempt to present and explain the Kilbuck and Yup'ik reactions to specific situations. The absence of a nineteenth-century Yup'ik scholarly tradition sets limits on the degree to which this can be achieved and is one of the reasons why the "conversion" of native peoples in general is so often presented as a unidirectional process. However, just as Sahlins[36] has been able to tease the meaning of Hawaiian history from acts recorded in the journals of members of the British Navy, I have endeavored to read the meaning of Yup'ik history from the love letters of a missionary husband and wife.

Over the years, the Kilbucks recorded myriad encounters between themselves and their Yup'ik cohorts, giving us insight into the cultural specificity of the Yup'ik encounter with Christianity and into the process of cultural conversion that their conversation with the mission engendered. The term "cultural conversion," as opposed to religious conversion, seems most appropriate to the situation. Although the Kilbucks' legacy was not an all-or-nothing commitment to Protestant ideology, they did effectively introduce the Yup'ik Eskimos to Western concepts of space, time, and personhood. Although the Yup'ik people strained Moravian theology through the filter of their culture, the impact on their consciousness was considerable.

In fact, a central issue in their biography is the question of how Christianity, as presented by the Kilbucks, interacted with and was affected by traditional Yup'ik ideology and action. Their biography challenges the unidirectional view of history built on the assumption of the eventual success of salvationist Christianity over traditional native belief. On the contrary, ideological change is a complex and creative process and, for the Yup'ik Eskimos, has led to the development of their own particular mix of Christian and native belief. There are a number of ways in which Christianity, itself internally fractured and changing, may be rejected, marginalized, absorbed, or transformed at the hands of the people it encounters.[37] This book attempts to map the dynamics of that encounter for the Yup'ik Eskimos of the Kuskokwim drainage.

A central concern is understanding how the Yup'ik people of the late nineteenth century dealt with a theology that contradicted many aspects of their everyday lives. The focus is not on macrohistory, but on the meanings the Kilbucks and their followers, as well as the Moravians and the Yup'ik people more generally, attached to objects that related to their understanding and behavior in specific situations. The meaning of the Kilbucks' message, as received, was as much a consensual product of their Yup'ik audience as it was the result of John and Edith's evangelism. Moreover, the journal references to sermons given and received indicate the symbolic, narrative, and rhetorical strategies by which the Kilbucks sought to confront Yup'ik men and women, strip them of their cultural assumptions, and invest them with the Moravian mode of interpreting experience.[38] Insofar as these strategies help to explain the process of religious and cultural conversion, they provide an alternative, and in some cases a direct challenge, to the sociological stance that takes external physiological and social conditions as an explanatory context.

An interpretation of two-score years of dialogue between John and Edith Kilbuck contributes to understanding the Kilbuck-Yup'ik dialogue which reconstituted its listeners during this same period and to understanding the Christian-native encounter more generally. During their last years on the Kuskokwim, John and Edith recognized that not everything had developed as they had planned. They often remarked on the disparity between what they taught and what the people learned. The recognition of this irony, however, is the beginning, not the end, of our understanding of the Kilbuck enterprise and the Yup'ik experience.[39] In fact, the results differed from both Kilbuck and Yup'ik expectation. This process, rather than simply the missionary and native misfirings, is what concerns us.

CHAPTER 2

THE KILBUCKS AND THE MORAVIANS

AN ORIGINAL BOND

On a wet spring morning in 1865, Joseph Romig, a Moravian missionary working among the Delaware Indians, baptized two children at the New Westfield Mission in Kansas. Twenty years later he would perform their marriage ceremony in the same chapel and for the next thirty-seven years save and store in tin bread boxes in an Ottawa bank vault the journals and letters they sent him from Alaska. However, on that day in 1865 the parents looked back rather than ahead, giving their children well-worn family names. One of the babies was the Romigs' own first-born daughter, whom they called Edith Margaret after her Swedish mother. The other was a four-year-old Delaware Indian boy for whom the baptismal name of John Henry Kilbuck already held a wealth of history.

John Henry's mother, a Mohican named Sarah, called her first-born son Chick-quatlt-e'-tak (Little Toenail of a Frog).[1] From his father's side John Henry bore the name Gelelemend before baptism. This was his birthright as the great-grandson of the Delaware chief of the same name, who had lived during the Revolutionary War and was the grandson of the Delaware chief Netawatwas (King Newcomer).[2]

This first Gelelemend was born in 1737 near Lehigh Gap, Northhampton County, Pennsylvania. He was a progressive man, desirous of following the English customs so recently introduced to the Delaware Nation. Consequently, he adopted his father's name "Kill buck" (Nihilajapen) as the family name,[3] so bequeathing his great-grandson a patronymic in translation.

The boy that Brother Romig held for baptism thus bore the marks of his heritage, both in his native names and in their translation. History also

16

enlivened the simple English names. Gelelemend's father was the first John. He was dubbed "an evil man and a friend of the Quakers" by the Moravian missionary John Ettwein, who apparently disdained what he took to be the man's easy marriage between Christian charity and heathen values. The addition of the name Henry was the work of Gelelemend. It was formally prefixed to the Kilbuck family name in 1775, three generations before John was born. Gelelemend took it for himself and all his descendants to come to commemorate the courage of Major William Henry, who had saved his life during the French and Indian War. The English had captured Gelelemend with a number of French sympathizers at Braddock's defeat and were about to put him to death. Major Henry saw him give the Masonic sign of distress and asked that his life be spared. The two exchanged names according to Delaware tradition. Moreover, Gelelemend declared that all his descendants, both sons and daughters, were henceforth to bear "Henry" as their middle name. This ordinance was kept for nearly two hundred years.[4]

Following his deliverance, Gelelemend remained faithful to the Americans and lived under their protection for the remainder of the war. More important for our story, he came increasingly under the influence of the Moravian missionary David Zeisberger, who baptized him William Henry on April 12, 1789. As William Henry embraced the white man's church, his wife Rachel and his sons Charles, John, and Christian Gottlieb soon followed him.[5] Moreover, his conversion opened the way for the charismatic Zeisberger to work among the Delaware. At Gelelemend's death in 1811 at Goshen, Ohio, he was remarked to be a "devoted Christian" of "irreproachable character" who had worked much good for the Christian faith.[6]

Gelelemend was an active and devout convert in the broad sense of the term, and his sons apparently followed in their father's footsteps. Before the war John, the eldest, had been in direct line for the chieftainship of the Unami, or Turtle Clan of the Delawares. A battle was fought within the tribe over the merits and dangers of sending their future leader to attend a white man's school. Again the progressive side won, and John was sent to Princeton. Of this decision Charles Kilbuck later wrote: "Great-grandfather (Netwatwes) was old at this time and did not realize what John's absence meant until he was gone. Then he regretted it."[7] How much did history repeat itself seventy years later when his twelve-year-old namesake was similarly bundled off to the Moravian academy at Nazareth Hall?

The first John Henry (1741–1837) eventually returned to Goshen. After the war John and his brother Charles helped lead what was left of their tribe to New Fairfield Mission in Canada, where they remained until 1837. White settlers constantly encroached upon their land, and drink and disease weakened their numbers. To escape these conditions, the Kilbuck brothers were instrumental in leading a faction of Christian Indians on a six-month trek west, eventually ending on the banks of the Kansas River in Indian territory.

THE MORAVIANS

The Moravian mission that was to develop on the west side of the Kansas River, and into which John Henry Kilbuck was born, originated far away in ancient Bohemia and Moravia. There, in present-day Czechoslovakia, the Czech reformer John Hus led a protest movement against the doctrinal positions of the Roman clergy and was burned at the stake for his presumed heresy in 1415. Out of his teaching was born the Moravian Church, or *Unitas Fratrum* (Unity of Brethren), as it has been officially known since 1457.

At its founding the guiding principle of the Moravian Church can be summed up as a commitment to a godly Christian life as evidence of saving faith. From the beginning such a life was conceived as materially unadorned yet spiritually rich. As with the followers of the Lutheran Reformation, it appealed to many seeking a more direct relationship with the Almighty over the dogmatic formulation of creed. Members originally banded together for the purpose of bringing about a reformation within the Christian church. However, persecution compelled them to withdraw from the communion of the churches they sought to reform, and they organized into a distinct ecclesiastical body.[8]

Although the Moravian Church enjoyed growth into the early sixteenth century, opponents subsequently subjected it to bitter persecution and drove followers of the faith into exile. The eighteenth century saw the renewal of the Moravian Church under the patronage of Count Zinzendorf of Saxony, and his estate became the focal point of Moravian activity. But persecution continued, and a dozen years later adherents were sent from Germany to America, where they successfully established communities in both Bethlehem, Pennsylvania, and Winston-Salem, North Carolina.

As one of the first Protestant denominations the Moravian Church stands apart in several essential respects. First, from its founding it has been characterized by evangelism, especially among peoples perceived as "underprivileged" or "heathen." The stated policy has been to work among the unbaptized, not to win souls from other Christian churches.[9] The intent was not to enter into religious controversy but to bring unchurched men and women to a knowledge of Christ. As early as 1732 the Moravian Church sent missionaries to the West Indies and subsequently established missions among the natives of Greenland, Lapland, Surinam, South Africa, West Africa, the Samoyeds in Russia, Algiers, Persia, Jamaica, Antigua, and Labrador. It is not surprising that the Moravian Church was active in mission work among John Henry's own ancestors during the eighteenth and nineteenth centuries.[10] Although not a large or well-known Protestant sect, through missionary efforts the Moravians have had immense influence.

A second feature of the Moravian church is its commitment not only to the community of believers, but to separate communities within the larger flock. This distinctive "choir system" developed in the eighteenth century to support the association of groups "naturally" drawn together by sex, age, and condition. As a characteristically Moravian method of curing souls, it was grounded in the theological concept that Christ, in passing from infancy to maturity, had sanctified every stage of human life and had given to each category of believer the example of his own faultless conduct. [11]

In its fullest development each congregation was divided into nine sets: widowers, widows, married people, single men, single women, older boys, older girls, little boys, and little girls. [12] Although Moravians upheld the fundamental importance of the marriage relationship, they gave equal weight to the spiritual relationship between the community of sisters and the community of brothers. This communal emphasis was apparent in the constitution of the Alaska mission field.

A third feature of the Moravian faith carried from Moravia to the Delawares and eventually all the way to the Kuskokwim. The plain-living, nononsense aspect of community life grew from the "brotherly agreement" around which the Moravians originally organized their fellowship. This doctrinal thesis set a practical standard for the life of community members in everyday affairs as well as in relation to the church. Briefly, it acknowledged the Bible as the only rule of faith and practice. From this followed a code of right living, including cordial relations with other churches; loyalty and faithfulness of members in attendance and support of their church community; an emphasis on training children in brotherly love, peace, charity, and economy; and a membership that was industrious and temperate, avoiding books and amusements which had a bad effect. In sum, the brotherly agreement stressed a godly life lived with "due economy" and industry. In dress, for instance, it emphasized simplicity, considering changing fashions an improper attempt to attract attention, and urged members to live within their means. [13]

The Moravians brought these values with them to America and taught them at the missions where John's father and grandfather grew up. A Kilbuck by blood and a Henry by decree, he was the child of this marriage of minds begun almost a century before he was born. Ideas that had been brought new to his father's people, he would, in turn, bring to the Yup'ik Eskimos of Alaska's Kuskokwim River. As the product of a conversion process, he had both learned and forgotten. The years ahead would act on both new converts and converters to awaken each to what had gone on before they were born. In the end, each would gain history, whether or not they gained salvation.

YOUNG JOHN HENRY

John Henry Kilbuck was born on May 15, 1861, on a plot of unsurveyed land near Fort Scott, Kansas. There the government had set aside a tract of land for the Christian Indians who had come down from Canada some years before. At the time of his birth, John's parents were living in a tent on the banks of Cowskin Creek. His father eventually built a cabin there, cultivated a garden, and raised cattle and ponies.

When John Henry was four years old, his family moved from the Delaware reservation where he had been born to a Chippewa reservation in Franklin County, Kansas. This move was sparked by the hostility that had developed between the resettled Indians and the neighboring white settlers of Fort Scott, who were not above violent tactics to discourage Indian residence in the area. Consequently, John's family moved, as they had so many times before, settling near Ottawa, Kansas. There the government made arrangements so that the landless Delawares could purchase allotments from the Chippewas and establish permanent homesteads. At the time the Kilbucks arrived, the reservation was already the home of an active Moravian mission, New Westfield, with Reverend Joseph Romig, John Henry's future father-in-law, in charge.

We know relatively little of John's childhood. He had brothers and sisters; although at least two grew to adulthood, none left offspring. There was apparently some trouble between John's father and mother, and Sarah Kilbuck eventually left for Indian Territory. Accounts conflict concerning the causes and depth of the break. William Henry kept John and his brother Joe and later remarried the older, some say richer, Catherine Caleb, by whom he had several more children.

John made only passing reference to his siblings and parents in his journals of later years. As he had not yet married Edith and was not writing to her, our major source of personal detail is lacking. Edith Kilbuck did, however, write a brief biographical manuscript in 1930. Although it is anecdotal, with the idealized quality of hindsight, the incidents she chose to highlight are telling. First, she described the character and strength of the Indian and missionary forces (Kilbuck and Henry) working to influence the boy. Second, she detailed John's leaving the Kansas reservation to attend mission school in Pennsylvania, where these same divergent influences continued to shape his experience.

A major turning point in John's life took place before he left the reservation. According to Delaware tradition, as first-born son of the first-born son's son of Chief Gelelemend, the young John Henry was in direct line to inherit leadership responsibilities and power. Appropriate instruction came from his father's sister, Rachel Henry Kilbuck. Edith recounted the character of Aunt Rachel's influence, as well as the conflict between traditional and contemporary demands John experienced.

> Old Aunt Rachel Kilbuck, the oldest person in the tribe, was rich in the lore of the past. She would teach him. Now it was customary for this *oldest person*, to gather together the interested members, and particularly the young men and boys of the tribe for instruction. . . . Before the fireplace Aunt Rachel

reclined or crouched on a blanket. Little Johnny Kilbuck was her choice so he must sit behind her while she crooned out the legends and folk lore of the past, the superstitions and taboos that had guided their ancestors before them, and which a true representative of their tribe must know.

Lest he fall asleep while she was talking and miss some of the lesson he must *scratch her back*. If the scratching ceased she knew he was drowsy and not paying attention, so she and others berated him soundly and he would waken up and go on with the scratching and learning.

At other times, and frequently in summer, she took him with her on her search for plants used as medicine. This he liked above everything else, and in time learned to know on sight the many herbs used as medicine. Many hours were spent in teaching him this preparation, and the pow wow was no small part of this.[14]

On the one hand, Aunt Rachel expected her nephew to learn the traditions of his tribe. On the other hand, the Moravian missionaries working at the mission encouraged him to attend the local school. What part John's parents played in resolving this conflict is unclear. His parents were both Christians and may have disapproved of Aunt Rachel's teachings on this account. Perhaps they encouraged him to forsake a traditional education or merely allowed him to attend the local school in response to his own wishes or the pressure of the missionaries. In a letter to his wife, John gave a brief account of his own attempt to sort out whom he should follow: "When I read [Hiawatha's] fasting, I called to mind a similar attempt I made, when I was about six years old. I went up on a hill and gathered some stones, placing them in a circle. I sat down in the enclosure, and waited for my particular spirit. Either I had no spirit, or I left too soon. I never knew, but hunger drove me home at supper time, and no one ever knew of my aspirations."[15]

Twenty years later, Edith wrote her own rather more self-conscious version of the same event and how John resolved the issue of whom he would follow.

After Aunt Rachel's training . . . he was to have the usual test of bravery as a child.

Building a crude shelter of stones he must remain there from one to three days and nights alone, without food. During the time the Great Spirit would visit him and give him his commission, and if no Spirit came to him he was free to pursue any vocation he might choose.

Having built the shelter, he walked around it again and again as night drew on, hoping the Great Spirit would not delay his coming. Piling on a few more stones, he went inside. . . .

Time passed slowly and yet no Spirit. What should he do? Choose to be a Medicine Man and live for the good of his people. . . . But perhaps he could be useful some other way. He could go to school and learn many things. Of course, Aunt Rachel would be disappointed and scold him for she had spent much time in his training. . . . Perhaps even his parents would be disgusted with him, and yet they encouraged his going to school. . . .

Finally he said to himself, "I'll go back home and I will be useful to my people in some other way. I will *not* be a Medicine Man." So up and away he ran. . . .

A few weeks later school began and no one was more eager to learn than he was. Truly, he was preparing to help his people in *"another way."* [16]

Edith's retelling of these two episodes captured a major factor at work throughout John's life: the relationship between his native roots and the white man's teaching he came to identify with so strongly. Instead of developing into a conflict that would work to pull him apart, John's life marked a marriage between the two. In the end the young Kilbuck was allowed to attend the mission school. The local missionaries identified him early as an exceptional child. Among those who took notice of him was the Reverend Joseph Romig, who served at the New Westfield Mission from 1861 until 1870.

When Joseph Romig arrived at New Westfield, he had approximately eighty parishioners divided almost equally between a group of docile and obedient Christian Delawares and a more intractable Chippewa contingent. Although the Delawares were loyal to their missionary, the Chippewas, originally from Michigan, had never had a missionary among them and were less than receptive to Romig's attentions. To complicate matters, each group spoke its own language and held to its own ideas. Although they eventually agreed that Romig might open his school and work a small farm to supplement his income, he toiled his first years among them under an uneasy truce. But Romig stuck to his business and, unlike his predecessor, declined to profit financially from them. [17]

When Romig left the mission to take charge of the English church in West Salem, Illinois, his father-in-law, Reverend Levi Ricksecker, took over the New Westfield Mission. Romig described Ricksecker as a restless, impatient, energetic man, generous to a fault in his dealings with others, and equally ungenerous towards the faults of his own family. With his boys he tried to whip the bad out and the good in, and it was often severely done. He never touched the daughters, although he did a huge amount of scolding. When everything was in motion he was all right, but when stopped or at rest he was like an engine with a superabundance of steam, hissing and ready to be put into motion again. He was disposed to extremes and freely used superlative adjectives. In partnership with his wife, a meek Christian woman, he served as a missionary for twenty-three years, eight of them on the Indian mission in Franklin County. [18]

Between Romig and Ricksecker, John Henry Kilbuck's future in-laws were instrumental in his early education. When the time came, Ricksecker was the driving force behind the effort to send the promising young Indian boy back East to school. While the missionaries were trying to educate John, a less than charitable effort was made to keep them from it. In a complaint addressed to the mission board, Mrs. Jane Donohoe pled her own son's case, holding that he, too, should have the right to go to school. At the height of her indignation she slammed home the query, "Who recommended the two lads [Kilbuck and Veix]? The reason they wanted to send them is because they want to keep them from running after girls, and fishing on Sundays and playing marbles, etc. Them boys are past controling. They come and go as it suits them. They are like men."[19]

The mission voice finally won over the combined objections of Aunt Rachel and the malcontent Mrs. Donohoe. At the age of twelve, John and his cousin George Veix were sent to school at Nazareth Hall, Nazareth, Pennsylvania. The tribe was at the depot in full force to see them off, and the boys were instructed to get off the train at Philadelphia and take another for Bethlehem. However, they missed their stop and were carried on some thirty miles. When they realized their mistake, they got off the train and walked back along the tracks. Just at sunset, they reached the Philadelphia suburbs, where an inquisitive stranger took them in and sent them on their way to Bethlehem the next morning.[20]

In Bethlehem, John began a testing as severe as the one he had endured alone at night as a child. After his eventful journey, he settled into a five-year stretch of schooling at Nazareth Hall. Not once did he visit his family in Kansas during this period. Years later, in a letter to his children on the occasion of their own departure for school, he intimated the bonds forsaken for school's sake: "It was my experience when I left Nazareth Hall, where I passed five consecutive years. Also when I left the Hills for the last time as a student I went to town on horse back, alone. Father and friends had gone in a wagon. I rode by the mission, slowly and when I passed the chapel I could not hold the tears back, but I let them flow freely. I have never been so overcome by my emotions since then."[21]

At the time that John attended, Nazareth Hall was run along the lines of a military academy. Moravians were already well known in Europe for their fine schools and commitment to education, and Nazareth Hall, established in 1759 as a church academy, proved no exception. Although it opened its doors to non-Moravians in 1785, its central purpose remained the training of young men for service in the church.[22]

Although the move East could not have been easy, John's recollections of the years he spent at Nazareth Hall were far from negative. He confided to Edith that the school and the surrounding country meant a great deal to him and that he hoped sometime he might return to the rolling hills of Pennsylvania to reexperience the sights and smells of his boyhood ramblings. These yearnings bespeak a man with good memories of his youth, strongly rooted in a place where he came to feel at home.

Neither John's nor Edith's remarks concerning the years he spent at school make reference to his feeling discriminated against because he was an

Indian. On the contrary, his special status as a Christian Indian seems to have acted more as a positive factor in developing his sense of self-worth. In a personal recollection to his sons in 1905, John wrote, "As an Indian I was more or less a curiosity in the days I spent in the east. Through this fact, I was often shown favors and almost any farmer around Nazareth would allow me to go into his orchard or fish in his streams before he would tolerate white boys."[23]

Just as John had been marked as special in the Indian world because he had aspired to learn white ways, he was equally marked in the white world, where he was treated as extraordinary by virtue of being Indian. His academic skills had singled him out at the mission school and led to his advancement, whereas at Nazareth Hall his athletic ability in archery, running, and high jumping led to special recognition. In a letter to his wife in 1910 he remarked that he could still jump almost seven feet, standing jump, run fifteen minutes without blowing, and "if I can jump eight feet without weights and without a run, I will about equal my average record when I was 20 years old."[24] He was also a good football player, captaining his college team for two years. Moreover, he was a fine baseball player. "Kilbuck's nine," so tradition has it, never lost a game.[25] Ironically, each environment chose to applaud a skill that was, in its context, special. As a result, John excelled in both, for different reasons.

By the time John graduated from Nazareth Hall, he was considered ready for further training. From Nazareth he went to Moravian College and Theological Seminary in nearby Bethlehem, Pennsylvania, where he took the full classical and theological course, receiving his B.A. in 1882 and his B.D. in 1884. His college mates called him "Squallie," as they could not pronounce his Delaware name.

Established in 1863, the Theological Seminary had by the 1880s solidified a connection with Nazareth Academy. Together, both institutions met a real need in the American Province of the Moravian Church as the only training ground for ordination into the Moravian ministry in the United States. Before the seminary and Nazareth Hall opened, all ordained ministers who served in the American Province were out of necessity foreign born and trained on foreign soil. American-born Moravians, let alone American Indians, were practically excluded from serving in the ministry.[26]

The character of John's training at Nazareth Hall carried into both the academic and social environment of the seminary. Camaraderie had been part and parcel of the sports and military drill that took place at Nazareth Hall. Similarly, fellowship with his ten classmates and five faculty members was as important in his seminary training as were the classical and doctrinal aspects of his education. One classmate, William Weinland, would remain a particularly close friend and colleague and would precede him to Alaska. While in Bethlehem, they formed an effective partnership in the practical work of church extension.

Billy and I worked together in gathering subscriptions for the building of the West Bethlehem Chapel [in 1883]—each one of us had a separate district—but Billy and I decided that a fellow needed a bolster—so we joined company. In his district he did the talking and I bolstered—and vice versa when we worked in mine. The thing was such an innovation among the hide bound Moravians—that the old trustees declared it could not be done. One of them shook a fistful of greenbacks, exclaiming—"See them"—and of course we expected at least a dollar, "not one of them do you get," and thrust them into his pocket. Where we expected to be ejected unceremoniously—a wad was thrust into Billy's hand—which he did not look at until we were on the street—and upon opening the wad—"Who'd a thunk it!" almost yelled Bombshell—and there was $50.00 in green backs. . . .

Billy and I wielded the pick and shovel, too, when the foundation was being dug—and this after working all day at the mills. This was however like going to a party for the women and young ladies of the neighborhood were there with their smiles and good cheer—sugar cake![27]

On April 16, 1884, the Central Moravian Church in Bethlehem recorded a "very interesting service." On that day Bishop Edmond de Schweinitz ordained John Henry Kilbuck a deacon,[28] the first Delaware Indian to receive ordination into the Moravian Church. At the same meeting, Brother Adolphus Hartmann and John's friend "Billy" Weinland shared their thoughts on the proposed exploratory reconnaissance to Alaska and the mission the Moravians hoped to establish there.

John's ordination signified that he had completed his training and accepted his first assignment as a missionary. He was appointed to the Canadian Indian Mission at New Fairfield (commonly called Moravian Town) to assist Reverend Hartmann. During Brother Hartmann's absence from his post, young Brother Kilbuck would serve in his place. Five months later, at a meeting of the Society for Propagating the Gospel (SPG),[29] Brothers Hartmann and Weinland returned a favorable report on the prospects for establishing a mission in Alaska. At this same meeting a letter from John was read, expressing his desire to serve in Alaska.[30] John Henry Kilbuck's career as a Moravian missionary had begun.

EDITH

John Kilbuck spent the summer and fall of 1884 at the Canadian mission; at Christmas he visited his old home at the New Westfield Mission in Kansas. There, on New Year's Day 1885, he met the nineteen-year-old Edith Margaret Romig, who was teaching in the mission school. John was often a special guest at the home of Brother and Sister Kinsey, where Edith was boarding. At numerous dinners he talked about his work in Canada and his plans to go to Alaska the following spring. All this must have intrigued a missionary's daughter who had lived and worked in missions from her early years; on Valentine's Day she agreed to be John's wife and to accompany him to Alaska.

Fig. 2.1. William Weinland in a three-seater kayak at the mouth of the Kuskokwim River. Taken during the 1884 expedition to seek a site for a Moravian mission station. (A. Hartmann, Moravian Archives)

That an educated white woman should marry a full-blooded Indian was not past remarking in the mid-1880s; however, the match had its own logic. For Edith, John embodied the best hope of her people's work among the Delaware, the more so as he now intended to go forth and do unto others what had been done to him. Given the standards of her youth and upbringing, this was certainly a piece, at least, of why she first loved him. On John's part, too, his quick courtship of this particular daughter of the mission may have grown from the fact that of all white women, she more than any other was no stranger to his people. In fact, Edith may have been as much the choice of John's father, William Henry, as of his son.[31] The girl had been born at the mission and had come back to the mission, and so was theirs already.

Briefly engaged, John and Edith married at Independence, Kansas, on March 14, 1885. Just as John's name figuratively enshrined the marriage between the missionary and the convert, Edith's name did so literally. She brought to their marriage a parentage historically linked to mission service to which she added her husband's Delaware surname.

On her father's side, Edith's people were blessed both with strong constitutions and a quiet turn of mind. They were rarely sick and seldom angry. Edith's grandfather, Jonathan Romig, was a tall, active man, born and brought up in the pioneer regions of Ohio where his father's father had migrated in 1803 from Northhampton County, Pennsylvania. Jonathan was fifth in a family of ten children. In mental disposition, he was the reverse of Grandfather Ricksecker, mild and easy. Only once did he lose his temper, becoming so distracted that he stopped speaking English and broke into rapid German.[32]

Jonathan Romig married Mary Ann Kinsley when he was twenty-six and she but sixteen. They had eleven children, Joseph being the eldest son. Mary Ann's father was as mild as his son-in-law, a model of Protestant virtue. He was a careful man, shrewd but not greedy. His lunch was typically bread and butter, rather than purchased gingerbread or the like. Industry and economy gave him his start, and in later years he was able to contribute $1,000 at one time for the repair of the church to which he belonged.

Jonathan Romig raised his children on a farm in Tuscarawas County, Ohio. The land was rich and food was plentiful, from homemade maple sugar to stoneground flour. Clothes were made of homespun wool and shoes of home-tanned leather. Joseph Romig went with his brothers to the small log village school where he received "lickin and learnin" side by side. He was not an overly ambitious scholar and stopped school after having acquired little more than rough reading and writing skills.

Injured at fifteen by a horse, Joseph had to walk with a cane. Kept back from games with his brothers during his convalescence, he took to reading and thus finished his own education with a slow persistence that carried over

into his life's work. At twenty he went away to school to study for the ministry. He subsequently entered the Moravian Theological Seminary in Bethlehem, Pennsylvania. At the end of two years he went on to Nazareth Hall
as a teacher and a year later began work as a missionary in the Kansas Indian
mission. That summer he opened a school with twenty-six Indian children,
only two of whom could understand and speak English. In November 1863
Joseph Romig married Margaret Ricksecker and brought her back to the
mission. There, on Easter morning, April 16, 1865, Edith was born, the
first of ten children.

Edith spent her earliest years at New Westfield. There, the story goes, a
young Indian boy visiting her parents' home was captivated by the two-year-
old baby girl playing on the clean wood floor. Although Edith may not have
remembered John from this period, years later she recalled riding to town
in a wagon driven by a colorfully turbanned, expansive Indian gentleman
whose demeanor contrasted with that of her own sober and restrained Papa.
This was John's father, whom Edith never forgot.

Although John and Edith crossed paths during their younger years, they
spent no time together. By the time Edith was six her parents had moved
away from New Westfield to southern Kansas. There her father continued
his work as an itinerant preacher, teacher, and farmer, with mixed success.
Ill health and bad luck several times forced him to deed back his lands to
the mortgage holder. Edith later recalled the positive aspects of her childhood privations: "We learned to appreciate His smallest gifts to the full.
Even now, I can work with my hands, and the things I need for my sewing
are not lacking. I have so much more than my poor mother had. She loved
beautiful things and her deft hands could fashion the most artistic creations
from almost nothing, even from a piece of white paper and a pair of scis-
sors. She had so little in her life but hard work and self denial."[33]

Although material riches were lacking, Edith remembered her homelife
as spiritually rich and self-sufficient.[34] When it came time to be educated,
Edith was taught first at home and later at the mission school by her father;
eventually she attended the County Teachers' Institute.[35] What Edith's education lacked in formality, it made up for in practicality. Beyond reading,
writing, and sums, she was taught "to do well whatever she did." Joseph
Romig remained convinced that this "thoroughness and accuracy" followed
her all through her life and was the foundation of her success. Romig thus
characterized his daughter for posterity:

> She was a tall young woman of fine open countenance and wonderful good
> health. Her chest expansion was five inches—that of a man. The doctor said
> after measuring her chest, "Go along, you will never die of tuberculosis if
> you take care of yourself." And this chest capacity has served her good in all
> the many years she has spent in Alaska.
>   As to their religious training, much might be said. But Christianity never
> was a somber or morose subject—in the home or in their lives. . . .

Fig. 2.2. William Henry Kilbuck's singular looks attracted the attention of an Ottawa, Kansas, photographer, who invited him to sit for the camera about 1870. (Moravian Archives)

As to the genuineness of her piety one needs only to be acquainted with her to see for themselves. And intimate acquaintance never lessens that esteem for her. Even myself, altho her father, I appreciate more and more the genuineness and depth of her faith and piety. Never prone to be positive and self-assertive, altho now at this state her strength has been much impaired from long residence in that climate, and from much hard work.[36]

As in Edith's description of John, Joseph Romig's description of Edith tells us as much about the father as it does about the daughter. Certainly, Joseph Romig was immensely proud of the accomplishments of his eldest. Later it was he who laboriously copied her Alaska journals and submitted them to *The Moravian* for publication, so that through her words the entire church community might read about the work. The large support that the Alaska mission received during its early years was, in part, a direct result both of Edith's compelling descriptions and the pride her father took in them.

Joseph Romig's description of Edith echoes character traits remembered by other members of the Kilbuck family, who also remarked her physical presence and capability. These same traits emerge from a reading of her journals. They are doubly impressive, as she often wrote from situations of isolation and hardship. However, she appears neither a stoic nor a saint, but rather a flesh-and-blood person with strong opinions and the intention to live them.

THE FIRST YEAR: SETTING OUT

However disparate their childhoods, in the years immediately following their marriage John and Edith Kilbuck were so closely bound to each other and to their work in Alaska that they cannot be separately described. They regularly wrote to friends and relatives about what they thought and saw. More significantly, as John's travelling kept them increasingly apart, they both wrote detailed journals of what went on in the other's absence so as to let each see what the other's life had been. John even set himself goals as to how many pages he would write for Edith during a given trip.

For the first year after their meeting at New Westfield, John and Edith were almost constantly together. Within ten weeks of their meeting they were wed at Edith's family's home in Independence, Kansas. There they stayed for the next ten days awaiting Weinland's summons to join the missionary party in San Francisco, preparatory to their departure for Alaska. It should have been nine days, but in saying their final farewells they missed their train.[37]

The visit was both a glad and a sad time. Edith's family and friends were happy to see her launched into mission work but sad to have her go so far away. Her family, including four younger sisters and five younger brothers, had always been a close one and enjoyed large gatherings on holidays and special occasions. Although Edith was not the first to leave home, she was the first to go so far and for so long a time.[38]

Edith's departure for Alaska might be seen as comparable to John's departure twelve years before from New Westfield, when he left the reservation for school. For this reason the move to Alaska may have been easier for John than for Edith. In fact, while Edith's journal entries for that first year are full of the newness and excitement of the work, they also contain ever-increasing references to small aches and ailments. Edith's complaints, which intensified over the years, were probably rooted in the combined physical and mental strain of mission life. That this stress manifested itself in debilitating bouts of "neuralgia," as well as in numerous other minor ailments, makes sense in the context of late nineteenth-century concepts of what were and were not acceptable outlets. Somatizing the situation was a culturally appropriate response. It is also likely that regularly describing and recording her trials and triumphs in her private journals helped her continue to function in a world very different from the one she had left behind.

John, too, had much to adjust to after his arrival on the Kuskokwim. He continued to have trouble with his eyes during his first year in Alaska and consequently wrote very little during this period. What he did write projected satisfaction with his new surroundings. All his considerable energy was focused on the work before him and what he had to learn to accomplish it. Skills necessary during the first year alone included carpentry, lightering, wood rafting, sailing, weather observation, linguistics, doctoring, and gravedigging. Although his seminary skills motivated his work, his success in the manual arts sustained him. He showed a zest for life and a pride in doing, coupled with a deep faith which grounded all his actions. That belief, and the assurance it gave him, both enlightened and blinded his actions.

John's first journals convey a piety, a formality, and a sense of missionary purpose that are not so much lacking in his later writing as taken for granted. His observations betray the energy and conviction of youth, containing no hint of hesitation or reservation. At the same time, from the very beginning, John describes, if not an affinity with, at least a desire to understand, the people he had come to convert. In a letter to Bishop de Schweinitz he wrote:

> You probably wish to know what I think of these people. My first impression is very favorable. Their personal appearance is, of course, not cleanly, but there is some degree of neatness about their dress. Their language, or rather their way of speaking, their intonations and accents are very much like that of the American Indians that I have met with. . . . Seeing that the vocalization of the Eskimo and the Delaware is so very similar, I personally do not anticipate very much trouble in learning to speak the language. Whether I shall be so fortunate in grasping their way of thinking and the mode of expressing their thoughts, I really can not tell.[39]

It is significant that John posed this critical question in his first written commentary on the Yup'ik people.

The mission party that arrived at the mouth of the Kuskokwim aboard the schooner *Lizzie Merrill* in June 1885 was small and close-knit. Along with John and Edith it included William and Caroline Weinland. Like the Kilbucks, they were young, untried, and newly wed. The party also con-

Fig. 2.3. The first mission party, 1885. Left to right, John Henry Kilbuck, Hans Torgersen, Edith Romig Kilbuck, Caroline Yost Weinland, and William Weinland. (Moravian Archives)

tained the lay missionary Hans Torgersen, a middle-aged carpenter who had left his wife and two children at the Canadian Indian mission to contribute his substantial practical skills to the endeavor.

After their arrival they made their way upriver to the site of the new mission, which they named Bethel.[40] The mission was located across from the trading station of Mumtreglak (*Mamterilleq*), which at that time consisted of little more than a store and several dwellings. Here the missionaries' job, first and foremost, was to build a base of operations from which they could begin work. A formidable challenge under the best of circumstances, the task was made even more difficult by the tragic death of Brother Torgersen, who drowned August 10 while returning to Bethel with the last load of supplies from the Warehouse at the mouth of the Kuskokwim.[41] The impact of his loss was substantial, as it forced John and William Weinland, both green in the art of construction, to raise the first mission building on their own. The wetness of the wood and the lateness of the season caused problems and delays; however, both John's and Edith's accounts of these trials convey the mission party's sense of camaraderie, which they sustained throughout the first year. In John's first letter home to his family he quipped, "I know you would have laughed to see me, running around, with a sunbonnet on [to protect his weak eyes]. The sisters had their fun, when Bro. W. and I were putting up the rafters. . . . They said that *Aunt Sally* looked dangerous with her hammer, and *Granny* looked rather timid."[42]

The missionaries' efforts and their need for a sense of humor did not end in October, when they were finally able to occupy their new home. Rather, the entire party continued to divide their attention between their two major concerns: the physical maintenance of the mission, and their effort to learn the Yup'ik language. Days they spent hunting, gathering firewood, cooking, and cleaning, while they devoted their evenings to language lessons, reading, talk, and prayer. As they had only hand sleds, they did little traveling during the first winter and then only to villages close to the mission. Weinland travelled farthest afield when he accompanied Edward Lind, the trader in charge of the Mumtreglak station and the missionaries' only nonnative neighbor, to Russian Mission on the Yukon.

Two noteworthy moments in the Kilbucks' personal biography occurred during their first year on the Kuskokwim. The first was John's internal debate concerning his commitment to the Alaska mission. In January 1886, having been in Alaska little more than a half year, John recounted a personal dilemma sparked by his allegiance to the New Westfield Mission in Kansas. Apparently, the present missionary had urged the mission board to abandon the field in Kansas. When he received this news, John told the mission party that he felt it his duty to take over the job, should that occur. This proposal marked the first and only time that John ever wrote about voluntarily leaving the Alaska mission field.

Fig. 2.4. The first trading post at Bethel, before it was Bethel. This post probably was located by Reinhold Sipary across the river from Mumtreglak sometime in the 1870s. Even back then, erosion of the riverbank was a problem; note the sea wall on the bank in front of the buildings. (Photo by A. Hartmann, 1884, courtesy of the Moravian Archives)

Fig. 2.5. The Warehouse, Warehouse Creek, 1884. On the riverbank—at right—newly arrived Alaska Commercial Company goods are awaiting storage. (A. Hartmann, Moravian Archives)

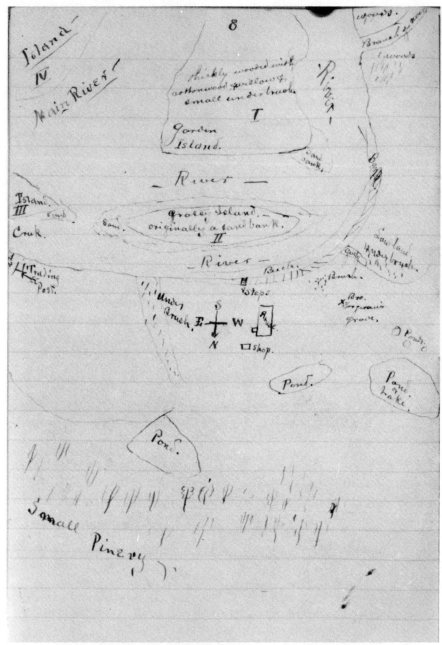

Fig. 2.6. Sketch of Bethel by John Kilbuck, 1885. (Moravian Archives)

The conclusion of the Kilbucks' first year of marriage found them both in good health and living in expectation of the birth of their first child. On their anniversary Edith wrote:

Although each year of my life has been a happy one, I never spent one with so much real enjoyment and pleasure as this last one. It is so nice to have a companion that is all your own. One in whom you may with confidence tell *every* little joy and sorrow, one who cares for *your* comfort and happiness above all others. It is a pleasure to work and manage for such a one. I constantly look forward to the time when we will be in our own happy home and I plan some new pleasure and sweet surprise for each day. . . . With health, home, and our dear little one and each other; what more could we ask. The world would not be more to me. When I look back one year and think of my happy girlhood days they certainly are a joy to me but not to compare with this joy.[43]

On this note of satisfaction and expectation John and Edith ended their first year together.

CHAPTER 3

SOMETHING ABOUT THE YUP'IK ESKIMOS

THE YUP'IK ESKIMOS

From their arrival in Alaska, the Kilbucks were committed to an energetic project of cultural conversion. Before this project can be described, however, the object of their energy must be presented: the Yup'ik Eskimos. Who were the people living along the Kuskokwim that John and Edith confronted on their arrival? John wrote his best description of the late nineteenth-century Yup'ik people in 1910, entitled "Something about the Innuit of the Kuskokwim River, Alaska."[1] Written twenty-five years after his introduction to the region, it contains his considered opinions on the Yup'ik way of life, including detailed descriptions of their annual subsistence cycle, history, family organization, and ceremonial life.

John was technically incorrect in referring to the natives of the Kuskokwim drainage as "Innuit." His title should have been "Something About the Eskimos (or Yup'ik Eskimos)." The natives of western Alaska are indeed members of the larger family of Eskimo cultures extending from Prince William Sound on the Pacific coast of Alaska to Bering Strait, and from there north and east along the Arctic coast into Canada, on into Labrador and Greenland. Within that family they are members of the Yup'ik-speaking, not Inupiaq-speaking, branch. As John himself noted, the natives of the Kuskokwim refer to themselves as *yuut*, not *inuit*.

Along with the other natives of the Yukon-Kuskokwim delta and Bristol Bay area, the Kuskokwim Eskimos speak the Central Alaskan Yup'ik language, which at the time the Kilbucks arrived in western Alaska was one of five Yup'ik languages internally divided into four major dialects.[2] The other four Yup'ik languages of historic times included three Siberian Yup'ik

38

languages which were spoken on St. Lawrence Island and the Chukchi Peninsula in Siberia, and Pacific Yup'ik (also known as Suk, Sugpiaq, and Alutiiq), which was spoken around Prince William Sound, the tip of the Kenai Peninsula, Kodiak Island, and part of the Alaska Peninsula. Inuit-Inupiaq-speaking Eskimos, on the other hand, occupied the entire Arctic coast, from Greenland west across Canada and northern Alaska as far south as Unalakleet on Norton Sound. Together the two language families (Inuit-Inupiaq and Yup'ik) constitute the Eskimo branch of the Eskimo-Aleut (or Eskaleut) family of languages. In this sense John was essentially correct when he spoke of Inupiat and Yup'ik peoples as "cast from the same mold." [3]

The name Yup'ik [4] (plural Yupiit) is the self-designation of the Eskimos of western Alaska and has the meaning of "real person" or not a sham. It is derived from the word *yuk*, meaning person, plus the postbase *-pik*, meaning real or genuine. The phenomenon of considering themselves real in contrast to unspecified and presumably less real outsiders is not unique to the Yup'ik Eskimos. The word Inupiat has the same literal translation, as do the self-designations of a number of native peoples the world over.

Although the relationship between the Inupiat of northern Alaska and Canada and the Yup'ik Eskimos of western Alaska that Kilbuck surmised was fundamentally correct, their common origin is in eastern Siberia and Asia rather than Greenland and the Canadian Arctic. Archaeologists date the original peopling of the New World from Asia by men and women moving across the low, flat, two-hundred-mile-wide Bering land bridge exposed during periods of glaciation and related low sea levels somewhere between twenty thousand and eight thousand years ago. [5]

The ancestors of the men and women John and Edith encountered in 1885 were originally shore dwellers, settling primarily on the coastal headlands of western Alaska as many as three thousand years ago. [6] Perhaps due to population pressure or perhaps in search of a more reliable food supply, they began migrations up the drainages of the coastal rivers some five hundred years ago. [7] By the time the Kilbucks arrived in Alaska, Yup'ik territory extended upriver to the vicinity of Pimiut (*Paimiut*) on the Yukon River and Crow Village on the Kuskokwim River, at which point they came into contact with the Ingalik, a linguistically distinct group of Athapascan Indians.

At the end of the nineteenth century, the Ingalik inhabited portions of the lower Yukon as well as small areas of the Kuskokwim drainage above Crow Village (*Tulukarnaq*). Relations between the Yup'ik Eskimos and Ingalik Athapascans of the middle Kuskokwim were largely amicable. Intermarriage between Indian men and Yup'ik women was common during the late nineteenth century and continues to this day.

The third and last native group living along the Kuskokwim drainage at the time the Kilbucks arrived was the Upper Kuskokwim Athapascans. These people were closely related to but culturally distinct from their Ingalik neighbors, with whom they were on something less than friendly terms. The Yup'ik Eskimos of the lower Kuskokwim inherited their share of animosity for this small and scattered Athapascan population and, according to John, referred to them as "Ingkelexlook" (*ingqilirrluk*, Athapascan, plus -*lluk* bad: literally, "bad Indians").

GEOGRAPHICAL CONSTRAINTS

On their arrival in western Alaska, John and Edith found themselves in a landscape very different from either the rolling hills surrounding Bethlehem or the sprawling Kansas bottomlands of their childhood. They disembarked in the midst of a seemingly endless alluvial prairie, the product of thousands of years of silting action by the Yukon and Kuskokwim rivers. On its 5,000-mile journey, the Yukon River annually contributes 88 million tons of eroded earth to the Bering Sea. Over thousands of years, the result has been the buildup of a broad marshy plain, the surface of which is as much water as land. Innumerable sloughs and streams criss-cross the lowland delta, creating the traditional highways of its native population. The only relief in the landscape is occasional low volcanic domes such as those which break the surface on Nelson and Nunivak islands and outcroppings of metamorphic rock in the vicinity of Cape Romanzof. Along the coastline the sea is as shallow as the land is flat.

Frequent storms as well as strong winds which gather force as they race uninhibited across the landscape have given the delta lowlands a less than attractive reputation. Although not as frigid as the interior (annual Fahrenheit temperatures range between $-3°$ and $62°$), wind chill can drive the temperatures to $-80°F$ in the winter. A sunny windless day in July can push the temperature to $85°F$ and bring children out to swim at the edge of the Bering Sea. Overall, the climate is dry, in contrast to the large proportion of surface water. Precipitation averages twenty inches a year, including fifty inches of snow.

Though observers have often remarked on the austerity and desolation of this broad coastal plain, it actually supports a wealth of plant and animal life. The subarctic tundra environment is replete with a rich variety of vegetation, including numerous edible greens and berries harvested in abundance by the local people. Shrubs and trees, including willow and alder, crowd the shores of streambanks. The river drainages are forested with a mixture of spruce and birch from above Bethel on the Kuskokwim and Pilot Station on the Yukon. Moreover, breakup brings an ample drift of logs down river every spring. Thus, though living beyond the reach of the rich forests of the interior, the Yup'ik Eskimos were well supplied with wood necessary to build their homes, boats, tools, and elaborate ceremonial paraphernalia.

Not only is the delta rich in plant life, but the fauna it supports is equally impressive. Smelt were the first to ascend the river after breakup, moving

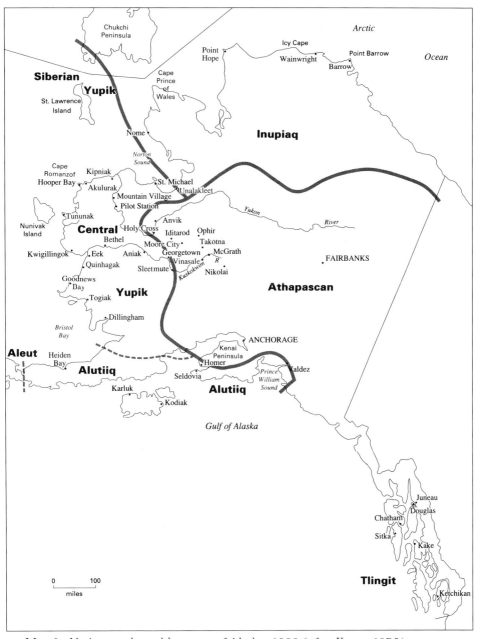

Map 2. *Native peoples and languages of Alaska, 1980 (after Krauss 1975)*

as far as 150 miles upstream. All along their way they were subject to a brief but intense harvest, marking the opening of the season of plenty. Along the Yukon and Kuskokwim rivers, smelt were followed in regular succession by five species of salmon, including king (chinook) salmon, red (sockeye) salmon, coho (silver) salmon, pink (humpback) salmon, and chum (dog) salmon. From June through August, millions of these fish ran the major waterways to spawn. As they began their ascent, thousands were taken in gill nets, dried, smoked, and stored away as food for the winter for both people and dogs.

The salmon were not the only fish species taken by the Kuskokwim Eskimos. As the summer came to a close, fishermen employed dip nets, spears, and traps to harvest an impressive variety of fish, including sheefish, northern pike, Dolly Varden trout, burbot, and along the coast Pacific herring, halibut, and flounder. Various species of whitefish, especially abundant in the region of the tundra lakes to the west of Bethel, comprised an important trade item from that subregion. Last but not least came the ubiquitous blackfish, which John described as having excellent flavor "even to cultivated palates."[8]

Though fishing provided the major source of food for people living along the Kuskokwim drainage at the turn of the century, hunting both land and sea mammals was also an important activity. Along the lower Kuskokwim sea mammals not only comprised an important element in people's diets, but also supplied the major articles of trade—seal oil and seal skins for boot soles and boat coverings. Species harvested included bearded seals, spotted seals, ringed seals, and an occasional ribbon seal. Walrus, beluga whales, and sea lions were also available as well as an occasional grey whale. Inland and upriver hunters pursued a variety of land mammals, including Arctic ground squirrel, snowshoe and tundra hare, Arctic fox, red fox, wolverine, marten, lynx, wolf, caribou, and black and brown bears. Muskrat, mink, river otter, and beaver were also common. As with seals taken along the Bering Sea coast, the caribou were particularly important for the skins and tallow they provided, and the two species shared the place of honor in nineteenth-century ceremonial distributions.

Finally, the delta coastline comprised an especially rich habitat for all manner of waterfowl, including geese, swans, brant, cranes, ducks, and sea birds. Thousands upon thousands of birds annually made the long journey north to nest and breed in the ample wetlands. In late spring and then again at the end of summer, their numbers darkened the sky, signaling first their approach and then their departure.

The rich natural resources of the delta environment notwithstanding, food shortage was a regular feature of the early spring season along the Kuskokwim. This period was more or less prolonged, depending on the weather as well as the people's success in putting up food during the previous season. John viewed Yup'ik subsistence as a constant Darwinian struggle

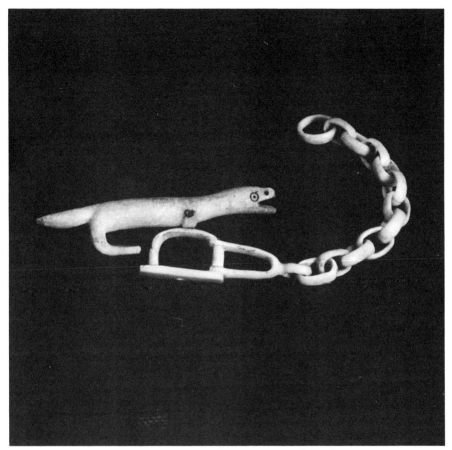

Fig. 3.1. Ivory otter and trap, length five inches. (Kilbuck Collection, Ottawa University)

for survival, attributing these shortages to technological limitations rather than to improvidence.[9] In fact, nineteenth-century hunting technology remained largely traditional. Only in the early twentieth century did increasing trade make firearms readily available to replace the bow and spear along the river. At the time the Kilbucks arrived, the only non-native goods used to any extent were tea, flour, and tobacco, plus some cotton clothing.

HISTORY AND TRADITION

Building on their rich resource base, the Yup'ik Eskimos of the Yukon-Kuskokwim delta were able to develop a complex and internally differentiated cultural tradition prior to the Russians' arrival in western Alaska in the early 1800s. Sometimes referred to as the cradle of Eskimo civilization, western Alaska supported and continues to this day to display a cultural

Fig. 3.2. Wooden tobacco box with ivory insets, length 9 inches, height 2.5 inches. (Kilbuck Collection, Ottawa University)

diversity and vitality outstanding among Eskimo peoples. The region is generally recognized as having been one of the most heavily populated areas in Alaska prior to Russian contact. There is good evidence that the delta population may have been as high as fifteen thousand in the early nineteenth century.[10]

Prior to the coming of the Russians, the substantial population of western Alaska was socially divided into a number of overlapping extended family networks which in turn were united into territorially centered village groups, ranging in size from 50 to 250 people. The rich resource base of the delta environment allowed for a relatively settled life compared to that of other Eskimo peoples. The picture that emerges is one of a nomadic population moving annually within a fixed range. Village groups demarcated minimal subsistence ranges, that is, fixed areas including one central settlement and a number of seasonally occupied sites within which people circulated throughout the year in the acquisition of seasonally and culturally appropriate resources.

Under normal conditions there was no need for travel between the territories of different village groups, as each group had access to a complete variety of seasonally available resources within its regular territorial range. Western Alaska was, however, subject to seasonal and annual variation in the availability of specific resources. Not only were there dramatic fluctuations in the populations of such species as hares, caribou, and salmon from one year to the next, but during a given year ice and weather conditions, including wind direction and tidal variation, could either enhance or restrict the harvest, making the difference between feast and famine. Because of the unpredictability of environmental conditions as well as species fluctuations, it was often necessary to travel between the territories normally used by single village groups. A number of social strategies facilitated this movement, including cooperative hunting ventures with related extended families from different village groups.

Exchanges of food, women, names, feasts, and visits also served to unify village groups into at least twelve larger, more comprehensive regional confederations. The literature often identifies these regional confederations as discrete units.[11] Although ideologically and socially bound, these confederations were not distinct politico-territorial collectivities but rather regional designations implying a potential alliance between more precisely defined village groups.[12] By the time John and Edith arrived in western Alaska these social boundaries had been muted by the impact of introduced disease, beginning with the smallpox epidemic of 1838–1839. However, John was still able to identify eight distinct regional groups, not including the population of Nunivak Island.[13]

Perhaps the most important context of intergroup relations in an otherwise neutral or negative situation was interregional trade. At the turn of the century, both Bethel and Sleetmute were major sites of such exchanges. There, walrus and seal skins and oil from coastal and lower-river people were exchanged for wolverine and beaver pelts, bundles of squirrel and muskrat skins, caribou skins, and sinew from the upper-river people.[14]

In two short manuscripts John also gave a detailed account of the interregional warfare that characterized delta life until the arrival of the Russians. He was one of the first and last to record as history what would later become the stuff of legends.[15] Aside from the limited information recorded by Edward Nelson and Lt. Lavrentiy Zagoskin concerning bow-and-arrow warfare, this aspect of Yup'ik history has been poorly documented.[16] Until recently, the image of the peaceful Eskimo, impervious to the horrors of warfare, has dominated our understanding of intergroup relations within

Yup'ik society. John's ethnographic manuscripts relate the oral history of specific incidents in four major interregional confrontations, and through his writing give them the status of history.

RUSSIAN IMPACT

Although John could record accounts of historic battles won and lost, by the time he and Edith arrived in western Alaska interregional confrontations were a thing of the past. All that remained as evidence of Yup'ik warfare were ruins crowned with luxurious plant growth fed by the ashes of villages put to the torch. As John noted, these violent confrontations had come to a halt with the arrival of the Russians in western Alaska in the early 1800s. It was neither imperial edict nor the force of Russian arms that put a stop to the conflict. Ironically, the killing was brought to a close by death itself. A dramatic population decline resulted from the diseases that accompanied direct contact with Euro-American peoples.

The period 1838–1839 was a major marker of change in western Alaska. Although the resident Russian population was almost nonexistent at the time, the larger Russian trade network to the south, to which the Yup'ik Eskimos were attached, contracted and subsequently introduced smallpox into the region. The epidemiologically virgin native population was devastated, and whole villages were wiped out.[17] As many as 60 percent of the Yup'ik people with whom the Russians were familiar in Bristol Bay and along the Kuskokwim were dead by the middle of June 1838.[18] Bitterness was intense; John recorded the narrow escape of the Russian trader Lukin at his trading station on the Kuskokwim from Yup'ik warriors intent on revenge.[19] Aside from a handful of incidents, the reaction of the Yup'ik people to the epidemic only rarely took the form of aggression against the intruders.

The effects of the smallpox epidemic of 1838–1839 and of subsequent epidemics of influenza in 1852–1853 and 1861 widely varied. Some villages were reduced to less than half their original population (for example, Pastolik went from 250 to 116 individuals in 1839),[20] while other settlements were bypassed altogether. The net effect, however, was a tremendous dispersal and shift in the population, as many individuals and family groups sought refuge with kinsmen or partners in other areas.

The population decline seriously undercut interregional social distinctions, muting the boundaries over which the bow-and-arrow wars of the previous century had been fought. Moreover, the tragedy worked to undercut the efficacy of traditional religious leaders, who could offer no cure or relief for the new diseases. Though the introduction of communicable diseases in the early 1800s damaged traditional social groups, authority structure, and patterns of intergroup relations in western Alaska, daily life proceeded much as in the years prior to the epidemic. Small bands consisting of bilaterally related extended family groups continued to move over the landscape in search of food and to gather in winter villages for an elaborate ceremonial round.

In the years following the smallpox epidemic, the region failed to attract Russian settlement to any significant degree. Though rich in the resources necessary to support a scattered and seasonally nomadic native population, western Alaska is notoriously lacking in significant amounts of any of the commercially valuable resources that first attracted non-native entrepreneurs to other parts of the state. The shallow coastline is blessed with neither the sea otters that first drew Russians to the Aleutians nor the bowhead migrations that later brought American whalers into arctic waters farther north. No gold or mineral deposits comparable to those found in either northern Alaska or the upper Yukon were ever discovered in the region. Although furbearers were present, both the scattered human and animal populations served to undercut the ability of non-natives to exploit their presence.

Because of its geographical isolation and lack of commercial resources, western Alaska was late, compared to other parts of the state, in directly experiencing the impacts associated with non-native contact. Though Russian traders and Orthodox priests were present in the region from the 1840s, in many parts of the region it was not until a hundred years later that people first experienced extended contact with a resident non-native population.

The first non-natives to come to western Alaska were the Russian traders and explorers who sought to extend the purview of the Russian American Company north from the Aleutians. Though the Russians established trading stations at St. Michael in 1833 and at Kolmakovskiy Redoubt on the middle Kuskokwim in 1841, in neither case did they facilitate dramatic technological innovation or a substantial increase in the non-native population. The traders were mostly Creoles, not Russians, and they settled down with local Yup'ik women. The availability of trade goods was on the increase during this period; however, the natives were more interested in luxury goods such as beads and tobacco than utilitarian items. Also, the scarcity of imports meant that Russian traders often dealt in local items.[21] Finally, the Russians failed miserably in their attempt to get the local people to increase the harvest of specific furbearers. For example, in the late 1830s the Russians introduced steel traps and raised prices in an effort to increase the number of beaver harvested.[22] However, the traps were dismantled for their valuable metal components, and the higher prices only served to decrease the number of beavers it took for a native to satisfy his wants. Cultural need continued to be the determining factor in trade relations, and the Russian attempt to foster a paternalistic pattern of dependence among the Yup'ik Eskimos largely failed.

Russian Orthodox priests working out of Ikogmiut (Russian Mission) on the Yukon River also attempted to teach the rudiments of Christianity to the Yup'ik people. Although their field was large and their numbers few, they

Fig. 3.3. *Kolmakovskiy Redoubt, the post built by Russian American Company traders on the Kuskokwim in 1841, 250 miles upriver from Bethel. (A. Hartmann, Moravian Archives)*

succeeded in increasing native awareness of the existence of alternative ideologies. This foreknowledge of other world views would be an important factor in the Kilbucks' ability to gain converts. John and Edith would indirectly build on the foundation the Orthodox priests had laid.

COMMUNITY LIFE

At the time the Kilbucks arrived along the river, the Kuskokwim Eskimos still followed the seasonal round of their forefathers. In early March they left their winter villages for spring camp away from the river. After breakup along the river, they returned to its banks for summer fishing, where they remained until the middle of August. At that point the people moved from their villages out into the tundra in scattered groups for fall fishing and hunting on small streams and lakes. Their principal catch consisted of white- and blackfish which they put raw into grass bags and stored in holes cut in the permafrost. On the lower river, hunters set traps for muskrat, land otter, mink, and fox, while interior natives hunted for deer, bear, beaver, marten, lynx, and fox. The women and children concentrated on gathering and storing roots and berries. In November the people began to move back to their winter villages, where they remained until February.

John noted that on his arrival the combined upriver and downriver population was divided into eighteen winter villages. All were located along the water. The small skin-covered *qayaq* and the larger *angyaq*, with a heavy wooden frame suited for longer journeys and larger loads, were the principal means of transportation. Within each riverbank hamlet, the bilateral extended family group, numbering up to thirty individuals, was the basic social unit. This unit consisted of two to four generations, including parents, offspring, and parents' parents. The parents' married siblings or their offspring might also be included. The extended families making up a single village and ultimately a village group were joined by an overlapping network of consanguineal and affinal ties, both real and fictive. Members of a village group were probably related to one another in several different ways within four or five degrees of consanguinity. In larger village groups most marriages were within the group.

Although during much of the year extended family groups resided together, they did not live in family compounds. Rather, the villages were residentially divided between a communal men's house or houses and smaller women's houses. At various seasons either married couples or groups of hunters might move to outlying camps for the purpose of resource extraction. During the more settled winter season, and in some cases during the spring seal hunting and summer fishing seasons, large numbers of extended family groups would gather together. Winter villages ranged in population from a score to several hundred individuals and one to a dozen extended family units. In the larger settlements, as many as three *qasgit*, or

Fig. 3.4. Yup'ik village near the mouth of the Kuskokwim, 1884. (A. Hartmann, Moravian Archives)

Fig. 3.5. Trader Lind's boat, circa 1890. (Moravian Archives)

Fig. 3.6. Children on top of qasgiq (men's house) at Akiak. (Moravian Archives)

men's houses, might be in operation, with resident populations of forty to fifty males in each.

The furnishings of the *qasgiq* were public property and consisted of an axe, maul, horn wedges, a walrus tusk pick used for splitting wood for the fire bath, from one to six tambourine drums, two or more seal oil lamps, a skin covering for the entrance, and a water bucket. Thus equipped, it was an important social as well as residential unit and was found in even the smallest permanent camp. The residents of a village sometimes gave their qasgiq a formal name, indicating the distinct character of this separate component of the settlement. In this structure all of the men and boys over five years of age worked, ate, and slept. The site of diverse activities and encounters, it served as the community sweat house, hotel, workshop, medicine lodge, and dance hall.[23]

Fig. 3.7. Bentwood water bucket, length 10 inches, with wolf design in black and a red band on top and bottom. (Kilbuck Collection, Ottawa University)

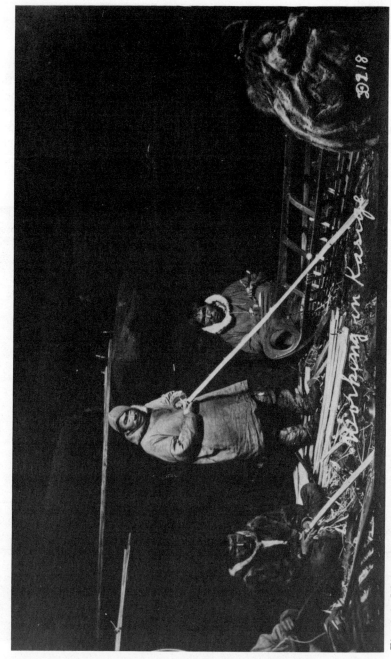

Fig. 3.8. Men at work in the qasgiq. (F. Drebert, Moravian Archives)

Men were astir in the qasgiq by three or four in the morning so they could set out on their day's doings and be home by sundown. When not directly engaged in subsistence activities, they often spent their time in the qasgiq working on wood. All men were carvers and spent hours making tools, weapons, bowls, kayaks, and masks. There the women brought them their meals, waiting demurely by their sides while each man emptied his own personal bowl. The qasgiq was also the scene of the ubiquitous sweat bath, wherein the central smoke hole was opened and the fire fed to an intense degree. After enduring this heat the men rubbed their bodies with urine aged in wooden buckets expressly for that purpose. The ammonia worked to cut the grease and, combined with a rinse of fresh water, effectively cleansed the participants. Women did not engage in sweat bathing.

Each man's place in the qasgiq reflected his social position. John wrote, "Custom places the aged—directly over the entrance, a tacit evidence of being ready to go out for good. The next in age occupy places on the right and left of the oldest and so on down the years to the youngest.—Generally speaking—the side of the Kashigi over the entrance is for the old men—and the two remaining sides are occupied by the middle aged—while the floor is for the boys."[24] The social structure of the qasgiq mirrored that of the natural world. The Yupiit believed that sea mammals lived in huge underwater qasgit, where they ranged themselves around the central firepit in ranked fashion comparable to that displayed by their human counterparts. From these underwater homes they could view their treatment by men and, based on what they observed, could choose or refuse to give themselves to human hunters. There they would also entertain powerful shamans who sought to influence their willingness to emerge from their home and give themselves up for human use.

The hunters who gave the most thought and care towards the animals they sought were richly rewarded, both socially and materially. John made mention of the power and authority of the good hunter (*nukalpiaq*) in the daily life of the qasgiq as well as in community life in general. The nukalpiaq contributed wood for the sweat bath and oil to keep the fat lamps lit. Successful hunters also figured most prominently in the distributions occurring during the winter ceremonial season, and through such gift-giving they both established and confirmed their power and prestige.

Although the extended families comprising a village group were not socially discrete, they were both economically and politically independent. There was no politico-economic hierarchy as described by anthropologist Ernest S. Burch, Jr., for the ranked societies of northern Alaska, where a whaling captain (*umialik*) and his wife collected surplus and much of the basic production of individual family members and later redistributed it.[25] Rather, a less centralized, although equally hierarchical, system worked to place every local extended family in competition with the others in their ability to accrue and redistribute surplus during both formal redistribution and informal hosting. For the Yup'ik Eskimos of the late nineteenth century, status and authority accrued to the one who could afford to give. Without the existence of a central authority figure, political integration was loose at best during times of plenty.

Although both political and economic integration focused primarily on the prowess and generosity of the nukalpiaq, his authority was mitigated by the counsel and valued knowledge of elders, who not only advised when to harvest but when to distribute. Dispute settlement within the group operated chiefly through ostracism and indirect confrontation of the offender through gossip and avoidance. Although the Yup'ik Eskimos did not possess formal government, as we know it, they were far from lawless. In noting that they had no law "except public opinion"[26] John inadvertently identified a diffuse yet powerful and effective force in traditional social control.

John went on to describe in general terms the tradition of oral recitation in the qasgiq by which elders transmitted hunting knowledge and rules for right living to younger community members. It was this tradition that the missionaries would enter into:

> The old men are the recognized monitors—and their suggestions bearing on general comfort in the Kashigi—are of the force of mandates.—They are the disseminators of knowledge as to the life the Eskimo lives.—These talks given as monologues or dialogues—bear on every phase of life. . . . These talks are handed down from one generation to another—and include such new accepted rules as later experience has proved to be sound and beneficial.—In this way truth and error—are confirmed in the young men—and the seeds of it planted in the youngest generation.[27]

John was accurate in his estimation of the degree of deference and respect shown the older men by their juniors in this social setting. While men worked, young boys watched attentively, fetching tools or raw materials when necessary. A young man might try his hand carving a scrap of spruce root, learning this necessary skill through success approximation. Young men were also admonished to perform helpful acts in the village at large, while keeping their minds filled with thoughts of the fish and other wildlife on whose goodwill their lives depended. By such thoughtful action they were believed to be making a path for the animals they would someday hunt. For instance, young men must keep the water bucket full at all times to attract the seals who were always thirsty for fresh water. Likewise, boys kept the water holes constantly free of ice, as it was the window of the world below. Seal spirits living in their underwater men's house could view the attention of would-be hunters by watching the condition of the central smoke hole in their abode. If hunters were giving them proper thought and care, the smoke hole would appear clear. If the hole were covered with snow, the seals' vision would be obstructed, and they would not emerge from their underwater world or allow themselves to be hunted. This belief motivated the young men as they carefully cleared ice from skylights and water holes alike.[28]

Although the lives of men and boys centered on the qasgiq, women and girls lived and worked in a different social setting. Each men's house was surrounded by one to a dozen smaller structures. In each of these *enet*, or sod houses, four to ten women, their daughters, daughters-in-law, and young children slept, worked, and took their meals. As cooking was often done in the entryway, and sweat bathing was reserved for the men's house, the sod houses were frequently cold and damp. However, given the small size of the structure and the large number of people often present, body heat as well as heat produced by the small seal oil lamps provided some warmth.

The residential division of the sexes that characterized village life had important ritual as well as social significance. In a variety of contexts, the women's house was likened to a womb in which biological, social, and spiri-

Fig. 3.9. Yup'ik girls, 1884. Note beaded earrings and belts. (A. Hartmann, Moravian Archives)

tual production was accomplished.[29] It was here that women worked to transform the raw materials supplied by their men into food and clothing for the people. A pregnant woman's activity within and exit from the house were correlated to that of the fetus within her own body.[30] In certain contexts, both the women's house and her womb were equated with the moon, the home of the *tuunraat*, the spirit keepers of the land animals. Spring itself was marked by the cutting of a door in the side of the women's sod house to permit ready egress.[31] A similar opening in the moon was necessary to release the land animals for the new harvest season. John noted that in the shamans' effort to insure success in the coming year they would "journey to the moon" (a euphemism for sexual intercourse), where they were said to use their power to induce the land animals to visit the earth.[32]

Not only was the women's house viewed in certain contexts as a symbolic womb, productive of animals as well as of people, women's activity (and inactivity) was also analogously tied to a man's ability to succeed in the hunt. Contact with women was carefully circumscribed so that a man could retain his power to pursue game. Men and women had distinctive eating utensils reserved for the exclusive use of each. In bed with his own wife, a man was warned never to sleep facing her back lest the braid of her hair appear hanging in front of his face and subsequently block his vision. Women's air was also considered polluting to young hunters, who were advised to pass on the windward side so as not to dull their senses.

At the same time that a hunter must protect himself from the debilitating effects of unclean air, socially restricted sight was necessary to produce powerful supernatural vision. Likewise, young women were admonished to avoid direct eye contact with hunters. A hunter's vision, like his thought and breath, must not be squandered. A man's ability to harvest animals as an infinitely renewable resource was contingent on his careful use of his own finite personal resources. Just as direct eye contact between the sexes was proscribed for successful hunting, successful hunting was the prerequisite for acquiring a wife.

THE FAMILY: COSMOLOGICAL REPRODUCTION

As a result of both residential and ideological separation, young Yup'ik men and women grew to adulthood in socially separate but closely related worlds. Young girls were taught at home by their mothers to weave baskets, mats, and socks from grass, to sew skins, and in other ways process the hunters' catch. Young boys, on the other hand, were sent at the age of five to live in the qasgiq with their father, brothers, and other male relatives. There they were schooled in woodworking and hunting lore. They tended the precious water bucket, shoveled the porches clear of snow, ran errands, and generally prepared themselves both mentally and physically for the day when they would ask the animals to give themselves to them so that they might supply the people's needs.

At puberty, or even before, a young woman's first marriage would be arranged. Both John and Edith noted, albeit with ethnocentric despair, that a number of trial marriages often occurred before a couple settled down to raise a family. Childlessness or incompatibility between the couple or members of their families often resulted in failed marriages. Although polygamous unions were infrequent, they did occur, especially when a hunter's harvesting abilities exceeded his wife's ability to care for his catch. Successive monogamous marriages were common, and a person often had three or four mates during a lifetime. Unlike polygamous unions, these were not particularly remarked upon in the oral tradition. A bride marked her formal acceptance of a suitor by the presentation of feast food to her new husband and his male relatives in the qasgiq. On that occasion, she would appear dressed in the new clothing that her husband's family had prepared for her.

The informality and downplay of the rite of marriage was countered by an elaborate set of prescriptions and proscriptions that came into effect after the birth of the couple's first child. Not only were the actions of both husband and wife rigorously monitored preceding and following the birth, but their names were changed and teknonomy (the designation of an individual as the parent of their child) was put into effect. Teknonomy is one of a number of ways in which the Yup'ik people to this day avoid direct reference and address. Another important means included referring to a child using a kin term reflective of the speaker's relationship to the person for whom the child was named. Thus a newborn baby might be called Apacungaq (literally "dear little grandfather"). Not isolated peculiarities, these practices had important and related cultural significance.

In the Yup'ik view of the world, procreation was not the addition of new persons to the inventory of the universe, but rather the substitution of one for another. Some spiritual essence passed with the name, and in an important way the Yupiit believed that the dead lived again through their namesakes. Out of respect for the namesake, however, the name was never used in direct address or indirect reference. Thus, at birth a person entered into a relationship with the dead based on shared name and a relationship with the living through terminological skewing. Later, when that person had offspring, the parent would enter into a relationship with the living child through shared name (teknonomy) while simultaneously entering into a relationship with the dead by way of terminological skewing in reference to the child. By means of this system a man became father to his father and offspring of his child, and alternate generations were equated. Here was more than a relationship between the living and the dead—a cycling between them and a consequent collapse of the system into two generations took place.[33]

John also observed that with the birth of their first child, a couple became subject to elaborate gift-giving requirements in the child's name. Besides

the relation through the name and the classificatory cycling between generations, at the birth of a child parents were bound to honor requests for the
bestowal of special favors by "nominal" relatives. This relationship was designated *cingarturluni* (from *cingar-* "to kiss or snuffle a child") and was most
often put into effect between a newborn and a member of the grandparental
generation. As John noted, a suitable return was also expected and might
occur either immediately or after the delay of many years when the child,
grown to adulthood, visited the home of distant relatives.

As the child grew, his or her first culturally significant accomplishments
(such as first bird harvested or first dance) also provided the occasion for
elaborate distributions. These distributions could occur during annual ceremonies or as a separate event accompanied by the feasting of the elders of
the community. Moreover, at all the major ceremonies the most valuable
gifts in the distributions were usually given in the name of the young children, who were, by name, their ancestors incarnate. Also, when guests gathered in the qasgiq for the distributions the shares were given out to the
eldest first on down to the youngest. At the very head of the receiving line,
however, were parents with babes-in-arms who received special gifts in the
name of their offspring.

John noted that for a girl the most important event was designated "putting away the doll"[34] in honor of her coming of age. On the occasion of her
first menstruation, a girl was sequestered, her condition approximating that
of the fetus in her social invisibility, restriction of movement, and prohibi-
tion of both childhood and adult activities. When she "stood up" after this
period of isolation, she must give her childhood playthings, including small
wooden dolls and their clothing, to other prepubescent females. Restrictions
surrounded the use of these dolls: forbidden from using them during the
winter or inside the house, young girls could only play with them outside
after the return of the geese. The dolls' dormancy in the interior of the
house during the winter and their emergence in the summer as the playthings of immature girls replicates both the transformation of their owners
through puberty restrictions into women capable of giving birth and the
birth process itself. Given the cyclical and interconnected Yup'ik view of
the world, what could have been more appropriate than requiring a girl to
put away her *irniaruaq* (literally "pretend child") between the time she could
play with it and the time when she could produce her own?[35]

YUP'IK COSMOLOGY: THE RINGED CENTER

The Yup'ik Eskimos possessed very specific ideas as to how the human and
animal worlds were constituted. They inscribed these ideas on the physical
world, which they viewed as the concrete manifestation of their cosmology.
Differences existed between men and women which framed activities in
everyday life and concepts about the sexually specific nature of the space in

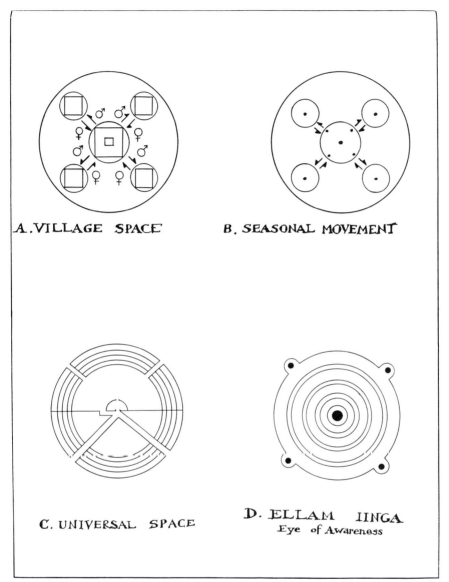

A. VILLAGE SPACE

B. SEASONAL MOVEMENT

C. UNIVERSAL SPACE

D. ELLAM IINGA
Eye of Awareness

Fig. 3.10. Yup'ik cosmology in cross section.

which these activities occurred. A major component of their annual cere-monial cycle was to effectively transform these relations so as to remake their world and their relationship to it. Through the ceremonies, the people ul-timately joined the domains of hunting and procreation as essential to assur-ing the reproduction of life and enacted reversals and inversions of the normal productive and reproductive relations between the sexes to recreate the world anew.

The image of the ringed center constantly recurs in Yup'ik cosmology and always with the connotation of vision as well as movement between worlds. As we have seen, the men's house was the spiritual window of the community, surrounded by the individual women's houses (Figure 3.10A). The spiritual rebirth and vision of an other-worldly reality accomplished there were the counterparts of the physical birth, female productivity, and seasonal rebirth symbolized by exit from the traditional women's house. It was largely, although not exclusively, in the men's house that visions of the supernatural were realized in material and dramatic form. However, physical birth and spiritual rebirth were not conceived as opposing each other. Rather the Yup'ik Eskimos were deeply committed to a cyclical cosmology and embodied their fundamental belief in the spiritual constancy underlying temporal flux in a multitude of forms.

As the men's house dominated the center of the community, the younger members of both sexes regularly traveled the space between public center and private productive periphery. Young women and girls dutifully brought cooked food to their male relatives in the qasgiq. Likewise, young men worked to sweep the porches and gather water for their mothers and sisters. In the evening a husband might visit his wife for social and sexual intercourse. The older men and women of the community, however, rarely breached the residential separation and left to the younger generation the job of going between. The winter ceremonials radically reversed this normal social separation.

The performance of a number of important ceremonies in the men's house dramatically reinforced the notion of this structure as the spiritual hub of the community, with its central firepit and smoke hole as passageways between the human and nonhuman worlds. Residents arranged themselves in ranked fashion around a central firepit in which the spirits of the dead (both human and nonhuman) came to reside during specific ceremonials. One of the most important traditional ceremonies was the Bladder Festival, held annually to insure the rebirth of the animals' *yuas* or "persons," thought to be located in their bladders. During the closing performances of the Bladder Festival, the shaman would climb out through the skylight to enter the sea, visit the seal people, and request their return. Likewise, at the end of the festival the men would remove the inflated bladders through the qasgiq smoke hole and take them to the icehole. There they would deflate them and send them back to their underwater qasgiq with the request that they return the following year.

In addition to serving as a passage permitting movement and communication between the world of the hunter and the hunted, the central qasgiq smoke hole served as a passageway between the world of the living and the dead. For example, in the event of a human death, the body of the deceased was pulled through the smoke hole, after first being placed in each of the hole's four corners. By this action the deceased, on the way from the world of the living to the dead, gradually exchanged mortal sight, lost at death, for the supernatural clairvoyance of the spirit world.[36]

The winter village was only seasonally occupied. As soon as the ice began to break in the spring, residents of the large winter villages dispersed to the mountains and the coast, then to the river mouths for summer fishing, and later in the fall to the tundra sloughs and streams for trapping and fall freshwater fishing. With the approach of freeze-up, families returned to the winter village, bringing with them the stores that they had successfully harvested from the tundra and the sea.

As in the daily cycle of movement between the men's and women's houses, the annual cycle of movement between small dispersed seasonal camps and the permanent winter village was a loosely bound movement from public ceremonial center to private, production-oriented periphery (Figure 3.10B). Moreover, the regional confederations that have been identified for western Alaska each centered on one or more of these winter settlements.[37] Each of these confederations, in turn, centered on the use of a loosely bound territory encompassing seasonal migrations around a fixed point. Crossing these boundaries for intervillage festivals was ritually controlled in a manner that replicated the movement between men's and women's houses within the village and the winter village and seasonal camp.[38]

Finally, the cosmological motif of successive levels of encompassment (a circle within a circle) apparent in the structure of daily life and movement in the world at large is also apparent in the Yup'ik conception of the universe. First, the world was believed to have originally been thin and permeable, hardening since its creation by Raven.[39] If a person journeyed far enough in any direction, he would eventually arrive at a point where the earth folded up into the skyland, the home of the spirits of the game.[40] This space between earth and sky was characterized by dramatic reversals of the normal seasonal cycle—men wearing parkas in the heat of the summer and, alternately, fish skin clothing in the snow. The skyland could also be reached by moving upward through the "holes" in the heavens (the stars). In one story recorded by Nelson[41] a shaman sitting on a hill had a vision in which the skyland came down upon him. He then climbed through three successive starholes, each of which provided access to another level of reality. From this vantage point he looked through the star holes and viewed the earth, just as the sea mammals viewed activity in the human domain by looking through the gut skylight of their underwater abode.

The earth not only was encompassed by a canopy from above, but below its thin surface resided the spirits of the dead, both animal and human, each in separate villages according to their social and biological affiliation. Four

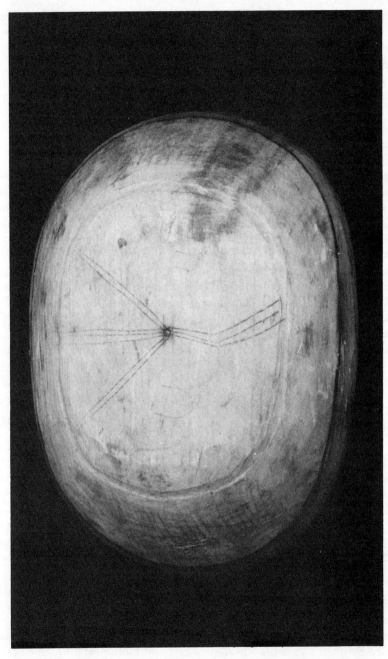

Fig. 3.11. Raven-foot design with rusted iron center on underside of wooden dish. (Kilbuck Collection, Ottawa University)

or five "steps" separated these two distinct but related domains. The numbers four and five recur in ceremonial transformation and probably refer to the steps required to move from one spatial domain to another.

Yup'ik cosmology can be schematically depicted as successive circles, each one simultaneously encompassing and encompassed (Figure 3.10C). In fact, this cosmological circle is a recurrent theme in both social and ceremonial activity and paraphernalia. The circle-and-dot motif so common in Yup'ik iconography is designated Ellam iinga (literally "the eye of awareness").[42] The use of this decorative motif is associated with both spiritual vision and the creation of a passageway between the human and spirit worlds. The central dot accompanied by four outlying dots has been identified as a means of both depicting as well as affecting the five-step movement between the world of the living and the dead. It is possible that the encompassing relationships described above were also a part of what was represented. Although both the smoke hole and the ice hole were rectangular rather than round, this does not diminish their significance as spiritual eyes. One variant of the circle-and-dot motif is, in fact, a circle with four small projections, one at each corner, within which was carved a dot surrounded by concentric circles (Figure 3.10D). The reference to square or rectangular holes and the quadrangle functioning like a circle and dot may form a logical symbolic complex with this added sacred dimension.

In cross section the human world can be seen to be encompassed by the spirit world. As we shall see, the nineteenth-century Yupiit annually enacted their ceremonial cycle to travel the distance between domains that they kept rigorously separated in daily life. If successful, ritual activity had the power to recreate the world anew. To perform this creative transformation, the ceremonies reversed the normal relationships between men and women, and between the human and spirit worlds.

THE CEREMONIAL CYCLE

Human action in daily life was controlled by the knowledge that the eye of *Ella* (the universe, awareness) was watching, literally, and that human activity was visible to the spirit world.[43] For the Yup'ik people, comparable visibility of game (its appearance, disappearance, and hoped-for reappearance) was a central problem and one which their ritual activity directly addressed. Ritualized movement in the ceremonies reversed the rules and rigorous separation between domains that daily life required. In so doing they powerfully recreated the passages between worlds as well as the power to see into and in some measure control them.

After freeze-up in November the people gathered in their winter villages to enjoy a "round of pleasure" which marked winter as the ceremonial season. In his ethnographic manuscripts, John gives succinct descriptions of all six of the major summer ceremonies, three of which focused on the creative reformation of the relationship between the human community and the

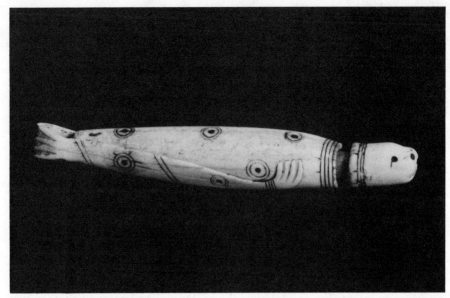

Fig. 3.12. Seal-shaped ivory needle case with wooden stopper decorated with circle-and-dot design. Length, five inches. (Kilbuck Collection, Ottawa University)

spirit world. In these three ceremonies (the Bladder Festival, the Feast for the Dead, and the masked dances known as Kelek) members of the spirit world were invited into the community, formally hosted, and finally sent back to their own domain. This ritual movement effectively recreated the relationship between the human and spirit worlds and placed each in the proper position to begin the year again.

One of the first ceremonies the Kilbucks described, and one that Edith would continue to remark upon into the 1920s, was the "Berry Festival" (Ingulaq). This ceremony is poorly documented and may have been much more important traditionally than either the Kilbucks realized or contemporary elders remember. What we do know suggests that along the Kuskokwim it was held in late summer or early fall after the berry harvest and just before freeze-up. It was marked by the invitation of one or more settlements by another to a dance and feast featuring different kinds of *akutaq* (literally "a mixture," including berries, seal oil, boned fish, tallow, etc.). The dances performed were also referred to as *ingulaq* in some areas and were characterized by short, slow songs performed by women who stood, eyes lowered, facing the audience, holding the edges of their garments and swaying from side to side. Both John and Edith participated in the event and on one occasion their first-born daughter performed a dance depicting John sawing boards.[44]

Often Ingulaq would also involve the rebuilding of the qasgiq. Men would remove its contents, repair the floor, and replace the benches. Then the women would hang new grass mats in the doorway and place a new gut covering over the central skylight. After the repairs had been accomplished, everyone would gather in the refurbished men's house for the Ingulaq. Given the social and ritual importance of the qasgiq as the locus of spiritual rebirth, in contrast to the birth imagery of the women's house, it is not surprising that its maintenance required such elaborate display and was necessary to open the ceremonial season.

John correctly noted that a major event of the winter ceremonial season was the Bladder Festival (Nakaciuq, from *nakacuk*, bladder, literally "something done with bladders"). At the time of the winter solstice, the people inflated the bladders of important animals killed that year and brought them into the qasgiq. The Yupiit believed these bladders contained the animals' souls, and during their stay in the qasgiq they treated them as honored guests.

The primary function of the Bladder Festival was to reverse the separation of body and soul effected at the time of the animal's death. As described above, a hunter worked to "draw" the animals through proper thought and deed. If successful, he returned to the village with his catch, which he immediately gave over to his wife or mother. The woman then greeted sea mammals with a drink of fresh water and land mammals with a drop of seal oil. Once this had been accomplished, she was free to butcher the animal. Though she might cook the meat and blubber, she carefully preserved the bladder, as it was believed to house the animal's soul.

At the approach of the winter solstice, the Yupiit performed a series of ceremonies which effectively reunited animal body and soul. The Bladder Festival was preceded by a ceremony known as Qaariitaaq in many areas. During Qaariitaaq the men painted the bodies of the village boys and led them from house to house each night, where the women gave them food. Through this ritual circuit, the children (perhaps representing spirits) opened the community to the spirit world.

Aaniq (literally "to provide a mother [for someone]") was held directly after Qaariitaaq and introduced the Bladder Festival proper. During Aaniq, two older men, dressed in gutskin parkas and referred to as "mothers," led a group of boys, who were termed their "dogs," around the village. The men collected newly made bowls filled with akutaq from the women, in a dramatic reversal of the usual pattern of women bringing cooked meat to their men in the men's house. This reversal of male and female roles marked the transition from the "inward" movement of Qaariitaaq, in which humans impersonating spirits prepared and opened the village to the spirit world, and the outward thrust of the Bladder Festival, which ended by sending the animal spirits back to their homes. In some areas Qaariitaaq and the Bladder Festival each lasted for five days, corresponding to the five steps that separated the worlds of the living and the dead.

During the Bladder Festival, the men's house and its residents were ritually purified by sweat baths and by the smoke from wild celery plants. They set aside routine activities and devoted the days to athletic competition between married and unmarried men, instruction in and performance of commemorative songs, and presentation of special feast foods. They performed all of these activities with the intent to draw out the souls of the animals residing in the bladders hung along the wall of the men's house.

On the last night of the Bladder Festival, the entire village, as well as invited guests from nearby villages, gathered in the men's house. Parents gave gifts to celebrate their children's accomplishments and distributed the wooden dolls of the young girls who had come of age. Finally, a huge villagewide distribution took place in which large amounts of frozen and dried fish and seal skin pokes full of seal oil were given away. John noted that, when giving these gifts, each donor stated that everything had been given to him. Giving gifts in someone else's name, particularly that of a deceased kinsman in the ascending generation, was a feature of a number of ceremonial distributions. It was one of a multitude of ways in which Yup'ik individuality was continually undercut by a sense of generational cycling and continuity. To this day in western Alaska, social ties between the living are both created and maintained through the relationship between the living and the dead.

Finally, at the close of the Bladder Festival, pairs of young men took the inflated bladders along with bunches of wild celery out through the central smoke hole and down to a hole in the ice (*nalugyaraq*). There they deflated the bladders and returned them to their underwater home where presumably they would boast of their good treatment and subsequently allow themselves to be taken by the villagers the following season. John's description of the Bladder Festival makes no reference to this last critical step in the ritual process.[45]

The central theme of the Bladder Festival was the regeneration of the hunted through ritually appropriate and respectful behavior on the part of the hunter. In turn, this focus on the return of the souls of the animals was part of a larger view of the world in which human and nonhuman "persons" alike were seen as but moments in a larger cosmological cycle. By this view the spiritual rebirth accomplished by the exit of the bladders through the qasgiq smoke hole opposed the image of physical birth, metaphorically accomplished through the cutting of a spring doorway in the woman's house. It was a view whereby procreation was not creation but one stage in an endless cosmological cycle of birth and rebirth.

The Bladder Festival was one of the traditional Yup'ik ceremonies most remarked upon, especially among the coastal people with their greater emphasis on sea mammals. There its religious significance was profound, and the period of its occurrence was a ritually dangerous time. According to John's description of the Bladder Festival as celebrated along the Kuskokwim,[46] however, it was a period during which the rules of the qasgiq were relaxed and everyone (including the children) took part, entering into the spirit of fun. Neither he nor Edith actively suppressed it as they did other elements of the traditional ceremonial cycle. Perhaps this was because the event was not as important along the Kuskokwim. It is also possible that the Kilbucks underestimated its importance in the traditional cosmological schema. It is noteworthy that John's knowledge of nalugyaraq, the last part of the ritual process, was deficient. Because he was a Christian missionary, the Yup'ik people may have been hesitant to include him.[47]

John and Edith's tolerance for the Bladder Festival was matched by their intolerance for the third major winter ceremonial, the Feast for the Dead. Known in some areas as Merr'aq (from *mer-*: "to drink"), this annual event was the public occasion on which the spirits of the human dead were invited into the human community to receive the food and clothing they required. Men initiated the event by placing stakes at the graveside, effectively "opening" the village and inviting the spirits to enter, as in the ceremonies prior to the Bladder Festival. As in the Bladder Festival, the people ritually cleansed the village in preparation for the arrival of the spirits. Moreover, they took great care during the ceremonial period to limit any human activity (such as sewing or chopping wood) that might injure or "cut" the souls during their journey to and from the center of the human world.

The Great Feast for the Dead (Elriq) was a much more elaborate event, held at five- to ten-year intervals. It attracted hundreds of people from the far corners of the Yukon-Kuskokwim delta and continued for four to six days. The major distributions took place on the fourth and fifth days of the ceremony, when first the women and then the men ritually clothed the living namesakes according to the sex of their deceased relative. Articles were required in sets of four, five, nineteen, or twenty (four sets of five totaling a person's twenty digits) to completely clothe the namesakes and, through them, the dead incarnate. Here again, the numbers four and five refer to the number of days after burial before a female and male shade finally departed, stepping down into the underworld land of the dead. The hosts often brought these gifts into the men's house through the central smokehole, reversing the route used to remove the human body at death. Just as the Bladder Festival reversed the separation of body and soul that occurred when a seal was killed, the Great Feast for the Dead effectively reversed the human mortuary process.

For the nineteenth-century Yupiit, the feeding and clothing of the namesakes at Elriq fed and clothed the dead as well. The event thus vividly expressed the relationship between the living and the dead and the Yup'ik belief in an essential generational continuity.[48] John and Edith early recognized this connection and in later years strongly opposed Elriq.[49] Moreover, they were appalled by the huge quantity of goods distributed and the resulting impoverishment of the host village. In the long run, they found this lack of economy more reprehensible than the ideology that motivated it.

Fig. 3.13. Yup'ik grave monuments a year before the Kilbucks' arrival on the Kuskokwim. (A. Hartmann, Moravian Archives)

John described a fourth important ceremony that he termed the "Masquerade," which probably is synonymous with the traditional ceremony Itruka'ar or Kelek. This complex ritual involved the singing of songs of supplication to the animal persons (yuas), accompanied by the performance of masked dances under the direction of the shaman. For the event carvers created ritually powerful masks that represented the spirits of the game as well as the tuunraat or shaman's spirit helpers.[50] Like the circle-and-dot motif, the large hooped masks functioned as eyes seeing into a world beyond the mundane. John accurately estimated the importance of the shaman in this event as an intermediary between the human and spirit worlds. He described his archrival as an absolute power, more feared than loved: "They frame the superstition in vogue; interpret signs and omens; dispel enchantments by conjuring; bewitch; predict future events, and regulate the supply of fish and game. A shaman with a reputation for success, gains quite an income by conjuring sick people. Like the Oracle of Delphi, the shaman's revelation bears two interpretations."[51]

In preparation for Kelek the shamans directed the construction of the masks that revealed the spirits as at once dangerous and helpful. Used in enactments of past spiritual encounters, the masks had the power to evoke them in the future. Kelek embodied yet another instance of the cyclical nature of Yup'ik cosmology whereby the past might be reborn in the future through appropriate action in the present. The missionaries, overwhelmed by Kelek's pagan implications and associated shamanic practices, failed to recognize the positive aspects of this point of view. Participation in Kelek was one of the first things forbidden mission converts.

A fifth ceremony that John described was the "commercial play" known as Petugtaq (literally "something tied on," referring to the stick to which small models of the gift requests were attached). This event is usually described as an intravillage exchange of goods between men and women.[52] By John's account the gifts were relatively small, the idea being to have fun rather than to play for great amounts. The men might begin the play by making tiny replicas of things that they desired, such as grass socks, birdskin caps, or fish-skin mittens. These replicas were hung from a wand or stick and taken to the women of the village. Each woman then chose one of the images and prepared the item requested. When all was ready, the women brought their gifts to the qasgiq, where they presented them to the men, who were duty-bound to provide a suitable return.

In some areas, at least, enjoyment derived from the pairing of both biologically and socially unlikely couples in the exchange because no one knew who had made a specific request until the actual distribution. In this context the pairing of cross-cousins (that is, cousins related through parents of the opposite sex, including mother's brother's and father's sister's children) was considered particularly delightful. In Yup'ik, the terms used to refer to cross-sex cross-cousins were *nuliacungaq* (dear little wife) and *uicungaq* (dear

little husband).[53] Marriage between cross-cousins was not traditionally prescribed; however, teasing, complete with sexual innuendo, characterizes the
relationship between cross-cousins to this day, as distinct from the much
more serious and respectful relationship between siblings and parallel cousins—that is, cousins related through same-sex parents, including mother's
sister's children and father's brother's children. The pairing of cross-cousins
during the distribution added spice to the event and provided the occasion
for endless banter.

As in the men's impersonation of women just prior to the Bladder Festival, the pairing of cross-cousins during Petugtaq derived its transformative
and cathartic power from its reversal of the proper day-to-day relationship
between husband and wife. In some areas the two who exchanged gifts were
reported to have shared each other's bed as well. Although this may have
occurred along the Kuskokwim, John and Edith were blissfully unaware
that any sexual activities were associated with the exchange. Over the years
they recorded their participation in numerous Petugtaq exchanges, towards
which they maintained a largely tolerant attitude.[54]

The sixth major ceremony that John described was Kevgiq, often referred
to as the Messenger Feast.[55] A mutual hosting between villages characterized Kevgiq, whereby one village would go to another to dance and receive
gifts. A host village initiated the event by presenting their guests with a
long list of wants, and the guests subsequently reciprocated with a list of
their own. Besides collecting the articles to be given, each village composed
songs which described the desired articles and the name of the individual
from whom the object was requested.

The quality and the quantity of the gifts given during Kevgiq excited
considerable rivalry, and in some areas the attending guests were designated
curukat or "attackers." A calculated ambiguity circumscribed Kevgiq, as a
fine line existed between friend and foe. Although Kevgiq shared features
with the other ceremonies, it stands out as a particularly elaborate display
and distribution of the bounty of the harvest, providing a clear statement to
the spirits of the fish and game that right had been done by them and that
the hunters were ready to receive them anew. Indeed, two important functions of Kevgiq were the redistribution of wealth within and between villages and the expression and maintenance of status distinctions.[56]

The details of the traditional ceremonial cycle that John recorded in 1910
represent the studied observations of twenty-five years living along the Kuskokwim. During the first years after their arrival, little of this was clear to
them. Although John and Edith gradually became familiar with the general
contours of traditional Yup'ik ceremony and framed their objections to it,
they never became fully cognizant of the unified cosmology that the ceremonies both embodied and empowered.

Individually, the ceremonies served to emphasize different aspects of the
relationship between humans, animals, and the spirit world. Ingulaq pre-

pared the community, opening it up to the spirit world and perhaps inviting their participation. The Bladder Festival (Nakaciuq), along with related ceremonies including Aaniq and Qaariitaaq, insured the rebirth and return of the animals in the coming harvest season. Dramatic ritual reversals of the normal productive relationships opened the human community to the animal persons, inviting them to enter and receive recompense for what they had given and presumably would continue to give in the future. Both the annual Feast for the Dead and the Great Feast for the Dead (Elriq) served the same function within human society as the Bladder Festival served within animal society; in the Feasts for the Dead the souls of the human dead were invited into and subsequently dismissed from the center of the human world, where they were ritually fed and elaborately clothed in the person of their namesakes. The Masquerade (Kelek) involved masked dances which dramatically recreated past spiritual encounters to elicit their participation in the future.

Finally, in the same way that the efficacy of the Bladder Festival derived from its reversal of the normal relationships between sexes and between hunter and hunted, the intravillage Petugtaq and the intervillage Messenger Feast (Kevgiq) played on, exaggerated, and reversed normal social relationships between husband and wife and between host and guest. The latter also served important social functions, including the display of status, social control, the initiation of the young, and the redistribution of wealth. At the same time, it provided a clear statement to the spirits of the game that the hunters were once again ready to receive them. Throughout, human action was represented as instrumental. Together the ceremonies indicated a cyclical view of the universe whereby correct action in the past and the present reproduced abundance in the future. Over the years the Kilbucks would dramatically challenge the expression of this point of view, although they would never fully replace it.

CHAPTER 4

GOSPEL OF SERVICE

CHRISTIANIZATION AND CIVILIZATION

Following an introduction to the world of the nineteenth-century Yup'ik Eskimos, consider the point of view of the nineteenth-century missionaries who came to transform them. What were the Kilbucks' goals and what were the means they employed to accomplish them? The Kilbucks came as activists bent on changing what they found. What ideals and policies guided them in their work?

Moravian missionaries sought to accomplish a two-fold conversion, in Alaska as well as in other foreign and domestic fields. First and foremost, they came to baptize and to Christianize; however, they believed this to be neither practicable, nor even possible, unless the people among whom they worked could be "civilized" as well. These two goals had run side by side in Moravian missionary policy for over a hundred years and continue in a modified form to this day. In a pamphlet written in 1927, dealing with rules and regulations of the Moravian mission in Alaska, the dual intent is clear: "Primarily, the object of the Mission is to promote the Kingdom of God, not to spread civilization. Yet this it also does incidentally and as a secondary result. Therefore the missionary shall encourage cleanliness, and thrift, and everything that elevates the mental and moral and physical condition of the people, whilst laying special stress on the truth that life comes first of all from above." [1]

The marriage between Christianization and civilization is not unique to Moravian policy and is venerably grounded in Western social thought. The Rousseauian view of natural man as born pure, and only subsequently corrupted by civilization, cannot be dismissed in the history of Western man's attempt to make sense of the "primitive." However, the Hobbesian perception of man as naturally brutish and mean and in need of being tamed by civilization has dominated Western thought. The evolutionary views of civilization popular in the late nineteenth century, and part of the intellectual climate the Kilbucks experienced during their growing up, were only the most recent manifestations of this Hobbesian perspective.

On their arrival the Kilbucks both overestimated and underestimated the Yup'ik people. While they admired Yup'ik simplicity, the view of them as pure arose less from respect for their culture than the romantic view of them as overgrown children with the missionaries as their parents. Ambiguously, this childlikeness implied both irrationality and unspoiled innocence. Thus, while the missionaries valued Yup'ik spiritual potential, they deprecated their actual state. Moravian policies in the field were based on a contradictory evaluation—the Yup'ik people were equal in God's eyes and worthy of salvation, but Yup'ik beliefs were inferior. Eskimos merited respect as individual people but not as a "race." The Kilbucks were impelled to missionize among them not only to communicate the word of God but to alleviate the presumed poverty of Yup'ik culture.

Though the marriage between Christianization and civilization that the Kilbucks endorsed can largely be understood within the broader framework of late nineteenth-century social thought, it also reflects a related ideological shift and gradual secularization that was at work within Moravian ideology. For example, in the Moravian community of Bethlehem, established during the early 1700s, the primary goal of life had originally been to develop an intimate relationship with the Savior. In this context death was joyfully welcomed and even sought after as the realization of this goal. Towards these ends, the demands of the choir system and the spiritual life that it made possible took precedence over nuclear family ties. One hundred years later Bethlehem had changed from a communal society of symbolic brothers and sisters almost monastically focused on simple living and religious service to a privatized community of socially stratified families whose cultural ideal was usefulness to family and society. A growing need for close relations with family and community had replaced the original intimate friendship with the Savior.[2] As a result, the relationship between life and death had also been transformed. Whereas believers originally welcomed death, later they submitted to it with resignation. They no longer perceived sickness exclusively as a means of bringing people closer to the Savior but now saw it as an affliction to be battled. This changed attitude found direct expression in the Kilbucks' work along the Kuskokwim, where they would put considerable energy into finding a cure for physical ills when they could and teaching the acceptance of death with resignation when they could not.

By the time the Kilbucks began their ministry the intensity of the original religious mission of the Moravian Church had taken a more routine place alongside everyday social and economic responsibilities. The nineteenth century had seen the transformation of the religious holism of the first Moravians into a privatized community, interested in the more permanent world beyond this one but cherishing their time together here on earth. Ironically, the Moravian mission as carried to Alaska by the Kilbucks involved a comparable transformation, where the spiritual holism of traditional Yup'ik cosmology was confronted by the cultural ideal of salvation of one's immortal soul primarily through service to family and society.

Edith gave the clearest view of the Kilbucks' secular responsibility as temporal "civilizers" in an unpublished article entitled "Do Missions Pay?"[3] Partly because of the reflective quality of the fifteen-page manuscript, it articulates what the Kilbucks thought they were doing and how, for them, it "paid off."

Edith began by describing the state of affairs at the time of their arrival as "primitive in the extreme . . . when ignorance, superstition and dirt reigned supreme."[4] She proceeded with a litany of the physical ills that plagued the Yup'ik people in the 1880s, including poor housing, lack of ventilation, crowding, unwashed bodies, uncombed hair, rotten food, diseases, and worst of all oppression by the traditional shaman, or medicine man. Under the circumstances, the course was clear: new homes must be built and the unhygienic manner of living eliminated.

After a brief description of the means used to accomplish these goals, she reiterated the fundamental mission policy:

> The gospel of service is the gospel that wins. . . . So hand and hand with the message of salvation went the duties of teaching better living here and now. Better homes, better food, better clothes, the use of soap, and water, and washtubs of dishes and spoons and knives and forks—of individual cups and towels—of reading and writing and singing and playing—of marriage and fidelity and the training of children—and the hundred and one things that go to make up the life of us all.[5]

The Kilbucks brought far more than a spiritual message to the Kuskokwim. With them came everything from soap to the institution of marriage—in that order.

Given the ends the Kilbucks hoped to accomplish, it is important to view the means they employed. Although the conversion process was a complicated one, from the beginning the Kilbucks' approach to their work was relatively straightforward. It can be divided into five basic activities: building, talking, healing, teaching, and traveling. If the formula was simple, putting it into effect was not always so easy.

BUILDING: RESTRUCTURING SPACE AND TIME

Although motivated by a desire to save souls, success in the manual arts was what sustained the missionary party during their first year in Alaska. John and Brother Weinland arrived clear on what they wanted to build, but "greener than new corn" in their ability to actualize their plans. They learned by experience and by following the advice of the natives. However, they did not seek to replicate local technology but to adapt Western building patterns to the tundra with as little modification as possible.

The process often frustrated them. Not trusting that suitable building materials would be available locally, they had brought lumber with them from California; but the late summer rain wet the wood and made it unmanageable. Moreover, when they tried to dig into the permafrost to lay the foundation for their house, the hole kept filling up with water. They persevered, however, and with the help of Mr. Lind, the local trader, the fruit of their first construction season was one small mission house. From this meager base, the mission would grow exponentially over the years.

Settled in a wood frame house, the missionaries next set about encouraging the Yup'ik people to follow suit. Traditional building patterns were judged both structurally primitive and functionally unhygienic, and whenever practical the missionaries encouraged converts to build and maintain log houses. They considered this new construction an essential part of the conversion process: "The first and most important thing to be done was to get them up out of the ground into more healthful and sanitary houses. Improvements along this line came slowly in the form of small log huts half out of the ground. . . . However, a beginning was made, and proud indeed were the owners of these first houses. They said, 'We are becoming like white people.'"[6]

In the same way that the missionaries introduced new ways of constructing space, they also structured their activities according to a very different sense of time. Days were regularly divided by periods of work and prayer, as were the weeks and seasons. Church activities and holidays punctuated life in Bethel. Both the calendar and the clock were introduced, and with them the objectification of time as a commodity that could and should be saved, not squandered. Making time measurable was the first step in the objectification and eventual commoditization of individual activity into labor.

John made efforts toward this end from the very beginning. He found it "trying and inconvenient" in the extreme that the Yupiit did not share his "civilized" concept of time as a scarce and limited resource and work as a means rather than an end: "It is certainly hardly to be expected that these people should work as steadily as the laborers of civilized countries, seeing that they do not know what it is to work year in and year out, from morning to night. The work necessary for their way of living is very little and is of a spasmodic character. . . . To have anything done quickly and thoroughly we must be on the spot, otherwise a small job will drag out beyond our patience."[7]

Although it would be many years before the Yup'ik people would be drawn into replicating mission building patterns and exploiting the concep-

Fig. 4.1. The sawyers, 1890. (J. Kilbuck, Moravian Archives)

tual framework that went with them, the model was in place, and the missionaries vividly presented the Yupiit with the possibility of "becoming like white people." The mission buildings, with their wealth of Western artifacts, created an image that helped in the conversion process as much as any word or deed. John explicitly used the image of technological progress to communicate the spiritual progress he intended: "I said their stone-axes were well enough, until they saw the white-man's ax. Now a native does not think of using a stone-ax, but prefers the white-man's ax. 'So the Gospel of Jesus Christ is to be and will be preferred above any other religion.'" [8]

In their work at Bethel the Moravians were not simply constructing buildings but were restructuring basic categories of space and time. At the very least, the construction of the first mission house introduced the Yupiit to alternate means of building the world (literally and figuratively) and was one of the many ways in which the Moravians made them aware that a way of life existed other than their own. [9]

TALKING

As mentioned again and again in both private correspondence and official reports, a primary goal of the first year was to learn to speak the language. Without this skill, nothing else was possible. Edith wrote:

> His [the missionary's] first great need was to learn the language—a language that had never been reduced to writing. In the whole country there was not to be found a single individual who could speak both English and the native tongue, so the task of acquiring the language was beset with difficulties at every turn. Finally, however, some progress was made. We were able to understand each other better as time passed, and in proportion to our ability to talk our influence grew. [10]

In recognizing the importance of learning the native language to facilitate the work of conversion, Edith echoed a fundamental tenet of Moravian missionary policy, one that had grown out of a hundred years of experience in foreign mission work. [11] John also maintained that linguistic competence was the key to effective conversion. In his first letter to Bishop de Schweinitz he confided his hope that his native knowledge of Delaware would help him to master the Yup'ik language. After a year's work, he reported their progress: "In all our dealings with the natives we have been able to get along without the aid of an interpreter. We have learned a great many words, but words are not all we need in order to speak the language. We hope to make a more rapid progress next year, as we begin to have an idea of the manner of speaking and the mode of thinking among the natives." Later that same summer, Edith added, "Natives were around us all Summer and we made fair progress at learning their language. We know about 200 words and can talk without an interpreter to them." [12]

The acquisition of vocabulary was a laborious process. In the beginning

Fig. 4.2. House building in Bethel, 1893. (J. Kilbuck, Moravian Archives)

no published Yup'ik grammar or dictionary existed to guide them in their efforts. The missionary party had to rely on word lists (mostly nouns) laboriously compiled during their daily intercourse with the natives and shared with each other at night. Their recording in the native language was largely written as a heuristic prompt, rather than in an effort at scientific documentation. As a result, each missionary developed his own idiosyncratic orthography.[13]

More problematic than inconsistencies in writing styles were the variable meanings the missionaries attached to individual Yup'ik terms. Moreover, as often as not, their initial understanding of a Yup'ik expression proved flawed. In his manuscript history of the Moravian Mission in Alaska, John recorded an example of this process of trial and error in the field. During the construction of the first mission house, Brother Weinland pointed to the building paper that was being put up and asked an old man what it was: "'Nathloaka [*nalluaqa*]' replied the native. Then Bro. Weinland by gestures informed the man that '*nathloaka*' would be put all over the house.—This was the truth, for 'I don't know'—(the meaning of 'Nathloaka') was plainly to be seen in every part of the building."[14]

Although the consequences of this misunderstanding were humorous, Edith recorded another more serious misfiring.[15] While John was traveling during their second summer in Alaska, he met a native from Bethel who reported that Edith had "died a little bit" in his absence. John was scared and prepared to come home at once. The native went on to say that when he had left, Edith was walking around again, and so alleviated some of John's fear. When John finally did arrive home, he found Edith hale and hearty, having suffered a spell of cramps.

Although the first year brought progress in the command of numbers of words, the issue of mutual understanding, especially on spiritual matters, remained unresolved. In John's second annual report he described the manner in which linguistic incompetence still comprised a major hindrance:

> For a time the [Sunday school] lessons were translated, but this method was far from satisfactory. The lessons were at first put into the simplest English and then Mr. Lind would translate it into the simplest Russian to his interpreter who, in turn, would translate into the Eskimo language. Somehow we could not get the idea of translating into the head of the native interpreter, and frequently we spent a whole evening over a few short sentences. Often the work of one evening had to be revised, as Mr. Lind's woman would declare that Foetka's translation was not correct. So I never was entirely certain that my lessons were entirely correct. Mr. Lind thought that Foetka had been instructed by the Greek [Orthodox] priest to mislead us if we required his services in studying the language of this country.[16]

Whether or not intentional problems in interpretation resulted from this roundabout method of instruction, a more effective means to confuse and deflect Moravian efforts is hard to imagine. Later in the same report, John recorded the native response to the dilemma: "More than one native has expressed a desire to know more of our teachings and are looking forward to the time when our tongues will be 'light.' They say that to-day our tongues are too heavy, and therefore they can not understand us." [17]

The missionaries made slow but steady progress in language acquisition. When the first school opened in September 1886, Weinland took charge of the classroom, freeing John for intensive work on the language, which he in turn was expected to communicate to the other missionaries. Although the job of mastering the Yup'ik language was a priority from the beginning, gaining the fluency required to communicate their special message was a slow task. Three years after their arrival, Edith voiced the frustrations of having a willing audience, but one as unable to understand their message as they were to express it: "Sometimes we think we know a good deal of their language; but when we come to explain the love of Christ Jesus, what we do know seems as nothing, and we find it impossible to make them understand us as we should. When, O when, will our tongues be loosed, that we may preach and teach unhampered by this great barrier! Soon, soon we hope and pray." [18]

HEALING

Their deficiency in the Yup'ik language initially prevented the mission party from sowing the seeds of salvation by preaching; healing, in the broad sense of the word, provided the bridge that language failed to supply. After the initial visits of curious Yup'ik and Ingalik men and women anxious to discover the reason behind the arrival of this strange entourage, the chief context in which the missionaries ministered to the people was in caring for the sick. A year after their arrival, Edith described the situation: "The natives call our place 'sick town' or 'the village of the sick.' We have had some sick person with us almost constantly, and often more than one. Others only came for medicine. . . . The natives bring all their troubles to us, whether it be sickness, an old broken ax or a canoe to be mended. They think if any one can help them out, we can." [19] Later that same year Edith gave evidence of the general in her description of the particular: "Our little patient's boil is very bad. His mother is with him night and day, caring for him very tenderly. Three other cases here today for treatment. Every day has some. Some we can cure, some we can only relieve, and others we can not benefit in any way. They have great faith in everything we do, and this is one advantage." [20]

On their arrival, the missionaries were caught between an epidemiologically virgin population on the one hand and imported infectious diseases on the other. The great need for medical services eventually led to the dispatch of a trained nurse in 1893 and the arrival of Edith's brother, Dr. Herman Romig, in 1896. The Moravians were ready and willing to respond to the situation because of their association of physical with moral healing. For them, health and wholeness involved the well-being of both the body and the spirit. They saw the physical ills of the Yup'ik people as a partial reflection of their moral inadequacy. As a result, they combined medicine with prayer to help the sick, using opportunities for healing the body to heal the soul. Conversely, they took the return of a patient's health as an external sign of inner salvation.

The Yup'ik people also interpreted physical well-being as both the essence of complete personhood and a reflection of proper mental state. An ill person was considered less than whole and guilty for either knowingly or unknowingly disregarding the rules for living. Though the Yupiit did not view illness exclusively as punishment, they believed a person's offenses eventually came back to him. To be cured a person must not only care for the body, but "think good thoughts" and act according to the rules. Similarly, the missionaries would teach that salvation must be based on an individual's desire to be saved and commitment to living the good life.

Traditionally, the Yup'ik Eskimos treated illness with a combination of plant and animal remedies, acupuncture ("poking"), and physical manipulation (a "laying on of hands") by their religious leaders, the shamans. They were initially receptive to the missionaries' connection between physical and spiritual healing, as the shamans likewise combined the healing of body and soul. Moreover, although they initially resisted any kind of operation, saying that they would not allow anybody to "cut their meat,"[21] they were not in principle opposed to new kinds of medicines. In their medical ministry the missionaries always held their skills as subordinate to and deriving potency from the "Good Physician," Christ himself. Their Yup'ik patients gradually came to share this view, deducing by their own logic that the missionaries' god made the medicines work.

TEACHING

From the beginning of the Moravian mission the goal was to establish a school as soon as possible. This policy, too, had its roots in time-tested mission policy, as it had proven a fundamental tool in the process of religious as well as cultural conversion. Throughout Moravian history the chapel and school stood side by side. Their faith was a faith of the Book and required commitment to the Word by their converts, that is, to a textualized truth. The school taught young scholars to read and write. In making available the written word, language would for the first time be taken out of its immediate context. Moreover, the environment in which the children were trained—schoolhouse space and time—was as significant as the skills that were taught. Through the schools the Kilbucks and their cohorts initiated the process of forming an analogue to Western culture along the Kuskokwim.

Fig. 4.3. The Bethel mission, 1887, with the first house on the far left. Drawing by John Kilbuck. (Moravian Archives)

Although Weinland occasionally referred to teaching children who gathered at the mission, the missionaries were unable to establish a school during their first year at Bethel because of their late arrival and subsequent need to devote their energies to maintaining themselves. Yet they had made enough progress by the following fall to allow the missionaries to open the doors of the newly completed schoolroom to half a dozen scholars, four boys and two girls, whose number doubled by midyear.

The Moravians established the school with the understanding that it would receive financial support from the United States Bureau of Education. This arrangement was mutually beneficial, as the mission needed funds and the government needed staff and educational facilities for the new territory. Although controversy developed over the number of days the school should operate per year and the support accorded each student, the school received sufficient federal support to maintain steady expansion over the next ten years.

Edith was matron of the school during its maiden year. Describing her duties to her father, she wrote, "I have the sewing on hand now, which means to make and mark for each boy two towels, two handkerchiefs, two shirts, two pairs of pants and a pair of mittens. They look quite neat and like white boys when they have their long, matted hair cut, and are dressed in white drilling shirts, blue denim pants and blue suspenders. They are proud of it, too." The following August she continued, "Our spare time is spent in planning and calculating for the school. Food and clothing, cooking, washing and ironing, mending, baking, and dividing off the victuals, all must be seen to by one of us if full satisfaction is to be had. All of it is such 'little work', but we are kept very busy." [22] Edith Kilbuck's impact lay in the cumulative effect of "such little work."

In a letter to Bishop de Schweinitz at the close of the school's first year, John proposed training school boys in "habits of industry" to better suit them for their adult lives:

> If the Government considers trapping a proper branch of the school, I will adopt the following plan: I will provide the boys with a competent trapper, who is to receive a part of the furs trapped by the boys as pay. At first I will furnish the traps, but eventually I will expect each boy, as he is able, to buy his own traps. . . . I will then expect the trappers to provide for their own clothing, and, if possible, pay for at least part of their board. The idea is to train the boys to habits of industry, so that when we send them into the world they may not only take their place among their fellows, but may push ahead and elevate their physical condition. I believe the notion prevails in some minds that the school will turn out Cossack [Kass'aq: Caucasian] people, who will not be able to get along as well as the native. I will do all I can to put this notion to utter confusion. [23]

John's goal of teaching native skills so that non-native virtues would be inculcated at the same time is visible in his proposal. In it can be seen, in microcosm, the trademarks of what became a lifelong policy of cultural conversion.

Ironically, while the missionaries focused on learning Yup'ik, the chief reason parents were willing to send their children to school was for the scholars to learn English and thus gain access to one apparent source of missionary power—the written word. In July 1889 John wrote, "Hitherto I have not been very successful in getting scholars from below, but as there is a prospect of a cannery or two being established at the mouth of the river next Spring, I hope to be able to secure quite a number of bright boys, by holding up the advantage they will have in securing work if they know a little English." [24] The desire to gain a degree of control through an understanding of the language of the other was apparently mutual. The features of the mission schools most criticized today (insistence on English, removal of children from their parents, imposition of scheduled order) were explicitly initiated with the best intentions of everyone involved.

Though they supported the mission school and were instrumental in the establishment of educational policy, the Kilbucks were not primarily teachers during their first fifteen years on the Kuskokwim. Weinland taught during the school's maiden year, and not until the next fall did John take charge of the boys. When the mission received reinforcements in the fall of 1888, the school was given first to the newly arrived Brother Weber and eventually, in 1892, to the experienced teacher Miss Mary Mack. John characteristically devoted himself to the maintenance of the mission as a whole, including the school, and as his Yup'ik improved, to carrying the word to the surrounding villages. John made it clear that if new missionaries able and willing to take over the school had not arrived, he would have given the school second place to duties he felt more pressing: "As to appointing the missionary a Government teacher, my idea is that it should not be done. Such an office will prevent him from looking after his people. The congregation that we may gather will be so scattered that a visitation will mean absence from home from a day to a week, or even the Winter, when the people are most likely to be at home." [25]

Finally, an important human exchange occurred concurrent with this aspect of their work. By the beginning of the school's second year, Edith pictured the reciprocal nature of the relationship:

> They are independent and jolly boys, yet there are times when they crave a mother's interest and care. Scarcely an hour passes but one comes to me for this, another for that, and yet another to tell me of some little unimportant joy or sorrow. I think they know I love them; for I have only to ask for anything once and any and all are ready to do it. . . . Indeed it is a great comfort to have the children so confiding and free. We often wonder how our time would pass if we were without them. They cheer many long hours and evenings. [26]

TRAVELING

> *Home is like a lodging place for him.*
> —*Edith Kilbuck, 1888*[27]

In his letter to Bishop de Schweinitz, John expressed another career trademark—his commitment to traveling. The mission field was vast, the population scattered, and he was convinced that rather than wait for people to come to the mission, it was his duty to take his message to them. With the advantage of hindsight, it seems inconceivable that a man aspiring to so profoundly influence the Yup'ik people could have done otherwise. However, the history of other Alaska missions, including the Moravian mission at Carmel,[28] indicates that not all missionaries were either able or willing to follow his example.

The Moravians had originally chosen Bethel as a mission site because of its central location and its proximity to a half dozen winter villages, each having a population of between fifty and two hundred. As they had hoped, natives visited the mission with increasing regularity as it became better known. Its proximity to the Alaska Commercial Company trading post of Mumtreglak attracted visitors, as did the medical aid available at the mission. Curiosity about the mission itself drew regular "customers," as Edith sometimes called them. Though the missionaries were glad to receive them at the mission, they recognized that for every visitor another ten natives waited in the home villages. From the outset John and Edith realized that to reach the people whom they hoped to convert they would have to go to them.

The first missionary trips were conducted as much to get to know the people as to introduce the gospel. During their first winter in Bethel, John and Brother Weinland traveled together to nearby Napaskiak (*Napaskiaq*) to attend a local celebration: "Feb. 23rd John and Billie went to Nepaskiagamute [Napaskiak] to attend an *Eckerushica* or dance. They stayed all day but as it was only the practice day they did not see much. . . . Feb. 26th. This morning John came home. He said the natives from below came in a body and the Kashima was jam full. They kept up this frolic until midnight, and then they tried to sleep."[29] Aside from these brief forays away from home, John made no major trips during his first year in Alaska. Weinland made a one-hundred-mile trip to Russian Mission on the Yukon with Trader Lind in March 1886. Their limited knowledge of the language, however, made preaching impossible and forced the missionaries to stay close to home, concentrating their efforts on building a mission base.

John did not begin the regular traveling for which he became famous until the fall of 1887. Also, he did not write his first major journal to Edith, detailing the ups and downs of his trip, until his seventy-three-day journey to Carmel in the winter of 1888–1889. We know of earlier junkets pri-

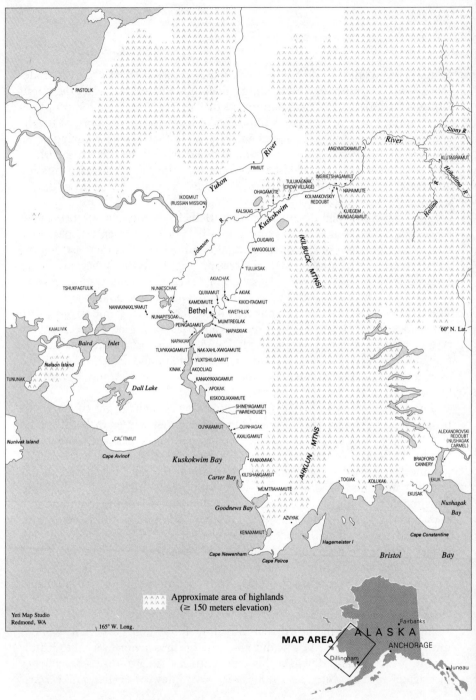

PASTOLIK

Yukon River

PIMIUT

IKOGMIUT
(RUSSIAN MISSION)

OHAGAMUTE

KALSKAG

Johnson R.

Kuskokwim R.

ANGYAXOXAMIUT

Stony R

KLUTAGRAMUT

INGRIETSHAGAMIUT

TULUKAGNAK
(CROW VILLAGE)

River

Hoholitna R.

KOLMAKOVSKIY
REDOUBT

NAPAIMUTE

KUIEGEM
PAINGAGAMIUT

OUGAVIG

KWIGOGLUK

TULUKSAK

AKIACHAK

QUIXAMUT   AKIAK

KAMEXMUTE   KIKICHTAGMIUT

NUNAPITSOAK   KWETHLUK

Bethel

PEINGAGAMIUT   MUMTREGLAK

LOMAVIG   NAPASKIAK

NAPAKIAK

TUVYAXAGAMIUT   NAK-XAHL-XWIGAMUTE

YUXTSHILGAMIUT

KINAK   AKOCLIAQ

KANAXYAXAGAMIUT

APOKAK

KISKOQUAXAMUTE

SHINEYAGAMIUT
("WAREHOUSE")

OUYAXAMIUT   QUINHAGAK

AXALIGAMIUT

CAL'ITMIUT

Nunivak Island

Cape Avinof

Kuskokwim Bay

Carter Bay

KANAXMIAK

KIL'TSHANGAMIUT

MUMTRAHAMUTE

Goodnews Bay

AZVIYAK

KENAXAMIUT

Cape Newenham

Cape Peirce

TSHUKFAGTULIK

NUNATSCHAK

NANVAXNAXLYAMUT

KAIALIVIK

Baird   Inlet

Nelson Island

TUNUNAK

Dall Lake

(KILBUCK MTNS)

ARKLUN MTNS

TOGIAK   KOLUKAK

EKUSAK

Hagemeister I

Bristol   Bay

60° N. Lat.

ALEXANDROVSKII
REDOUBT
(NUSHAGAK
CARMEL)

BRADFORD
CANNERY

EKUK

Nushagak
Bay

Cape Constantine

∧∧∧∧ Approximate area of highlands
      (≥ 150 meters elevation)

Yeti Map Studio
Redmond, WA

165° W. Long.

MAP AREA

A L A S K A

Fairbanks

ANCHORAGE

Dillingham

Juneau

Map 3. The Yukon-Kuskokwim delta, 1885

marily through Edith's journal entries to her father. On August 3, 1886, she wrote, "John and Abraham start up the river to collect a raft of logs some twenty miles from this place. . . . John wishes to bring a raft of sixty logs if he can find so many. I hated to see him go, when Katie [born July 15, 1886] was so young and I not strong yet; but it was necessary, and so he went. He expects to be gone about three weeks."[30] John came home on August 22, but in less than a week he was off again. Although the fortuitous arrival of a raft of logs aborted the second trip, the pattern of arrival and departure increasingly typified their life along the Kuskokwim.

The winter of 1886–1887 saw more traveling on John's part than during the preceding winter, though not for the purpose of preaching to the people. As breakup had been late, and food was in short supply, John made a number of trips during the winter, mostly to the tundra villages to buy fish for the mission and school. Weinland probably would have made more of these trips had he been able, but his health continued to fail all through the winter. As a result, in the spring of 1887 the mission party decided that the Weinlands should return to the States when the supply ship arrived in June. This was not an easy decision, especially for William Weinland, who had worked continuously for the Kuskokwim mission from its inception three years before. It also posed serious difficulties in staffing the mission station, as the Kilbucks would be alone. The missionaries agreed, however, that the mission would provide the Kilbucks a secure base of operations for the coming year. Although both John and Edith were sad to see their companions go, they chose to stay, and the summer found them moving ahead with plans for the coming year.

After the departure of the Weinlands, John and Edith spent the summer fishing, gardening, wood gathering, and planning for the school. While John managed the work around the mission grounds, Edith had her hands full maintaining the home, which, after August 30, and the birth of William Henry, included not one but two babies. The birth of William, named for his Delaware grandfather, was difficult, and Edith almost died as a result. Even with this trauma, the first letters written home after the Kilbucks took charge of the mission gave no sense of flagging spirits.

In the fall of 1887 John again set out traveling to nearby villages to secure logs and fish. In a letter written to Weinland, he mentioned a growing desire to go further afield, perhaps as far as "primitive" Nelson Island. In this same letter, John described a beluga kill, giving the first of what would be innumerable ethnographic digressions through the years and journals to come.[31]

As the scope of their work increased, illness again beset them, restricting John's travels. First baby Katie became ill, followed by both John and Edith, who were taken with dysentery. John was still anxious to visit the people in their villages, and Edith resigned herself to the separation: "It will be hard enough when the time once comes but I will gladly see him go. It would be worse if I had no babies to keep me company." [32]

John was not the only person traveling on the mission's account. That year more than fifty natives from up and down the river traveled to Bethel to attend the Christmas celebration. That traditional native celebrations could draw as many as eight hundred visitors did not undercut the Kilbucks' sense of accomplishment at the arrival of so many visitors. [33] In response to this well-attended Christmas service and the interest it signaled on the part of nearby villages, John finally began his missionary traveling in earnest.

Not surprisingly, as John's traveling increased, Edith was left alone more and more often. Already, in the fall of 1887, she wrote, "I will stop for this evening. Bro. Kilbuck is at home and I only have his company after nine o'clock at night and at meal times in the day. . . . December 22.—School closed today for one week. Bro. Kilbuck will be at home now more than usual, for which we are all now very glad. We haven't had much of a home this year. I've been alone most of the time." [34]

Thus began John's career as an itinerant missionary, circling out from the Bethel mission in his effort to transform the Yup'ik people. Traveling by boat in the summer and by dog team in the winter, he averaged several thousand miles a year for the next decade. Together he and Edith became expert at preparation for this constant journeying. In November 1889 Edith described his traveling kit:

About John's starting out—I would say, that he is all but ready. He only has five dogs and the first thing he must do is buy some good ones. He has a sleigh. "Cassack" has a *fine* rabbit skin blanket about finished for his use. Sr. Bachman has been making him some extra heavy clothing. Procopi's wife has made water or travelling boots and I have packed one valise with clothing. In a second one he has his bible, hymn book, catechism, native vocabulary and grammar, medicines, salves, plasters, bandages, and a blank book and pencil for writing a journal for me. The only extra clothes he takes along are, a change of underwear, plenty of dry socks, extra boots, and soap and towel and fine comb. His bedding is a pillow, rubber blanket, woolen blanket, fur blanket, and a grass mat. Besides this he takes a small box with cup, saucer, plate, knife, spoon, candles, matches, salt, bread and tea. In water tight sacks he takes sea-biscuit, sugar, bread, meat, and flour. Lying loose in the sleigh are some dry fish for the native that travels with him. He also has his small bundle of bedding, and snow shoes for both. Then comes the boiling pot in case he should get fresh fish or game, the tea-kettle or "Chinek" [*caanik:* from Russian, *chaynik*] and an ax. All is wrapped in the sleigh sheet and well lashed over the top so nothing can be lost. Now every thing is ready but tent and tent poles which are fastened on top to be handy. He will try to have nine or eleven good dogs and then I think his outfit is complete. These are the necessaries for travelling in Alaska. More than this would only be a burden. [35]

From the beginning John's energy and personality led to an approach not only practical but compatible with the Yup'ik way of life. Just as the Yup'ik people moved annually within a relatively circumscribed area in their search for sustenance, so John moved from place to place in search of "customers" to listen to his talk. Just as the nineteenth-century Yup'ik Eskimos regularly returned to winter camps and summer fishing sites, so John lived those years on the trail to and from the home and family that Edith kept for him at Bethel.

The couple that had spent their first year of marriage within earshot of each other came increasingly to spend their lives apart. Remaining alone at home, Edith began to feel the strain: "My mind seems to get more weary than my body and that means a good deal." She gave eloquent testimony to the "Catch 22" that came to characterize their marriage: "[The weariness] vanishes when John is with me for he is cheerful and happy. We are always happy when together. But most of the time he is not at home." [36]

The strain of their enforced separation may account in part for Edith's continuing, persistent medical complaints. At the same time that John began to travel in earnest, Edith's health seriously declined. [37] Whatever the physical and mental strain of separation, the marriage remained a close one. Although they increasingly led their daily lives apart, their relationship continued to provide strength and comfort, as did growth of their family. In a letter written in 1889, a pregnant Edith wrote, "We take every interest in our people and our work, and we need not complain of loneliness as long as we are spared to each other, and have our little ones." [38]

Finally, as traveling continued to pull them apart, first Edith and then John found in their letters and journals a way to mitigate the separation. In so doing they wrote their own story.

THE WRITTEN WORD

All of our love letters have been written since we were married.
             —*Edith Kilbuck to John Kilbuck, 1896* [39]

Over two score years John and Edith penned dozens of journals and hundreds of letters describing the establishment of the Bethel mission and the work in progress. These journals are descriptive documents of historic value; however, they were not written primarily to inform an anonymous public or future generations.

Each entry in John's journals was, above all else, a love letter affectionately addressed to his wife. Many of his journals were later published in Moravian periodicals to aid the mission cause by supplying details of the trials and tribulations of life at Bethel. Often the published versions give a false picture of impersonality and change what was originally intended as a private conversation into a report. In all cases the editor removed personal references, including the opening greeting to Edith.

Just as Edith was John's partner in life, her journals comprise the companion to those of her husband. Describing the nuances of life in Bethel, her journals are much more than a supplement to the writings of her hus-

band and are a testament in their own right. They convey an entirely different voice from that found in the journals of her husband and in so doing
give us a strong personal sense of what she felt herself as well as her husband
to be about.

In his early reports, especially before he began keeping travel journals
for Edith, John focused on the public side of mission life. In this formal
correspondence, he described various plots and plans in the process of acquiring workmen, building buildings, learning the language, establishing
the school, and traveling out to visit and convert the people. It was not until
the winter of 1888 that he began regular journal writing. John's style re-
laxes, becomes more humorous and spontaneous, recording small cameo
accounts of his experiences, including a description of the impression his
journal writing made on the Yup'ik people who observed him: "To pass the
time I have brought in the Century Magazine. . . . They were surprised
when I explained to them that the print represented the conversation of some
one. I told them that my journal was for you to read, and from it you would
know about my entire trip, without being present to tell you. I gave them a
sample of what I had written and you should have seen their faces covered
with astonishment."[40]

Edith's writing can also be divided into two periods. During the early
years we know her chiefly through her letters to her father. Whereas John
intended his early writing as a monument, Edith's functioned as an outlet
and personal testimonial. Her journals are characterized by a remarkable
openness and are both insightful and opinionated. She had strong expectations as to what a Christian life entailed and strong opinions about those who
failed to live up to them. Some of these opinions Joseph Romig discreetly
omitted when he recopied his daughter's journals for publication.

Along with the journal that Edith regularly wrote for her father, in 1888
she began to keep a journal for her husband. She did this so that he might
read about what had occurred at the mission while he was traveling. These
private journals give a clear, sometimes funny, sometimes tense picture of
how Edith felt as well as what she saw and bring to life the personal experiences that accompanied the accomplishments described by her husband.
They were written while she worked at the mission in John's absence and
describe the events, both small and large, that took place at Bethel while
John was away.

The Kilbucks were not the first or only Alaska missionaries to keep a
written account of their experiences. What makes Edith's and John's descriptions valuable is not merely the fact that they wrote nor what they wrote
about but how they chose to say it. Taking the form of a confidential dialogue
rather than a description for an anonymous public, their styles are both
vivid and familiar. Neither self-conscious nor intentionally literary, the information conveyed sometimes takes second place to the quality of the story.

Edith's account of her trip to the Warehouse in the spring of 1887 de-

Fig. 4.4. Trader Lind's skin boat, used for hauling supplies from Warehouse Creek up to Bethel, as seen in Kuskokwim Bay, circa 1900. (Kilbuck family)

scribed the composition of her journal and the pleasure its creation gave her: "I must now close my journal for this year. Much has been written with Harry in my arms, or late at night. Just now I am seated in the tent keeping mosquitoes off of my sleeping babies. Look with charity on the blunders and may it be as much pleasure to you to read, as it has been for me to prepare it for you."[41] Although the description was typically candid, the circumstances surrounding it were not, as the journey marked Edith's first trip away from Bethel since her arrival two years before.

In her account of the trip to the Warehouse the following year Edith remarked further on her journal writing, as well as her reaction to their publication in *The Moravian*:

> We got no Moravians and we are so anxious to see what parts of my journal were published. I never dreamed they would be published else I might have written them more carefully. I generally write when I am tired or am in a great hurry. I don't mind that they were published if they did any good. If John's eyes were stronger I think he has the education and ability to write a better one than I can. I like to write exceeding well but feel the lack of ability very often.[42]

Not only did Edith describe the pleasure she took in writing, but also the satisfaction that reading family journals and letters gave her. In her entry to her father for June 19, 1889, she wrote that his journal was one of the things she lived for and one of her greatest enjoyments when it came. On another occasion she described the comfort they took in rereading his journals: "I've been a whole week at it. I would read sometimes and John sometimes, then we would talk it over. O! Papa it is such a good journal . . . because it is full of home news . . . and when you speak of spending a social Sunday . . . I think of how impossible it is for me to go anywhere or even have company come to the house." In fact, writing provided the respite it described.[43]

Not only was writing tremendously important to them, but the exchange of letters played a huge role in their lives. Edith's descriptions convey the drama of receiving a year's worth of news in a single day. They also communicate the excitement and anticipation preceding the mail's arrival, as well as the mixture of pain, relief, and satisfaction in the aftermath. In June of 1886 she described the mail's arrival:

> June 26 . . . The boys went up to the post and from there could see Mr. Lind and the scow coming along very slowly on account of low tide and a calm. John soon returned with another sack of mail and Billie staid to help unload. We anxiously opened the mail bag and divided the letters. . . . I hurridly ran over the postmark of mine and saw that one in dear papa's handwriting was bordered in black. This I knew was sad news for me and I opened it and commenced to read the sad message it contained. I soon saw that sickness and death had visited our dear home and my heart raised a prayer for them and for myself, even before I knew which one was gone. . . . All too

soon I learned that it was my *dear, dear* mother. . . . June 27 . . . We learned from . . . our letters that: Aunt Nellie and Ida are still alive, Emma and Jim married and, Mrs. Taylor a baby girl, . . . news of . . . storms, murders, railroad wars and strikes, and general and political news from every where. The mission chapel at New Westfield burned and Br. Kinsey withdraws, Grandpa's well but very feeble. Many deaths all over the world by collisions, earthquakes, storms, disease and accidents of all kinds.[44]

In the spring of 1887, Edith described her letter-writing efforts, which were as important to her as receiving letters. Though she wrote primarily as a wife and eldest daughter, this was not exclusively the case. Spring found her expending tremendous energy on her extensive correspondence: "thirty three letters, with an average of thirteen pages each." The journals that followed continually referenced the anticipation she endured. Finally the boat arrived, the mail was delivered, and the time of reading was at hand: "I closed the tent, put the children to bed, and then tried to read some letters, but the children were so tormented by the swarms of mosquitoes that I was obliged to keep them away with a bush, while lying by me were sixty-five letters. This I did nearly all night, and you do not know how hard it was to do."[45] No fabricated description of the importance of mail to an isolated missionary group could better convey this tiny drama. Again and again, both Edith and John gave voice to the fragility and strength of the missionaries' fiercely maintained connection with each other and with the world they had left behind, through the written word.

CHAPTER 5

WORK IN EARNEST

ON THEIR OWN

During their first two years in western Alaska, the Kilbucks accomplished a great deal. Above and beyond their mission work, they built a home, started a family, and made a good beginning at learning the Yup'ik language. Not only that, but the young seminarian had been initiated into the arts of carpentry, sailing, hunting, and fishing in the subarctic tundra environment. John quickly revealed himself as energetic and disciplined. As for Edith, "She has the gift of managing any work that has to be done; even if she is not able, at times to do a great deal. She is a very practical person, and I feel that it would be hard to carry on the work without her."[1]

Although the Kilbucks had much to hearten them after their first two years, the departure of the Weinlands at the close of their second winter marked a turning point in their lives and work. Until the arrival of Ernest Weber the following spring, they were left alone to manage the mission. The isolation was severe, and Edith's health seriously declined. All the mission party had had bouts of sickness during the first years; however, it was only after the departure of the Weinlands that Edith's condition became chronic.

In spite of Edith's precarious health the Kilbucks believed that they were making progress in their work. In January 1888 John conceived the plan of building a chapel thirty miles up the Kuskokwim to serve the three large villages on which their work was already focused: Kwethluk (*Kuiggluk*), Kikichtagmiut (*Qikertarmiut*), and Akiak (*Akiaq*). The response to this plan was encouraging. As soon as John made public his intention of building a chapel upriver, the natives expressed interest in the project. Moreover,

96

the tundra village of Peingagamut (*Paingarmiut*) as well as another unidentified village, indicated that they, too, were eager for a chapel and pledged
themselves to furnish building material if John would oversee the construction.[2] This active cooperation was more than they had anticipated.

The Kilbucks thought they could discern beginnings of a spiritual awakening among the people in response to John's Christmas sermon of 1887
and the traveling he did during the rest of the winter. Following the Easter
services for that year, John wrote:

> During the Easter week, although I had no prospect of having an audience
> . . . I began my native services on Palm Sunday. In a few days strangers
> began to drop in, and none went away until the Easter services were closed,
> and this in spite of the fact that the time for their Spring migration was at
> hand. These services were all held in what native language I could command,
> and if it had not been for the deep interest and evident desire for something
> to satisfy a craving already awakened in their hearts, these services would no
> doubt have been wearisome to my audience. But . . . I was able to hold their
> attention twice and even three times a day; and each service was from one
> hour and a half to two hours long.[3]

After nearly three years in Alaska, John Kilbuck had begun to preach in
earnest. In the same letter, he gave voice to the message conveyed: "On
good Friday the audience was deeply stirred when we reached the crucifix-
ion. When I explained to them that the blood shed on the cross by Jesus
Christ, was for the taking away of our badness (sin), the older men exclaimed 'Kou-ja'-nah!' [*quyana*] (Thanks [we are thankful]) And added,
'we too, desire to have our badness taken away by that blood.' "[4]

A new phase in the work of the mission had begun. John never intended
to wait in Bethel for the people to come to him. Instead, he went abroad to
preach and encourage them toward the erection of their own churches by
their own effort on their home ground. Also, he had begun to preach, in
halting Yup'ik, a deceptively simple message. Beyond what he was able to
communicate verbally, his approach forcefully conveyed his expectation that
people not merely receive him but begin to work for their own conversion.

During the same year that John initiated work abroad, he and Edith were
also solely responsible for continuing the work at Bethel. In the spring, he
reported slow but steady progress on the home front:

> I only had the walls of the new house up, when cold weather set in, which
> stopped the work. Besides this, I fixed up our first log house and made a
> dwelling house out of it for us, and the frame house I turned over to school
> purposes. I also managed to persuade natives to bring us logs and fire-wood,
> and in this way I had fuel all Winter, besides I was able to have about 1,500
> feet of rough lumber sawed in February and March of this year. The buying
> of food for the school, also looking after our own fishing, took up some, and
> not a small portion of my time last Summer. With the fish that I bought from

Mr. Sipary (2000) I had about 3,300 salmon, besides quite a number of whitefish. In the Fall I bought thirty bags of blackfish, and three of frozen whitefish. This amount of food has been sufficient for eighteen natives and nine dogs, and I have some salmon left for dog food. . . .

Finally, I think I have a warm house, and one that we can live in with comfort. I am, therefore, ready for work abroad, for we ourselves have a good warm house.[5]

The school's progress was also gradual. As John had been unable to travel to distant villages, he had only seventeen scholars (including twelve boarders) during the entire year. He closed school in April so he could begin preparations for the busy summer season.

The arrival of Brother Ernest Weber with the annual supply ship in June 1888 marked the end of the Kilbucks' solitary duty in Bethel. Glad as they were of his coming, Edith admitted to disappointment that no woman had been sent to balance out the mission party.[6] Her chagrin constituted much more than a complaint against the *de facto* division of labor. True to the Moravian practice of a spiritual life focusing on groups defined by age and sex, sisterly fellowship had always been an important part of her life. The absence of other white women constituted a real deprivation and forced her to rely increasingly on her family, her Yup'ik neighbors, and herself.

At the same time that Edith was disappointed by the absence of female companionship, she was exuberant in her admiration for the goods that the vessel brought for the mission that spring.

We are so wild with delight at the good news and the many pretty presents, that I can scarcely settle down to write. Clothing for the School in suits by the dozen! One full set of beautiful clothes for Katy. This saves me much hard work this Fall. Even some clothes came for John and me. For Katy and baby were cards, books, blocks, dolls, rattles, balls, combs, brush and soap, and tooth powder; toy dishes, vases, six boxes of candy, dried cherries, dried raspberries and apples, 1 peck walnuts, 1 1/2 peck hazlenuts, some hickorynuts; one good old-fashioned home-cured ham; hoods for Katy and myself, carpets, upholstery goods for home-made furniture. Sunday-school cards and charts, photographs, and many more things which I have not time to mention. Suffice it to say that we have every thing our hearts would wish. But we miss the long-looked for potatoes, also no butter was sent, no coal-oil and no yeast and no windows for the new home.[7]

Years later, their daughter Ruth recalled the yearly arrival of the vessel and the delight such unlooked for presents continued to evoke. She remarked especially the annual gifts her mother received from a close friend in Bethlehem, who always had the wisdom to send something frivolous and fine, such as a framed piece of embroidery or a hand-stitched satin sachet. As practical and unadorned as Edith was, her daughter remembered the enjoyment she took in these small luxuries.

As the work in Bethel grew, these boxes and barrels from home became an important source of gifts for the people who visited the mission. From penny whistles to picture cards to mail order catalogues, what the Kilbucks received often entered, at that point, a wider circle of distribution than the senders might have imagined. Given as Christmas gifts to the school children or as small tokens to visitors or even to partners in feast exchanges, the caps and thimbles sent up from Bethlehem spoke eloquently of the rich world beyond the Kuskokwim.

Within a month of Weber's arrival, John was on the trail again—going upriver in search of logs and food for the school. At the same time he was always on the lookout for new scholars. Edith remained at the mission, kept company by Weber. There they received an endless and unbroken stream of visitors: "July 17 . . . Natives are here from both up and down the river, nearly forty strangers, one party here and the others at the Post. There are five tents pitched around Bethel, which make it look quite town-like. . . . July 20 . . . Several bidarras arrive each day from below, yesterday six arrived, but they are all gone again. They come with oil, but Mr. Lind already has all that he needs."[8] Besides coming to the post to trade, visitors constantly requested medical help from the mission: "It is my luck [crossed out and replaced by "misfortune"] to have some one sick to care for at such times and I think I would worry myself sick if I dare for the responsibility often seems more than I can bear."[9]

Trade goods and medicine were not the only things that drew people to Bethel. John himself began to be sought after: "Another party is here and say they wish our God to be their God. They wish Bro. Kilbuck 'was at home to baptize them and make them good.' They have very little idea what baptism means; but they want something, and we hope by the little we now are able to say to in part satisfy their longings for something good."[10] Although continually vexed by the limits of their knowledge of the Yup'ik language, as well as by the Yup'ik peoples' comprehension of their full intent, their doctrine of right living was beginning to make an impression. The year before, John had reported, "At present the lessons are drawn more from our daily lives than from our precepts."[11] Twelve months later the goal remained the same: to try to live their faith, even before they could communicate it verbally.

The Kilbucks made steady progress in their attempts to minister to the material needs of the people as well as to teach Christian love and charity through example. They remained firm, however, that no one be made a member of the church until having demonstrated, through Christian conduct, an understanding of the duties as well as the rights associated with church membership. In the beginning, the Kilbucks hoped to see the requisite evidence of godliness demonstrated by the school boys who "talk very often of how they are trying to live right so that God will 'take away their bad.'" However, full church membership continued to be withheld: "None of the natives were allowed to take the communion yet, though, if they continue to live as they have started, John says he can take them as full church members this summer some time." [12]

During the summer John wrote that he received nine requests for admittance into church fellowship. Finally, on September 9, 1888, the missionaries received the first Yup'ik converts into the Moravian church by the right hand of fellowship, as all had been previously baptized and confirmed in the Russian Orthodox church. John wrote, "We were greatly refreshed by this evident awakening among the natives. Although it is not conversion from heathenism that we can report, yet we have now a nucleus for a congregation." [13]

After Weber arrived, the school also prospered and during the fall averaged eighteen to nineteen scholars. John continued optimistic over its growth as well as its ability to weather the withdrawal of federal support. Against this necessity, he calculated the expense attached to maintaining the school at just over four hundred dollars a year for the feeding and clothing of up to twenty scholars.

During the fall of 1888 Weber tended the school while John cared for the sick and continued his traveling and preaching. Weber's inability to speak the language limited his effectiveness as a teacher. Just as she had during the year before when John was traveling, Edith shouldered the burden of the daily affairs of mission life. In the fall she wrote that she found herself lonelier than in years past: "What was new and interesting other years, is becoming an old story and we feel the monotony more than ever." Her health, which had improved during the summer, also began to decline: "It takes a constant battle to keep my mind off of my ailments yet I am becoming more reconciled to being sick. The hardest is to see my work undone and just sit still all day long and look at it." [14]

TRIP TO NUSHAGAK

All hope is gone of ever seeing my own dear John again. . . . They say I am a Widow.

—Edith Kilbuck, 1889 [15]

While Edith worked to maintain the mission, in December 1888 John commenced what was to be one of his more dramatic expeditions. Following an overland route, he set off by sled for Nushagak, where he hoped to make contact with Lord Lonsdale. The notorious "Yellow Earl" was sojourning in western Alaska to dissipate strained circumstances in his native England, where his philandering had earned him royal disapproval. John hoped to send mail down to the States with Lord Lonsdale's party, which was continuing south from Nushagak, across the Alaska Peninsula, and then down the coast to California. More important, John's visit was intended to give much needed encouragement to the small missionary band that had arrived at Nushagak the previous fall. Although he knew he would be gone at least a month, bad weather on the coast drew out his trip for an interminable seventy-three days. His journal conveys his growing weariness. Nowhere did he suspect, however, the tragic entries Edith was writing back in Bethel, where she was convinced that he had perished on the trail and would never be seen again.

Edith left us three somewhat different accounts of the anxious wait that comprised the home experience. These included a journal kept for John, one written for her father, and a long letter written for the home folks on April 23, 1889, and later published in *The Moravian*.[16] In these accounts she transcended her time and place, betraying in the particular the universal plight of waiting, not knowing, and no longer daring to hope. In her letter to *The Moravian*, Edith wrote:

> I knew I would be lonely while John was gone and it was a little hard to see him start, but I was not in the least unwilling to have him go. . . .
>
> Almost immediately we began to have ugly, stormy weather and high winds with intense cold and we were often forced to think of him and wonder how he was getting along. . . . We did not expect John home until the first of January, so our holiday season was very quiet and unpretending. . . . Our thoughts by that time were also turned to his coming and we counted the possible number of days in which he would or could return with as much interest and longing as the school-children did.[17]

Though Edith's trials appear fairly circumscribed in her retrospective account, the journal written for her husband gave voice to escalating stress: "I get so anxious that I don't dare think about it too much. Dear John, what would my life be worth to me without *you*!" As the days passed, Edith's journals lost their typical mix of trials and triumphs. More and more they concentrated on her expectation of and longing for his safe return: "I am just existing and nothing more."[18]

The days passed slowly, and Edith's health continued poor. Her only real pleasure remained her journals, which she turned to several times a day. Then, on January 14, the arrival of a team from downriver threw the whole mission into turmoil. In her journal to her husband, Edith declined describing the traumatic incident: "I can never write the experience of this morning but will tell you all when you come."[19] In her journal to her father, she pictured the cause of her distress. The natives who had arrived had brought the news that the Russian Orthodox priest Zakharii Bel'kov had returned from Nushagak but that John was not with him. This was cause for alarm, as the two had been expected to return together. Trader Lind "could not understand the natives very well" and headed down the river immediately to find out all he could. While Edith waited for his return, "bowed to the very earth with sorrow," a second party arrived at the post. This was Bel'kov himself, bringing letters from Nushagak, including one from John, which was "short but cheering": "He [Bel'kov] had said nothing to the natives so they made their own story and told it to us, which was that Mr. Belkoff had waited at Nushagak three days for John and then had come home, not seeing him or hearing of him all the way. We knew there was only one road and every one felt sure he had been lost." [20]

Although the arrival of John's letter temporarily relieved Edith's anxiety, days and then weeks of interminable waiting continued to crawl by. The weather was stormy without intermission and bitterly cold. Time, "long, anxious time," passed, and he still did not come: "The thirty-five days he expected to be gone were long past. Forty, fifty and sixty days were also gone and everybody began to hint to me that I must live without him." [21]

During this last period the waiting proved close to intolerable: "Only a prayer between every word I write keeps back the tears." Edith's February 1 journal entry consisted of three words: "Is it possible?" Reality was cruel; dreams even crueler: "I dream of your coming every night and once I got so far as to kiss those warm loving lips four times. They thrilled me with the hearty response you gave and I heard you say in your loving tone '*Papa's poor little girl, Papa's girlie*' when told of Katies toothache and sickness. Then I awoke, and cried my eyes nearly out." [22]

On February 4, Edith closed her journal and packed it along with fresh provisions and dry clothing to send downriver. Although everyone assumed John was dead, one last effort was made, and a team was sent out to try to find him. Edith wrote of the anxiety she felt as she prepared a box she was sure would return untouched: "*Oh! John, my own darling*, can you know how my heart *aches* for your return. *Surely* the Lord will hear my fervent constant prayer. . . . If you ever see this, and when you get close to home, let me know some way of your approach. This morning . . . we send Wasca and Lomuck to meet you. . . . I must pray almost constantly to drive away fears and heart rending doubts. . . . You know my heart to you. What more can I say." [23] Still the days dragged, and the mission party was prepared to pack away John's clothing, papers, books, and unfinished bits of work. His coming was no longer anticipated. The school reopened, Edith's health returned, and life carried on as before.

Then, finally, on February 15 John arrived home. By that time he had been so entirely given up that he almost reached the door before he was recognized, and the surprise was near complete. Mr. Lind, who was visiting, spotted him first, and handing Edith his binoculars called out, "*It's Kilbuck! Don't you see his cap and his brown coat? See he waves his hand.*" In a moment the sleighs had mounted the river bank, and John was home. "It was such a happy, such a blessed meeting for *us*. We at once retired to our own private room and as best our feeble tongues were able, we poured out hearts of gratitude and praise. . . . It seemed too good to be true yet here he was. . . . Harry was decidedly afraid of him and cried, while Katie only partly recognized him and has been very shy all day." [24]

John's safe return from Nushagak marked a personal triumph for the Kilbucks. It was also the cause of renewed success in their work. When John finally waved his cap, signalling his safe return, the tower of doubt that had been building while he was away was visibly shaken. Among those who appreciated his reappearance, and also among those who did not, a new acceptance was apparent. More eloquently than any sermon, John's safe return spoke of the life-giving power these Christians commanded. Where words were insufficient to earn converts, successful acts were taken as evidence by the Yup'ik people that here was a man (and perhaps a faith) worth their attention.

John recounted the moral defeat of an antagonistic shaman that his unexpected return accomplished:

> During my absence to Nushagak . . . he tried again to keep two wives, but could not induce any one to come and live with him near us. When my return was unusually delayed, he began to rise in power.
>
> Thus far his power had been greatly impaired, because he had been unable to harm one. But now he began to plume himself upon his powers. He declared that he was the one that was making all the terribly bad weather. Now the people would see who was the most powerful, he or that priest. He had called up these storms to overwhelm me, so that I should not return to meddle with his affairs. His former power and influence increased so much the more, as I was given up as lost. How quickly his glory and power vanished when unexpectedly I returned, after being absent seventy-three days, hale and hearty! Since then he has turned spiritualist. He is not likely to trouble us any more, for he has left for parts unknown.[25]

A struggle between native and non-native sources of power was under way, and the success or failure of either party in any context fueled the conflagration.

At the same time that the old shaman lived in anticipation of John's defeat, two old women "shammaned" for good weather for his benefit:

> One said he would come home soon, which he did not do, and the other said for some reason or other she had no power with the weather but finally came to the conclusion that because we were disrespectful to fish we had killed and left some few exposed to the bad weather it was no use to shamman for good weather for *us* until we had put those fish under shelter. She sent us word to take them into the house, but we were too busy to bother with that. However the next morning when we arose we found the fish safely stored in our fish house and no questions asked. All this done and yet the storms raged as bad as ever. I feel sure the power of the Shammans around Bethel is damaged greatly and their future does not promise well for them.[26]

Edith later described how the burden of John's absence was shared beyond their immediate family. The school boys had notched pieces of wood to keep count of the nights he was away from home. As hope began to fail, one after the other gradually put away their sticks, until when he did come only one out of thirty boys had kept the full count. Older natives also took notice.

> For about a week before he came the old women and men began to call on me saying "Our hearts are sick when we look at your little children for now they have no father. Our hearts are also sick for you and we cry plenty of tears but that don't do you any good, we know. We loved the one that is gone, more than we can say we loved him, but now that he is gone you must not leave us. We *will not* let you go. *No, no.* You are ours and you must stay here with us. . . . This touched my heart and I said to them I *would* stay and not leave them until our place had been filled; which relieved them greatly.[27]

If the Kilbucks had been mistaken for traders during their early years on the Kuskokwim, their standing four years later was significantly more ambiguous and, at the same time, complex. As they increasingly laid claim to the people living along the Kuskokwim, the people claimed them in their turn.

AFTER NUSHAGAK: THE WORK CONTINUES

After John returned from Nushagak, he continued his missionary trips. By March, however, he was forced to remain in Bethel when his eyes grew sore from the bright springtime snow. There he helped Brother Weber with the school and began preparations for the summer building and fishing season.

Unbeknownst to the Kilbucks, plans were being made on their behalf on the other side of the continent. Assuming that Edith was too ill to remain in Bethel and would come down on the vessel in the summer, the mission board was busy making arrangements for her replacement. Caroline Detterer had already volunteered her services, and it was decided that a second sister should be sent to accompany her. As a permanent missionary could not be found on such short notice, Sarah Bachman, wife of the prominent church leader Bishop Henry Bachman, volunteered to come for the year, accompanied by her teenaged son Johnny.

Pleasure and excitement followed the arrival of the women at the Warehouse in June. Edith's journal entries picture how much the renewal of sisterly companionship meant to her as well as the help they promised in the tasks required by school and mission home. This was especially true, as Edith was six months pregnant with her third child. Keenly aware of what their help and companionship would mean to the work and to his wife, John, too, was glad for their arrival. In a formal yet enthusiastic letter to Bishop Bachman, he thanked the bishop for the loan of his wife and promised that he would do his best to see that she "return to you none the worse for the wear and tear of a Winter spent in Alaska."[28]

The immediate upshot of the arrival of the two sisters was a rearrangement of accommodations. Following a Moravian custom practiced in the early religious communities, the missionary family was residentially divided into a brethren's and a sisters' house. Edith shared the frame building with

Sister Detterer (Carrie), Sister Bachman, and the Kilbucks' two young children, Katie and Harry. John, Brother Weber, and young Johnny Bachman shared the log building.[29] This arrangement, rooted as it was in Moravian tradition, was also compatible with the Yup'ik residential pattern, whereby men and young boys lived and worked together in the qasgiq or men's house and women and young children stayed in individual sod houses. Although the arrangement was not instigated in a conscious attempt to emulate the Yup'ik pattern, it is unlikely the coincidence was lost on Yup'ik visitors to the mission.

During the year following John's trip to Nushagak, the work in Bethel underwent considerable consolidation. What had originally been a rather tentative plan of action, worked out in direct response to the perceived conditions of the mission field, solidified into an energetic and effective battle plan worthy of experienced proselytizers. The plan consisted of the same five basic components that had surfaced during the missionaries' first year in Alaska: building, talking, healing, teaching, and traveling. With some of these goals well in hand, the Kilbucks were able to expand on aspects of mission work that had from the beginning been entirely beyond their reach.

John and Edith's persistence had paid off, and both were now able to converse in the Yup'ik language. In the fall of 1889 Carrie Detterer commented on John's command of the language, noting that once when he preached, an interpreter had to make only two corrections. The Kilbuck children were also fluent. Both Katie and Harry spoke almost exclusively in the Yup'ik language. Many funny stories were told of their comical English, as when Katie dubbed Mr. Sipary's calves, the first she had ever seen, "rabbits." Edith wrote to her father that "the children say many a cute and smart thing that I would like to tell you if it were not so hard to translate it into the same in English."[30] As well as providing a tool to facilitate mission work, the linguistic competence of the Kilbuck family did much to endear them to the people among whom they lived. Although other missionaries gained varying degrees of fluency, the Kilbucks remained outstanding in this respect.

By fall 1889 the mission party had grown to five; however, the job of talking with the people continued to fall primarily on the Kilbucks. After the annual Christmas service, John wrote, "I have hardly been in the house, except to eat and sleep, spending my time with the natives, talking and looking after the wants of the inner man. As my wife and I are the only ones who can hold any converse with them, whenever we have such a lot of visitors our time is not our own." In describing the natives who visited for the Christmas celebration, Edith remarked to her father, "Many no doubt of the women and girls are here for the first time and seem surprised to hear the children and me talk to them in their own language."[31]

Though Brother Weber and Carrie Detterer, his bride-to-be, would eventually gain a better command of the language, it was hard for them in the beginning. Describing Brother Weber's experience teaching during his first year, Edith's dry humor betrayed her sharp sense of human frailty: "It has been pretty hard for Mr. Weber and for them, on account of their not being able to talk more with each other. At times it came very near distracting him, not the school alone but the general management of the place while John was away from home. I am sure his first year in Alaska has been a very busy one, but not, as he may be inclined to think, the busiest and darkest year in the history of Bethel." [32]

Not only had the Kilbucks achieved success on the linguistic front, glad for "the open door that is now really open." Their limited medical ministry was also reaping a rich harvest. John wrote:

> The administering to the bodily ailments of our people has contributed not a little to the winning of the people. . . . [W]e have been able to so help the sick, that the people nearly always come to us first, and do not go to their "shamans." In fact, the people come to us eventually, even if they have employed a "shaman," and in nearly every case we either effect a perfect cure, or at least afford some relief. . . . Last Summer quite a number of natives, from the mouth of this river, came up especially to be doctored, and in every case our medicines effected a cure. This fact will be fully appreciated when I say that at the mouth of the river the people tenaciously cling to their shamans, and firmly believe in them. [33]

As in John's return from Nushagak, their successful actions commanded attention and gave evidence of a power to be reckoned with. Yet John made it clear that they still felt limited in their ability to minister to the sick: "Would that we could also have a medical missionary. This is the earnest cry that is going up from the natives, and is one of our earnest desires. There is no doubt about our being in a measure successful in looking after their bodily ailments, but a skillful man could do so much more." [34]

During the three years since the departure of the Weinlands, the school had also grown. In January 1890 John described it as the mission's "main dependence for a rapid progress." Due to the scarcity of food, however, no special efforts could be made to seek out scholars. He noted, "We have 30 names on the roll. The attendance will probably average 25 for each quarter of the year. Our supply of native food will hardly enable us to keep four full terms of school." [35] Along with limited resources, management problems also beset the work. In January 1890 John recommended a solution:

> I see the need of a man who will be fully qualified to take entire charge of the school. This Bro. Weber cannot do, for he himself admits that he cannot manage the boys. You know very well what kind of a man is needed to keep 20 or 25 boys well in hand. He must be a man who understands boy nature, with patience and a heart large enough to cover his entire charge. He must likewise be a leader. Boys are hero-worshipers and will readily gather around a leader and gladly follow him in life and work. If you can find such a man who feels a God-given call for this station, send him up. [36]

In describing the qualities a teacher must possess, John gives us a preview of the attitude he would bring to the profession fifteen years later in his work for the Bureau of Education.

For the present, though he recognized the importance of the school, John's primary concern remained traveling through and ministering to the mission field at large: "My work is among the people, and hence little time is spent at home. As the territory which I now visit becomes more fully developed I really will have no abiding place." [37]

In the same letter John gave his first full description of that territory and its regional variations:

> Our present immediate territory consists of ten villages distributed as follows: three villages up the river, three below, and four over the tundra, to the west and north-west of Bethel. It takes two weeks to make the round trip. A full census of the three villages above us shows a total of 359 souls; of these 186 are children. A full census has not been completed of the other villages, but an approximation gives 1100 or 1200 for the entire territory.
>
> The work is most encouraging up the river owing probably to their frequent contact since our arrival. . . .
>
> Down the river the people are willing to accept the word but are unwilling to give up their old ways. . . . Over the tundra, the outlook is the most discouraging. The people listen out of respect to me, but my preaching is nothing to them. They say our religion will do well enough for white men, but not for them. . . .
>
> Those tundra people are the only real, downright heathen that we come in contact with. The work among them is arduous and requires our utmost powers of spiritual endurance. [38]

In response to these regional differences the missionaries developed a strategy to solidify the work along the Kuskokwim. Although not solely responsible for deciding the direction mission work would take, John's knowledge of the field was a major determinant in the manner and means proposed.

The first proposal was to send two Yup'ik boys down to the States for further education. Although admittedly a small step, John considered it critical in the creation of a native leadership capable of furthering the work at hand. In the proposal John put his indelibly practical stamp on a work that by definition had cultural as well as denominational implications: "Our idea is, if possible to place these two boys with some families, where they will learn what home life is. We think that being able to read and speak English well, is quite a sufficient training for the present in the way of education for the brain. For the hands, we would suggest that if possible they should be taught carpentering, this is the trade for a pioneer station." [39]

The second step in extending the work along the Kuskokwim was John's appointment of Brothers Hooker, Lomuck, and Kawagleg as native helpers in the upriver villages of Kwethluk, Kikichtagmiut, and Akiak, respec-

Fig. 5.1. Togiak, 1884. (A. Hartmann, Moravian Archives)

tively. These appointments put into effect the plan proposed in the summer of 1889 to establish preaching stations up and down the river, manned by native helpers and regularly visited by brethren from the home station.

> [These are] the three villages in which we have been the most active, and which are also the most promising . . . more than others [that] have been under our influence for the past three years, and as there was an eager desire for instruction, I appointed a helper in each village. These . . . I instructed especially, and they in turn instructed their people. Moreover, in my visits, they assisted in the services, by repeating in better language what I had said.[40]

Given the immensity of the territory, the limited resources of the missionaries, and the goal of establishing a native church, a more effective plan is hard to imagine.

The third step, one intended to extend their work beyond the Kuskokwim, was John's proposal to establish a mission at Togiak. In his 1889 report to the board he detailed the advantages and disadvantages of such an endeavor. After visiting Togiak (*Tuyuryaq*) in March 1890, John concluded that because of the disease-weakened and scattered character of the population, the plan was, after all, not sound and should be abandoned. Throughout the debate, John displayed strategically as well as ethnographically astute reasoning: "It is uncertain how long this emigration will last, but it is certain that it will be many years before there will be an immigration from this river. Hence we think that for the time we must devote our entire attention to this river [the Kuskokwim], especially as it really is the key to Togiak. All the people from there, come from here, and from the very people with whom we come in direct contact."[41]

The Moravians developed the plan to establish a mission at Togiak in response to the problem of the tremendous size of the territory they were working in. Although this particular plan was not feasible, John was fundamentally correct that the only reasonable approach, given the size of the mission field and the limited resources they had to work with, was to establish discrete missions. These must be surrounded by satellite chapels and mission stations staffed by native helpers and must be regularly visited by non-native missionaries. Towards this end, his role as itinerant preacher remained critical.

CHAPTER 6

THE REAL PEOPLE AND THE CHILDREN OF THUNDER

THE REAL PEOPLE

The process by which the Kilbucks and the Yupiit came to know each other, and were changed by that knowledge, is the heart of our story. Although fraught with misapprehensions, it was never one-sided. As the "real people" watched and listened to the missionary couple, the Kilbucks' "thunder," while always a part of them, was modified by what they came to understand.

At the time the Kilbucks came to work in western Alaska, they found a people possessing a highly developed sense of themselves and their place in the world. Yup'ik values and notions of history, society, and eternity were grounded in a view of the world fundamentally different from the Kilbucks'. Though not always conscious of these differences, actions and interpretative interactions described in the journals give evidence of their existence. The journals, in turn, cannot be understood without reference to these differences.

The uniqueness of the Yup'ik view of the world is particularly visible in the notion of personhood. Every society possesses a definition of what a "real" person ought to be. A careful look at the attributes ascribed to a person provides insights about how people think of themselves and their relationship to others.

On the most basic level the Yup'ik people at the turn of the century viewed society as primary. The life of the individual took on meaning only in the context of a complex web of relationships between humans and animals, both the living and the dead. This idea contrasts sharply with the Hobbesian view of Western society in which every person is seen to confront every other as an owner. According to Hobbes, social relations result from

110

the actions of a multitude of individuals seeking to serve their own needs, and a person is a bound, unique, dynamic center of awareness. Although this Hobbesian perspective was but one part of the cultural baggage the Kilbucks brought with them to western Alaska, its impact on the Christian-Yup'ik encounter was considerable.

For the Yup'ik Eskimos, society included both human and nonhuman members. They extended personhood beyond the human domain and attributed it to animals as well. They did not believe that only humans possessed immortal souls in contrast to and dominant over the mute beasts that served them. On the contrary, the Yup'ik Eskimos viewed the relationship between humans and animals as collaborative reciprocity; the animals gave themselves to the hunter in response to his respectful treatment of them as persons (albeit nonhuman) in their own right.

According to the world view of the Yup'ik Eskimos, human and nonhuman persons shared a number of fundamental characteristics. First and foremost, the perishable flesh of both humans and animals was belied by the immortality of their souls. All living things participated in an endless cycle of birth and rebirth in which the movement of souls of both animals and people was contingent on right thought and action by others as well as self.

For game animals, the rebirth that followed their mortal demise was accomplished in part through the ritual consumption of their bodies by the men and women to whom they had given themselves in the chase. During the midwinter Bladder Festival (Nakaciuq) as well as the masked dances performed during Kelek, the spirits of the game were hosted and feasted as honored guests at the same time that as victims they were totally consumed. Given the missionaries' relatively circumscribed concept of personhood, it is no wonder that they had difficulty in comprehending the double meaning of the endless winter feasting that characterized traditional Yup'ik ceremonial activity. They interpreted as profligate and irrational squandering of scarce and limited resources an active attempt by the Yup'ik people to become worthy subjects of a reciprocal generosity on the part of the spirits of the game to whom, in the capacity of guests, they had given everything.[1]

Along with the belief in an essential spiritual continuity that bridged the gap between the past and the future, the Yup'ik people held that men and animals alike possessed "awareness." According to Joe Friday of Chevak, "We felt that all things were like us people, to the small animals like the mouse and the things like wood we liken to people as having a sense of awareness. The wood it is glad to the person who is using it and the person using it is grateful to the wood for being there to be used." The existence of such awareness was simultaneously indexed by and allowed individuals a sense of control over their destiny. This awareness was felt to be the product of experience. People lacked a sense of self at birth. Gradually, however, they became aware of their surroundings.

As they matured, both human and nonhuman persons received a multitude of prescriptions and proscriptions for the culturally appropriate living of life. Three related ideas underlie the elaborate detail of these rules: the power of a person's thought; the importance of thoughtful action in order not to injure another's mind; and, conversely, the danger inherent in "following one's own mind."

First, regarding the power of a person's thought, attitude was as significant as action. Thus, elders instructed young men to "keep the thought of the seals" foremost in their minds as they performed daily duties. In all these acts, by the power of the mind, they "made a way for the seals" they would some day hunt. Animals were also subject to this stricture. For example, young seals were said to be admonished by their elders to "stay awake" to the rules, both literally and figuratively, so that their immortal souls could survive the hunter's blow. If they were asleep when they were hit, they would "die dead, forever."[2] In all tasks the appropriate attitude was considered as important as the action. Conversely, both humans and animals gave help to individual elders and avoided their displeasure because of the "power of the mind of the elders" to affect their future.

Second, as proper thought effected success in the domain of human and animal interaction, so careful thought had to reign over thoughtless action in order not to injure the mind of another.[3] Just as a person's mind was powerful, it was also believed vulnerable. A reticence to hasty verbalization as well as the value placed on a person's ability to retain equilibrium in a tense situation derived from this belief. Ideally, smoothness and acquiescence were the appropriate mask for a person's emotions.[4] The value placed on the appearance of agreement partly explains the verbal assent missionaries sometimes received to their proposed reforms, often followed by no real change in a person's behavior. The Yupiit probably deeply resented (though they did not say so) the rude intervention of the missionaries which ran counter to their own highly refined system of indirect, yet nonetheless effective, interaction.[5] From the Yup'ik point of view, people were supposed to admonish a recalcitrant person without injuring the offender's mind in the process.

Third, and corollary to the belief in the power of human thought and the importance of thoughtful action, Yup'ik ideology maintained that one should refrain from following one's own mind when a person's ideas conflicted with the collective wisdom of the spiritually powerful elders. Individuality, as we understand it, was not a valued attribute. On the contrary, the pursuit of individual ends was often seen as conflicting with the good of the whole and was considered reprehensible.

A metaphor for what it meant to be a real person, according to the Yup'ik conception of reality, can be found in the opposition between sleeping and waking. Those who possessed powerful minds were said to be aware of or awake to their surroundings. Conversely, those who paid no attention to the rules and led thoughtless lives were considered to be unaware or asleep. The opposition between sleeping and waking is a frequent theme in Yup'ik moral discourse and signifies a spiritual as well as a physical condition. For example, a young boy who paid attention to what he was told was said to be awakened by the words of the elders. Elders encouraged young people to live on little sleep and to rise early and quickly. To be a lazy person or a sleepyhead was disapproved on moral grounds, as inordinate sleep was considered the outward sign of inner flaccidity and weakness.[6]

This same opposition between sleeping and waking also characterized animal society. For example, if a seal killed by a hunter's harpoon was awake when hit, its soul was said to retract to its bladder, where it would lie dormant until, well cared for by the successful hunter, it was returned to the sea to be reborn the following year. In the same way, when a person was dying, relatives would watch over the person, never going to sleep. Directly following a death the mourners set up a loud wailing to wake up the spirit for the journey ahead. Were the spirit allowed to sleep, like the seal it would be barred from rebirth in the future. Ironically, the Kilbucks deplored these funeral lamentations, taking them as signs of heathen grief that they would alleviate with their message of eternal life. In fact, a perpetual cycling between birth and rebirth characterized Yup'ik ideology; nothing ever finally passed away unless, through mental slumber or thoughtless action, one allowed oneself to "die dead, forever."

As can be seen, a number of specific attributes went into the Yup'ik definition of a real person and how a person might act in relation to others. These attributes differ significantly from the definitions of personhood and society that the Kilbucks held. The Western view of society, Christian and otherwise, can be characterized as a gathering of separate parts, which we know as individuals, each with distinct needs and desires and each seeking to augment its own ends. Consequently, individual freedom is generally considered a virtue and society a constraint. Within a Hobbesian framework, society is inspired by individual self-interest, tempered by fear of other people. Reason dictates that people get together because they cannot satisfy their individual needs unless they do.

These two different views of personhood and of society entail two different views of history as well. In the Western view, society originates in the unification of natural diversity. Although the Moravians stressed the community of believers, they saw this unity as forged from an original diversity. Western history depicts society as resolving, or at least as increasing control over, individual needs and desires. The Kilbucks manifested this view in their belief that people were born in sin, and life was spent controlling ever-present tendencies toward evil in the frailties of the flesh. This belief, in turn, ties back to the Western definition of culture, both individual and societal, as one's increasing control and refinement of oneself.[7] In its specifically Christian form, this epistemology guided the Kilbucks. Their work among the Yupiit paralleled their contemporaries' work in the marketplace to the extent that they abstracted Yup'ik culture as a thing that people did and had and could lose. On the contrary, for the Yup'ik Eskimos culture was a means of knowing, not something to be known, and as such was much more abiding than the Moravians allowed.

The view of society as the unification of an original diversity stands in direct contrast to the Yup'ik view of the origin of society and of history. By the Yup'ik view, as given in their oral tradition, society begins in peace and unity and coactivity. Traditional tales (*qulirat*) explain how this original reciprocity among human beings, and between humans and animals, was in specific instances broken. These stories usually tell of a person in pursuit of individual gratification, who loses sight of the rules and, as a result, either figuratively or literally loses humanity. Conversely, in the Western view, the pursuit of individual ends is taken for granted as a condition of being human and (to the Kilbucks) was evidence of humanity's original sinful state. To the Yup'ik Eskimos it was not. To them, people were social beings first and individuals only if they forgot themselves, in which case their downfall was assured.

For example, by one account, warfare among the Yup'ik people originated in an incident that occurred in a coastal community, sparked by the antisocial behavior of a man from the Yukon Delta who had married into another group. This particular hunter, eager to succeed but lacking the requisite skills, killed his hunting companions and stole their catch. His crime ultimately engendered armed conflict between the coastal and Yukon villages. This account is also given as the reason for the emergence of distinct social groupings out of an original unity, as Yukon and coastal Yup'ik Eskimos subsequently constituted two separable endogamous groups. Conversely, the conflict was laid to rest during a period of famine when a man from the Yukon and a man from the coast shared in the catch of a seal and saved each other's lives.[8]

Together, these two tales provide a cyclical view of history and, ultimately, a unified view of society. Whereas the original conflict divided a group united by marriage, the resolution brought about the rapprochement of two originally distinct groups. Though beginning in theft and the refusal to cooperate, the conflict ended in a return to food-sharing and trading. And although it began with the in-group murder of several successful hunters, it ended with the revival of an outsider who was close to death. Finally, the breach centered around the food quest and the relationship between humans and animals as well as between humans. Again, people's proper social relations were not seen as isolatable but as dependent on the correct relationship between hunter and hunted.

Although the Yupiit possessed a view of humanity fundamentally different from that of the men and women who came to "enlighten" them, in the interchange apparent similarities often masked the larger differences. In a number of important respects the Yup'ik code for right living is comparable to the Moravian "brotherly agreement," with its emphasis on a Godly life lived with "due economy," industry, and rigorous training. Edith's careful needlework drew moral as well as practical approbation from native women, who connected the quality of their stitchery with the quantity of their husband's catch. Both camps deplored waste, though defining it differently. Also, the Yup'ik definition of laziness bears a marked resemblance to John's own standards.[9] When the Kilbucks preached industry, they reached open ears, as the Yupiit were already committed to thoughtful action as an expression of one's proper spiritual state. On the other hand, the missionaries' emphasis on individual thrift often cut against the elaborate social reciprocity through which the Yupiit expressed a multitude of social and spiritual relationships.

To a certain extent both the Yupiit and the Moravians conceived a person's resources as finite, as opposed to the infinite resources of the universe (Ella) and God, respectively. Just as the Yupiit taught their young men and women not to squander their sight or breath, nineteenth-century Moravian parents advised their children not to read too much in order not to hurt their eyes and not to masturbate as it would waste their seed. Use of the spoken word was carefully circumscribed by both the Yupiit and the Moravians, as it was considered powerful and potentially hurtful.[10] Just as the Yupiit believed themselves dependent on the impersonal but all-powerful person of the universe (Ellam yua), so the Moravians saw themselves as unable to succeed without God's aid. A fundamental but independent similarity might also be suggested between the Yup'ik idea of the conscious and willing sacrifice of animals for the sake of human hunters and the Christian belief in the sacrifice of the lamb of God to redeem mankind. These congruences subtly aided and abetted the conversion process.

The Kilbucks also played on a significant isomorphism when they spoke of "waking up" the heathen, with its connotation of increased awareness. In 1889 John wrote, "The school children are quite awakened this winter. . . . Another young man came into our sitting-room . . . and said: '. . . While I sat listening to your words, it seemed to me that I was just waking up from a long sleep. I am indeed thankful, for now my eyes are open.'"[11] A fundamental tenet of Moravian doctrine is that death is a transition rather than a final state. Old Moravian church registers headed the column for the date of death "Fell Asleep."[12] Thus when the Kilbucks taught that to know God was life eternal, they hit a responsive chord, playing as they could on the Yup'ik belief in ever-cycling and, in this sense, everlasting life. These congruences, though historically accidental, were highly significant. They originated in different views of the world but provided a framework for mutual comprehension.

Although the Kilbucks were the harbingers of Western civilization in significant respects, their devout Christianity set them apart from their fellows. Along with the nineteenth-century Yupiit, they shared the belief that a person's material state manifested that person's spiritual condition. Visionaries within their own society, they deplored the *de facto* Western separation of the sacred and profane. Also, they shared a belief in personal responsibility. For both the Yupiit and the Moravians, the connection between action and ideal was fundamental, and harmony was the expressed ideal. Likewise, both admonished against vaunting good deeds in public. A contemporary Yup'ik account of traditional rules for living provides a striking parallel to (or perhaps culturally appropriate translation of) the advice given in Matthew 6:1–6 that a person not pray and perform charitable acts standing on street corners to be seen by others, but rather do so in secret to be rewarded by God:

> Only at night he clears the paths.
> If he does it during the day,
> letting the people see him
> already then,
> through the people he has his reward.
>
> But if he does that with no one watching him
> and nobody is aware of him,
> only the one watching him,
> the ocean or the land, . . .
> the Ellam yua [person or spirit of the universe] will
>   give him his reward.[13]

In the same way both the Yupiit and the Moravians placed a high value on personal encounter with an unseen power through prayer, as well as the use of ritual performance to insure the success of future action. Moreover, from the beginning, rather than suppressing traditional rhetorical forms, the conversion process employed the elders' practice of perpetually speaking out to advise the young people of their responsibilities. Just as discourse in the men's house figured as a central element in the traditional Yup'ik socialization process, the Moravians preached that continual public restatement was necessary for the Word of God to be received.

Another point of congruence can be found in the great importance Yup'ik tradition placed on the power of the human mind. The Yup'ik people used this fundamental ideological tenet to make sense of, restate, and understand the Moravian message of Christ's love. Many years later, in a sermon John delivered on gift-giving, his emphasis on intention approximated Yup'ik admonitions concerning the relation of thought and deed. He wrote, "My sermon was on the Widow's mite, as recorded by Mark. . . . In giving with the heart in it, we give a double portion."[14] In another sermon, John's reference to the hardness of the human heart was interpreted by his Yup'ik audience in terms of their belief in the power of the human mind.[15]

In the same way, though the concept of original sin was foreign, the

Christian emphasis on salvation and life eternal fit with the traditional belief in rebirth made possible by proper action in life. The conquest of death is one of the ultimate goals of Christianity and an important element in Moravian theology. This victory is achieved when sinners are "born again" in this life and the spirit of God is instilled in them. For the Moravians this spiritual rebirth cancels out the original sin that is part and parcel of human physical birth. On the contrary, in the Yup'ik view of the world, rebirth is physical birth writ large.

The people of the Kuskokwim partially resolved contradictions between Christian theology and the collective aspects of nineteenth-century Yup'ik daily life by practicing Christianity so as to give less attention to individual salvation than to harnessing divine help in supporting the well-being of the community of believers. Although the differences between the Yup'ik and Western views of the world were profound, the Kilbucks' Christian ideology proved to be a powerful intermediary in the process of religious conversion, which was also a process of cultural translation. A century later, the extent of their success was voiced on the occasion of the ordination of a native deacon, Bob Aloysius, in Bethel. According to Aloysius, "It had to take the Son of God to teach people to live like the Yup'iks. The main command of the Yup'ik people is to love one another and never put yourself above other people, and to look after your fellow man. What is the difference between true Christianity and the Yup'iks? I don't see any myself." [16] Although Aloysius did not speak the whole truth, he spoke a portion of it worth keeping in mind.

THE CHILDREN OF THUNDER

> *Civilization is one immense interrogation point standing up before them. Is it not to any one?*
>
> —*Edith Kilbuck, 1888* [17]

Although the resemblances between Yup'ik and Moravian ideology and action may have aided the initial presentation of Christianity, they also masked profound differences in expectation. To the Kilbucks, action in this world was preparatory to life in the next. For the Yupiit the meaning of existence was already given in the here-and-now, and the purpose of following the rules was to maintain the proper social and spiritual relationship between the human and spirit worlds. Whereas Yup'ik ceremonies sought to re-create essential relations already in place, the Moravians sought to participate in God's intended transformation.

On their arrival the Kilbucks viewed the Yup'ik mind as a blank slate as far as religion was concerned, ready to receive their message of eternal life. The self-imposed task of civilizing and Christianizing the indigenous "heathen" consumed their energy and imagination. During the early years, when the differences between the aboriginal and "civilized" worlds stood out in sharpest contrast, the Kilbucks wrote their harshest judgments, condemning the "barbarism" and immorality they found:

> They as a rule are very kind to each other. . . . One crime they do commit which none of them recognize as such, and that is, to kill off unwelcome infants, especially girls; and they also kill old and helpless persons. . . .
> They sometimes club to death and burn with oil a "shaman" or "witch" who is suspected of killing too many innocent people. Such dreadful deeds are shocking to us.[18]

Infanticide, ritual execution (for that is probably what the killing of the accused witch signified), and abandonment were, in fact, part of a cultural complex and survival strategy both foreign and abhorrent to the Kilbucks.

Traditional Yup'ik sexuality also drew sharp criticism. Exasperated by the apparently fickle and overindulgent character of Yup'ik sexual activity Edith wrote, "I fully believe that some of these women have ten to twelve husbands before they settle down and even when they have children and are old enough to be steady they think nothing of leaving their husband and taking some one else. . . . My heart aches for the girls of our part of Alaska. They are made perfect prostitutes by their parents from the time they are nine or ten years old."[19] Culturally committed to monogamy and to the ideal of repressed sexuality characteristic of late nineteenth-century Western culture, Edith especially saw Yup'ik sexuality as unregulated desire, rather than desires regulated according to a cultural logic very different from her own.

True to the late nineteenth-century evolutionary view of human history, the Kilbucks assumed that the Eskimos were at a lower "stage of spiritual development." They judged Yup'ik beliefs to be superstitions that could not be based on "higher impulses" such as love or morality: "The affection that has developed could hardly be termed love—in the usual acceptation of that term. . . . The kashigi has robbed the family of homelife—for the father and son virtually live in the kashigi—not even being regular boarders at what should be their home."[20] In their contradictory evaluation of the Eskimos, individual Yupiit might merit respect, but their way of life did not.

More distressing to the Kilbucks than the specific acts condemned by their sense of right and wrong was the Yup'ik people's apparent lack of recognition of the inherent evil of their actions. Edith wrote, "The people are not vicious or dangerous in any way, but they continually practice so many of the evils found among uncivilized people that it is shocking at times how little they think of the wrong there is in it all. This is one more of our hard tasks, to get the people to *sufficiently understand the vileness of sin* to leave off from doing it."[21]

Initially, the Yup'ik response to this condemnation was totally frustrating to the missionaries, striking them as duplicitous: "They may say 'yes' and agree that it is all wrong, yet they will not give it up, but only try to hide it from your view; and with this they are satisfied."[22] For the Yupiit, however, verbal assent acknowledged respect for the speaker or recognition of the speaker's power, not necessarily agreement. Behavior interpreted as duplicitous was in some cases no more than a limited attempt to be civil.

The Kilbucks were also grieved that initially they could not elicit condemnation of their fellows from those natives who verbally expressed agreement with the missionaries. Edith wrote, "Even those who have never done such a deed and say it is wrong, think no less of those that do, and treat them the same as other persons. . . . They think little or nothing of the cruel deed itself, not even giving it a second thought."[23] This supposed indifference was more likely the manifestation of the Yup'ik people's highly developed sense of personal responsibility and, the other side of the coin, the inappropriateness of direct interference with the actions of others.

Just as presumed indifference on the part of the Yupiit irritated the Kilbucks, their own directness was incompatible with Yup'ik etiquette. Blithely unaware that their own blunt talk might appear "barbarous" to the Yupiit, John and Edith did not hesitate to catch questioners in contradictions or to ridicule traditional taboos by word and deed. While the Kilbucks' emphasis on personal responsibility and lived faith was perceived as appropriate, their interference, which the Kilbucks saw as saving the people from themselves, was not.

Another aspect of the "thunderous" nature of the Kilbucks that never lessened was their poor opinion of those who lacked their sense of the inherent value of work. They were extremely critical of what they took to be Yup'ik lethargy and lack of motivation. Edith's criticism of one of the schoolboys is an early example of this evaluative absolute: "Johnny has all the good intentions in the world but very little ambition to carry them out. He never does anything exactly bad, but will scarcely exert himself to do anything beyond what is daily required of him. To tell the truth, he is decidedly lazy."[24] Rather than reflecting natural passivity, the child's reserve may have been a culturally appropriate reaction to the decisive and opinionated character of the missionaries. In the beginning, especially, the Yupiit responded to the Kilbucks' "thunder" by watching and withholding active judgment. The Kilbucks, in turn, interpreted this reserve as "natural ignorance" and stupidity.[25]

Along with their perception of the barbarity, immorality, duplicity, and indifference of Yup'ik attitude and action, the Kilbucks also believed that the Yup'ik people were inordinately superstitious. This behavior was particularly frustrating, as they saw no reason for it. To them, ritual acts of cleansing and purification, such as holding one's breath or averting one's gaze in particular contexts, were nonsense, and they taught strongly against them. In so doing they undercut the system of ideas of which the acts were but the visible manifestation.

Haircuts given to the children who came to the mission school provide a good example of such a battle. To provide protection from sickness, the Yupiit traditionally refrained from cutting children's hair, and they vehemently resisted the Kilbucks' insistence that young boys cut their hair before entering the mission school on the grounds that if they did so the boys would sicken and die:[26] "We have one boy . . . whom we had a task to get. . . . His mother would not agree because we would cut his long hair. . . . Whenever I came out she would shake her fist at me and say '*don't you cut his hair; not one bit of it. I don't want him to die.*'"[27]

The Kilbucks unremittingly condemned what they viewed as a groundless superstition connecting cutting hair with illness. Ironically, Edith voiced a reverse cultural logic, also couched in natural terms, to justify her own actions: "We have cut off [our daughter] Katie's hair. . . . She got rush of blood to the head and we thought best to have it short. . . . It was too long and heavy for a growing child to support. She did look sweet with it though."[28]

Another example of a misunderstanding was the Kilbucks' response to Yup'ik coastal traders' insisting that John drop what he was doing to trade with them immediately on their arrival. Although he usually complied, Edith deemed these requests uncalled-for impositions. In fact, Yup'ik etiquette required that a young man or woman (Edith and John were twenty-three and twenty-seven at the time) respond to the demands of their elders, regardless of how inconvenient from their point of view. What the Kilbucks perceived as unreasonable was probably no more than what common courtesy required.

The character of their enterprise limited the degree to which the Kilbucks could accurately interpret, let alone empathize with, the Yupiit as they found them. They are perhaps more impressive in the extent to which they described an increasing sympathy for, if not positive understanding of, the Yupiit. The whole of John's descriptive manuscript "Something about the Innuit" is characterized by this sympathy, which is a primary reason it remains valuable. For example, his comprehension of the traditional custom of wife-lending is remarkable for a member of the nineteenth-century American middle class, especially a missionary: "This is not promiscuously done—but two men may agree to do so—and thereafter hail each other by the title—Kathoon [*qatngun*: half sibling]."[29]

Another example is John's description of the situation underlying the annual food shortage that plagued life along the Kuskokwim. Although not devoid of a certain patronizing tone, John's explanation is less biased than that of a number of his contemporaries, who uncritically condemned all traditional ceremonial distributions because they were felt to provide an opportunity for "wasteful and wanton distribution."[30] Even so, when John contended that Yup'ik "improvidence" could be accounted for by the exigencies of primitive methods of meat preservation, he betrayed an ethnocentric and characteristic functionalism. In fact, the Yup'ik people viewed themselves as engaged in an endless cycle of reciprocal exchange with their animal compatriots, such that the more game they consumed, the more they would have. According to Robert Brightman, the midwinter ceremonies and elaborate gift exchanges in which they distributed and consumed tremendous quantities of food comprised an essential act of reciprocal hosting, rather than a practical way to use up leftovers. More than a mechanism for rationally equalizing excess, the nineteenth-century Yupiit believed these feasts to be the prerequisite for a successful harvest in the coming year and, as such, essential sacred acts, whatever their social cost.

Certainly the Yupiit worried over food shortage and the limitations of their own technology. Yet, if individual families expended great effort to provide for their future needs during one season, all their stores might be put at the disposal of the group the next. Kilbuck and his cohorts fought long and hard against what they viewed as impractical and "irrational" generosity. What the missionaries failed to understand was the larger social need the distributions functioned to supply. If the game failed, then villages must break apart and families separate in search of food.[31]

In contrast to the Kilbucks' commitment to the concept of an individual household boasting a full larder to which they had exclusive rights, their Yup'ik parishioners repressed individual hunger and persisted in incomprehensible social feasting that effectively exhausted the food at hand. Similarly, the Yupiit expressed sexuality much more freely and even celebrated it as a principle of both reproduction and production (for example, women baring their breasts when nursing and dancing with the explicit intent of enhancing their own and their community's reproductive capacity). Between their converts' perceived mismanagement of natural resources and overindulgence of sexual appetites, the Kilbucks had difficulty being sympathetic, let alone comprehending.

There are, in the journals, passages that make particular Yup'ik people appear foolish; Edith once described a woman holding a picture magazine upside down and then loudly blaming the senseless illustrations on the Kass'aq author rather than the turn of her hands. However, both Edith and John wrote their observations in the same tone that they used to describe human failings in general. As deeply religious as they were, humanism increasingly transcended the evangelism of their early letters. Years later, their daughter Ruth recalled that the only time her father ever spanked her was as punishment for slapping a Yup'ik playmate. Although the Yup'ik and the Kilbuck definitions of humanness remained disparate, that did not prevent a mutual respect.

THE RESPONSE

As John and Edith's letters and journals reveal their feelings about the Yup'ik people, they also reveal the Yup'ik response to their presence. On their arrival, John noted an initial confusion: "The first work has been, to

Fig. 6.1. Children at Bethel, 1896: Joe Kilbuck, Bertha Helmich, Ruth Kilbuck, Carlie, and Fritz. (J. H. Romig, Moravian Archives)

make them understand the object of our coming: that we have not come to trade with them, but to teach them. . . . The majority still believe that we are traders, and this in spite of our protestations to the contrary, and our absolutely refusing to buy their furs." [32]

The separation between the spiritual and the material involved much more than an issue of classification. Though their goal was to raise the standard of living of the people, the Kilbucks did not do so by giving goods directly as the traders might but by teaching a new attitude toward life in the present as well as in the hereafter. This issue was long standing. As late as 1895 the newly converted native helpers successfully played on the distinction between the traders' load of costly goods, which are soon gone, and the priests' spiritual load which "never is lost, will not wear out." [33]

Four years after their arrival, in the journal written to Edith on his trip to Nushagak, John described how far from a trader he had come in Yup'ik eyes: "I now have learned why the natives believe that I belong to their country. Their supposition is that some one of their number was carried off on the ice, as it frequently happens, and that this man was rescued or landed among the white people and that I am his off-spring." [34] Probably no higher compliment could have been paid John than the supposition of common descent. Yet it is not surprising. As a full-blooded Delaware Indian, John's dark complexion belied Caucasian ancestry. Also, his command of the Yup'ik language set him apart from white traders and explorers with whom the Yup'ik people had contact.

Nor did he stay at home during the winter, instead preferring to travel and visit. Traveling on his own, having a good knowledge of the language, John was able to see and hear things that helped him understand the significance of Yup'ik ideology and action in ways that a monolingual, stay-at-home missionary never could. Moreover, when he arrived in any village he was ready and willing to accept Yup'ik hospitality, bed and board included. In the same paragraph in which he described the Yup'ik claim of common descent, John remarked his first taste of seal meat: "It was killed in the morning, so it was quite fresh. It was fine." [35]

Edith attracted her share of notoriety. She was appalled when she learned of a rumor that described her as no less than common property of all the men on the Kuskokwim. The natives as well as the traders on the Yukon River circulated the rumor, and she expressed some, perhaps justified, concern that it would spread to San Francisco. Known as Suchdullera (*Sugtulria*, literally "one who is tall") because of her stately figure, she increasingly presided over the social life of Bethel, where visitors brought her small gifts of berries and fish and continually sought her out for aid and conversation.

In gifting, especially, the Yupiit tried to engage the young missionaries in their world, not without success. Even before they had seen their first change of season on the Kuskokwim they were receiving tokens of hospitality: "An old man just came with a nice fish for a present. We get 'Pinch-

Fig. 6.2. John Henry Kilbuck, 1897. (J. H. Romig, Moravian Archives)

Fig. 6.3. Edith Romig Kilbuck with daughter Katie, 1893. (Moravian Archives)

tamkins' (presents) nearly every day." When the children were born, the natives asked gifts in their name. Joe Kilbuck, especially, served to pull his parents into the distribution process: "Little Joe snared his first ptarmigan today, and the natives clamour for a treat. . . . Ice cream and fish were dealt out and games were played." [36] Yup'ik parents also gave Edith gifts as special thanks for her work on behalf of the schoolchildren. For instance, she received a wooden bowl in the winter of 1888 in thanks for making clothes for the schoolboys. Another time a woman made her a calico cap and said she must wear it because she was a married woman too: "They were much pleased when I wore it all day." [37]

As the Kilbucks were pulled into traditional social exchanges, they increasingly distinguished themselves among their missionary cohorts. During their first years in Bethel, John, along with William Weinland, visited nearby villages especially to witness major ceremonial events. However, the missionaries' early participation in and comprehension of these events were, by their own admission, minimal. At the end of the first year John wrote, "We have learned something about their religious belief, something about their customs, and their plays or *eckeruschkas* [38]; but as we are not quite satisfied with the information and desire to examine these subjects more carefully, we have decided not to write anything about them at present." [39]

In the years that followed, as the missionaries began to understand the meaning of the ceremonies, they became openly critical. They rigorously suppressed the overtly "pagan" ceremonies, including the Great Feast for the Dead (Elriq), the Bladder Festival (Nakaciuq), and the "Masquerade" (Kelek) as soon as they began to awaken to their full implications.

At the same time that these ceremonies came under heavy attack, other less offensive exchanges were spared. Both Edith and John wrote lively accounts of their participation in traditional exchanges during their early years in Bethel. John, especially, seemed able to enter into the spirit of what he witnessed. At the end of a detailed description of the dramatic reception of guests at what was probably a Messenger Feast (Kevgiq), he wrote, "Somewhere in me, there must be some of the old Injun left, for I was strangely stirred, and I could not but help thinking of my forefathers, who not so many generations back, were such proud boasters. I think it is on this account, that I feel so drawn to these people, and helps me enter into their feelings." [40]

Even in declaring personal identity with the natives, John's description was that of an observer. Edith's rendition of a Petugtaq exchange, however, is typically down to earth, describing in detail her family's part in the festivities:

> The present excitement is the friendship Ekrushica being held between our place and the Post. . . . Two nights ago Mr. Lind and the two men came over to present their gifts. . . . They placed everything in the kitchen then Wasca came in to me with a *large* grass mat, then went out and brought in a grass basket. Next time a large wooden dish, then four nicely dressed rabbits in another dish and last of all several lbs. of dried venison. Then came Kiack-shack with grass mat, *very large* and fine, wooden dish, grass basket, another dish with four large whitefish in, (something rare for so late in the Fall) and

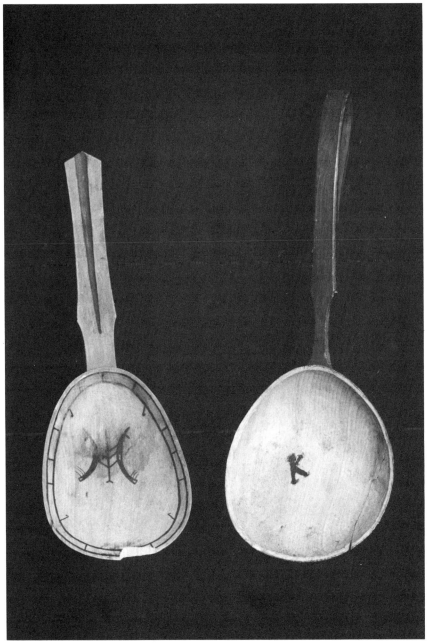

Fig. 6.4. Wooden ladles, length 16 inches. Note initial "K" for Kilbuck. (Kilbuck Collection, Ottawa University)

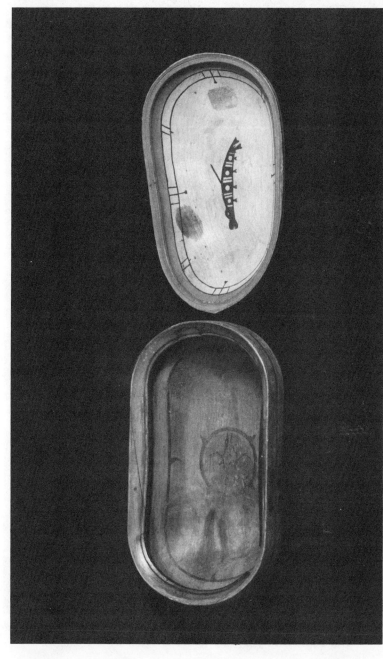

Fig. 6.5. Wooden bowls, length 10 inches. Bowl on the left is decorated with a turtle design signifying John's Delaware clan affiliation. (Kilbuck Collection, Ottawa University)

dried venison. Mr. Lind gave me a pair of new deerskin boots. Katie two pr. of boots, a panful of cookies and a large piece of corned beef. Procopi gave me two small lap boards of use in fur sewing, a grass basket and a sealion skin and fresh fish. He bought the skin of Mr. Lind purposely for me. It is used for bootsoles, has a market value of $1.25. . . . Today I returned the giving.[41]

John and Edith's writings testify to their family's early integration into community life, at least as far as the post and mission were concerned. When they understood the sexual exchanges associated with the exchange of gifts during Petugtaq, this event also came under attack. This revelation did not occur until 1896, however, by which time the Kilbucks had, to some extent, internalized the structure of Yup'ik gifting.[42]

John and Edith were most successful in their ability not to think but to *act* in Yup'ik ways. They took part in a number of vital cultural exchanges, including speaking, eating, traveling, visiting, and gifting. Although the Kilbucks assumed that it was the Christian character of these acts that won converts, it was, ironically, their Yup'ik quality that gave them their efficacy. Insofar as John and Edith acted in a Yup'ik manner, their parishioners assumed that they were thinking in a Yup'ik manner as well and that their appropriate acts were the product of "appropriate" Yup'ik motivation. It would be many years before Christian charity and sacrifice in God's name would be understood as such. In the beginning, however, the Kilbucks' participation in Yup'ik meals, plays, and gift exchanges was likely the chief means by which they won both converts and respect.

Although they certainly never became Yup'ik, no more than the Yup'ik people became Kass'aq under their tutelage, the cultural exchange the Kilbucks engaged in was impressive. John, especially, was able to participate in this exchange because the ambiguity of his own background served over and over again as a bridge in the conversion process. In the summer of 1890 Edith was able to use John's background to translate her message concerning the value of education into comprehensible, if not acceptable, form:

I explained to a houseful of them that John was taken away from his home and relatives in order to be educated, just as we wished to do with their children. White people did not kill or harm him and today he was thankful to them for what they did for him. This was news to most of them. They think he is *blood of their blood*; and love him accordingly but they had never thought anything about this past life. Some of them immediately said that it was foolish to be afraid of white people and object to send their children to school. I hope it *will* soften the parents hearts towards us a little.[43]

Over the years both John and Edith became more and more personally connected to the people among whom they worked. John acquired trading partners and regular hosts in a number of distant villages. As he continued to travel, he was increasingly grounded through gifts and formal social obligations: "At Crow village I met what the natives call 'Ah-la-nax-lux' [from *allaneq*: stranger] i.e. a stranger literally, but it really means, a stranger with whom you make a permanent friendship. Those holding this relationship always treat each other extra well, the best they can. I have three such relationships." [44]

Although Edith rarely traveled, she received a constant flow of visitors, whom she increasingly valued until, in the summer of 1893, she could write, "Nearly all the old neighbors have come to visit me. Women are here from eighty miles up the river. They help me out with sewing and I spend as much time with them as I can. The newer members of our party must often wonder why I leave the work that seems endless and sit and talk first in one tent and then in another. O, if they could only understand our conversations, if they loved these people and could talk, they would do just as I do, I am sure." [45] In the spring of 1890, in response to a child's plea that she not leave on the annual trip to meet the supply ship at the mouth of the Kuskokwim, Edith voiced her commitment to remain among the "real people": "You can hardly realize how bound we feel to our work and how thoroughly one we are with our people. It is no light thing that will cause either one of us to leave." [46]

As the Kilbucks became increasingly tied to their work along the Kuskokwim, their influence and stature among the Yup'ik people grew to the point where their name became synonymous with that of the mission itself. In the fall of 1890 two white men traveled from the Yukon, where they had taken the census. At Bethel they told the missionaries that "the natives farther up the river had talked so much about the 'Kilbuchamuks' that they expected to meet another tribe, not known as yet. As the natives were only referring to those living about the mission station, they were disappointed." [47] Not only had John and Edith received Yup'ik names, but their own surname was used to designate the small missionary band in the manner of a unique subgroup of "real people."

CHAPTER 7

THE TESTING

Experience realizes that for every plan accomplished there have been many trials to be borne, many obstacles to be removed, and many sacrifices to be made.

—*John Kilbuck, 1891*[1]

TENSIONS MOUNT

In letters and reports the Kilbucks painted an encouraging view of the Yup'ik response to the message that, after four years along the Kuskokwim, they were able to preach in earnest. As the language barrier melted away and as their own sense of foreignness dissolved into a feeling of familiarity, their strategy of traveling, preaching, teaching, and healing began to bear fruit. Tasks became routinized. Before the end of the first half decade Edith would report boredom settling over her life as the newness wore thin and her circle of work without end became fuller and more fixed.[2] This placid situation was not to last.

The positive Yup'ik response to the Kilbucks had never been unanimous. In fact, some of what they interpreted as supportive contained subtle and not so subtle clues that the ranks of dissension were already filling out. John found that he was no longer interrupted when he went to the men's house to speak. However, he often elicited a silence heavy with the tensions building within Yup'ik society. The hush that followed his arrival was perhaps not so much indicative of a lack of conflict but the degree to which such conflict had been internalized and made synonymous with tensions present and already at work. As the Kilbucks' momentum increased, it was matched by an increased identification by some Yupiit with what had come before them.

The antagonistic responses that the Moravian missionaries elicited can be divided between two camps: the traditional shamans or *angalkut,* and the Russian Orthodox. Although strife between these two groups existed before the Moravians arrived, their mutual hostility to the active intervention

131

of the newcomers served to heighten the depth and drama of the conflict to come.

With an eye on the positive fruits of his newly acquired ability to speak, John wrote Edith in January 1890 of a well-attended meeting in one of the nearby villages: "These people say, shamaning and masquerading must go, because they want to follow Jesus Christ. Edith, this is good news, something to brace the heart." More to the point was the response John received a month later at another village, when a spokesman said that though the people wanted to "go with Christ most of the time," they still wanted some of their customs. John, however, was firm that they must decide, and Edith reported that they chose "for Christ and the new over the old."[3]

The all-or-nothing commitment that John sought was certainly appropriate to the depth and character of his convictions. The fact that the Kilbucks had not been so audibly ambitious in the beginning reflected the tenuousness of their mission rather than theological laxity. After their arrival the Moravians had moved slowly to insure that when conversion came, it would be sincere. Even church service had been postponed in order that understanding accompany desire and that participants perceive religious acts as meaningful and not as mere ceremony.[4] The missionaries also displayed tolerance towards the schoolboys' attendance at winter festivals. Edith wrote, "Of course we would prefer to keep them here but we dare not be too hard on them. We must regard their wishes to some extent when no harm will come of what they ask for. If we are too strict we would soon lose all our scholars." From the beginning, however, Edith was adamant on what she took to be essentials: "John . . . is going with one of the young husbands tomorrow to get back his wife. I imagine that wicked old mother will fume considerable and maybe shamman him for so doing, but let her do so, so long as we are in the right. I am in fighting trim at all times. I have no mercy on the shammans, no more than I have for old satan himself. They are bare-faced liars, deceiving the people and living off of the poor."[5]

Although the Kilbucks' emphasis on personal responsibility was profoundly appropriate, this all-or-nothing attitude was not. Corollary to the Yup'ik concept of personhood, noninterference was the ideal. Just as each person was ultimately responsible for his or her own life, each must decide how to live it. When the Kilbucks began to do more than present an alternative and to actively prescribe how life's choices should be made, they ran head-on against a fundamental tenet of Yup'ik ideology. Significantly, they violated a tolerance of many traditional Yup'ik practices that the Russian Orthodox had already established and so provided grounds for a subtle joining of forces between their opponents.

ADVERSARIES

> *It is better to die from hunger than to convert from Orthodoxy.*
> —*Iakov Korchinskii, Russian Orthodox priest, 1896* [6]

The initial choice of Bethel as the site for their mission was in part based on the Moravians' view that no other denomination had representatives living along the river. This was an important consideration, as Moravian mission work typically focused upon the "totally benighted." Although their initial analysis of the situation accurately reflected the lack of a full-time missionary serving the Kuskokwim district, it was fundamentally flawed. In fact, the Russian Orthodox, also referred to as Greek Catholic, Church had been established at Russian Mission on the Yukon River for more than fifty years and laid nominal claim to almost the entire population of the Yukon-Kuskokwim Delta.

A handful of Creole priests, including Iakov Netsvetov and Zakharii Bel'kov,[7] had devoted their lives to winning converts in western Alaska and by 1890 had made significant progress in this direction, especially along the Yukon River in the communities immediately surrounding Russian Mission. Bel'kov's successor, Iakov Korchinskii, who served the Yukon mission from 1896 until 1900, concluded, "With the question 'of what faith are you?' even now throughout the Kwikhpak [Yukon] and Kuskokwim mission, the Christian Natives respond 'Zakhaliam', that is, in the faith of Zakharii."[8] Although the success of the Russian Orthodox had not been so great along the Kuskokwim, they had at least nominal converts in most of the major settlements. Less than two months after Hartmann and Weinland's reconnaissance, Bel'kov recorded conversions among the people living at the proposed site of the new Moravian mission.[9]

The Moravians can hardly be blamed for their mistake, as it was originally perpetrated by the Russian Orthodox priest Vasily Shishkin, whom they had encountered at Nushagak. To send them out of what he considered his territory, Shishkin, who was not himself an ordained priest, had falsely advised Hartmann and Weinland that the Kuskokwim comprised an open field.[10] In the winter of 1886 Weinland traveled to Russian Mission, where he had his first opportunity to talk to Father Bel'kov. Although he was able to make only one annual visit to the Kuskokwim branch of his parish, Bel'kov stoutly defended both the Yukon and Kuskokwim rivers as part of his diocese and claimed four thousand communicants on the two rivers.

Such territorial disputes were common in the foreign mission field; behind them lay a more fundamental animosity between the Russian Orthodox and Moravian churches. This situation was historically grounded in the inhospitable reception Moravian immigrants had received in Russia during the late eighteenth and early nineteenth centuries. Moravians had originally been invited to settle in Russia during the reign of Catherine the Great. To

Fig. 7.1. Russian Orthodox clergy, Nushagak, 1884. Shishkin is seated in the middle. (A. Hartmann, Moravian Archives)

encourage settlement in the Russian wilderness, they were promised both ownership of the land they cultivated and religious freedom in the communities they established.[11] As the Moravian communities flourished, however, the Orthodox hierarchy increasingly perceived them as a threat, and the early promises of religious freedom were not kept.

The ill will born of these encounters, although not part of the personal experience of either the Kilbucks or the Orthodox priests working at Russian Mission, set the stage for the denominational conflict that would characterize the Alaska mission. Moreover, the historically close association of Orthodoxy with the Russian government made it seem more foreign to the Moravians and therefore more suspicious than the other denominations working in western Alaska. Other Protestant denominations shared this view, and the appointment of Presbyterian minister Sheldon Jackson as the United States Commissioner of Education in Alaska in 1894 served to turn denominational bias into federal policy. Jackson personally inspired a number of Protestant denominations to support mission work in Alaska, his explicit goal to enlighten and "civilize" its "heathen" residents, many of whom were baptized Orthodox. The anti-Moravian attitude of the Orthodox priests must be seen in this global and national context.

Last but not least, the Moravians labored under the not entirely false assumption that since the withdrawal of Russian administration from Alaska, Russia had withdrawn financial support for its missions as well. In fact, the Orthodox missions still received financial support from the church of the motherland. However, support was so limited that even where the Orthodox mission wished to oppose the Moravians, it lacked the financial resources necessary to do so.

Animosity between the Moravian and Orthodox churches had a theological as well as historical basis. The chief characteristic of Moravian doctrine was its emphasis on "vital Godliness" and the direct relationship between the converted and his Savior. By this view, when an individual's life was touched with saving faith, it should be transformed to reflect the Christian love and charity at its core. The need for membership in a church was secondary to this experience of a personal spiritual relationship with God.

Moravianism had originated in an attempt to add vital content to what was perceived as the increasingly empty forms of the Roman Catholic Church. Initially, it developed as an ecumenical movement, committed to reasserting vital Godliness into Christian belief and practice over and above winning converts to their particular denomination. In contrast, Russian Orthodoxy, as it existed at the end of the nineteenth century, was territorially and denominationally exclusive. As it was practiced in western Alaska it emphasized the teaching and administering of the sacraments as the mystical representation of Christ's sacrifice. The Orthodox believed that if they provided patience and example, change in existing patterns of living would follow. For the Moravians, however, the result was the appearance of "empty ritual."

The Moravian response to Orthodoxy reflected a basic theological disagreement regarding the manner in which one became a Christian. The Russian Orthodox envisioned conversion as the completion of nature by grace operating through the sacraments, the gradual elaboration of an originally primitive whole. They viewed conversion as a continuing process and at least initially could tolerate local customs, as they would eventually be replaced. The Moravians, on the other hand, professed a theology that stressed complete and sometimes sudden transformation. For them conversion was a definite step rather than a process. As historian John Webster Grant pointed out, these theologies of continuity and discontinuity contributed to different missionary emphases in the field, with strikingly different practical results.[12] This divergence resulted in polarization, with each denomination convinced that the other was leading its native converts to perdition.

The Moravians' apprehension of the Russian Orthodox encountered in western Alaska can be explained by the discrepancy between Orthodox policy and practice in the field. A sensitive policy of tolerance of native practices instituted by Ioann Veniaminov (Bishop Innocent)[13] in the mid-1800s guided the Orthodox clergy. In this ecumenical policy, native ideology was left intact where it did not directly conflict with the administration of Christian rites. In his famous 1841 "Instructions" concerning the treatment of natives Veniaminov decreed that priests "on no account show open contempt for their [the natives'] manner of living, customs, etc. . . . . Ancient customs, so long as they are not contrary to Christianity, need not be too abruptly broken up; but it should be explained to converts that they are merely tolerated."[14] Orthodox policy prescribed gentle but firm pressure in the direction of salvation and tolerance wherever this was not in conflict with the ultimate goal of Christianization.

The Orthodox attitude towards the sacraments also helped determine how their policy was put into practice. Like the Moravians, their ultimate goal was careful and thorough conversion before baptism. In the same instructions, Veniaminov decreed, "Thou shalt not proceed to administer holy baptism to natives before they have been thoroughly instructed by thee in the above-named matters, nor then, unless they shall have expressed the wish to receive it."[15] However, the extreme importance placed on the sacraments, and their character as essential acts capable of transforming the lives of those who received them, meant that in the field instruction often took second place to their administration. Ironically, the Orthodox view of the sacraments of their church as essential to salvation meant that they were as intolerant towards other varieties of Christianity as they were tolerant towards the customs of those they were working to win; they viewed the Moravians, along with other Protestant denominations, as dangerous schismatics and the Roman Catholics as out-and-out heretics. While the Moravians perceived the Orthodox as lax foreigners, the Orthodox took them to be non-believers sent by Sheldon Jackson to persecute them.

Though the negative reaction of the Moravians to the Orthodox working in western Alaska is understandable, it is also ironic, given the common objectives of the two denominations. First of all, the initial break in 1457 from the Roman Church by the followers of John Hus in Moravia was rooted, in part, in their objection to the replacement of the Slavonic language and Orthodox liturgies in the worship services by the exclusive use of the Latin language and Roman rites.[16] The Moravian use of the vernacular in worship services is a clear reflection of their historic link with the early Eastern Orthodox Church, which had originated in a break with the Roman Catholic Church four hundred years before the Moravian–Roman Catholic schism. The two churches shared a commitment to spreading the gospel in words that the common people could understand. Second, what appeared to the Moravians as empty ritual and a lax attitude toward "heathen" customs on the part of the Russian Orthodox were rooted in this shared commitment to a broadly comprehensible faith. Orthodox tolerance partly reflected their practical realization of an inability to drastically alter the lives of all of their converts; however, it was also a product of church policy.

At the same time, the Orthodox early advocated native ecclesiastical involvement. They employed lay readers to hold the services at the St. Michael and Kolmakovskiy chapels, and native clergymen were the rule rather than the exception. What the Moravians critically viewed as "empty ritual" performed by "heathen priests" (that is, Orthodox Creoles of mixed native and Russian ancestry) was bred of the same broad vision that produced the Moravian willingness to modify Christian denominations through the addition of vital Godliness, rather than through the replacement of one denomination by another.

In the end, among all the missions in Alaska, the Russian Orthodox and the Moravians stand out in their tolerance and incorporation of the native language as well as their emphasis on and development of a native clergy. Ironically, although joined in their original commitment to a church of and for the people, historical divergence was such that when they met again in western Alaska, bitter conflict characterized their relationship.

The Moravians did not, however, rail exclusively against Orthodoxy. Although they lived on amicable terms with the Episcopal mission which had been established at Anvik in 1887, they were on less than friendly terms with the Roman Catholics. The Jesuits had established a mission on Nelson Island in 1888; they subsequently moved it to Akulurak at the mouth of the Yukon River. In 1891, when the Jesuit Father Paul Muset passed through Bethel enroute to the Yukon post, Edith remarked, "The Jesuits do not let any chances go by for securing new fields of labor, no matter if they step on the toes of others." Sometime later, she referred to another Jesuit, Father Paschal Tosi, as the "deceitful Catholic priest" who had apparently openly criticized the Moravians for having wives and being mercenary: "He said to the people, 'What kind of priests are they? They have wives.' He also said that we were here to make money, and that John was just the same as a miner and was no priest whatever." [17]

Over the years, the Kilbucks' opinion of the Jesuits seems to have mellowed. In 1896, Edith wrote, "The Roman Priests certainly have not done us any harm. They speak kindly of us and our work, nor do they interfere with the villages in our district." Where the Russian Orthodox were concerned, direct contact and subsequent conflict continued. As a consequence, the chasm widened. [18]

CONFRONTATION IN THE FIELD

In western Alaska, a profound difference existed between Orthodox and Moravian views concerning the conversion process. [19] From the beginning, the Moravians were more demanding than their predecessors in emphasizing personal belief and commitment over formal acceptance of the sacraments. In part, this was a matter of resources. The Russian Orthodox Church in western Alaska had never received support for more than a single priest to minister to the Yukon-Kuskokwim diocese since its establishment in 1838 by the Unalaska priest Gregory Golovin. With the removal of the Russian military and administrative apparatus accompanying the sale of Alaska in 1867, even this minimal support declined. Hieromonk Ilarion, the single fully ordained priest serving at Russian Mission, locked the church, removed the vestments, and returned voluntarily to Russia, leaving the spiritual maintenance of the mission in the hands of the Creole servitor Zakharii Bel'kov.

Three years after Ilarion's departure Bel'kov wrote to the Bishop of the Aleutians and Alaska that the churches in his district totally lacked means of support, as they received nothing from the Novo-Arkhangel'sk Consistory. In that letter he demanded return of the church utensils, which had been taken in 1868: "Our spiritual fathers have offended us, they have laid waste to our churches! We lament [our loss]." In this situation it is understandable that other Christian churches working in Alaska, including the Moravians, might assume that Orthodoxy in Alaska was dying, if not dead. The Orthodox priest Ioann Orlov at Kolmakovskiy Redoubt complained bitterly of this attitude in his annual report to the Bishop for 1900: "Last winter one [Catholic] Father let out during his preaching to a gathering that 'The Russian faith soon will be here no longer, the savages are no longer Russian but American and therefore the Americo-Roman faith should soon prevail here.' " [20]

In line with this opinion, the Moravians, upon their arrival in western Alaska, found an Orthodox Church almost devoid of external support. It existed through the commitment of a handful of Orthodox clergy. These men, although aspiring to accomplish a fuller conversion, were in practice preoccupied with the administration of the sacraments to a vast, far-flung constituency and did not have the resources to do more. It was not until 1901 that Father Orlov, at that time superior of the Orthodox Kuskokwim mission, could report the successful eradication of "polygamy, the matrimonial tie with close relatives, the harming of people [by sorcery], calling upon unclean spirits and belief in their power, dancing for the dead, etc."[21] Though he had always desired the elimination of such practices, none of these goals had been within his reach during the previous decade. Over the years he and his fellow priests had worked out a compromise with their Yup'ik and Athapascan parishioners: local practices not antithetical to Christianity were left intact, while men and women retained membership in the Orthodox communion. The importance that their theology gave to the ritual acts of baptism and communion made this a practical, if not ideal, solution.

Given the length of Orthodox occupancy, their arduous mission labors, and their sense of territory, the Russian Orthodox missionaries' consternation at the arrival of the Moravians can be imagined. In 1888, following his trip to Bethel, Bel'kov wrote the first of several anxious letters to the Alaska Consistory in which he announced that the "heretical Moravians" were trying to undermine Russian Orthodoxy, and to combat them he needed both travel funds and teachers. Though the Consistory denied the latter, they granted $150 (the amount requested) to support his itinerant efforts. No other provisions were made to combat the "alien preachers, whom it is necessary to follow every step of the way lest they play some sort of dirty tricks against Orthodoxy." The Orthodox were left with little more than their own convictions to support them.[22]

In the beginning, in confronting Orthodoxy the Kilbucks were to some extent confronting a native religion. At the time the Moravians arrived in 1885 the Orthodox clergy working out of Russian Mission were not full-blooded Russians, but Creoles raised in western Alaska and completely conversant in the native language. After the departure of Netsvetov (an Aleut trained by Veniaminov) in 1863, a true "Russian priest" would not serve the Kuskokwim until Father Iakov Korchinskii arrived in 1896. Not only was Orthodoxy largely administered by native-speaking Creoles, but the Yupiit identified the Orthodox priests to a limited but significant extent with the traditional Yup'ik religious leaders, the shamans. Father Iakov Korchinskii wrote that natives counted Hieromonk Ilarion, who had preached to the Yupiit from 1861 to 1868, among "those people who could damn, the shamans, and so is every Russian priest."[23]

Although never confusing the Orthodox priests with the shamans, the Kilbucks themselves complained of the former's tolerance for the latter. In his retrospective account of the missions entitled "The Hindrances," John wrote, "We openly attacked the shamans, and made a determined effort to discredit them before the people. Here is where we differed from the Greek church.—The priest did not approve of shamaning, but he was so weak on this point—that the people said that they could be good Greeks and still practice shamanism."[24]

While the Orthodox were placed within the Yup'ik scheme of things, initially the Moravians were negatively associated with white intruders. An excellent example of this is John's description of Bel'kov's dramatic association of the Moravians with the Americans, who, Bel'kov maintained, would soon come and steal Yup'ik women, take over the country, and turn it into a "Cossack" place. Edith continued in a similar vein, "They use the word 'white-man' to scare their children into obedience or silence as people in the states would say goblin or robbers. When the old priest wishes to intimidate the people he says 'scores of white men will come and take away the women' etc. The priest himself is a native."[25]

John reported another rumor, purportedly circulated by Bel'kov, which identified the Moravians with white soldiers and caused the Yupiit to shun them: "The opposition of the Greek Church, represented by a half breed Russian Priest [Bel'kov], living at the Russian Mission on the Yukon was felt at the very outset. As soon as this man heard of the advent of Protestant Missionaries—he circulated the report that we had come to make soldiers of the boys.—The native people lived in mortal terror of soldiers.—This report kept the people from sending their children to school.—The first scholars we got were orphans—for whom no one cared."[26]

The first direct encounter between the Orthodox and the Moravians over Kuskokwim parishioners took place in the winter of 1888, while John was away traveling to Nushagak. Bel'kov described his reception:

> We descended to the Kuskokwim River right where the missionary camp of the Moravian United Brethren is established; here I stopped at the Company house which is 3/4 mile removed from the mission. I stopped for two days to perform religious rites during which time I had the fortune twice to visit them at home, on the invitation of the wife of Mr. Kezbok [Kilbuck] who was not at home himself. . . . She received us kindly and already speaks the Kuskokwim language sufficiently.

Further along his pleasant remarks gave way to conflict:

> On my arrival here, where the mission of the Moravian United Brethren is, I found some Orthodox natives who had come for trade with the Company. They came to me without a summons and explained to me that allegedly these preachers of propaganda assembled them through fraud at their house, having read a little they gave them the Eucharist . . . and performed three marriages on the spot, about which they excused themselves to me in that they [the preachers] had convinced them [the natives] that their and our Orthodoxy is considered all one religion. "And later we learned from our own people that this is not correct and thus we violated the Word of God." After

which, leading their repentance for their mistake, I explained to them . . .
what their Eucharist means as opposed to our Eucharist. . . . No matter what
temptations he sees and hears, he should cast it all out of his head and remember only that he is a baptized Orthodox person.[27]

In her journal to her father, Edith described the encounter from her point
of view:

I thought they surely would leave our immediate neighborhood alone, at least.
But after they had received every kindness at our hands we were told that [the
Priest] had baptised numbers of our own people going so far as to do so with
one of our school boys from here. . . . Those that have been with us most,
and are of our little flock were also beguiled and now are on his church roll
as his members, as are all who are baptised and partake of the Lords supper
with him. He does no choosing. All who are taken by the ceremonies and
comply with these two things are his "faithful?" members and are saved.
What he has said I do not know. I hope he has not hurt us too much. We feel
sorely what he has done.[28]

Later, in a report to the Provincial Elders' Conference, John reiterated
the manner in which Bel'kov had "managed to frighten" the natives into
taking the sacraments at his hands, tried to dissuade parents from sending
their children to the mission school, and declared that the marriages the
Moravians performed were void. He concluded that the net effect of the
priest's visit was to increase, rather than decrease, Moravian veracity and
influence.[29]

John's account evokes the confusion that must have beset the Yupiit in the
face of two such different denominations, each convinced of its own legiti-
macy. For them, perhaps, there was originally no contradiction in acquiesc-
ing to both denominations. Etiquette supported at least an external show of
agreement and acceptance, whatever contradictory claims might result. The
missionaries made compliance with both denominations unacceptable, however, forcing the natives to choose between the two. Although the majority
of Kuskokwim Eskimos eventually converted to Moravianism, Orthodoxy
is still very much in evidence along the river.

This particular incident illustrates in microcosm the larger conflict between the Moravian and Orthodox views. On the one hand, John decried
what he felt to be the empty rituals of the Russian Orthodox, given without
sufficient instruction and unaccompanied by conversion to a Christian life.
Bel'kov, on the other hand, talked past the issue of formalism versus lived
faith and defended the Orthodox as the one true church, the only route to
salvation. Edith wrote:

[The priest] said that "John had no right to marry any of them. He was no
priest and they were no more married after he performed the ceremony than
before that." "If they listened to his teachings he would lead them to everlasting darkness and night." That "If they sent their children to our school our

teachings would do them more harm than good for they would be like something tangled in a big net." And compared *them* to a "dog turning again to
its vomit" if they had *anything* whatever to do with us.[30]

Edith did not exaggerate the extent to which the Orthodox perceived the
Moravians as a threat undercutting the sanctity of their sacraments. The
ecumenical character of Moravian preaching appeared to Bel'kov as a fraud
and an unscrupulous attempt to win converts. In this situation it is not hard
to imagine the consternation of the Yupiit caught between opposing camps.

Over the years the conflict continued between the Moravians and Orthodox. As the Kilbucks gained command of the native language and as the
Orthodox clergy became increasingly Caucasian or Russian, the conflict focused less and less on native–non-native differences and more on distinctions of ideology and practice. In 1895 Edith described the terms of the
dispute:

> More things . . . arose from the visits of . . . those that slandered us, those
> who say that we are blind leaders who will take others to destruction with us.
> Wolves hunting down the people, following them up and finally catching
> them in time to shove them down into the home of the devil. That we have
> no cross, and therefore no Christ, that instead of looking up to God when we
> pray, we bow down and look into hell, praying to the devil, that we pray after
> dark, therefore are of the darkness, and not of light or we would pray in the
> light. [This refers to evening chapel service as does also the following.] That
> we do not fear and stand in awe of God enough, but pray to him much too
> often, using his holy name—which is disrespectful and should not be done.[31]

Russian Orthodox service journals confirm that Orthodox criticism focused on the formal differences between the two denominations, particularly
those concerning the significance of the cross. Father Orlov wrote in 1895,
"Having gathered all those willing in the Kazhim, I engaged in sermons
with those who have fallen away and those who are vacillating from the
True faith about the Holy Cross and about honoring icons of the saints,
about the sign of the cross, all of which they do not honor in the presence
of the Moravian pastor."[32]

Just as the Orthodox were suspicious of Moravian disregard for what
they felt to be essential ritual acts, so the Kilbucks expressed equal dissatis-
faction with perceived Orthodox formalism. Edith wrote concerning their
chants, "I do not approve of our people learning them. There is too much
of Mary in them and of bowing and crossing." Edith also described John's
response:

> Since the Greek Catholics have been saying so much because we do not wor-
> ship the Cross as they do, John studied up the subject the past week and used
> that as a subject in the English and native sermon. It is impossible to tell you
> all that the Greeks say and do. They are worshipers of the cross rather than
> worshipers of Christ. In sickness a cross is dipped in water and the water

is given to the patient to drink. They wear them on the neck. The whole amounts to the same as the native superstitions. This John tried to explain and if ever he preached a powerful sermon in Eskimo he did it today.[33]

To help their native converts better understand the differences between the Moravian and Orthodox faiths, John also developed a sermon explaining the historical separation of the Greek and the Roman Catholic churches. For the Yup'ik people, however, the similarities between the Moravians and the Russian Orthodox were probably as impressive as the doctrinal differences that comprised a regular focus of missionary discourse during the 1890s. After all, both clergies performed marriages and baptisms, administered communion, sang songs, lit candles, and offered prayers to the one true God. Just as the Yupiit could not initially distinguish the newly arrived Moravians from traders and soldiers, in important respects all missionaries resembled each other.

The missionaries ultimately sought to reinforce the Yup'ik perception of them as sharing a common spiritual goal, and a shaky truce came to characterize internecine relations on the Kuskokwim. Interdenominational bickering still caused confusion amongst the Yupiit. Perhaps they wondered how the two bearers of light could so darkly condemn one another. As John headed upriver to Kolmakovskiy in 1892, his journal reports a tentative cease-fire between the Moravian and Orthodox camps: "The Russian Priest is either changing his tactics or else he is forced to recognize us. Instead of running us down he says it's alright for us to preach and that he is glad that we do preach God's word, *but*, he would like to hear me, *so that he could correct me, when I made a mistake.* On that last is contained his opinion of us. In other words, we mix the true and the false so well, that it would take him to correct it." John did not credit this to a true change of heart, but rather to the arrival of the Jesuits on the Kuskokwim: "I have an idea that his friendliness is brought about, because the Roman Catholics are going to establish on this river too, and the Russian Priest would rather make friends with us, in preference to standing between two fires."[34]

In 1896, Iakov Korchinskii described his professional relationship with John: "On first acquaintance, I tried to ascertain all the reasons which could serve toward misunderstanding between us. Mr. Kilbuck was very kind and agreed with the fact that it is better for each to shepherd his own church without meddling in the internal life of the church." Even during this amicable exchange, doctrinal differences intruded: "[Kilbuck] long insisted that people who are married should certainly adhere to the religion (in a mixed marriage) which the male partner alone professes; but I did not agree, and insisted that it be left to the people getting married themselves to unite in one religion. . . . All were on my side and the matter ended peacefully to our common satisfaction."[35]

Korchinskii concluded with a unique account of an attempt by the Orthodox and Moravians to explain themselves to each other. During a get-together in Bethel, Korchinskii described Orthodox doctrine to the Moravian missionaries, who "began to ask questions about the Russian church with great interest." Following this exchange, John invited Korchinskii to speak before the Moravian congregation, which he did:

> I began with a trope to the Birth of Christ and said that the Son of God had brought peace to the earth and after the Ascension of the Lord all Christians formed one church, as one body, but then the people began to heed their own reason more than Christ and divided; then I said that all should pray about that which the Orthodox Church prays: that the Lord help people again to join together in one true orthodox faith, in order with one mouth to sing, as did the angels in heaven when Jesus Christ was born: glory to God in the highest and on earth peace, goodwill toward men. My words made a good impression on the listeners. [36]

In the end, the Yupiit were confronted with a historically irreconcilable opposition: on the one hand were men who felt themselves to represent the true apostolic church and who were committed to forging an Orthodox unity out of the spiritual variety of humankind; on the other were the Moravian brethren, equally committed to creating Christian unity through the introduction of vital Godliness into existing denominational diversity. Korchinskii referred to this opposition in July 1897 when, on a boat trip, he tried to convince his oarsmen, who lived at the Moravian mission, that they should not believe "various teachers who allege that all faiths are the same." A year before he had grudgingly but accurately attributed Moravian ascendance to the combination of their material assets (including their school, hospital, and sawmill), the virtual absence of an active Orthodox defense, and last but not least, their ecumenical emphasis: "Many adhere to Moravian teaching only because of, on the one hand, material dependence and constant preaching in their language and the principal assurance of the Moravian missionaries that the faith is the same and the priests are the same (even the symbols of faith, song-singing, crosses, icons, and even the names remain unchanged)." [37]

Although the Orthodox continued to advocate one true faith, the Moravians persisted in their message that all faiths are one. Opposition frequently led to friction, but the possibility of a reconciliation was built into the terms of the conflict. This possible, although not always practicable, solution was realized in the idealized description of Brother Weber written by Korchinskii. According to Korchinskii, when Weber learned that Korchinskii taught people to stand firmly in Orthodoxy and not to exchange it for the "false Moravian fable," Weber told the surrounding natives, "Only God knows where the truth lies, perhaps [Korchinskii] speaks the truth." [38]

Although theological differences were significant, the degree to which each denomination expressed itself in practical terms was ultimately the determining factor in their success. The Orthodox journals for the last decade of the nineteenth century indicate that the Russian priests concentrated on explaining their doctrinal supremacy. The Kilbuck journals, on the other hand, emphasized "repeated attempts to teach them to live the new life and not only to believe it."[39] Where the Orthodox had laid the groundwork, the Kilbucks were able to advocate a new, active Christianity.

Although the Russian Orthodox tried to change the way of life of the people whose immortal souls they sought to win, their scant resources limited what they could accomplish. But material constraints did not prevent them from introducing literacy and an understanding of the rudiments of Christianity. Hymns had been translated, and the Moravians borrowed them for their own services.[40] John recognized the contribution Orthodoxy had made: "The people on the river from Bethel up to beyond Kolmakoffski have been nominal Christians for over twenty years, and . . . though they are almost entirely ignorant of the Gospel-story, they still have a good idea of it. This fact has loosened the bonds of superstition, even before our arrival."[41]

Standing on the shoulders of the Orthodox, the Moravians proceeded with a far-ranging program of cultural reformation. On their arrival they strongly objected to what they felt to be the Orthodox priests' empty formalism and lack of stress on practical religion. John wrote, "Those who had been baptized by the Greek Priest—were the same as the unbaptized—so far as their manner of living was concerned."[42] Critical to their approach was the belief that a change in the way people lived was essential to changing the way they thought. For example, to support their belief in the sanctity of the nuclear family, the Moravians built a sawmill to provide the lumber necessary for the construction of individual dwellings to replace the traditional multifamily sod structures. In contrast, the Orthodox were in practice unable to modify the Yup'ik way of living and focused primarily on drawing people into the sacramental life of the church.

The Moravians strove to accomplish conversion from within by thoroughly winning a handful of converts who in turn could spread the word among their own people. Moreover, they expected the Yupiit to take responsibility for their own reform. The Kilbucks did not see themselves as doing something for the people as much as inspiring the people to do something for themselves. Though admirable within a Christian schema, this activism was in painfully sharp contrast to the more culturally comprehensible conversion presented by Yup'ik-speaking Orthodox Creoles that had gone before. The resulting pressure brought to bear on the communities closest to Bethel must have been enormous. Wittingly or not, the Moravians violated a tolerance of many traditional Yup'ik practices that the Russian Orthodox had already enshrined.

CHAPTER 8

THE INSANITY EPIDEMIC AND THE "MARTYRDOM" OF BROTHER HOOKER

*When I tell you that I am recovering from a nervous shock that nearly pros-
trated me, you will doubtless wonder why, but if I can make you in a slight
measure to understand the burden of our hearts, you will not wonder much.
My hand still trembles and my heart beats wild, but I will try to go back to
last Saturday night and tell you all.*

—*Edith Kilbuck to her father, 1890*[1]

THE EXORCISM

During Easter week of 1890, tensions that had been building since the
Kilbucks' arrival resulted in a series of events vividly displaying the conflicts
associated with the conversion process along the Kuskokwim. The clash was
the most dramatic challenge to the rapid growth of the Kilbucks' power and
influence, both personal and professional, that they experienced during their
entire career. John described it as an open dispute between the Moravian
"New Way" on the one hand and the Orthodox and shamanic influences on
the other.[2] As such, it came to symbolize for him, as well as for Edith, the
perpetual battle of good over evil, a battle to which they had dedicated their
lives.

The Kilbucks wrote at least three full accounts of the incident.[3] Although
containing many of the same details, the effect of the repetition is to underscore not only the importance of the incident but also the symbolic value it
took on for the missionaries in years to come. In the Kilbucks' accounts the
Yupiit appear largely as pawns moved by the influence of false prophets.
Ironically, however, in their descriptions of this violent reaction by the
Yupiit to the Moravian intrusion, they leave us with a rare view of the depth
of feeling at work within the community during the last decade of the nineteenth century.

During the early months of 1890 their work appeared to be going well.
John was traveling in earnest, preaching in the nearby villages, and claim-
ing the fruits of the awakening he perceived among the people the previous
fall. The three native helpers who had been appointed the year before were

also hard at work, including Brother Hooker in nearby Kwethluk. Edith gave a telling description of Hooker's evangelism:

> His whole soul is *absorbed* in the one great work of *saving souls*. He came along home with John for he said his work was becoming too great for him. He needed more instructions. He felt his weakness so, because he wanted to do a thorough work among his own people. He wanted to talk on so many subjects concerning the spiritual welfare of his people. . . . O, Papa, I . . . wish you could see this man and hear him talk. . . . He talked to strangers, talked to crowds, talked to our boys and the men and women about us. Everybody heard him pleading and many gave close heed to his word.[4]

Partly due to Hooker's efforts, John was able to rebaptize a number of Orthodox in late February. Several young men from Kwethluk also visited the mission to tell the missionaries that "they as a whole village" were trying to be Christian: "They said that when Sunday came they would not work or travel, and that the women also observed the day, by not so much as sewing even one small skin. They said they were anxious to know and do what was right. I am so glad that they are free to talk of this new religion. Old and young, they talk it over between themselves and are constantly talking of it to us. As the one young man said, it made them glad."[5] Although the people of Kwethluk had always been the Moravians' most "ardent and attentive hearers," a new active inquiry and "speaking out" by both evangelized and evangelist had apparently gained sway.[6]

Most encouraging of all, the natives of Kwethluk broke new ground by being the first village along the Kuskokwim to abandon the midwinter celebration of the "Masquerade," designated in Yup'ik as Kelek or Itruka'ar. John noted in his annual report that the people of Kwethluk had burned their masks, forsaken every heathen rite, and "diligently inquired how to walk as the redeemed."[7] The masked dances performed as part of Kelek comprised an extremely complex ritual event and a critical part of the traditional ceremonial cycle. Briefly, Kelek involved the singing of songs of supplication (*agayuliluteng*) to the spirits of the fish and game, accompanied by the performance of masked dances under the direction of the shaman. The ritually powerful masks, created especially for the event, represented the yuas or "persons" of the game as well as the tuunraat or shamans' spirit helpers.[8]

John understood the importance of the shaman in the "Masquerade" as an intermediary between the human and spirit worlds. Shamans directed the construction of the masks to reveal the spirits as at once dangerous and helpful. Using masks in enactments of past spiritual encounters had the power to evoke the spirits' participation in the future. Thus, among other things, Kelek was an embodiment of the cyclical nature of Yup'ik cosmology, whereby the past might be reborn in the future through appropriate action in the present.[9]

Fig. 8.1. "Heathen Masks": Yup'ik ceremonial masks. (F. Drebert, Moravian Archives)

The Moravians failed to recognize the significance of Kelek or understand the necessity of its annual performance from the Yup'ik point of view. Instead, motivated by the "pagan implications" of its associated shamanic practices, the missionaries included participation in Kelek among their first proscriptions for converts. Needless to say, the Kilbucks were gratified when the residents of Kwethluk set Kelek aside.[10] In contrast, although the Russian Orthodox also disapproved of Kelek, the Kuskokwim natives were too far removed from Russian Mission for the Orthodox clergy to suppress its performance. Thus, the Kwethluk people had been able to profess acceptance of Russian Orthodoxy without giving up Kelek.[11]

Against the background of burgeoning interest and consequent high hopes of the missionaries in Bethel, the "shocking news" arrived on April 3 that Brother Hooker had gone "insane," was very talkative, and was sometimes violent. He was but one of a number of cases of what the Kilbucks labeled "temporary insanity" suffered that winter along the Kuskokwim.[12] Hooker's condition was preceded by the death of his only son at spring camp early in March as well as by a seizure of what John had labeled "vertigo" earlier in the year. However, his breakdown was completely unexpected, as he had just left Bethel two days before, on April 1, after spending close to a week there receiving instruction in his duties and responsibilities as a helper.[13] Doubtless, the physical and mental strain of the past months contributed to his deterioration. It is possible that Hooker recognized that the people of Kwethluk did not accept him as a new religious leader. Their reminder that he had transgressed the old way unforgiveably by acting as a helper to the missionaries was very likely the beginning of his guilt, fear, and final acceptance of their judgment.

When the message arrived that Brother Hooker was ill, John was upriver tending a woman who was likewise afflicted with insanity. Edith wrote of her anxiety while awaiting his return that evening. When John did return, he immediately began to prepare for the long day's journey to Kwethluk's spring camp in the foothills where Brother Hooker lay sick. He set off the next morning, leaving Edith, the two sisters, and Brother Weber to conduct the Easter week services without him.[14]

After writing to her father to describe her husband's hasty departure, Edith recorded nothing in her journal for ten days. When she wrote again, it was with both disappointment and grief. The mission party had anxiously awaited John's arrival home on the Saturday before Easter. When he finally came into view, he was running and appeared to be tired. More puzzling, he was accompanied by only one man and a small team, rather than the eleven dogs that had been sent down to fetch him from Bethel. After he arrived and came into the house, he sat for a long time and all he would say was that he was "so glad to be home!"[15] What had gone wrong?

After a full day on the trail, John had arrived at the Kwethluk camp at nine in the evening. He went immediately to the place where the sick man lay. Silence greeted him; Brother Hooker's relatives stood around like "so many statues." Edith recounted that no one spoke to John when he entered the place where Hooker rested until the younger brother of the "Mountain Boy" said a few words. But then all was quiet again. Odd enough under any circumstances, this stony greeting must have been all the more striking after the unusually loquacious response John had received from these same people on his visits during the previous months. Combined with the "vacant and frightened look that alternated itself on the sick man's face," the contrast between the past enthusiasm and the present cold reception went "through him like a knife." [16]

Shortly, John was left alone with the sick man, to whom he gave several morphine pills to help him sleep. John also slept until some time after midnight. Then Hooker's younger brother awoke him, hastened him outside, and told him that he must leave, by order of the "Mountain Boy." [17]

The Kilbucks knew the Mountain Boy. Up until that night he had been friendly to the mission. Edith first mentioned him in her journal on September 10, 1888, and commented that he "has always been a good friend to us, is industrious and intelligent." His Yup'ik name was Alamanak. Edith described him as Hooker's half-brother, who, together with Hooker, had held leadership of the Kwethluk people, "and what he said was law." [18] In the Kilbucks' opinion the Mountain Boy had slipped into the "temporary insanity" that they stated afflicted him during the crisis.

Ethnohistorian Wendell Oswalt contends that the Mountain Boy was a shaman. [19] The Kilbuck journals never say so directly, although they indicated that the people believed him to be "divinely inspired." It is possible that the Mountain Boy was considered to be a shaman or to wield shamanic power insofar as he was attempting to cure the insanity of his half-brother, a task that a shaman traditionally might have performed. Anthropologist Margaret Lantis states that for any strange behavior not explicable by normal experience, the shaman was called in to try to bring the individual back to normal. [20] Moreover, shamans were, by definition, persons who could organize and control their abnormal behavior, while someone who could not was deemed "crazy" or "insane." A shaman sometimes cured by consuming the contagion or by being consumed by it and then reborn. What appeared to the missionaries as "insanity" on the part of the Mountain Boy may have been part of this attempt to cure.

The Kilbucks wrote that the Mountain Boy ordered John to leave because he blamed John for his half-brother's illness. Although this order was delivered indirectly through an intermediary, the message was clear. John was even denied the opportunity to give medicine to the sick man: "All the medicine they wanted was for him to leave, leave in a hurry too." [21]

From the Yup'ik point of view, the Mountain Boy may have been following protocol in ordering John's banishment, thereby punishing or shaming John for his part in Hooker's illness as well as for the offense to the animal spirits his suppression of Kelek entailed. Traditionally, the Yup'ik Eskimos responded to aberrant or dangerous behavior through either flight from or banishment of the offender. Both were forms of abandonment, a severe punishment in any society but particularly harsh here. Whether or not John was cognizant of Yup'ik concepts of justice, his forced departure was probably banishment, as traditionally defined.

Not only was John's dismissal abrupt, but the terms were hard. He was to go at once, on foot, and must carry his grub box, valise, and medicine chest on his back, as no one would convey him. This he refused to do until a man visiting from downriver stepped in and said he would take John along with him.[22] Moreover, the Mountain Boy ordered that on his departure John cross the Kwethluk River, turn around three times, and then shake himself to drive off evil spirits. John considered this a "senseless performance" and refused to comply. He loaded his gear and left the village, walking slowly behind the sled. Edith later commented, "These people who always were so friendly and kind, how hard it must have been to hear all this, and be alone."[23]

Before John could leave, however, a ritual cleansing of the village took place whereby the Kwethluk people abandoned every material thing received from the mission:

> When the sleigh was loaded several persons came and put something in it. These things proved to be articles they had either bought or gotten from here. Some soap he found in with his bedding and a hood I had made as a Christmas present for a little girl, was stuck in his grub box. They disposed of everything that they had gotten from here. Even the smallest thing was thrown away. Needles, combs, etc. They took off shirts and pants and threw them away also because they came from here. We and all we had was bad.[24]

So John left the village. However, no more than a hundred yards down the trail, just as they reached open tundra, he and his companion were pursued. While his partner ran ahead, John turned around and faced his pursuers, who only stopped when they reached him. The whole village was following John, led by the Mountain Boy. At first they made no sound but upon approaching began to make strange cries. "The Mountain boy abused John, called him a 'Crow' that is a liar, said he was bad and that he belonged in the bad place, where they would now throw or put him. [Mountain Boy] called himself God, and crossed himself, where upon all the people bowed and crossed *themselves*. Much more was said, and they all sang some [Russian Orthodox] Easter pieces."[25]

This use of Russian Easter chants and the act of crossing themselves by the people, combined with the Mountain Boy's invocation of God, adds support to Edith's contention that the people believed the Mountain Boy to have been divinely inspired. Earlier in the same sequence of events, he invoked evil spirits and prescribed cleansing actions for both John and the villagers; these acts were rooted in the traditional Yup'ik view of the spiritual nature of the material world. The Mountain Boy's leadership style and the actions he prescribed thus drew elements from both traditional Yup'ik and Orthodox Christian ritual activity.

Even the disposal of goods on John's forced departure had roots in Yup'ik cosmology—the traditional Yup'ik requirement that the personal possessions of the deceased be abandoned to insure that the spirit of the dead would not return to haunt the living. The requirement that John cross the river and turn around three times (a significant Yup'ik ritual number) was probably related to Yup'ik beliefs concerning the means of spiritual exit from and entry into the human world. The ritual cleansing of the village of European-made goods was also a form of banishment. Traditionally, an offender might be sent out "into the wilderness" without the benefit of indigenous survival equipment as punishment for a serious transgression or infraction of the rules. In the same way, the people of Kwethluk sent John away from the community without sled or guide. Instead, he was laden with the products of Western manufacture, and these "dangerous goods" were banished as well.

The Mountain Boy was not alone in shaping the response of the people to the situation. Apparently, an old native woman described by Edith as a "fanatic Orthodox" also made use of the incident to turn the people against the Moravians.[26] She, in turn, may have taken her cue from the bitter complaints of the Orthodox priests, who deeply resented the Moravian intrusion, convinced as they were that the "Moravian heresy" endangered the hard-won salvation of their "baptized heathen." Orthodox priests had baptized many of the people of Kwethluk prior to the coming of the Moravians, and Father Bel'kov had visited them a number of times since then.[27] Thus, when some of the people turned toward Moravianism in the winter of 1890, the active fervor and constant verbal testimony of the newly enlightened ran up against bitter opposition, both from the actively Orthodox and the non-Christians. John was probably unconscious of the irony that, although he viewed himself as a bringer of light, in this case a community of believers essentially exorcised him from their midst through a creative mixture of both Orthodox Christian and traditional Yup'ik mechanisms of disposing of the proverbial powers of darkness.

THE DEATH OF BROTHER HOOKER

> *Eternity and time are joined in our Immanuel's name.*
> —*John Kilbuck, 1898*[28]

On the Saturday before Easter, John arrived home, too worn out to hold Easter sunrise service the next morning. A large crowd had gathered for services, and their anticipation and anxiety for his return were turned to anger by the incident he described. The missionaries were shaken, and Edith especially was distressed:

I was very weak and nervous from the strain on my mind. It seemed I could not get away from it. Every where I turned I heard some one talking about it. . . . Our minds too were weighed with the trouble at Quichtlamute, and we were anxious to hear from them, although what might be the news and how they would feel towards us, was a question that was always present with us. . . . This village in which we had placed our brightest hopes, was it all for naught? Were they all turned against us, and did they throw off the religion that but a short while back they had so warmly embraced? Would they make life bitter for us in the future by opposing us?[29]

On the same day that the mission received John and his astonishing news, events continued to unfold upriver. Brother Hooker recovered slightly after John's departure and was able to walk around the village as usual. The day before Easter, all the men in the village, including Hooker, took a sweat bath. Cleansed in this manner, the Mountain Boy announced that Brother Hooker was now prepared to leave them, that he was a saved man and would go to heaven: "With this they [the Mountain Boy and another Kwethluk man] led Bro. Hooker out, without any clothing and commanded the rest to follow. They went quite a distance from the village, when the two men ordered the people to stand still, and shut their eyes and bow their heads, while the three would go farther on. What happened my informer could not say, but suddenly there was a howl, a shriek, and when he opened his eyes, he saw Hooker surrounded by dogs, who were literally tearing him to pieces."[30]

Just as John was expelled through a combination of Orthodox and Yup'ik ritual exorcism, the events surrounding the death of Brother Hooker combined Christian and traditional Yup'ik ritual acts of purification in the people's effort to invoke all possible power. Within traditional Yup'ik ideology the sweat bath was believed to effect spiritual rejuvenation as well as physical purification, following which Hooker was "prepared to go to heaven." At the same time, as with John, the community sent Hooker into the wilderness because of the threat he posed.

As in John's expulsion, elements of Christian meaning were also at issue. Hooker died on the Saturday before Easter, April 5, 1890. Within Moravian theology this day is dedicated to the rest of Jesus in the grave. On the day before Easter the Moravians often celebrate a love feast as an appropriate transition from the thoughts of the passion of the Lord to the glory of his resurrection.[31] The early Easter service, celebrated on the following morning in their cemetery, God's Acre, has always comprised one of the most impressive Moravian ceremonies of the year and one of the first that was introduced to the new converts. For the four previous years Easter had been celebrated at Bethel, and natives had come from near and far to participate and look on. On this occasion the mood was one of spiritual renewal as the Moravians filed out from their township to their burying ground to give praise for Christ's resurrection and his message of everlasting life.

The Orthodox, likewise, stressed the crucial significance of the resurrection and considered Holy Saturday an important church holiday, celebrating Christ's conquering of hell prior to his resurrection. However, due to the fact that the Orthodox church followed the Julian, rather than the Gregorian calendar, the date on which this celebration occurred was a point of contention between the two churches. Although both denominations claimed Easter as a pivotal celebration, they did not agree on when it should occur, a fact that must have further confused the Yup'ik congregation. Although Easter Sunday fell on April 6, 1890, for the Moravians, the Russian Orthodox located it almost one month later, on May 1.

Hooker's death and the events surrounding it were therefore played out in the context of a highly charged and hotly contested Christian ritual celebration, centering on the fundamental belief in Christ's death and resurrection. In an important sense the events re-create these archetypal Christian events. Certainly, there is a structural similarity between the sequence of the Easter passion and celebration and the purification, betrayal, and death of Brother Hooker.

Traditional Yup'ik ideology possessed a complex and extremely articulate belief in an endless cycle of birth and rebirth, whereby no living thing ever finally passed away. Although the Yup'ik concept of spiritual rebirth is by no means isomorphic with the Christian view, it is in this concept that the two views of the world come closest. For the Christian, Christ died and was resurrected, and therefore, man has the possibility of rebirth and eternal life. For the Yup'ik people the life of the individual is the result of the proper life and death of the generations that came before of which the individual is but a temporary incarnation. The Protestant view emphasizes the individual relationship between the Savior and the saved, the one dying a mortal death to insure the spiritual rebirth and immortality of the other. The Yup'ik view emphasizes a cosmological cycle of birth and rebirth in which each person is but a small part by virtue of right thought and action. Although originating from different world views, the concept of spiritual rebirth after physical death emerged as common ground. It was on this common ground that Hooker's ritual slaying was accomplished.

The comparison between the death of Brother Hooker and the death of Christ goes beyond the formal similarity between the two events. They are also alike in that both were subject to conflicting interpretation by those directly involved. Christ was not exorcised by the Romans. He was viewed as a political prisoner and his death as an execution. Christian followers, however, saw his death as expiation—the sacrifice to God of God's own son as an offering for man's sins. The Kwethluk natives may have viewed Hooker's death as both an execution and expiation, using Yup'ik and Christian meanings as alternate explanations or guides from which they could select.

Critical to understanding the nexus between the death of Hooker and the Easter passion is the fact that this particular Easter was the first celebrated in the absence of the masked dances characteristic of Kelek and the shamanic vision quests sometimes associated with it. As noted, that very winter the people of Kwethluk had dispensed with the dances that for centuries they had considered the necessary prerequisites to successful harvests in the coming year.

An important feature of Kelek was the performance of agayuliluteng, or songs of supplication. The Yup'ik Eskimos believed that these songs had the power to actualize the events they depicted. Among some of the more fearsome and respected masks used during Kelek were those known as *tukarautet*. These masks made ominous noises when struck, and the people wearing the masks sometimes began to "act suddenly strange but would soon be all right."[32] Thus Kelek traditionally incorporated a small degree of prescribed or institutionalized temporary insanity. Also, in casting out shamanic activity during Kelek the people of Kwethluk mortally challenged shamanic authority in general, including the annual journeys made by the angalkut to the home of the fish and game for the purpose of requesting good treatment during the year to come. Often this spiritual journey was portrayed as the ritual dismemberment or bodily disappearance of the shaman, who then rearticulated himself and miraculously reappeared after visiting the spirits of the game.

The performance of Kelek embodied the fundamental belief that the enactment of power, through songs and masked dances, evoked real power. Directly tied to this was the belief that the future drew life from the past. In the winter of 1890, for the first time in their lives, the people of Kwethluk disdained the performance of Kelek and trusted instead in Christ's mercy for their future well-being. Unhappily, the result was a poor hunting season and an inexplicable outbreak of sickness and insanity among prominent members of their community. Something had gone terribly wrong.

In the face of these troubles the people of Kwethluk enacted a creative mixture of their past and present. Under the leadership of the Mountain Boy they celebrated Easter as if it were Kelek. Just as in Kelek they had acted out the prerequisite to the successful hunt in order to produce it, in the execution of Brother Hooker they literally acted out the passion and martyrdom of Christ so that their community could be purified and made whole again. In this dramatic event a Christian form had been enlivened with Yup'ik cosmological content. In the performance of Kelek and associated shamanic activity, the people had danced and the shaman had died so that the spirits would allow continued human life. The enactment of the shaman's death and rebirth created power to successfully attract fish and game during the coming year. Hooker's death was accomplished as part of a comparable attempt to influence the future. Not only was Hooker's death a figuration of

Christ's death, but through institutionalized insanity and prayers of supplication, it was an attempt to exorcise and empower an entire community. Together with John's expulsion, the death of Brother Hooker formed a ritual sequence (purification followed by supplication), an historical incidence of the mythical reality embodied in the traditional ceremonial cycle.[33]

Although the outbreak of so-called insanity that foregrounded these events may have arisen out of personal frustrations, the resulting acts had ceremonial qualities and were, in part, performances that required an audience and served a communication function. Far from the disassociation of meaning from action that the label "insane" implies, the sequence effected a transference of meaning from one mythical reality to the other. This was possible because both the death and resurrection of Christ in Christian cosmology, as well as the death and rebirth of the shaman in Yup'ik ideology, were events that involved individual action as well as collective representation. Both the celebration of Easter and the celebration of Kelek were events that were absolutely unique yet repeated every year.[34] Though embodiments of a cultural order, each was open to historical contingency and to the sense that living individuals would make of them. During the winter and spring of 1890 participants altered their meaning absolutely.

In the eyes of the missionaries the death of Brother Hooker was the murderous act of a madman; however, it dramatized a fatal cultural logic. It was primarily an attempt to purify a community plagued by insanity, the ultimate "illogic," in part brought on by the juxtaposition of irreconcilable differences between the Yup'ik and Christian views of the world. In addition to expelling alien influences the people of Kwethluk attempted to recreate them as their own.

The suggestion for the specific form employed was implicit in the Christian enshrinement of the Easter drama. Newly awakened to the truth that Christ had died for his sins, Brother Hooker had been "reborn" as a Moravian convert and was, by Christian logic, himself prepared to die. By the nineteenth-century Yup'ik view, rebirth was also of vital importance. But by Yup'ik logic, it must be preceded by right action in life. Because Hooker was a convert and an active evangelist the Yupiit may well have perceived his proselytizing as profoundly inappropriate and ultimately the cause of his own illness. His attempt to gain Christian salvation was jeopardizing his, and possibly the entire community's, life as traditionally defined. When the harvest proved poor after the postponement of Kelek, the community was seriously threatened. Hooker's death was in part a lawful execution prescribed as punishment for his part in offending the spirit world.

Moreover, his transgression was viewed as a sin as well as a crime (an offense against society) that would receive divine retribution.[35] The people of Kwethluk, as well as Hooker himself, may have interpreted his illness and his son's death as both proof of his transgression and an indication that the spirits had been offended. The community's response was not murder but abandonment, sending him out, defenseless, to die in whatever way would occur.

Christian ideology contended that for Brother Hooker to be truly saved, as he maintained he was, he must be purified and spiritually reborn. At the same time, by traditional Yup'ik ideology, for the community to be made whole, Hooker had to be expelled. The sweat bath prepared Hooker for his death. His clothing, the outward sign of his humanity, was not returned to him. Instead, the Mountain Boy and his followers led him out of the village, out of the human world. His own kin led the procession, reinforcing the interpretation of Hooker's death as execution. Had the act been performed by non-kin it would have required retribution and might have initiated a blood feud.

Hooker was probably not led forward primarily as punishment, but because he was a threat to others' survival. According to oral tradition, a lone, apparently defenseless person confronting the spirit-powers could survive and even conquer the dangers only with supernatural help. The person lacking and not deserving such protection and helpful action would die. This is reiterated in the oral tradition, in which guilt for offending the animals and anxiety for not following the rules is a central theme. That Hooker was literally torn to pieces also replicates both the ritual death of the shaman during Kelek as well as the manner of disposing of a person (animal or human) believed to be possessed. Only by cutting the body into pieces could its reanimation by the spirits be prevented.

Just before Hooker died, the Mountain Boy told the villagers to bow their heads, but even this was an ambiguous act. Was this, as the Moravians later assumed, in prayer? Or was it for the practical purpose of not letting them see? Or was it a ritual act in some way bound to the traditional Yup'ik belief in the opposition between powerful supernatural sight and restricted human vision? Whatever the significance of their withdrawal, the Mountain Boy led Brother Hooker forward and gave him over to his death a saved man. By the Christian view, Brother Hooker had attained life eternal in God's kingdom. For the Yup'ik residents of Kwethluk, the ritual exorcism of their community had been accomplished.

Grieved and shocked by the event, the missionaries nevertheless only half-consciously perceived the significance of the exorcism. They would, in retrospect, categorize the incident as an isolated tragedy resulting from weak men following a deranged leader. John likened it to the martyrdom of Stephen.[36] For him it was symbolic of spiritual progress gone awry, rather than a fatal attempt by one world to comprehend another on its own terms. John attributed the derangement to a direct physiological cause:

> I have come to the conclusion that this loss of reason is due to repressed cutaneous eruptions, as I notice that in the case of the "Mountain Boy," now that he is better, small pimply eruptions cover his body. Also in the case of a young man . . . we feared . . . was losing his reason, but a few doses of

homeopathic medicine relieved him considerably, and not long after, he also broke out with eruptions. During the winter cutaneous eruptions were the common and principal afflictions of the people.[37]

What the Kilbucks termed insanity became a recurring phenomenon, and they often remarked on it in their journals over the next four years. The helpers Lomuck and Kawagleg both temporarily succumbed, along with a number of other men and women associated with the mission. In the fall of 1890 Edith noted that insanity had struck the Yukon River as well, the victims including an Episcopal missionary, two white miners, and several natives.[38] In December 1892 John wrote to Edith concerning a strange sickness in the school: "Alice has been acting quite *looney* for several days, and now Oscar is beginning to act strangely this evening. I do hope, and I have prayed God, that there be no serious sickness in our midst like the Quiechlohxamute affair a few years ago."[39]

In January 1894 Edith noted a new "wave of insanity" in the school:

The boys jump on the stove, dance, whistle, sing and often cry. One of them threw down a lamp. They must be watched night and day for they are inclined to get out and wander away. I have them sleeping in my dining room at night. There is no place to put them and they need such close attention. One night when John was gone we had to shut the door and then unscrew and take off the knob to keep them in. Yesterday two more began to perform. It is not good to have them together. When one begins to hop and jump the others all follow suit. They think that is the proper thing to do.[40]

Finally, the following fall, she wrote her father concerning a native who was "out of his mind":

Sometimes he is afraid, at other times he cries, or laughs and sings. In all the varied forms of this disease it is connected with heart disease, or possibly produced by it. It is common to men and women, boys and girls. One of their remedies is to bleed the patient, which does at times seem to relieve them. Nearly all natives have suffered from it at some time in their lives, but it is not permanent, lasting from six weeks to two years. Others are then off and on all through their lives.[41]

Edith's description echoes John's attempt to give the insanity epidemic of 1890 a physiological explanation. However, descriptions of the features of the insane behavior and its causes have no clear common denominator that can tie them to any currently understood physiological or psychological condition.[42] It is probable that the Kilbucks used the label insanity as a blanket term for separate conditions. However, in the journals the numerous references to insanity occur almost exclusively between 1890 and 1894 during the period in which the conflict between the Moravian, Orthodox, and traditional Yup'ik views of the world was probably the most intense and, for the natives, the most confusing. During the years prior to 1890 Moravian effort had been aimed primarily at establishing a base at Bethel. After 1894 their ministry took on the character of an established work. In the years between, however, they preached in an environment of hostility and doubt.

Although the insanity epidemic of 1890 and the events stemming from it may have been rooted in a physiological problem, they probably took this particular form because of a more generalized ideological conflict and the associated stress. John understood this in part; he described the crisis in classical terms:

It may be mentioned that at the time of the Mountain Boy's spell of temporary insanity—there seemed to be a sort of an epidemic of this malady. . . . A possible explanation may be this:—That the crisis of the conflict between the Gospel and the powers of evil—proved too much for the minds of these simple minded Eskimos.—The strain was undoubtedly great—for the shamans were active—and so were the Greeks—and the missionaries.—The shamans stood up for Diana of the Ephesians—and the Greeks for the tradition of the fathers—and both combined against the New Way.[43]

Hooker's death subsequently figured as a turning point in a number of John's reconstructions of the history of the region, and he returned to it in several retrospective accounts. In each successive rendition the reasonableness (under the circumstances) of native "unreason" is made more apparent. The uniqueness of the Yup'ik reaction to the situation is lost in his eagerness to have the incident make sense in Western terms, and a mode of being in the world very different from our own is presented as a primitive manifestation of ourselves.[44]

The Orthodox priest Iakov Korchinskii's description of learning of the incident six years later suggests that the Kwethluk Eskimos also assigned great significance to the events of that Easter weekend. Korchinskii wrote that "Kilbuck tried in every way to convert people to his own faith, but none of them agreed except for the people he was feeding. They took his faith, the chief [Hooker] and his brother [the Mountain Boy], and they were the first to die. The chief's own dogs tore him up on the first day of Easter, and the brother went to Kilbuck [reference to the Mountain Boy's subsequent conversion]. Now nobody listens to Kilbuck."[45]

Phillip, an old native man from the Yukon area, gave Korchinskii this account in broken Russian. Phillip, in turn, had heard the event described by Kuskokwim Eskimos. His account testifies to the enduring significance of the event for at least certain members of the native community.

Incorporating the story into their oral tradition, Kuskokwim elders passed it the length and breadth of their delta world.[46] Almost one hundred years later, villagers could still remember hearing about the incident as children. Joshua Phillip, of Tuluksak, recalled conflicting interpretations of the epidemic of insanity:

At that time, especially at Kwethluk, people were possessed with insanity [usviite-: to be insane, crazy, foolish]. Some of the people were told by the

shamans that "It is because you are misled by your religion that you are
insane." But because he understood, he [Kilbuck] had answered, "When the
devil is going to come out of the people, it is in panic because he would no
longer have control over people, he goes insane with the evil spirit." He told
us to know that over at the Holy Land when Jesus did something there were
insane people then at that time. And Jesus had answered them at that time
that he had seen the devil cast down from heaven to hell.

It was like that when Kilbuck was working. Then the people were insane,
when a devil was no longer to rule the people. That is what happened to the
people. Because of that they almost killed him across there but he was
delivered.[47]

To missionaries and missionized alike, Hooker's death became history
because the incident was meaningful by virtue of some larger cultural reality. For the Kilbucks, Hooker's death took its place in history as a "martyrdom" in Christ's cause. The incident was a sad accident of fate, a case of
the inexplicable effects of an epidemic of insanity among people under
stress. For the missionaries, Hooker's death occurred outside of the bounds
of rational action. For the people of Kwethluk, the Mountain Boy's act
became meaningful as it took on positional value in a very different cultural
schema. Far from "insane action," the horrific act was the product of a fatal
clash of cultural logics and demonstrated an attempt to resolve an intolerable
conflict of meanings.

Few incidents in the Kilbucks' careers demonstrate so vividly the complex
process by which the Yup'ik people attempted to make sense of the Moravians' presence. Having been visited with disruptive behavior and a poor
harvest season, the people of Kwethluk mustered the ritual tools of an already Christianized tradition; they performed ritual acts (both Yup'ik and
Orthodox) intended to exorcise the bad influences (in this case personified
by John and Brother Hooker) and invocations intended to reestablish a lost
order. The sequence failed to protect them from the persistent and unsettling effects of change along the Kuskokwim, and they bitterly blamed the
Moravians.

AFTERMATH

> *Those who stubbornly cling to heathenism he [the Mountain Boy] compares
> to a stake frozen in the ground. "You can maul," he says, "and you can
> hammer, but not an inch deeper will you drive him. The stake will be com-
> pletely destroyed by the hammering and mauling, and so with some of the
> adherents of heathenism."*
>
> —*Missionaries' Report, 1891*[48]

Less than a week after Easter, a handful of men from Kwethluk came to the
mission, bringing with them the Mountain Boy as well as the story of
Hooker's death. While there, they demanded an indemnity from the mission for Hooker and engaged in threats and wild talk. Apparently, the

people of Kwethluk held the mission at least partly responsible for Hooker's demise, as the mission had originally inspired Hooker's mad acts, which in turn led to his death.

The missionaries ignored what they took to be an absurd demand on the part of the Kwethluk contingent.[49] According to Edith, the Mountain Boy wanted to be taken to the Orthodox priest on the Yukon so that the latter might help him out of his trouble. After a brief stay at Bethel, the natives continued down the river with the Mountain Boy, hoping that the change would do him good. No sooner had they left than the Mountain Boy changed his mind and returned to Bethel, where he remained in the care of the Moravian missionaries (primarily Edith) throughout the summer. Although the "veiled threats" of the people of Kwethluk were a source of worry for the missionaries, Edith predicted a happy resolution to their troubles:

> The poor people of that afflicted village, grief stricken, worn out and excited, followed their crazy leader until they were made to know that he could not be followed, in a most heart rending manner. . . . It was after their deed that the people lost faith in their leader and came to us to be friends again and to ask for advice and help. . . . We thank God that they were led to us again and we can now call them friends. The crazy man is the only one that is against us and he is not accountable for what he says.[50]

Ironically, and unfortunately for the mission, Edith's conclusion was premature. In the months that followed, the Mountain Boy continued to stay at the mission, where he became increasingly friendly; meanwhile, the relationship between the village of Kwethluk and the mission remained strained. Early in the summer his wife and child came down from Kwethluk to stay at the post: "The Mountain Boy and his family visited us too. How glad we are that so soon he will be friendly. He is pretty well and seems natural. He apologized for his ill treatment of John and was quite friendly all afternoon."[51]

References to a "reformed" Mountain Boy, however, alternate with continual mention of his relapses: "The 'Mountain Boy' has been crazy again and is tearing around and talking as unkindly as ever about us. . . . He himself and several others still retain the ugly feelings they had in the winter. . . . He has asked for medicine and now claims that John gave him something that made him worse. He charged me with the same thing a few days ago and he and one brother were quite wrathy for several days towards me."[52]

Later in the fall, the Mountain Boy, always prone to extremes, took a strong stand for Christ.

> Last Sunday after English preaching our "Mountain Boy" wished to say a few words, and he then told the houseful of natives and us all that he truly believed in Christ Jesus. He wanted all his brethren to understand that his

Fig. 8.2. Mountain Boy is designated by an X in this photograph of a marriage scene in 1902. The inscription in faded ink on the photograph states, "The Mountain Boy tried to kill Kilbuck and did kill his [the Mountain Boy's] brother." (J. H. Romig, Moravian Archives)

desire was to be *true Christian*. He confessed that his heart was full of bad, which was continually trying to get the upper hand of him. But he now gave it to God, and asked Him to put it far from him. He again asked John's forgiveness for the wrong he had done him this Spring. He said the people of his village had done very wrong to follow him, when he was crazy, and he often tells them so. It was very hard for him to speak. His face was sad and his voice trembled with embarrassment, but he would not stop before he had said that much. Another time he says he will "open his heart" more fully to the public. [53]

The Mountain Boy subsequently recovered his senses and became an ardent supporter of the mission. The Kilbucks repeatedly mention his progress, both spiritual and material, in their journals. The annual report of 1891 went so far as to declare that the winning of this one man for Christ, if that were the only fruit of their six years' stay, would be sufficient to encourage and strengthen their faith. However, various comments indicate that the Mountain Boy remained somewhat peculiar. Although the missionaries eventually accepted him as a true believer, they never gave him the same responsibility or friendship as other close mission associates such as Lomuck, Kawagleg, and Neck. [54]

Although the Kilbucks were encouraged to see the Mountain Boy giving testimony of his renewed loyalty and faith, they could not help perceiving the increasing distance between the people of Kwethluk and the mission: "Our people of Quichtlamute . . . blame our God for their siege of trouble this spring and say that is what comes of their believing in our God. They now have thrown him and us off and have a "God of their own." They come here and want favors but beyond that they are not friends to us. Many times they are forward and insulting." Equally bleak was Edith's observation in January 1891 that "the Greek Priest likely would stir up old troubles for he had talked a great deal to the Quichtlamut people about their last years trouble. He gave them all [baptismal] papers and blotted the names of Hooker and his boy from his book." [55]

The Kilbucks continued to receive mixed messages from the village for years to come. The annual report of 1893 firmly declared the worst: the villagers had "gone back, and there seems to be no way of awakening them once more." In 1894 John wrote that the Kwethluk people "have determined to come back to us for good this time." Yet a year later, the animosity recurred.

[At Kwethluk] the Greek Catholics are very unkind to our people. For which reason Brother Weber will build a chapel away from this village and at a better place, where our members are only too anxious to move and settle. We had a good service at the Kashima, and the Greeks came in and were very friendly to our faces, but they kept several little boys to guard us, who would watch very closely everything we said. But we were particularly on our guard, and said nothing that they could be offended at or make trouble of. [56]

In the end the community remained devoutly Christian—but predominately Orthodox.[57]

The repercussions of the incident at Kwethluk were prolonged and far reaching. Though a creative and dramatic response to the missionary presence, the events of the spring by no means marked the beginning of the end of Moravian influence on the Kuskokwim. On the contrary, they marked the point at which the initial ambiguity to the missionary presence was replaced by a clearer perception on the part of the Yupiit of what was at stake. More significant than either the violence associated with the Kwethluk incident or the active turn towards Orthodoxy, was the general consolidation of forces that resulted.

Edith and John both perceived the distance that increasingly separated the mission and the people.

> The work is not so encouraging as it had been. Since our trouble last Spring, there is a decided luke-warmness in the desire of the people, in general, to become Christians. Some are weak, and would like to follow our teachings, but are afraid to do so. The shamans scare them by holding up the calamities of those who did listen to us. Others are trying to serve both God and the devil; so our hearts are burdened with their many wanderings.
>
> We still hear many reproaches and must bear the overreaching and scheming of the hardened ones, for they crowd around us for the "loaves and fishes," instead of living water and heavenly bread.[58]

John observed the same division and battle lines clearly drawn: "The nominal Christian is also one of our worst banes, but we rejoice that the time is at hand when those who are not with us are becoming more openly against us; in other words, the people are showing their true colors."[59]

CHAPTER 9

AN ESTABLISHED WORK

The awakening of a year ago is by no means at an end; but instead of spreading, it is deepening, growing downward, into the very bottom of individual hearts.

—*John Kilbuck, June, 1891* [1]

PUTTING THE PEOPLE ON PAPER

As far as the Kilbucks were concerned, the years immediately following the incidents at Kwethluk were full of the gains and losses of an established work. They accepted the Easter events as a setback, although how profound they were not immediately aware, and continued to travel, teach, and talk as before. More than ever, they saw themselves engaged in a spiritual sorting process by which the weak and ignorant were separated from the actively hostile and given the encouragement they required.

After the events of the spring, John made his first major journey for an ostensibly temporal purpose: to gather information for the federal census of 1890. He had been employed as a special agent for the Census Bureau by the infamous Ivan Petroff, whom posterity remembers for his creative fusion of fact and fiction in the documentation of Alaska's history. [2] Unaware of his employer's idiosyncracies, John was one of a number of special agents employed to gather information in a specific area. He was glad for the opportunity to explore the upper Kuskokwim as well as to speak to the people along the way. He received funds enough to employ two men to accompany him to act as guides in the winter and paddle his boat in the summer. Traveling on and off from July 1890 through February 1891, the trio covered an estimated 1,000 miles by boat and 1,560 by dog team, traveling through the entire Kuskokwim drainage, as well as the coastal region from Cape Smith to Cape Newenham. [3]

John started his first trip in mid-July 1890, traveling upriver as far as Vinasale. [4] In his entry for July 27 he noted the natives' "superstitious fear that some evil would result from my travels among the people and 'putting them on paper.'"[5] This he ignored, attributing it to distrust related to the troubles at Kwethluk the previous spring.[6] As John continued to travel up-river, he recognized an abundant opportunity to speak the Gospel story and, parenthetically, the degree to which Orthodoxy had laid the foundation for his message: "The Kaltschanies [Upper Kuskokwim Athapascans] are particularly glad. . . . No priest or missionary has been amongst them for a long, long time, and yet they are living up to the few Gospel truths they have managed to pick up."[7]

The journal that he wrote for Edith during this trip includes a detailed description of Vinasale, as well as numerous references to the Athapascans of the upper Kuskokwim, whom he liked and compared favorably to the Kuskokwim Eskimos. At the journal's end he commented: "I try to give all honor and glory to Him. It is a great temptation to take the honor that these people willingly and heartily lavish on a benefactor."[8]

John finished his enumeration of the Upper Kuskokwim Athapascans on August 23 and arrived home on the twenty-seventh. Though the published census data that resulted from his efforts remain,[9] a fire in the Commerce Department Building in Washington, D.C., in January 1921 destroyed the actual population schedules and the detailed enumerations that they contained. This was a loss, as John's command of the Yup'ik language had allowed him to make fine distinctions within larger population groups which were dismissed in the published version of the report. All that remains is his travel journal and a summary of the health conditions of the Kuskokwim natives written into the Annual Report to the Provincial Elders' Conference: "The census shows that not less than 50 per cent of the people are afflicted with some chronic disease. The affection of the lungs takes up about one half of the 50 percent, followed by rheumatism, scrofula, and heart disease. From the data gathered, it shows that about two thirds of the children born do not live or rather do not outlive the parents." Later in the same report, John continued, "It is true that sometimes we happily succeed in relieving or even in curing. But it would be vain boasting to even hint at entire satisfaction with our present arrangements; hence we are desirous of putting the practice of medicine into intelligent and experienced hands."[10]

Healing remained an important mission concern, as did teaching. While John continued his census travels, the fall of 1890 found the missionaries, including the newly arrived Lydia Lebus, regarding the school as their main business at Bethel. Weber was in charge, and Sisters Lebus and Caroline Weber taught various subjects. When he was home, John also gave special religious instruction, as well as taking Weber's place to free him for periodic travel.

The management of the school, including the support services and temporary helpers it required, comprised Edith's chief work during these years. Her journals picture her capability in this department. At the same time John worked to communicate the spiritual goals of their mission, Edith's management of the "loaves and fishes" comprised an essential aspect of that work. She was both specific in her requests and profuse in her thanks for the boxes and barrels that the mission received to help the Yupiit help themselves. The last clause is important, as true to Moravian mission policy in general, she viewed her job as both more and less than charitable gifting:

> Words cannot express our gratitude for this great help in our work. . . . But it is not our idea to furnish clothing to the native people. Second-hand clothing is not suitable on account of the make, and then it is very unwise to give clothes away. It is apt to make them proud, or to create hard feelings. It is our idea to simply work amongst these people for the good of their souls, and we do not wish to create any jealousies amongst them, or to raise them out of the destined way of living, and then after a season see them discouraged when they must again come down to their old level.
>
> Be it far from us to attempt to change the costumes or customs of these people. We only try to Christianize them, and persuade them to live more cleanly and in accordance with the laws of health.[11]

At the same time this "civilizing" effort was Edith's chief work, it was also the context in which her personal life took on a new dimension: "This afternoon I cut out boots for John and Mr. Weber, and [Mary], Cassock, Martha and Nancy sewed them. We were talking and having such a good visit, that we each made a mistake in our work and had stitches to rip out and sew over. John said when he came into the house, he heard us talking and laughing, so he came up stairs to where we were and learned what was so amusing."[12] In years to come, during a period in which the closed society of the isolated mission began to take its toll, these relationships took on increasing importance. During these years Edith consistently found refuge in the relationships she established among the Yup'ik people. For the present, they formed one dimension of a rich and satisfying personal life.

Not only did Edith have the support of the native women, but her fellow sisters in the mission family comprised an essential part of her life, especially when John was away from home. This can be gauged indirectly from innumerable journal references to shared experiences and sisterly exchanges. Direct testimony is also contained in Edith's description to her father of her feelings for Sister Bachman after the latter returned from the field: "She was like a mother to me and I long to see her, and tell her my whole private heart, as I used to do when she was here."[13] Given the importance these relationships held for Edith, it is no wonder that the arrival of white sisters at the mission, as well as her growing ability to communicate with the native women with whom she worked, provided increasing personal support and allowed her to make substantial gains in her health.

With John traveling and Edith managing the work at home, 1890 drew to a close. Influenza ("la grippe") had caused many deaths in the fall. There was also a food shortage, as few fish had been taken during the summer. As a result, the school closed in February. Not only was there physical distress during the winter, but recurrent episodes of insanity continued to claim victims, both native and white, into the new year. Sickness notwithstanding, in letters to Sister Bachman, Edith described an exuberant Christmas celebration followed by a midwinter trip upriver with John: "The thought of *really* leaving the sights, sounds, responsibility and work of home for a few days so excited and overjoyed me that I could not sleep last night. . . . As we came rushing through the village, the natives came rushing out . . . some child was sent into all the houses with the news that *"He is here and his wife too."* [14]

Although this trip away from Bethel was a rare occasion for Edith, her journals are replete with references to John's comings and goings. Even when he remained physically in Bethel, he was still consumed by the work at hand.

> We have so much work to be done and John has most of it to do with his own hands. All last week he worked until nine and ten o'clock at night before he came in for the night, and then he was up early the next day. . . . He is trying to do all he can while he is at home. He may be gone this summer, and of course his great interest and thoughts will be with us and the needs and general progress of this place. I wish you could step in since our house cleaning is done. We are comfortably and neatly fixed for the Summer. The rooms are cozy and homelike. [15]

Here, in typically understated style, Edith's work of homemaking is inextricably bound to John's "larger work" of mission building. The two were played out separately, yet side by side.

VISIT OF BISHOP BACHMAN

By the summer of 1891 the Kilbucks' work along the Kuskokwim had gained both a momentum and style characteristically their own. As a paradigm of the virtues of Western industry and the sexual division of labor, they were superbly suited to the job they had set themselves. Not only were they able, but they were willing and apparently well satisfied with their lot.

It was, then, a minor triumph in their lives that at this point, rather than the traumatic year past or the trying year to come, that the home board sent Bishop Henry Bachman, president of the Society for Propagating the Gospel, to inspect the missions in Alaska. The purpose of his visit was to reestablish a direct tie between the mission builders and the mission fathers at home in Pennsylvania. Not since the spring of 1885 had the Kilbucks had direct contact with those men and women ultimately in charge of their work. John wrote to Reverend Schultz, the vice president of the Society for Propagating the Gospel, "The value of this visit is incalculable, both to us and to you. Now you will get a clear understanding just how this Mission stands, and its prospects. Although we have endeavored by writing to keep you well posted, still seeing with one's own eyes is much more satisfactory." [16]

From the time the bishop debarked from the native kayak in which he had come up the Kuskokwim, he was inundated with the accomplishments of the missionaries. Before him lay the mission buildings, spread out in a seemingly random arrangement. Native dwellings were interspersed with the half dozen frame and log structures that housed the school, the storerooms, and the living quarters of the missionaries. Seemingly grown straight out of the brown-green tundra, their stark quality was softened only by the cold frames and cabbage patches that attended them. Later in the summer the bishop would contrast this to the Carmel mission, where an iron fence tied together and enclosed the main buildings with the native dwellings on the opposite side.[17]

The mission's internal operations confirmed the relative informality and easy working relationship between the Yupiit and the missionaries that was apparent in Bethel's physical configuration. During the first church service he attended Bachman heard the native converts singing translated hymns. He also wrote a formal portrait of John preaching:

> The opening exercises were conducted in English by Brother Kilbuck, and it was pleasing to notice how well the boys and some older mission people joined in the responses and sang our hymns. Then Brother Kilbuck preached a sermon, with remarkable fluency, in the Eskimo language, and as he did so the deep significance of the work that is being done in this sorry little building forced itself upon my mind with overpowering effect.
>   . . . Brother Kilbuck spoke with ease, slowly and calmly, with no unnatural attempt at oratory. Of course, I could understand nothing of his sermon, excepting the name Jesus Christus, pronounced as in German. But his tone and manner were those of a teacher seeking earnestly to inspire and instruct his scholars, or of an honest witness striving to convince his hearers of the absolute truth of his testimony. His audience was very attentive too, and on some faces there were signs of sorrow and wonder and gladness, although the majority seemed to be merely debating the whole matter, message and messenger, in their own minds, as whites also do in noble temples of worship and under the ablest and most accomplished preachers.[18]

Not only did Bishop Bachman observe John at work; he also formally advanced John from the rank of deacon to that of presbyter. As a presbyter, John was able to administer all the sacraments of the Moravian Church. This was a great honor and a clear indication of the Church's regard for his part in the establishment of the Bethel mission. Just as John had been the first native American to be consecrated a deacon, his advancement to the rank of presbyter was also a landmark achievement. He had risen from the grass roots of the recently converted, which distinction served to enhance the esteem of the church for his accomplishments. Bishop Bachman described the service held in Bethel on July 5, 1891: "About ninety people attended the impressive service. After an intermission of fifteen minutes a service was held in the Native language, in which both Bro. Kilbuck and

Fig. 9.1. *Bethel Mission, 1896, showing the first house in the center, immediately behind the ship's mast, and the sawmill to the right. (J. H. Romig, Moravian Archives)*

the Native Helper, Lomuck, made addresses. It was a strange experience for me to listen to an address by a newly converted heathen, but Brother Lomuck's calm, thoughtful, and yet earnest delivery was deeply impressive." [19]

Bishop Bachman left Bethel the following week, traveling to Carmel to complete his inspection of the Alaska mission. He left with a strong sense of the accomplishments and the promise of the work at Bethel. The mission district he had visited was estimated to hold over a thousand Yup'ik Eskimos, scattered in scores of small camps and villages. Of these, fifty-three men and women were active church members. Two native helpers had been appointed, and Bachman himself had listened to one of them speak. The missionaries requested reinforcements to establish a mission station at Quinhagak to reach an additional 840 "heathen" who were too far downriver to be reached from Bethel, yet not close enough to Nushagak to be served out of Carmel. Although a huge variance remained in the spiritual condition of the converts, the missionaries were optimistic and morale was high.

IMPS LOOSE AT HOME

Following the Bachman visit, the missionaries experienced steady progress with no major victories or setbacks. John continued to travel, and both he and Edith continued to write. The texture of their journals is richer than ever. Small events take on mythic proportions in the hands of these two opinionated story-tellers. This was especially true where the management of mission goods and people was concerned.

On August 6 John left on his first trip of the summer to procure wood for the mission. This was less than three weeks after Edith gave birth to their fourth child, a daughter whom they called Ruth. While John was gone Edith tended the trading parties that came to the mission, cared for the children, and still found time to write small portraits of mission life. On the tenth she described a boatload of Nelson Islanders coming to the mission to trade. Shortly after their arrival, Edith caught one woman red-handed filching her new bolster cases and white cotton flannel. With righteous indignation, Edith reclaimed the stolen goods, amazed that the woman remained unabashed and "as brassy as ever." [20]

The next day, the traffic at the mission continued, and Edith again confronted the would-be traders: "Nepaskiogamut [Napaskiak] is about to have an Ekrushka with Nepachioshagamute [Napakiak] and the house has been full of tormenters all day. They would sell their all, for something to give. . . . I did not give them anything. It is not *for their* good to pander to their practices and wants and I *never* will do it. If they were in *need* of anything very badly I would be reasonable; but *no debt* and not even buy what they will need before the year is over." [21]

Here Edith gives us a cameo of the motivation and process of what in grander terms is referred to as cultural conversion. Striving as she was to replace the Yup'ik conception of social obligation with the Western concept tying need directly to individual biological survival, the impact of her management policy was both immediate and far reaching.

In both instances the Yupiit failed to involve Edith in social exchanges, which her Protestant individualism perceived as either senseless debt or brazen thievery. Moreover, she profoundly misunderstood the meaning and intention of these acts. It is likely that the Nelson Islander remained unabashed because she had not committed an offense by Yup'ik standards. Rather it was Edith who had acted badly in refusing the request of a stranger, guest, and elder. John's frustration with the constant raids made on the mission wood pile reflect the same conflict in notions of reciprocity and exchange. What the Kilbucks took to be stealing was a justified reaction on the part of the Yupiit to stingy missionaries and their antisocial propensity to hoard wood.

At the same time that the Kilbucks were critical of Yup'ik concepts of ownership, reciprocal exchanges characteristic of the Yup'ik ceremonial cycle also came under suspicion. Although the Kilbucks still viewed Petugtaq exchanges as legitimate recreation, they appraised the annual "Masquerade" (Kelek) and its associated distributions as the direct manifestation of man's naturally sinful state. John ended a powerful sermon to this effect: "Close with an exhortation to accept God's way of salvation. Also exhort all professors of the new faith to give up, *shamaning* and the *masquerade*." [22]

It is not surprising that the Kilbucks would distinguish between Petugtaq and Kelek exchanges, allowing the former while vehemently opposing the latter. Petugtaq was much more social in orientation than Kelek, which was blatant idolatry as far as the missionaries were concerned. Though Petugtaq was thought to be at worst bawdy, Kelek centered on the performance of masked dances to propitiate the spirits of the fish and game. This use of "graven images" inflamed the missionaries and inspired them to active intervention in the years to come. For the present, the war they waged was less systematic, if equally determined.

The immediate response on the part of the Yup'ik people was not to abandon their ceremonies but to take them underground. The past winter had witnessed new evasive tactics on the part of ambivalent Yupiit: "One sign of the weakening "shaman" in our own neighborhood, ie Mumtrekhlagamute [Mumtreglak] was the holding of the annual masquerade without masks. This was a compromise and was intended to catch, as it did, some of our members." [23] The missionaries disciplined the offenders by not allowing them to take communion during the Easter services.

While John was busy preaching the doctrine of natural sin abroad, Edith kept busy battling its recurrent manifestations on the home front:

> It seems as though I can hardly do any writing, even for you. Just as I thought, Mrs. Lind had a dance on Sunday evening where they also had their masque ball. She got nearly everybody to go, too. She first started the Ptochtuk [Petugtaq] game and after nearly every one was up to it she had the other

added on and by that means she got them to go. I only knew of it after *some* of our folks had already gone but Lydia [Sister Lebus] and I sat up until nearly midnight to entertain the rest and keep their minds off of the "fun" that was so close.[24]

The natives had reason to feel "held down," as Edith was relentless in forbidding participation in "their foolish, wicked games." Although her efforts did not always meet with success, still she saw her course as clear and unalterable. "The imps were loose at home," she wrote her husband, and would be made to know their error.[25]

SEPARATION

You are to the women what I am to the men.
                          —*John Kilbuck to Edith Kilbuck, 1822*[26]

After seven years of continuous service, the mission board granted John and Edith their first furlough in the spring of 1892. With the mission now established and the work at Ougavig and Quinhagak begun, the Kilbucks could finally be spared from their post: "Brother and Sister Kilbuck have fully earned a period of rest. Seven years of sub-arctic life, especially amid the peculiar trials which they have known, mean a strain on any constitution. Moreover their presence home will be of service to the cause. We are convinced that their story, as told by themselves will arouse enthusiasm and call forth new support."[27]

To keep the mission fully staffed during the Kilbucks' absence, the board appointed two replacements: Mary Mack, an experienced teacher, was sent to manage the Bethel school; a carpenter, Edward Helmich, was chosen to accompany her. Although both arrived in San Francisco in the spring of 1892, before they were able to set sail for Alaska, Brother Helmich contracted pneumonia and was unable to continue. As the board could not find a replacement on such short notice, they decided to transfer the Carmel missionary, Brother John Schoechert, to Bethel so that the Kilbucks might still take their furlough. However, the boat bearing Miss Mack sailed into the mouth of the Kuskokwim before the board's written instructions arrived. On meeting the vessel, John assessed the situation and made the decision to remain in Bethel alone, sending Edith and three of the children down without him.

John's decision to remain behind was a last-minute one. He and Edith had made elaborate plans for their year on leave, plans it must have been hard to let go. Although they had lived their daily lives increasingly apart ever since their arrival in Bethel, still they lived for the same purpose. Edith, perhaps more than John, lived for her partner, translating the wind into his need for a tent or eying wild rhubarb with his appetite for pie in mind. John, although always on the go, inevitably hurried his step on the home stretch, anticipating his wife's welcome. Though the work and the children might be seen to have impinged on their marriage, by their own admission their growing family added strength to it.

If John and Edith could have looked into the future, one wonders if they would have allowed their work to part them that day on board the *Dora*. In retrospect, it was an ill fate, or a mean accident, that sent them four thousand miles apart. Had not Helmich taken ill, John would have gone. Had the board's orders arrived in time, the family would have stayed together. Their marriage would never have been tested as it was in the aftermath of the year ahead. More important, only once again after their farewells on board the *Dora* would they and their children find themselves all together again. But this they could not know.

While still on board the steamer, John wrote to Brother Bachman concerning his decision to remain. He listed as a major factor the Webers' inability to carry on alone due to Sister Weber's ill health. John's own unwillingness to let the work he had managed so long go into other hands also may have played in his thinking. He wrote to the board, "After making the above decision there was a great weight rolled off my heart, and now I feel that I am standing on my feet on solid rock." [28]

While this published statement presented an optimistic view of the situation, John's first entry in his journal to Edith after her departure was uncharacteristically despondent. Likely he had no idea beforehand how such a separation, so different from anything preceding it, would actually feel: "Since I left you and the dear children there has been a strange tight feeling about my throat. . . . Many provoking things have happened but somehow even these have failed to rouse me up. I am as it were in a dream which will not be broken until you are once more at my side." Later he queried, "What will life be to me without you?" [29]

Not only did John's sudden decision produce surprising effects within himself, but it also received a quizzical response among the residents of Bethel. Although glad to have John return, they missed Edith. On his arrival in Bethel, in company with his young son Joe, who had also remained behind, and Miss Mack, he wrote, "Everyone was strangely moved. After the first excitement was over, one and all, but especially the women lamented because you were not here with me. The women feel that you are to them, what I am to the men." [30]

John's unexpected return to Bethel also had repercussions within the larger mission family. No sooner had he arrived than Brother Weber informed him that he and his wife desired to go to Ougavig, eighty-nine miles upriver from Bethel, and establish a mission station where originally only a chapel site had been intended. As the Webers' inability to manage without him had been a factor in John's decision to remain in Alaska, the turn of events was ironic. John confided to Edith that he was hurt by the move, as it intimated either that the Webers did not "fancy Miss Mack, or it is because he does not want to work with me any more." [31] Rather than a negative rejection, Weber may have been anxious to try his own wings in his own place, independent of John's dynamic, and probably overshadowing, presence.

Whatever the reasons, the Webers made the move, leaving John, Lydia Lebus, and Mary Mack alone to manage the Bethel mission. John described the latter to Edith:

> Miss Mack, has a good deal of go ahead about her, and with all she is not officious. I like her very much, and when you are with her awhile you will find her a good companion intellectually, as well as a great help in actual down right hard work. . . . She takes hold anywhere, washes, darns stockings, mends, scrubs, in fact pitches into any kind of house work. In all her ways she is methodical and expeditious. She is not trying to take it easy, by any means. . . . You will see from this that Joe and I will be well cared for, and if you are comfortably fixed, you must put all care away and enjoy yourself to the utmost and take a good rest.[32]

During the year, Miss Mack was in charge of the school, which she succeeded in holding open for the full two hundred days. On her return the next year, Edith would write that "the boys have learned more in this one year under her teaching than in any other three years since they came to school."[33] Sister Lebus, on the other hand, was put in charge of the housework, which she apparently managed with difficulty.

As the weeks passed, John's written style eased and became less constrained, regaining its old vitality and humor. For example, he gave a comfortably detailed description of his new bachelor apartment:

> My quarters are ready, paint and all. Last evening the sisters tried to steal a march on me, by fixing up my bedroom, without my knowledge. I, however happened in on them in the midst of their frolic. . . . Before Miss Mack got back, Lydie found me, and we had a good laugh. My bedroom is cosy and homelike. Over my bed on the west wall, hang, my class picture, Sam Smith and family, and the Norway scene. At the head are a few chromos, colored, a harvesting scene, and a young woman resting under a shade tree. On the other side, where the light from the window is good, hangs the photo of your beloved self. Lydie kindly gave me this, and I fully appreciate her tho'tfulness. The floor is covered with home made carpet, some of our own, and two pretty mats, sent by Bro. Eberman. The furniture consists, of a spring cot: the top quilt is a new one sent this year by Mrs. Stadiger of Bethlehem.[34]

Joe was also a comfort to his father during the year his mother was gone. While John was more fully occupied with mission work than ever before, Joe was cared for by his native "Anni" (from *aana* "mother"), Miss Mack, and a Yup'ik girl, Nancy. Sometimes it made John sad to see Joe playing alone, seeming "so much like a poor orphan." However, Joe, too, regained his ease, although he was still unusually clean and quiet, with the air of an only child. John wrote, "At home Joe is my comfort. He is getting so sweet, and is so cute. He says, he is Lydy's little man, Aunt Mamie's (Miss

Mack's) pet, Nancy's nuisance, papa's son and Mamma's big boy. He is learning to spell Dody the name Miss Mack generally calls him by." [35]

Though mission life continued as usual, and John's work with it, his journal for the year is like none other. Replete with references to her absence, he commented at one point that he feared she would get sick of hearing "just one thing." He pardoned himself, giving the irresistible excuse that whenever he sat down to write "everything else seems to away, and all I can think of is yourself." In the same vein, he wrote, "I wonder how close we do come together without seeing each other. How thick is the vail that separates our spirits. It can't be very thick I am sure. Sometimes I think we all but jostle each other." [36] And again: "How strange that I should be separated from you just at a time when we expected to have so much pleasure together. Sometimes my heart rebels and I begin to ask, why did I ever stay back, and then again I feel that being in duty's path it will yet be for some good." Finally, commenting on her work lecturing for the mission, he added, "I would be more worthy of you. I sometimes feel so small, and really of little worth, compared to what you are, or what I might be." [37]

For Edith, the year was a full one. After a brief visit in Carmel she and the three children arrived in San Francisco in August. She wrote stories of the children's wonder at the place. Having never been beyond the Kuskokwim and speaking little English, six-year-old Katie, five-year-old Harry, and Baby Ruth must have been impressed by what they saw and heard. Ruth learned to walk on the ship and later attacked the San Francisco sidewalks at an angle that made passersby wonder.

By October Edith had arrived in Bethlehem, where she met with the Home Board to report directly on the work in Alaska. She detailed the needs of the mission, requesting a wood boat with a sail (opposed to the steamboat then under consideration) as well as a sawmill. From there she went to Philadelphia and environs to lecture and raise money for the cause. In one instance, printed fifty-cent tickets announced a talk entitled "The Manner and Customs of the Eskimos of Northwestern Alaska." In November, after an engagement with two Christian endeavor societies, Edith described the content of her talks: "My talk was about learning the language, giving numerous specimens and then gave a detailed account of dog teaming and your trips, your reception in the village, your camping out in severe weather, eating frozen bread without even hot tea at times and your long trip of 73 days and hardships. Your hearty reception by all at home when you return." [38] Here, as elsewhere, her talk focused on John's dramatic exploits, rather than her own quieter accomplishments.

Finally, Edith was able to return to her father's home in Ottawa for a good visit and rest and then, in the spring, on to California and back home to Alaska. On her return voyage three new missionaries accompanied her: Brother and Sister Helmich, as well as Miss Philippine King, a trained nurse. The native boys, George and David, also traveled home after three years of school in Carlisle, Pennsylvania.

Before she left, however, Edith kissed her two oldest children good-bye, leaving Katie in Salem, North Carolina, with the Clewells, and Harry in nearby Clemens. The year before she came down, she had written to her father about the necessity of sending the children away from the mission: "The worst forms of sin and immorality are as open as daylight before them. . . . If I were to leave the work all to John and others, and do nothing but care for and amuse them, we might keep them longer, but now that I can talk and have influence over the Natives, I can not be spared by any means."[39]

However resigned Edith may have been to the necessity of the separation, it cost her a great deal: "The last parting with little Katie was not an easy one. . . . I controlled my feelings for the dear child's sake, as long as she was in sight, and then my worn and weary body gave way." Her parting with Harry, whom she bade farewell at the Kansas mission, was no easier: "Poor Father [Kilbuck]; for him it was *hard* to think John . . . would not come down this year. . . . How *proudly* he held in his arms my Harry, *his first grandson*, on whom the *honors* of the tribe rest: By right its future Chiefton. He, dear child, did not realize that 'mamma' was going far away, and for so long a time. He was anticipating a rabbit hunt with bow and arrow in company with Grandpa Kilbuck and asked me to tell his papa so. We then passed out of sight."[40]

Years later Edith maintained that these partings comprised the one real sacrifice their work demanded: "They who had been our joy and consolation, cheering our darkest days with their sweet sunny lives—must have the advantages of education which were denied them in the mission field, so in His dear name we gave them up, and turned to our work with hearts that, but for His sweet grace had well nigh broken."[41]

Although the leave-taking was hard and the return trip tedious, Edith described the high drama of the reunion. After the ship anchored, a storm came up, and it was four long days before John and Brother Weber were finally able to meet the ship. Edith wrote:

> The hours seemed a day long each one of them and thus we waited until the fourth day when in the distance a sail was seen to seaward, but headed for our ship. It was soon recognized as the Bethel Scow, and O, how we shuddered as we saw her blown by the wind, and mercilessly tossed by the angry waves. I knew that our dear ones were on board, and I could not bear to watch her coming in such a terrible storm, and yet I could not keep my eyes away. Two hours of this anxiety, and they came along side. I saw that John and Br. Weber were there, but as they had hard work to come close enough to catch a line and yet not run into the ship I stayed inside until all was over and everything made safe. It was pretty hard to do but I did it. As soon as they came on

board the Captain invited them to his room where we were all sitting. John had never heard that I had come and when he saw me he was almost too surprised and glad to speak.[42]

Writing again from on board the *Dora*, John formally thanked the brethren for her return: "I do not exaggerate, when I say that the tears often ran down my cheeks, while listening to Sister Kilbuck's account of her reception in every congregation she visited. An Indian does not weep often for pain or grief, but kindness will touch him in the quick." John closed his correspondence: "Thank God for the happy end of a long year of waiting, my wife and child are again with me, and now I begin to feel as though I were a whole man again."[43] Their separation was over, and their life together resumed.

BITTER TEARS

> *Every thing has changed so in the year I was away. I must often regret that I left what once was all I lived for. I have not turned against the work or the people; but everything looks so different now. I try and try. . . . but I have shed more bitter tears since my return, than in all the seven years I was here before.*
>
> —*Edith Kilbuck, 1893*[44]

Edith found a warm reception when she returned to Alaska after her year's furlough. As soon as she stepped ashore, she and John resumed their active partnership in the work of converting the Yupiit, and the official reports and letters written after her return reflect the extent to which their combined energies met with renewed success.

The gains experienced by the mission were not without their personal cost. The mission to which Edith returned was propelled by a very different dynamic than that which had characterized it in its infancy. During the first seven years no more than half a dozen missionaries had lived and worked together at Bethel at one time. No sooner had Edith left than the already depleted forces split. The Webers moved upriver to Ougavig, while John remained at Bethel with Sister Lydia Lebus and Miss Mary Mack. When Edith returned in the spring of 1893, Brother and Sister Helmich and Miss King accompanied her. With these new recruits, the mission force expanded to an unprecedented size and capability.

Although there is little question that this growth had a positive impact on the work of the mission in general, it also changed the character of that work. In the past the Kilbucks' whole energy had been focused on their relationship with their "people," supported almost exclusively by their relationship with one another. Now when she wrote to her father of "unlooked for tasks and trials" and "defeats and failures, without and within,"[45] more often than not she referred to strains generated by conflicts among the missionaries themselves.

That interpersonal conflicts existed among a group grown so large and of such varied background and experience is easy to understand. What is more remarkable is the degree to which the Kilbucks' correspondence refrained from directly expressing these strains. Typical of Edith's understated criticism is the following journal entry, in which her emphatic description of what she thought people should do probably reflected, at least in part, what she felt was lacking around her:

> People who for duty's sake simply put up with these heathen and in a martyr spirit live each day as a sacrifice—know nothing of the joy of cheerful service.
>   What one needs up here is to *forget your self* and honestly *give up everything*—to *delight* and *rejoice* in the *little* daily, hourly tasks and not be looking forward to some grand or heroic thing to do. Heroic deeds are few and far between—but [not] *humble, willing* service day by day.[46]

In the same journal she greeted her father, after almost a month's silence, with the following: "I can't say much about things that have happened. . . . You must read between the lines. They hold *far more* than the lines do no matter how often I write. . . . I would rather be silent than to have it seem that we clashed in any way. In speaking thus, I refer to the *whole* of our combined work."[47]

Edith's discretion reflects not only her own standards, but also stated mission policy. According to the official instructions for the Moravian missionaries in Alaska: "If anyone be overtaken in a fault, or be unjustly treated by his associates the matter must never be the subject of correspondence with friends in this country, as the circulation of such reports only does harm to the cause."[48] Harmony was the expressed ideal of mission life, and the missionaries both disdained and repressed evidence to the contrary.

Due to an internal sense of propriety reinforced by external regulation, the correspondence of John and Edith contains only fleeting reference to the troubles that burdened them during the years immediately following their reunion. Where their public voice fails to describe their trials, their private journals, especially those written to each other, functioned as a vent for growing frustration. Although not always naming the cause, the journals, especially Edith's, betray the blackening mood. In so doing they shed light on what, by the spring of 1894, was an increasingly tense situation. Miss King's sharp tongue was apparently a source of trouble.[49] In August Edith wrote that "feeling in our midst is not very good just now," as ill will had also developed between the Helmichs and the rest of the mission party.[50] As the work prospered and deepened, so did the strain.

THE MARRIAGE FALTERS

Although 1894 found the mission party experiencing internal conflicts far beyond anything that Bethel had known before, perhaps the most traumatic breach was in the Kilbucks' marriage. No doubt the separation had been a strain. However much John was accustomed to being away from home, his family, particularly Edith, functioned as an anchorage, firmly grounding his work along the Kuskokwim. Her departure left him adrift in ways that, for all his traveling, he had not experienced since his arrival in Alaska.

In retrospect, their marriage takes on a mythic quality, spanning as it did thirty-seven years in which they lived through and witnessed so much. Because of the central role their marriage played in both their lives, perhaps the most difficult period they endured were the years during and immediately following their enforced separation in 1892–1893. Although close scrutiny reveals them as fallible and human, their failings and the way they chose to deal with them underscore the strength of their marriage.

Though well matched in energy, John and Edith differed markedly in temperament. Edith was more highstrung. Her journals certainly, and her nervous complaints probably, served as outlets for a tremendous emotional reserve. She was largely successful in coping with the strains that accompanied her move to Bethel by both turning them into stories and journal entries as well as by medicalizing them to an overwhelming degree. In so doing she effectively came to terms with John's interminable absences and coped with a life in which she sometimes felt the noise and disorder would kill her.[51] At the same time her repeated illnesses, culminating in her need for a year's furlough, ultimately placed a physical constraint upon her married life.

Early in her writings Edith revealed herself as both active and outspoken, a woman of high standards which she imposed on herself as well as others. A spiritually ambitious woman, she aspired to be an exemplary wife and mother. At the same time that her demands on herself were great, her needs were also tremendous. In a moving and intimate passage written for John, she expressed her desire for a more intensely spiritual relationship:

> Oh, how I have longed for you to feel as I do about some things. It would do me so much good, if every day you are at home, and every time you saw me tired and worn, you could say some little word of exhortation, if you could clasp my hand with a grip that told of the love of Christ in your heart burning toward me, and say,—say anything, Say "*cheer up, look up, God will help you*" or say "be faithful, be patient, the reward is great." And oh, if *often*, you would kneel beside me and *pray,—pray for our own selves, pray for faith; pray for zeal* and pray for strength in the spirit of God to do our work. It seems to me, if this we did often, and felt at home in doing so, we would then truly be one more so than ever. To live, *more* in the spirit would make living in the flesh more blissful.
>
>   You are doing *grand* work for the Master. You have your time well filled. You have numerous duties and responsibilities at home and abroad, *but I believe you could help me to save my own soul by doing this*, some times I feel so loaded with sin and neglected duties that I despair of reaching the longed for goal. Moreover I feel that I could be a better half to you, a better worker for

the Lord and a better example to these people around us. I know you love me
and for that loves sake, a love that is *so dear* to me would you help me this
much.[52]

Though rarely so intense, the journals Edith wrote to John during their first
years of marriage are replete with references to her need for his support.
These alternate with descriptions of fretful children and infinite small tasks,
all accomplished to sustain him.

While Edith's life revolved around her husband, John's life centered on
his work. The work filled his days, and as much as Brother Helmich's
pneumonia, was directly responsible for their year's separation: "I can never
get over it that Bro. Kilbuck was not along. He is so deep in the work."[53]
Finally, his work came to life in what he wrote. Unlike Edith, John rarely
used the written word to unburden himself in a spontaneous manner.
Rather, his entries present a picture already thought through and delivered
to some timeless audience. One imagines that this was also true of his oratory, said to have been eloquent.

Although John's expository style was characteristically less spontaneous
and introspective than that of his wife, it was hardly less affectionate. This
was especially true of journal entries written during their year of separation,
when this remarkably private public figure freely and repeatedly expressed
profound emotion. After Edith's return, John's journal entries continued to
evoke a romantic vision of their marriage: "You will always be the only
woman that shall find a place in my innermost being. You know I often said
before and now say again consciously that should the Lord take you home
before me, I will never put another woman in your place."[54] At the same
time, he decried their having to be so much apart, calling it "hard."

More troublesome were John's increasing expressions of self-doubt and
unworthiness, feelings never apparent before. In December 1893, several
months after Edith's return, he wrote to her from Akiachak, where he was
helping with the Christmas celebration: "Surely the Lord is gracious, to
bless such work as mine, yet after all it is not what *I* have done, for I feel
too too sinful. I feel, that I come far short of what I should do and what I
should be." Five days later, a solitary entry occurs describing an indiscre-
tion that would change John's life: "Dearest Wife, I have tried to be faithful
in tho't, word and act, and this is my constant petition to Him, who hears
and answers prayer. Last year, after you left me, for months I hardly smiled
because I felt as one bereaved by death. This did not go away. As some men
take to drink to drown the one thing that weighs upon them I erred."[55]

This stark reference to error is the only mention in the journals of an
event that was to have serious repercussions for John's career and personal
life. We know from later entries in the formal minutes of the mission board
that adultery was supposed to have taken place during Edith's absence with
Miss Mack and several native women. Under what circumstances we are

never told, nor was Edith, at least in the beginning. Rather, the period between the close of 1893 and the fall of 1897 is characterized by a gradual and painful revelation by John of the extent of his fall.

The circumstances of John's adultery remain obscure. He may have been engaging in the common but discreetly unstated double standard character-istic of late nineteenth-century sexual mores[56] and the tautological distinc-tion between procreation and recreation that it harbored. His "fall" may also be attributed to a too-zealous conversion to Yup'ik sexual standards, as he perceived them. Certainly, his Yup'ik parishioners would have sympa-thized with his celibate condition and may have provided him opportunities difficult to resist.

Whatever the context of his infidelity, at first John deeply regretted it. His confession ultimately seemed necessary for his own peace of mind. He believed that the Christian in him had been conquered because his work as a missionary had taken second place to fleshly desires. Although Edith was a responsive woman, her lingering illness before she left and then her long absence probably proved too much for John's more demonstrative affection.

When Edith returned in 1893, she was at first ignorant of anything amiss and threw herself back into her work, happy to be home again. She found Miss Mack a dear and good companion. During the first year after her return she made no mention of trouble between her and her husband. Rather, her distress focused on the general ill will beginning to build within the mission as a whole.

In retrospect, one telling entry occurred in the spring of 1894, when Edith wrote to her father, "*Actually*, even John got the '*blues*.' I have had them some time already. He *never* gives way—but last week he was worried almost sick. He said several times that he was worn out and homesick—and I never before in my life heard *him* say a *word* about being homesick."[57]

Edith was a straightforward person. That she made no direct reference to John's infidelity during the first year after her return is fair evidence that she had no knowledge any such thing had occurred. By the fall of 1894, however, more appeared to be going wrong in Bethel than minor tiffs and spats within the mission party. By the new year she perceived trouble, al-though its cause remained shrouded. She began to speak of herself as "sigh-ing" and the Webers as "wondering." She wrote, "To live thus always in a cloud of mystery and grief, is no less than slow dying of another kind."[58] The summer found John sick in body and soul and Edith confused and distressed.

Edith kept her private journal for the year 1895–1896 in a tiny diary in an equally tiny hand. Entries were short and sparsely drawn. Not until September did she write, "John is much better. We have hard feelings but do not say anything." The next day she added, "John and I talk of our troubles and plan to do differently in the future. I am so sensitive that I often take too much to heart what to him seems as nothing."[59]

By November, the weather outside had turned cold, and Edith's entries betray hard times within. Following his confession to Edith, John faced his peers: "John opens his whole heart to Brother Helmich. . . . Stephen arrives and John tells him about our trouble. . . . John writes to Brother Weber relieving his mind of its heavy weight, by telling them everything. At night I myself write to them."[60]

The last stage in John's confession was a letter written to the Provincial Elders' Conference in which he admitted his transgression. Upon its arrival in Bethlehem, his case was brought before the mission board: "Brother Kilbuck informs us that in the year of 1893 he was guilty of immorality, which he has confessed to his fellow missionaries and the native helpers, who pardoned his offence, as he has also sought and received pardon from the Lord himself who has graciously owned and blessed his work since that time." Because of the confidence John retained among his fellow missionaries, he requested that the church retain him as a lay helper. The conference, however, declined immediate action, preferring to wait until they knew "if it was an overt act or a continued evil practice."[61]

In August the conference received letters from both Edith and John expressing their thanks for the consideration shown them thus far. John acknowledged that his sin was more than an overt act; it was a succession of acts, but he believed his repentence had restored him to God's favor. As a result of this confession, the conference voted to relieve him of the superintendency of the Bethel mission, while allowing him to continue to serve until a successor had been appointed and the transfer of authority completed. Subsequently, the board received more petitions attesting to the unshaken faith of John's fellow missionaries and asking for his continuance as a missionary. The board finally resolved to allow John to continue to serve in the position of assistant superintendent, while calling for Miss Mack's "early retirement" from mission service.[62]

Although the aftermath of his confession could not have been easy for either John or Edith, it became a shared burden once confessed. Edith spoke of it alternately as "our trouble" or "our sorrow," and only rarely as John's personal "fall." After his confession Edith stood firmly on the side of her husband and testified to the undiminished strength of her affection. Hard feelings gave way to sympathy: "How I pity him, for he has lived a worthy life, save this fall, and now all his faithful work seems to be covered by one sin."[63] Some years later, on the anniversary of their engagement, Edith would recall "eleven years of happy marriage."

CHAPTER 10

BARRIERS CONTINUE TO WEAKEN

There is a wonderful movement in quite a number of villages; Not only one or two persons, but the majority are coming out boldly on the side of Christ. From Bethel to Ougavig not one village will hold their "masque ball" this year.

—Edith Kilbuck, 1894[1]

STEADY PROGRESS

In spite of personal strains between the missionaries in general, and John and Edith in particular, the years immediately following Edith's return were characterized by substantial progress by the Kuskokwim mission. With Edith's return and the arrival of reinforcements, the prospects for the coming year looked good. It was soon decided that Brother and Sister Weber would return to Ougavig, accompanied by Sister King as a companion for Sister Weber. Brother and Sister Helmich would be stationed in Bethel, along with John and Edith and Miss Mack. Though no specific recommendation had been received from the church board, John felt that, given the strength of the Bethel mission, the Schoecherts should return to Carmel, and he wrote accordingly to the board.

The arrival of the sawmill was as significant as the arrival of human reinforcements. Pleased as they were, the missionaries were thrown into temporary consternation when they found that this miracle worker had been shipped without a belt. Under Brother Helmich's direction, however, the missionaries sewed seal skin to the proper dimensions and cut more than 2,500 board feet of lumber that fall. Edith wrote, "On August 8, we sawed our first logs, and John's eyes almost filled with tears, as he stood off and watched the boards drop off every two minutes, and then looked at the old frame where he and Harvey ground out with hard labor the few we have had heretofore."[2]

On her return to Bethel, Edith reasserted her willingness to live with the people and teach through example: "John and I would be willing to give up

184

every comfort and live *with* the people, if more might be reached by doing so. . . . I am sure to begin as they begin, and by example teach them industry, economy and thrift, would be wiser a hundred fold than to simply tell them how to do it." [3]

Edith's actions lent support to her vision, as can be seen in her description of overseeing the women gathered together to sew the school children's fur clothing: "The work, to be sure, demands my attention, but there is a grander work at such times, a greater opportunity to influence these women for good than is afforded in all the year besides. They come to visit as well as work. It is the only time in the year when so many of them can come, and now, especially since my return do they wish to talk with me." When the sewing was done and the women prepared to depart, Edith made it clear that, although trying, the presence of her native visitors was of personal as well as practical support: "I have enjoyed their visit. I would not miss it for anything, and it will seem lonely when they are all gone." [4]

At the same time that Edith affirmed conversion through lived faith and immersion on the part of the missionary in the world of the native, John voiced a pragmatic view of the implications of immersion of the native in the white man's world. Commenting on the two native boys who had recently returned, he wrote, "I see now that they were too young when sent down, and they have returned too soon. . . . I think that with proper management and training, we will have in them lay helpers in the spiritual work that will be valuable. My idea is to put them in such a position, or rather to help them to a position, where they can be recognized as members of the mission party. . . . I am going to try to keep them away from their people, so that their ideas and character may grow under our influence." [5]

Later that fall Edith painted a comical picture of John's continuing efforts to reform the character of the school boys. While Miss Mack worked to teach them English and Sister Helmich to keep their clothes starched and ironed, John undertook to teach them to step and march.

> I was over the first evening to watch how they took to it. . . . It was worth no small sum. I never tried as hard to keep a straight face as I did that night. . . . Several of the larger boys almost fell over when they tried to turn; Others hopped around. It is simply impossible to describe the ridiculous positions they would take; all the while thinking they were doing well. It was *certainly* the funniest performance I ever witnessed, but they *did* get some idea of what was wanted before the hour was over and now they march quite nicely. They go to their meals in regular order, two and two. [6]

The missionaries were successful in their effort to transform the outward behavior of their pupils. Two months later Edith commented on the native audience's response to the annual Christmas performance: "The school performed their part well—to the surprise and pride of all. Everyone exclaimed, 'They are *just* like white people.'" [7]

Fig. 10.1. Rolling building logs down the Bethel beach, 1894. The trading post can be seen in the distance. (John Kilbuck, Moravian Archives)

While the school experienced steady progress in the cultural conversion of their charges, the work at the mission enjoyed equal success. At the same time the children's growth was measured in their ability to speak English and "walk" in *kass'aq* ways, the mission's progress was directly linked to the missionaries' hard-won proficiency in the Yup'ik language: "Now that preaching, singing and praying can be done in their own language, they take more pains to be present each time. I often wonder how we held our first audiences. Our speech was so imperfect and we were so unacquainted with their ways of thinking and talking."[8]

Although the future gave hope for steady progress, nature chose to complicate the missionaries' comprehensive plan of cultural conversion. The summer was wet, and the catch of fish was impossible to dry. The winter was long and hard, and breakup was late the following spring. Consequently, John began travels in earnest over the tundra to buy what fish he could and during the winter of 1893–1894 made a total of nine trips. In most cases a native helper accompanied him to aid in acquiring souls as well as fish. They were rewarded on both counts.

As usual, John kept a detailed travel journal for his wife. One of the incidents that he described was a funeral he witnessed in the village of Kikichtagmiut. There mourners laid out the corpse with due decorum, lit the lamps, and gathered around the body for prayer and song. John pronounced the benediction: "What a contrast to eight years ago, when I was almost distracted by the lamentations of the bereaved at Napaskiagamute [Napaskiak]. This time there was nothing of the kind, and I also believe that the words spoken were comforting." Three years later, Edith made a similar observation: "I did not see one tear shed. We have told these people not to mourn for their lost ones, for they were not lost but gone before. Like children they obey, while in their heathen state they would howl more like dogs than human beings."[9]

Given the noisy reception of the spirits of the dead in traditional Yup'ik cosmology, the change the Kilbucks observed marked no small victory. To this day the Yup'ik cultural ideal is to greet death stoically, without noise. This attitude coincides with both traditional and contemporary attitudes toward pain, which is to be met resolutely, without emotion. Later Edith remarked how she could not forbear so at the death of a loved one. Here she indicated that the Yup'ik people did more than adopt a Christian attitude toward death. Perhaps as they altered their view of death they came to treat it differently, yet still according to traditional standards, as pain to be met quietly, rather than the presence of spirits to be greeted with a clamor. They had come to accept the Christian point of view; however, the noise-lessness that the Kilbucks took as the demonstration of a remarkable stoicism may have had its base in yet another domain of the traditional Yup'ik schema.

As remarkable as the reformation John witnessed in funerary practices was his successful confiscation of traditional ritual paraphernalia the following day at Ougavig. There Brother Weber had discovered the existence of "idol worship" the preceding winter.

> They have quite a number of false faces hung upon a tree in the timber, to these masks there is attached a roll of birchwood, and in the rolls there is a wooden doll; toward spring they take these things into the kashima and open them and they say they find all kinds of things in the rolls. If there is a deer hair in it there will be many deer, if there is fishskin in, there will be an abundance of fish and if human hair, many deaths of persons and so on: in fact they look to see what there is going to be during the year. They also bring presents to their pieces of wood while they are in the kashima, but I suppose these they afterward take and deal out amongst themselves. The people say that if anyone handles these objects that the one that touches them will die; they say some men once burnt some of these masks and that these men all soon died. I want to burn them if I can get the consent of the people for I think it is a sin for Christians to have anything to do with them. So far even those that profess to be Christians still fear them and I think they still have faith in them. If we did not live so near the village, I don't think we would be able to see into all such customs as we do now. Heretofore we did not know that they had idols and as that idol worship takes place only once a year one is not so apt to find out.[10]

During John's visit the following winter, the men presented him with a small bundle of fur clothes that they maintained was the "last of the idols, these being their garments."[11] John's description of the encounter eloquently testifies to his ethnocentric estimation of the worth and value of the natives' point of view:

> After [the service] a lot of people remained and Bro. W.— said they wanted to talk, so we sat down. After a few desultory remarks, one of the men bro't a little bundle of fur garments, and handed them to me with the remark that this was the last of the idols, these being their garments. Then a protest was made at the way in which the images were taken from here, and that without money, or being paid for, we had sent them to the states, where they were of great value. The people tho't we ought to pay them well for these images because nothing in the states, however small, was ever taken without first being paid for. We asked them how they knew that these images were sent to the states. They said the boys that Bro. Weber left with his raft last Spring opened the box containing the images and saw them. We then condemned such a practice as that of opening boxes and meddling with other peoples' property. This cooled their ardor a bit, and then I explained to them that the images were at Bethel, and had not been sent down. So far as pay was concerned, as they profess to give up their heathen practice, I did not see how I could pay them; and another thing, those images will never be sent anywhere with the idea of making money by them. If they were still heathen and be-

lieved in these things, and I wanted those images, then I would be willing to pay for them, but under the circumstances I could not and I would not. Some approved of this decision, and others were not satisfied. It leaked out that every village from Quixoluck [Kwigogluk] to Ekaluxtahlugamute [probably above Napaimute] had similar images, but these of Ougavig were the oldest. The bundle handed to me consisted of a little drum, parkas and caps, belonging to the images, and the people said that was all they had that belonged to the idols, and in giving them up, they let go for good this superstition of theirs.[12]

While the missionaries continued to suppress "idolatry," as embodied in the midwinter doll ceremony, they increased the purview of Christian replacements. The Christmas celebration for 1893 expanded in significance. The missionaries set the precedent for such an expansion and transference of meaning by taking Christmas gifts to the outlying villages. Whereas in years past they had given cakes, candies, and small presents to the people gathered around them in Bethel, that year John and his helpers took the cakes and picture cards abroad.

Not only did the missionaries give to their converts, the helpers expanded the event into something resembling a traditional feast or *kalukaq*. Describing the Christmas celebration at Kikichtagmiut, John wrote, "After the Christmas service Brother Lomuck and two others made a play [distribution]. They gave out oil, frozen black fish, ice-cream [akutaq], fish skin boots, parka belts, pieces of calico for handkerchiefs, and small kantucks [singular, *qantaq*: wooden dish]. The dealing out took up most of the night. I was not in the Kashima, still I got food for my dogs and a pair of fishskin boots."[13] Three days later, after a comparable celebration at Akiak, the father of a baby girl whom John had just baptized received John's permission to present boiled rabbit legs to all the village children.[14] The other parents followed suit and the next day feasted the children on ice cream and fresh boiled fish. While the celebration of the doll festival began to decline, the significance of Christmas was on the increase.

At the same time the missionaries strongly opposed specific events in the traditional Yup'ik annual ceremonial cycle, they allowed other activities to flourish. Not only did they permit "social" feasting, but they left both the Bladder Festival and Petugtaq intact. Although Edith would proudly declare the following February that not one "masque ball" (Kelek) had occurred from Ougavig to Bethel, the Bladder Festival still flourished, accompanied by acts of ritual purification and spiritual hosting which, had the missionaries been fully aware of them, would have drawn their disapproval.[15] Their ignorance ultimately worked to their advantage, as it allowed them to focus their negative attacks on one "heathen rite" at a time.

Along with their selective attacks on the traditional ceremonial cycle,

190

John and Edith, as well as their missionary cohorts, were bent on the transformation of traditional Yup'ik sexual mores. Their targets included the
easy attitudes of the Yupiit toward premarital and extramarital sex, as well
as the regular occurrence of both successive and simultaneous sexual part-
nerships, including cases of divorce and polygamy. Edith described the effort this required:

> Then comes a man and says he has left his wife. He tells me why, and
> repeats all the little and big grievances from away back: Then they come
> together and I talk to both. I dare not stop to eat or rest; but while I am at it
> and they together are willing to listen I keep on. . . . I talk, persuade and
> pray until at last they decide to live together again. Then they say "People
> will make fun of us for parting and then making up so soon. They will say
> we are like children and there couldn't have been much wrong or we would
> not make up at once. We don't know how to begin. We feel so ashamed."
> Then I take them over with me and let them drink tea together before other
> natives, while I sit and talk with them all. Since then they have been quite
> happy together. We try to help them to do what is right. They however are
> not the only couple that need constant encouragement and help to keep the
> home together. [16]

Behind their efforts lay the Kilbucks' firm belief in the value of the home.
Edith wrote, "More than this, one of our dearest families has been having
trouble which threatened to break up the home. . . . If there is anything I
grieve over; it is to see a husband slight or neglect his wife, or to see a wife
treat her husband with less deference and love than when she first knew and
took pride in him." She concluded, "If one only has the *home* pure and filled
with love and tenderness, they can bear *anything* that comes from outside." [17]
What the Moravians deemed hasty marriages and divorce cases proved one
of the most troublesome and persistent barriers to the full conversion they
sought to accomplish, causing more converts to stumble and fall than any
other single "sin."

Though John and Edith had much to be pleased with as 1893 came to a
close, they also experienced substantial setbacks as their efforts in the villages surrounding the missions became more intense. Upon visiting the
tundra village of Peingagamut in February, John found that the people had
"fallen back" and had held the annual masquerade: "They said that their
neighbors made so much fun of them, and not wishing to be the laughing-
stock of the tundra, they decided to hold, as it were, a farewell dance. . . .
It was a sore blow." [18]

Any setback must have seemed particularly hard, as gains had been made
at such a cost. Edith painted a striking picture of the pace of their life
during this productive but intense period:

> *Just before* the service another call came for John. The old Shamman so
> recently converted was nearing his end and wanted the *"priest"* there at the

last. . . . John staid until the celebration service was over. Then the people hitched up his dog team, and in the dark, in a driving snow storm he started for the village. . . . but John was about an hour too late. He did what he could to comfort the people then started home arriving in the rain and wet through and through.

After changing his clothes and drinking a cup of hot coffee, the bell was rung and he held the main service of the day all of which was in the native language.

He then lay down and I gave dinner to near two hundred people. Another service was held at 6: P.M. after which he talked with the helpers and a few of our leading men. We fairly *dropped* into our beds that night. We were so, so tired.

The following morning he ran hither and thither, giving out medicine and getting the folks started for home.

I made ready his clothes and provision box for another long trip.[19]

Edith was also stretched to the limit: "Since he is gone I find that all I can do is to look after the house work and in a manner hold the lines of the whole place. I would often gladly put my tired head on some one else's shoulder and take a good cry, but instead of that I must hold others up and cheer and comfort *them*."[20]

In January the general food shortage, combined with an outbreak of insanity among the school boys, forced the mission school to close. John, usually so resilient, began to show the strain. In February, Edith wrote:

His face is very sore yet where it was frozen. He suffers great pain and I have not seen him so hollow cheeked and thin since I knew him.

He has traveled so steadily this winter that he like his poor team of dogs is completely worn out. . . . It *is* discouraging sometimes, but he tries to bear it and not murmur. It is not *all* bodily pain that hollows his cheeks and sprinkles his head with gray hairs.[21]

In late March, John stopped traveling because the frostbite on his face stubbornly refused to heal. Food was short, and people gathered around the mission for support. John spent his time hunting while the women set snares for ptarmigan, simultaneously providing themselves with a much-needed change and fresh air. Edith wrote, "In all thirty persons look to us now, to keep them alive until the river opens and fish come. I don't know how we have fed them this long, but with each day something comes, and no one is starving. . . . Strange to say, the very day the ptarmigans left, the geese came."[22]

While the winter had been arduous, the mission emerged stronger than ever. Following Edith's return, John recommended his circling out from the mission. Edith took great pride in his energetic itinerant ministry: "His description . . . was intensely interesting. I long to be with him in these experiences. I want to travel with him constantly as soon as I can. I love this work and all the people and nothing will bring me more joy than to share in *his* work, not only the job, but the hardship and discouragements as well." [23]

By the spring of 1894 John and Edith had been working for almost nine years in what had come to comprise the Bethel district. Their larger congregation, including members from Akiak, Kikichtagmiut, Kwethluk, Napaskiak, Peingagamut, and Kolmakovskiy, boasted 102 members with an additional 35 from Ougavig and its surrounds. Bethel also had a small school, where up to 30 students worked their lessons in English. At a tremendous personal cost, more often than not left unstated, their work was bearing fruit.

THE SHAMANS' POWER

As the mission's power in general, and John's power in particular, increased along the Kuskokwim, the power and prestige of the shamans fell proportionately. When John had first attempted to preach in the men's house, the shamans had ignored him and with their followers silently vacated the building, leaving John with only his voice to keep him company. On John's annual visit to Peingagamut in the fall of 1890, the people abandoned the men's house as he began to preach. John attributed the lapse to an unusual dearth of fish, which the Yupiit blamed on the use of iron axes to chop ice on the river. Owing to this rudeness, the fish had refused to swim upstream, and the people went hungry.

Allowing for occasional setbacks, by 1891 the tables were turning, and a native helper reported that the shamans and their followers were the ones left alone when he called the people to his home for services. By the winter of 1894 John had essentially taken their place. Now it was the shamans who were forced to retreat, leaving their followers to witness John's traveling pictures and translated stories depicting Christ's birth and rebirth: "When it was time to call the meeting, one of the men took a maul and thumped the Kashima floor with it, and in a few minutes the women and children began to come in. . . . I spoke first—taking note of the fact that the people of this village were at last coming out of darkness into the light." [24]

Shamans, or angalkut, played an important part in nineteenth-century community life, functioning as intermediaries between the human and spirit worlds. During ceremonies and dramatic trances they communicated with the spirits of the game through drumming and chanting. During cataleptic trances they were believed to die and subsequently be reborn, or they might be killed and come back to life. While dead they traveled to the all-important spirit world. These experiences marked them as men apart, and shamans were the only men who lived permanently in the houses of their wives. In times of food shortage they acted as food locators and foretold the future through the exercise of their clairvoyant powers. In case of bad weather they might be asked to divine its cause. In addition to their role as seers, they also acted as healers in cases of unusual or prolonged illness. They were both necessary to and feared by the community they served, as they had the power to affect both its physical and spiritual well-being.

The missionaries constituted a direct challenge to the power of the shamans. Their way had been paved and continued to be softened by the social and ideological disruption attending the epidemic diseases that ravaged the Yup'ik people during the nineteenth century. The death toll resulting from the smallpox epidemic of 1838–1839 alone may have run as high as sixty percent of the Bristol Bay and Kuskokwim population. Although the more isolated coastal and tundra groups were left more or less intact, social disruption and reorganization accompanied the numerous deaths.

Introduced diseases continued to plague the Kuskokwim Eskimos into the late nineteenth century and produced a situation in some respects ripe for the changes the Moravians advocated. The young scholars that the Moravians obtained from the outlying villages were frequently orphans, the social artifacts of this situation. Elderly individuals without community support, attracted to Bethel for its "loaves and fishes," were a product of the social stress produced by the high mortality. The mission also attracted men and women whom debilitating diseases had left crippled and incapacitated. As the Yup'ik people traditionally placed great emphasis on physical well-being as essential to becoming a whole person and a productive member of society, the new diseases wrought social as well as physical outcasts. Had disease not paved the way, the Kilbucks' message would probably have taken much longer to find fertile ground.

Though the traditional shaman's role had been inextricably bound with healing, epidemic disasters alone would not necessarily have undone their claims to power. On the contrary, increased disease might have produced a comparable increase in people's reliance on their traditional healers. What the shamans' claims could not withstand was the combined impact of death without precedent and the arrival of men and women who carried both the hope of physical cure as well as an ideologically comprehensible explanation. Conversely, John and Edith rightly feared the association of the arrival of disease with the arrival of the missionaries: "We have heard of many sick and 22 deaths in our own vicinity. . . . We hope and pray this may not get into the school for we might not be able to bring every one through and the Shamans are anxious to get hold of some excuse to run us done. They and the Greek Priests try hard to spoil our plans."[25] The epidemics that followed the arrival of the missionaries put a hard edge on the natives' suspicions. Missionary power was ambiguous at best, as it could both help and harm. The attention the Kilbucks focused on the sick and dying reinforced these fears. Where their medicines worked a cure, however, the effect was profound.

The power of the *kass'am inrua*, or white man's pill, was eloquently attested by one "Bad Heart" whose "name should be Light Heart now":

> He gave the solution to the problem, why we had such a hold on the people, and why they so rapidly gave way to the Word of Light. He said: "When these missionaries first came, they did not command our attention by what they preached. But when they gave us medicine, and said this and that disease and ailment would be cured, we looked on to see if what they said was true. And in the end because their medicines proved to be just as they recommended them, we learned to believe that what they preached was equally true. We learn now, that the Saviour Jesus, when on earth, not only preached, but He also healed. So I would recommend, that whenever missionaries set out to work among heathen, that they take the Word of God in one hand, and medicine in the other."[26]

Although disease provided a sober backdrop to the arrival of the Moravians, the missionaries' imperviousness to shamanic ritual action was also an effective tool in their behalf. In "The Hindrances" John noted that the shamans cut pieces from the missionaries' clothing and used them to make "bad medicine" with which to spoil the mission's power. To the extent the missionaries ignored these threats and demonstrated their impotence, the efficacy of these shamanic acts of power was inverted and turned against the shamans themselves.

Finally, in the several instances where a shaman was converted, both John and Edith testified to the extraordinary impact this event had on their membership. One of the first and most widely remarked shamanic conversions occurred in the winter of 1894, when the recalcitrant shaman known as "little Whetstone" died "repenting his sins." Ironically, sickness had played a part in softening the man: "His stubbornness is melted away, and now he is an infant. The long sickness has been a blessing to him, and will be a blessing for his fellow villagers. If his change of mind becomes a fact . . . we will have a help stronger and more powerful than Brother Lomuck."[27] Singlehandedly, this Kikichtagmiut elder had worked long and hard against the missionaries and their converts, including his own son. His change of heart represented a tremendous victory. Edith wrote:

> The New Year for us has had a glorious beginning. There has been *steady* awakening amongst our people. The conversion of the wicked old shaman who died a happy and peaceful death, has done more to strengthen the faith of the undecided and wavering ones, than many a sermon could have done. The people *wonder* for they say "he was an old man, set in his ways, and in our eyes immovable." Nearly the whole of his village have since come forward and professed a sincere desire to be such as he was at his death.[28]

After the shaman's death, the missionaries appointed his son assistant helper in the village; this act had full community support. This one conversion, with its transference of power between the generations, might be taken as exemplary of the death and replacement of shamanic power in general.

Another important victory occurred during the winter of 1895, when a young shaman from Napaskiak publicly "gave up his black art." Edith wrote:

> He tells the people that he has been a Shamman and their tricks are all lies deceiving people and stealing their goods without doing them any good. His fellow Shammans are displeased with him. They say, if he wishes to give up well and good but that he ought not to spoil their means of support. They will thus have to earn the bread they eat and their clothes they wear. He says he does not know how to teach the people about God and Salvation, but he *can* and *will* tear down their faith in the Shammans. He sat for nearly one whole day explaining the tricks which to the people seemed more than wonderful. Not a soul stirred even to eat until he was through. The whole village is so disturbed over this that they do not know what to believe. We have not discouraged his talks, for they are worth more than a sermon. To tear down their old superstitions and beliefs prepares them to accept the Gospel. How widely different the people are to what they were. The older men are none the less bitter, although they are quiet, yet they do not chop wood and make noises to hinder others from listening.[29]

Although shamans initially put up stiff resistance, on conversion they became some of the most zealous proselytizers.

THE HELPERS' CURE

> *Some of our own . . . have not only given themselves to Christ, but also given themselves to his service.*
>
> —*Edith Kilbuck, 1890*[30]

> *When I work among those who have already been won by the Word, I am under a strain for they are often like deer corraled, but ever looking for an exit.*
>
> —*Helper Neck, 1921*[31]

Though John and Edith and their fellow missionaries worked hard to demolish the shamans' power, they could never have accomplished so much so rapidly without the disruptive effects of epidemic disease and the Orthodox conversion experience that had preceded them. Both of these situations undercut the power and efficacy of their adversaries within the traditional schema. Perhaps more important in the conversion process than this negative denial of what had gone before was the creation of an alternate focus for power within native society itself. This alternative took the form of the native clergy.

The Alaska mission early recognized the valuable role native brethren could play in the conversion of their fellows. Official mission policy actively

Fig. 10.2. "Raw Eskimo Helper: Kawagleg Speaking." Kawagleg was one of the first three Yup'ik Eskimos recruited as Moravian helpers. (Moravian Archives)

sought such helpers along the Kuskokwim: "The true conversion of individuals within easy reach of the established stations should be considered the first object to be gained rather than the securing of a large number of adherents merely, and the extending of operations over a large territory . . . thereby gaining efficient helpers who may then carry the gospel to more distant points, inaccessible to the missionary himself, for want of time, strength, or means."[32] The missionaries were few in number and the territory demanding their attention of tremendous scope and size. Their ability to "gain efficient helpers" was essential for success.

The appointment of three native brethren as Moravian helpers in 1889 was the first formal step in the creation of a native clergy. Their labors were a key element in John's strategy for effective cultural conversion. The early helpers were the eyes and ears of the missionaries, acting in their place between their visits. The helpers led the regular prayer meetings and organized the local celebration of religious holidays. Helpers dispensed the medicine the missionaries provided. When the missionaries visited, they looked to the helpers to tell them who needed special help or reprobation. Although John no longer required their assistance in understanding his Yup'ik parishioners, he still relied on the helpers as translators in a larger sense.

During the years immediately following their appointment the helpers worked primarily in their home villages, although they also occasionally accompanied both John and Brother Weber in their work abroad. However, as John especially became more pressed by the demands of the growing mission field, the helpers were commissioned to pick up the slack. In fact the helpers were largely responsible for missionization on the lower Kuskokwim. During a trip to the coast John noted one case where the people specifically asked for a helper instead of a white missionary, as they said it would take the latter too long to learn to speak.[33]

By the fall of 1894, mission resources were stretched as far as they could go in ministering to the huge field that comprised the Bethel district. Yet the missionaries were reluctant to postpone the establishment of a station at Quinhagak, at the mouth of the Kuskokwim, and so decided to send out their first native missionary. As a result Brother Kawagleg, who over the years would become one of the Kilbucks' closest Yup'ik friends, left his home village of Akiak and moved with his wife and children to serve at Quinhagak. Although traveling less than one hundred miles downriver, he would be living among virtual strangers. In his farewell address in Bethel he said, "As every soul is precious, I can not refuse to go. We who have light ought not to deny the light to those in darkness."[34]

Following Kawagleg's departure John increased his efforts to train the native brethren left serving in the Bethel district, including previously appointed helpers as well as several older school boys.[35] Although he began

Fig. 10.3. Helper Kawagleg and his wife, 1915. (F. Drebert, Moravian Archives)

formal instruction in October, the onset of what was diagnosed as pleurisy thwarted his efforts. He was up and about in a few days and was strong enough to attend the Thanksgiving services, where in gratitude for his recovery he rededicated himself to service along the Kuskokwim, not for a season, but for life. After his recovery John continued his work with the helpers. In retrospect this was timely, for on December 11 he was back in bed with a near-fatal relapse of pneumonia.

The result of John's illness was twofold. First of all, his condition served to draw an increasingly fragmented mission family together as well as to evoke signs of concern and devotion from his followers. When his fever was at its worst, the school boys offered up a prayer that they credited with saving his life. John apparently thought he was dying, but after the natives prayed for him he revived. Edith wrote, "When he heard of the many prayers offered for him by our people, he said, 'I have not been able to do much for the Lord but surely this is a little.' Then he cleared his trembling voice and through tears of joy exclaimed, 'It is almost worth being sick to see this, is it not?'"[36] Later, Edith contrasted the prayers offered in this instance and the shaman whom sympathetic people had prescribed for them seven years before when their elder daughter Katie had been ill. As a consequence of the perceived miracle of John's recovery, the mission's influence was stronger than ever.

The second and perhaps more profound effect of John's illness was the active response it drew from the native helpers he had trained. Though John had passed out of danger by Christmas, he remained at the mission most of the winter. This left the outlying villages virtually undefended against backsliding.

The missionaries were especially anxious at New Year's 1895 when the Great Feast for the Dead (Elriq) was celebrated at Kwethluk. As Kwethluk was a wealthy and prestigious community with broad social ties, guests from the coastal area between the mouths of the Yukon and Kuskokwim rivers, as well as from the Togiak river drainage, had been invited. The missionaries anticipated that emissaries of the Russian Orthodox priest would attend, and John had wanted to be on hand to counter their claims. As he was still too ill, the native missionaries went in his place. When all had gathered, religious argument took precedent over the celebration of the native ceremony.

> The Greek adherents and those of the shamans combined in an endeavor to confound the children of Light. The Greek helper from Kolmakoffski preached abuse and damnation, and the shamans directed their ridicule against us. Our people did not fling back retorts, but took their turn at having services, and preached the Word of God as they knew it. David Skuviuk was there, and he preached a powerful sermon. It was so striking and convincing, that the opposing elements ceased to make public efforts. Many a heathen

Fig. 10.4. Moravian helpers, 1903. Standing from left to right, Helper David, Hallelujah, Tuntuk; seated, Helper Lomack and wife, Helper George and wife. (Moravian Archives)

said, "*Nutan* [*nutaan* (exclamation): fine, very good] now we begin to understand." Even one of our young school boys offered a public prayer in a Kashima crowded full of men. After the service, one of the men from the sea coast, who had been one of the principal scoffers said, "I have argued with men, but they have never shaken my determination to hold to the old tradition; but that little boy, in the presence of all this audience, by his prayer unsettles. There is something more than human that enables that boy to stand up and speak like that." Many of our own people who had been weak and lukewarm, were roused up to greater strength and activity.[37]

This account strongly contrasts to the Easter execution described for this same community five years before. In this case the same forces clashed, but with very different results. Previously, John had been evicted and Brother Hooker killed; now the people of Kwethluk and their guests sat and listened in the qasgiq while mere school boys proclaimed the new faith. They found the boys' performance "more than human"—it was not appropriate Yup'ik behavior for young boys to speak out. Later trips by the younger brethren elicited similar comments: at Lomavik, the people greeted them heartily, saying that "because they were boys, they did not at first guess their errand."[38] As John's young students spoke, his instruction reaped rich rewards through the striking form as well as the comprehensible content of the delivery.

In the wake of this encounter the native brethren began their winter missionary trips to the villages upriver and downriver from Bethel. These were the first, but by no means the last, missionary encounters of the kind. The trips stand out not only for what they accomplished at this juncture in the conversion process, but for the record they left of how the work was done. Aside from this one episode, the early helpers left no written accounts. Although none kept travel journals, through notes jotted down by John and anecdotes recorded by Edith, the eleven journeys that the helpers accomplished during the winter of 1895 have left strong, although filtered, images of the dynamics of their work.

Wassili and Eddie made the first missionary trip, leaving Bethel on January 11 and visiting the villages of Kikichtagmiut, Akiak, and Kwethluk. Although they were no more than advanced school boys, they were well received.

> From what they report the meetings must have been good. . . . The recent stir created by the Greek Catholics from the Yukon has done little or no harm to us, or the people. Rather has it stirred up our people and brought them out more firmly on the side of right. There seems to be a wide spread awakening such as the Kuskoquim district has never seen. Every Christian has turned into a worker of the Lord, not being ashamed to speak in public or lead in prayer. The topic of conversation everywhere is *how to live a Christian life* as well as to confess it as good.[39]

This visit represented the first time that the Bethel missionaries sent natives out alone to make a missionary trip.

In the ensuing months, various combinations of helpers and older scholars made other trips. During these visits the helpers spoke on a variety of topics, including the story of creation and the fall, the commandments (for example, the sanctity of marriage and the duties of husband and wife), the cross, heaven and hell, the necessity of baptism, the true faith and the separation of churches, attendance at church, and the coming of Christ.

Normally, a group of two or three native brethren arrived at a village unannounced. In the evening they would hold services in the men's house. First, one would speak, followed by another, with a third leading in prayer at the close. The native helpers carried on their talks at length, often beginning on one evening and concluding the following morning. In cases where the people were receptive, the brethren made return trips. Although a single meeting would focus on two or three topics at length, over the winter most topics were presented in most of the communities.

Quickly, however, it became clear that not all villages were anxious to listen to the brethren. For example, on January 31, 1895, Brother Neck, accompanied by Robert and Wassili, visited Napaskiak. Their visit was inspired by the rumor that the villagers had hosted a "Masquerade" during which they had openly ridiculed Christianity. Someone was rumored to have played God while others prayed to him. On their arrival, the helpers found the people about to start out for Napakiak to attend a return feast. On entering the near-empty men's house the occupants greeted the brethren with the remark, "You come of course to talk. . . . If you were related to me, I would not let you talk." Although few listeners remained, Wassili did as John had told him and announced that though the Moravians would not take notice of their previous acts of profanity, "God himself will answer them in his own way."[40]

Later, a man testified that their rumored sacrilege had been a half truth: "Two [boys] said to each other, pointing to some calico—said—You sinner look what will become of you. The boy's mother told him to stop that. The other then made out/believe to pray—saying he wanted to live until evening—and even to Sunday." Nonetheless, the brethren were something less than warmly received. The villagers singled out Neck (whose father had been a shaman) for special abuse: "To think I see a shaman that refuses to shaman. Come, the weather is so stormy, make the weather better"[41] Then, just as they were ready to speak, one man threw down wooden masks. Another began to split them up for use as firewood, and the commotion prevented the brethren from holding their service.

Although overt hostility characterized their reception at Napaskiak, Tshogijak and Lomuck's visit upriver was more encouraging. Tshogijak's comments during their talks throw light on the manner in which the native brethren chose to deliver their message. For example, his rendition of the Protestant ethic is peculiarly Yup'ik and contains imagery unlike anything John would have chosen: "God's gift to us of all things He had created—to us especially it seems that the fish is our gift—hence we must use them in the right way—however abundant not to *trample* on them. To work in the fish season—and to sell only what they can spare." Later, his sermon on the duties attending Christian marriage also carried a familiar Yup'ik metamessage and was probably all the more acceptable because of the familiar means it employed: "Tshogiak—spoke to the women about the care of her husband's food and possessions—the man works to collect food for the women and children—she must respect her husband as her head, and that she must not try to be the head of the family."[42]

Later, at Kamexmute, Tshogijak employed a well-conceived metaphor to communicate his message: "Don't ask why does this man try to make us let go our custom when he himself, has used it. I tell you because it is like pulling off an old parka and putting on a new one,—we advise to put on the new, because it is better."[43] At the same service, he likened the Christian message he carried to a spiritual load, more valuable than any sled full of trade goods: "Don't say why do these men— tho' not priests, go around preaching. We do the best we can—Priests travel without a sledful of stuff—but simply—bedding—food—and in the end of the box—a little book—that is their *load*. Trader's travel w. sometimes 21 sleds of stuff—costly—and nice—and we buy them, but they are soon gone. The Priest's load never is lost and will not wear out."[44] In both instances, the culturally appropriate form into which Tshogijak molded his Christian views probably contributed to his ability to influence his audience.

To add to the drama of the winter awakening, on February 28 word reached the mission that the Russian Orthodox priest had arrived on the Kuskokwim. Receiving a mixed reception at Akiak, the priest moved downriver to Kwethluk. Here again the helpers proved their worth, and Brother Neck, whom Edith deemed the brightest of the native brethren, dogged the priest, determined to hear all he had to say: "Bro. Neck is too wise to interfere with the Priest, but he will see him out of our district, and know what he has said and done before he leaves his side."[45]

Although Kwethluk proved "as unstable as water," the people of Akiak stood firm. There Neck directly confronted the priest with his presumed inability to make meaningful changes in the way of life of the people whose souls he sought to win.

> In speaking to the Priest before all the people, he said, "When we were Christians according to your way of teaching we never tried to live more pure lives, we did not know the meaning of faith or hope, and we did not leave off one of our old heathen superstitions and practices. But these teachers have taught us; we have awakened from darkness; we have found the true light; we

are new beings, and we will not now leave or turn from those who have opened our eyes. You may talk, you may say we are on the road to hell, but we will keep right on; we cannot be very far out of the way if we do what the Bible tells us, and that is our Guide. You never taught us from the Bible, and you never taught us to love. If you will preach to us we will be glad, but if you talk about us and our Priest, it will not go through the Skin—it will never reach our hearts."[46]

An influential elder at the tundra village of Peingagamut reiterated this accusation. Along with Neck's diatribe, testimony of a native convert likely had more impact than half a dozen visits from a non-native missionary.

Whether helpers or not, the native converts were increasingly able to present the Christian message in powerful and comprehensible terms. When Neck declared that "the people are getting awake to Christianity," the traditional imagery of personal awareness was employed in an innovative, effective, and powerful way. All of the evidence indicates that a significant isomorphism existed between Moravian and Yup'ik imagery, which the concrete images of the native brethren successfully invoked.

By the mid-1890s the missionaries' success created the context for a profound conversion: "I spoke of not using Xtianity for a cloak, or as mere covering, but of using it and that it become a needful article."[47] In accepting Christianity as useful and "needful," the Yupiit were beginning to redefine their conceptions of need and value. Previously, an object such as a ceremonial doll or mask had been accepted as the repository of social relations and as such was valued not for itself but as part of a ritual act. Now it "had no value." At the same time, these same masks entered the realm of Western political economy to become "private property" and, as such, objects over which rights of some indeterminant legality might be exerted.

Conversely, Neck and others reiterated Tshogijak's testimony concerning the nonmaterial nature of the missionaries' load. Thus, they placed value on a spiritual and relational dimension: "At Apokagamut [Apokak], Neck had what amounted to an open air meeting. One of the men said to Neck 'Now you are chief, you will take all of the duties of a chief. We hear that a chief looks after the temporal affairs of the people, seeing to it that the traders do not over charge the people for goods.' Neck replied 'We have nothing to do with the goods of anybody, but we are here to teach the Word, that is our work.'"[48]

THE POWER OF PRAYER

The helpers' work was to teach the Word, and in their own minds and the minds of the missionaries they were presenting their listeners with a choice. This view has been shared by the majority of analysts who depict the conversion process as an all-or-nothing encounter in which the native culture is either left intact or totally transformed.[49] On the contrary, the encounter between the Yupiit and Moravians produced neither total commitment nor total rejection, but an internalization of categories which the helpers' performances vividly display. In accepting the Moravian message, the helpers and their audience both performed a deliberate act of innovation as well as supplemented a familiar store of responses.

The encounters between the missionaries and their opponents during the winter of 1895 involved a struggle for control. They also constituted a dialogue between two different systems of meaning. By the Christian view, the individual was powerless and must pray to God to make power available through Jesus. John wrote, "We commend ourselves and our work to the Church's intercession, confident that our prayers will be heard and that the answer may reveal the saving power of Christ, working in the hearts of all the natives."[50]

The Yup'ik people, on the other hand, expected the spirit world to provide them direct access to useable power. Their initial reaction to Christianity may have been to use Christ as an additional source of power, rather than a means of salvation. Instead of viewing the missionary as a mere dispenser of the sacraments over which he had no proprietary right, they may have apprehended him in terms of the traditional shaman who gave and withheld his blessing at will. The natives dubbed Dr. Herman Romig, the first doctor to serve in Bethel, Angalkuq (the shaman) because of his demonstrated power to heal. His explanation of the limitations of his skill did little to undercut this apprehension. When he was asked why he sometimes succeeded and at other times failed to cure a patient, Romig explained that the "germs of death flew from man to man like invisible birds"—he could control some, but not all.[51] The Yupiit likely accepted his story in terms of their own belief in spiritual encounter and possession, which simultaneously accounted for both his failures and success.

Nothing in the principles of Yup'ik cosmology limited access to spiritual power or prevented borrowing the Moravian's "technical means." Along with medicines, one of the first things the Yupiit embraced was verbal testimony and prayer. The Yupiit had always valued oral performance, and when John preached in the men's house, he entered this tradition. While gaining efficacy in this arena was no easy or speedy process, a decade after his arrival he had the satisfaction of hearing native men and boys follow in his footsteps to preach to their own people: "This evening in our Chapel service, Martin, one of our school boys, offered voluntary prayer."[52]

This use of the public arena to witness for Christ was tremendously important. Though direct confrontation of the individual and the attempt to invest the audience with the fundamentalist mode of interpreting experience was not appropriate, the less confrontational tactics of the native helpers allowed them to gain entrance into this arena; it also helped the audience to make sense of the message. In this way the helpers were able to communicate the rhetoric of the Moravian daily texts in a manner comparable to the indirect comments of the elders. Public prayer meetings were not unlike the

Fig. 10.5. In creating this ivory bible, a Yup'ik carver used a traditional technique in an innovative way. Length 2.75 inches, width 2 inches, 1 inch thick. (Kilbuck Collection, Ottawa University)

perpetual speaking out of the elders to advise the young people of their responsibilities; in the same way, the Moravians believed that the Word of God would be received if continually restated. The Yup'ik response was enthusiastic: "When I explained to them that the blood shed on the cross by Jesus Christ was for the taking away of our badness (sin), the older men exclaimed 'Kuyana!' [*Quyana*] (Thank You), and added, 'we, too, desire to have our badness taken away by that blood.'"[53]

John often wrote concerning prayer and what it entailed: "It is by His grace that we can send this news of our work. . . . We would indeed be as John the Baptist, only 'a voice' proclaiming the salvation of God, as worked out by our Lord Jesus Christ. Help us then by your prayers, that we may have humble hearts, filled with patience and wisdom from on high."[54] The direct relationship between heartfelt prayer ("humble hearts, filled with patience and wisdom") and earthly rewards was not unlike that associated with traditional rituals performed to ensure the success of the hunt. When the school boys offered prayers for John's recovery, they were not, as Edith surmised, engaging in a qualitatively different activity from their sympathetic attempt seven years before to help the Kilbuck's ailing daughter by offering the help of a shaman. When the helpers spoke out in public places, they were not merely displacing the traditional world view with Christianity but were appropriating it in Yup'ik terms. Similarly, the helpers did not simply replace the shaman, they appropriated his position through a deft transformation of the concept of spiritual power.

Traditionally, a person with religious experience was not described as either a leader or a believer, but as someone who "knew" or "saw." This knowledge and vision were analogous to and spoken of as spiritual power. Although this power was recognized, it did not always entail the authority to coerce. Rather, authority was based on consensus and a fundamental respect for autonomy rather than on superordinate position. Ideally, power was truth rather than control,[55] and a leader, whether spiritual or secular, was someone who followed the people.

When the Kilbucks arrived, the Yupiit did not abandon traditional concepts of knowledge and power, they asked the shaman to explain the source of the Moravians' power. The Kilbucks correctly judged that if they could influence these prominent individuals, such as the infamous Little Whetstone, their own influence would grow. At the same time they recognized the lack of a political structure fostering positions of leadership in Yup'ik society. Ironically, by Yup'ik standards the missionaries ultimately lacked authority to perform their self-appointed task of leading the people out of darkness into the light.

What did conversion mean to the Yup'ik people in the mid-1890s? More than a rebellion against tradition, Christianity was probably initially accepted by the Yupiit as they might have added an additional song or ritual to their repertoire when they perceived it as a helpful source of spiritual power. This does not imply that conversion was superficial, a mere addition to existing means of relating with the spirit world. Nor was it the radical change that Edith's contrast between the people's offer of a shaman versus their subsequent offer of prayer on the Kilbucks' behalf would seem to imply. Conversion constituted a legitimate appropriation in the face of changing circumstances.

The Yupiit originally accepted John and Edith because of their ability to act in Yup'ik ways. Ten years later their acceptance constituted a deliberate break with the past as well. The Yupiit heeded the Moravian message both because of and in spite of its association with Western society and technology, which they increasingly recognized as a source of power. Though the culturally appropriate terms of Moravian oratory helped to make their

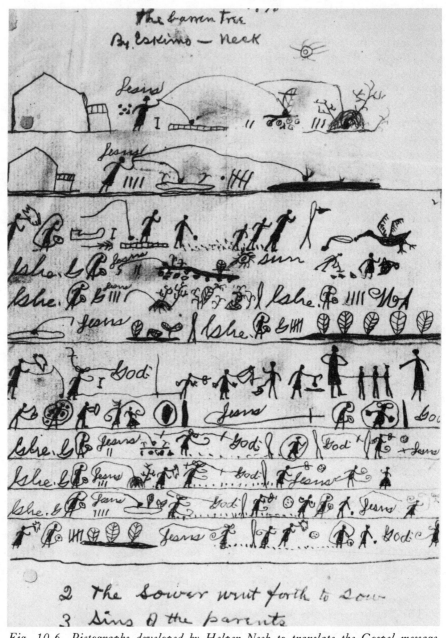

Fig. 10.6. Pictographs developed by Helper Neck to translate the Gospel message, 1898. (Moravian Archives)

message clear, in part the Yupiit accepted the missionaries and helpers precisely because they were so different and because they gave access to European goods and medicines.

Though the Western association of Christianity was an obstacle to acceptance, it was also an attraction. In opting for religious conversion the helpers were consciously opting for Western "technique" and the power it entailed. Traditionally, there was no sharp distinction between material and spiritual realms, and the means of production were mental as well as material.[56] If Western guns were superior, the Yupiit reasoned, Moravian rituals and sacred books might provide new sources of spiritual power. As Sahlins described for the Fijians, the Western presence was a "total" social fact, "religious" at the same time it was "political" and "economic," while Yup'ik theory "stood Marx on his head by its insistence that . . . the economic base depended on the spiritual superstructure."[57]

By the turn of the century the Yup'ik people increasingly viewed conversion as a means of sharing in the exercise of superior spiritual power and, conversely, protection from harm. Crosses and holy water replaced amulets and medicine bags as curing devices. The attachment to guardian angels recalled personal helping spirits and enabled the Yupiit to retain their belief in a familiar spirit world. Traditionally, a person's name might be changed to effect a cure. In the same way, people suffering from illness were not above rebaptism from Moravianism to Orthodoxy, and vice versa, if the power of a particular faith was insufficient to heal. John and Edith expressed concern at these carryovers and waiverings, seeing them as signs of superficial Christianity. Indeed, rather than a rejection of traditional ends, conversion represented a conviction that Christianity offered more powerful means, as traditionally defined.

One of the most dramatic instances of a helper taking an aspect of the missionary message and making it not only rhetorically, but literally, his own, was Helper Neck's development of a unique hieroglyphics. In the spring of 1896 Neck stayed in Bethel to learn to better communicate his message. Because he could not read English, he took down his lessons in a form of picture writing that he worked out for himself. By the time he left he had recorded almost the entire passion week manual and many parables in this manner. His calligraphy enabled him to speak from his notes and to teach others to use them.

Through the years Neck refined his "picture writing." His unique script played an effective role in his ministry, and his act transformed as well as translated the Moravian message. The Yupiit (Neck in particular) were impressed by the acts of reading and writing that they witnessed at the mission. Likely, they considered these acts the evidence, if not the source, of the missionaries' efficacy and power. Some came to the mission to learn to read and write, thereby acquiring for themselves the missionaries' powerful tool. Neck, however, chose a more independent and creative route. Rather than adopt the missionaries' alphabet, he took from them only the concept of the written word and successfully developed his own technical system. As he had done with the translated messages he preached, he was able to transform what had been brought to transform him.

The events of the winter and spring of 1895 marked a dramatic finale to the Kilbucks' first decade on the Kuskokwim. Edith wrote that the "minds of most everyone have been disturbed by the visit of the Greek priest."[58] However, the concrete images employed by the native helpers, combined with the dramatic testimonials of "enlightened" shamans such as the young Napaskiak convert, provided an effective counter.

The tension between the Orthodox, the nineteenth-century Yup'ik, and the Moravian points of view was by no means resolved in the course of the winter sermons of 1895. Other conflicts in other contexts arose, throwing the Yup'ik people into uncertainty. In 1897 Edith described the people of Quinhagak as "in the same state as a vessel, as a pan or kantuk [qantaq: bowl] brimful of water, the least jar will cause it to spill, hence must be handled very carefully."[59]

Nevertheless, the Kilbucks' journals from this period convey a very different picture from that depicted five years before when shamanic and Orthodox opposition had erupted in the Easter execution of Brother Hooker. In the spring of 1890 the people of Kwethluk had bowed their heads and blindly followed their leader in the ritual killing of one of the first native helpers. Five years later, the people of nearby Akiak listened with attention while another native helper urged them to be faithful "to the sight they have . . . to remember that our Master watches over us at all times."[60] The opposition, central in traditional Yup'ik cosmology between fallible restricted human sight and powerful supernatural vision, had been realized in social action. A powerful piece of the Yup'ik view of the world had been vindicated at the same time that it had been transformed.

The fate of the son and heir of the "wicked old shaman" whose conversion so heartened the Kilbucks, provides a final image of the impact of their first ten years on the Kuskokwim. Not only did the old man die a believer, but after his death his son was appointed an assistant helper in his village. In this instance, at least, not only had power been transferred from the shamans to the Moravians, but power was given over to a member of the younger generation. Which transference was the more significant is hard to judge; however, in many ways this was still power as traditionally defined.

On this note the Kilbucks' first and perhaps most dramatic decade of work together drew to a close. They had helped establish the Moravian mission along the Kuskokwim and had learned something of the language and ways of the people among whom they had come to live. Their marriage had borne four children, withstood the public disclosure of adultery, and sustained long separations. Among his Yup'ik parishioners, John's energy had earned an acceptance and respect in which Edith shared a full part. Although nearly three decades of work lay ahead, at the end of their first ten years most of the major external barriers to their mission had begun to fall. Ahead lay the nurturing of the transformation they had helped set in motion along the Kuskokwim, a task more difficult and telling.

CHAPTER 11

CHANGING OF THE GUARD

COASTAL TRAVELING

The Kilbucks' second decade on the Kuskokwim began with their work well in hand and their marital problems in the process of resolution. Although strains remained between individual missionaries from the personal disclosures of the past year, John's public confession in November 1895, of adultery committed three years before, temporarily cleared the air in Bethel. Following his confession, John focused his attention on traveling on the mission's behalf. During the winter of 1895 the missionaries covered more than 2,500 miles in their work, John making the majority of the trips. An epidemic of whooping cough claimed dozens of lives during the summer, followed by a relatively minor but still distressing siege of "la grippe." Although freeze-up was early, shortening the critical fall fishery, whitefish proved plentiful during the winter, and a food shortage was averted.

By spring the missionaries eagerly awaited fresh stores as well as the words from the home board that would, they hoped, clarify John's official position. The missionaries also looked forward to the arrival of the first medical missionary on the Kuskokwim. In the spring of 1896 Edith's brother, Dr. Herman Romig, had been ordained a deacon of the Moravian church and together with his wife, Ella (a trained nurse), embarked for Bethel. Plans for this addition to the mission party had long been under way and were the fruition of innumerable pleas on the part of the Bethel missionaries for qualified medical help. The hope was that many souls seeking care for their afflicted bodies might come to seek the healing power of the Great Physician whom they served.

Following Herman and Ella's arrival, the mission did in fact receive more and more calls for medical help. As the demands on Herman's time increased, John gave orders that Russian Orthodox patients must pay for treatment. A barrage of what Edith termed "instant Moravians" was the immediate consequence:

[Helper] George's father is sick and wants treatment. . . . Herman said he would do what he could for him, but being a *greek* [Orthodox] he would have to pay for the medicine, although he would not charge for the treatment. This of course was a pill, for he says we have his only child working for us, which is the same as if he were working for us. He turned Moravian at once, and talked around until for George's sake, Herman examined him and promised to give him treatment.[1]

John's policy had to be rescinded to protect otherwise heaven-bound Orthodox from perjuring their immortal souls.

Edith's journals to her father during the year after Herman's arrival often make mention of his work. He performed his first successful operation in May 1897 on a man who was later discovered, to everyone's amazement, to have had a chew of tobacco in his mouth.[2] Later that year, John commented that Herman's success was fast growing into a confidence in medicine downriver. Soon, John predicted, the shamans would be forced to take a back seat.

Although in Bethel John increasingly shared the spotlight with his brother-in-law, it was still his responsibility to journey in the mission's cause. When Sister King was transferred to Carmel at the end of the summer, John transported her down the Kuskokwim in the mission sailboat *Swan*. Though not nearly as long or as worrisome as his sledge journey to Carmel eight years before, the voyage of the *Swan* was one of John's more memorable trips. Perhaps relieved after the mental stress of the past winter, or perhaps because traveling was one of his great loves, John's journal for this trip, later published in *The Moravian*, struts and swells with the tide. Obviously delighting in the act of telling the tale, he described his mastery of the boat as it took to the high waves as easily as the sea ducks that were swimming and diving around them. However, no sooner had they left the mouth of the Kuskokwim than they ran aground while attempting to escape a line of breakers.[3]

The scrape over the bar caused a leak along the keel of the boat, temporarily crippling her. However, the *Swan* was beached, the leak caulked and mended, and she was soon sailing towards Nushagak. A week later, on rounding Cape Newenham, he wrote, "Oh! Edith, but it was a most enjoyable night for me, being also elated over the safe rounding of the Cape, and our little ship, like a thing of life, bounding along, without a leak. Actually I seemed to feel her glorying in the fact that she did not have to carry an unnecessary load of water. Sr. King was out as we rounded the Cape and we sang some Gospel hymns." The conquest of the next cape proved even more exhilarating: "Look is that really the Cape, wait, may be there is more land beyond. No? Sure enough there is the Cape. . . . See how much rougher it

Fig. 11.1. Bethel missionaries, 1896. Standing from left to right, John Kilbuck, Herman Romig, Lydia Schoechert, John Schoechert, Edith Kilbuck, Ella Romig, Ernest Weber. Seated, Mary Mack, Phillipine King, Caroline Weber. (Moravian Archives)

Fig. 11.2. Bethel landing at high tide with the Swan at right, 1900. (J. H. Romig, Moravian Archives)

Bethel Landing 1900

is here. Watch out for breakers, now, these little mountains of water are all right, we are acquainted with them, but the breakers,—we don't want to have anything to do with them. Hello! what's matter! I look around and look back—Hurrah—we have rounded the cape, and there is quiet sea ahead. Here Frank, in these quiet waters—take the helm—Ha! but that was work."[4]

During this voyage John displayed a renewal of the personal power that had lain dormant during the winter of confession and repentance. The jubilant journal he brought home to Edith supports the claim. Carmel was in sight, their goal at hand, and their reception enthusiastic. Ten days later, John set sail on the home stretch. Through false leaks and turnings, the *Swan* pushed steadily north into the Kuskokwim. On his safe return to Bethel, John received a hero's welcome, and he felt the part. Though she would later declare the trip "fool hardy," Edith also gloried in his success: "Before he left, he said that if he reached Carmel and got back in safety, he would feel about as big as Columbus, and by his log you will see that it is no small thing to undertake. There is no one else who would have undertaken it, and it is doubtful if any one else would have accomplished it."[5]

Immediately after his return from Nushagak, John resumed his travels and his journals, free from introspective comments. Later in the winter he described an interview with a group of native brethren who had gathered to ask his advice.

> The object of their visit was to request the establishment of some kind of government, and to this end, ask for a governor from the states. I tried to explain . . . all that their request involved. . . . The principal reason for this request was because of slow progress of Christian living, an unwillingness on the part of some to listen to and to obey advice and warning. I explained, that the remedy was in those who did believe to lead an earnest and conscientious life—outside the Power of the Gospel, there is no higher power, for doing good.[6]

Although it was not the first time that John's advice had been sought, this incident marks a subtle transition from evangelist to interpreter. Once rudimentary conversion had been accomplished, John's role as spiritual guide gradually evolved into that of counselor and arbitrator in a more comprehensive sense, a role that would dominate his work into the 1920s.

Back in Bethel the event of the winter was the arrival of a train of thirteen reindeer and seven sledges. The party, which included several Lapps, was led by Mr. Kjellmann, superintendent of the Teller Reindeer Station. Their purpose was to explore the country, with the idea of sending out herds to the different missions. Although Kjellmann found the Kuskokwim drainage to have good forage, the deer would have to be kept in the uplands on account of the wetness. The party remained a month in Bethel and apparently created quite a stir, people taking the deer for dogs with trees growing out of their heads and the men for soldiers.[7] This visit was to have an impact

Fig. 11.3. The Kilbuck dog team leaving Bethel, 1896. (J. H. Romig, Yugtarvik Regional Museum)

on John's future work along the Kuskokwim, as he soaked up information concerning the possibilities and logistics of starting a herd along the river. Fifteen years later, when he returned to the Kuskokwim to begin his work at Akiak, deer herding would be a central element in his strategy for cultural conversion.

Less than a month after the deer had departed, John received official word from Bethlehem that he would be retained as assistant superintendent. Although the future brightened for the mission on this score, Carrie Weber's health appeared to be seriously and steadily failing.[8] Due to her ill health, the missionaries decided that the family should leave for a year's rest. When the annual supply ship set sail for home that July, the Webers were on board. At the same time, John and Edith received instructions reassigning them to Carmel, while Herman Romig was put in charge of the Bethel mission. Though they were sorry to leave Bethel, they were glad to be able to continue working for the mission.[9] As the call to Carmel arrived too late in the summer to allow them time to make the move before freeze-up, they decided to stay one last year in Bethel and leave the following year, after the Webers' return. Some still hoped that the Kilbucks would be able to remain

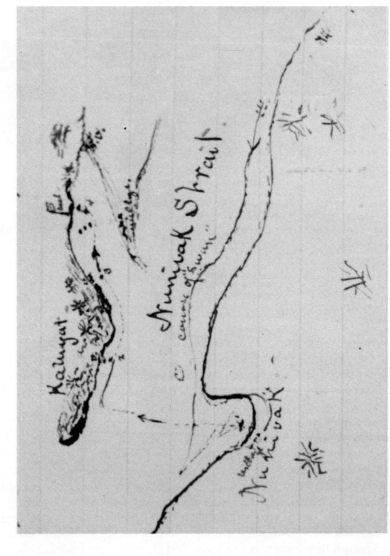

Fig. 11.4. John's journal sketch of trip to Nelson Island (Kaluyat) in search of "dusty diamonds." (Moravian Archives)

along the Kuskokwim, and the helpers wrote to the mission board on their behalf.

Late summer 1897 found the people again suffering from the grippe. Food was short, and the school was forced to close after only four months. Winter weather proved good for traveling, however, and John was able to make eighteen missionary trips, covering more than eighteen hundred miles by dog team. He also traveled up the coast three times, twice for supplies and once for coal. The coal reconnaissance comprised a major exploratory and entrepreneurial adventure, as John hoped to mine coal on Nelson Island in quantities sufficient to fuel the mission throughout the year.

With this goal in mind, John set sail down the Kuskokwim on the *Swan* on August 8, traveling to Quinhagak. A week later he wrote Edith, "Here we are on the other side of the Kuskoquim, on a *mudbank*. I suppose Ruth thinks I have no business to be on land . . . but it is human nature to be contrary." On the seventeenth he resumed sailing but by early afternoon found himself in shoal water again. The day following he arrived at the point where the tides divide, between the Kuskokwim tides and those toward the west and north. From here on up the coast was blocked by a chain of banks within which there was no deep water. John sailed south and upon successfully clearing the banks, he wrote, "Oh! Edith, I enjoyed the day, as I have never done, for I do not know when—and your presence attended me, and pervaded the air I breathed, that nothing but your actual presence at my side, could have filled my cup of pleasure. Darling, were you thinking of me, all that live long day?" [10]

The *Swan* sailed steadily north up the coast, with John at the helm through the night. When at last he finally did lie down to rest, he was almost immediately awakened and informed that Nunivak Island lay dead ahead. An immediate concern was a line of breakers extending towards their path "with jagged rocks showing here and there, like hungry teeth." John safely cleared the reef, however, and continued to sail up the coast of Nunivak, carefully steering clear of the hidden rocks guarding the headlands: "According to descriptions, we judged that we could not be very far from a village. But, however close our lookout was, we did not see any signs of people until, in crossing the mouth of a bay, and the extremity of the island was raised above the horizon, and then in making a tack into the bay, we saw a kyack, coming for us." [11]

A number of Nunivak Islanders interested in trade soon boarded the *Swan*. John was struck with the ways in which they differed from the people of the Kuskokwim; theirs was a distinctive carriage, clothing style, vocabulary, and pronunciation. John gave a full account of the culturally appropriate means he employed to conquer the apprehensions of his visitors, who were generally not on friendly terms with the Kuskokwim Eskimos because of historically grounded animosities between the two groups. When they asked for trade goods, he countered with a request for hospitality. Gifts of food passed between the two parties and "after that they acted as tho' we were not strangers."[12]

After remaining at anchor overnight and trading with the Nunivak people, John set sail across Etolin Strait toward Nelson Island. At the head of what is now known as Toksook Bay he successfully located and mined a load of the long-sought "dusty diamonds." Although the coastal camps were deserted, news of his presence reached the people. Nelson Islanders visited the ship while it was anchored in the bay. One old man regaled John with the story of the creation of Nelson Island, which John fortunately recorded in some detail.[13]

After they had successfully loaded the coal, the *Swan* set sail for the mouth of the Kuskokwim, arriving at Quinhagak on August 30. There John witnessed the arrival of guests invited to participate in what he labeled an Eckrushka and what was probably actually an Ingulaq or Kevgiq exchange. John responded enthusiastically to the display and contended that he had been "strangely stirred" by the event, which caused him to recall his Delaware forefathers. At the time when his standing within the Moravian mission was at its most ambiguous, he was, through recollections of the proud boasts of his aboriginal forefathers, enabled "to enter more fully into the feelings of the people" whom he had come to convert. Although an awareness of his ancestry heightened his ability to empathize with the Yup'ik people, there was never any question that he was "becoming" an Eskimo. His empathy only served to fit him better for his role as cultural interpreter and transformer.

John's abilities as translator, in a broader sense, were constantly called upon during the end of his tenure as missionary-in-chief along the Kuskokwim. No more than a handful of days after the experience at Quinhagak, Helper Lomuck sought John's counsel concerning the proper way to honor a deceased daughter with gifts in remembrance:

> Bro. Lomuck also, asked about his expected deal out of oil. Before these people became Christians, it was a custom, that something like a *totem* was erected to the memory of some dear departed one. As I understand the custom of the deal out or potlatch, stress was laid on the erection of the *totem*. Now [in] the place of the *totem*, is placed the cross, and with us the grave stone or slab. The custom is hard to deal with, in as much as memorials are erected in Xian communities the world over, and just what part of this native custom to condemn, is difficult to settle. The greatest difficulty is, to remove all idea of superstitious belief, as this is no doubt firmly fixed in the mind of the people, and still to forbid the natural desire to express in some way affection for the dead, would not be fair as Christians every where else do so, where the means are at hand.
>
> In a certain sense I forbid Lomuck, telling him it is not good to continue heathen customs (are they heathen is the question) under the banner of Christ,—but if he wants to, he can take a part of his intended deal, and put it into the chapel. Now he has four bags of oil to deal out,—say he gives one

bag to the chapel, by paying that bag to one or more men, who will hew so many logs of the chapel, and the rest he can give out in the name of the little girl, and not because of the *totem*.[14]

In proposing that Lomuck use part of the goods he had intended to give in the name of his daughter as pay for building logs for the chapel, John displayed a typically practical solution to a culturally complicated situation. It was also one which had important implications for the concept of value within traditional Yup'ik ideology. As the original meaning of the gift was a spiritual feeding of the departed through the living, John's apparently benign and effortless conversion of the gift to a form of currency required a fundamental transformation of the significance of the entire event. Years before, Weinland had recorded the rationale for such ritual feeding of the living in the name of the dead: "They did not believe that death put an end to existence, but that there is a life beyond the present. The departed descends to the other world by four stages, each stage being one day's journey. Thus far he still retains his terrestrial nature, and must be fed from this world."[15]

As in his attack on the noise and clamor traditionally attending mourning, John's complaints touched at the core of Yup'ik cosmology. In suppressing the gift, as in suppressing the cry, he was not merely arguing about the manner of living, but about life's resolution in death as well. That some Yupiit, at least, realized the depth of the desired changes is intimated in a comment reported by one of the helpers. He said that when he would call the men of the village from the men's house to his home for service, the shaman would start up a meeting in opposition, "endeavoring to dissuade those so inclined from attending the church service, by saying that their old way of living is much better, and that they will get into a good place if they remain good natives while living."[16]

On a missionary trip upriver later in the fall, John made several observations concerning the Yup'ik response to the current food shortage. At Akiak he noted that people were hard at work on the fish traps on which they depended for daily fare:

All the talk is about traps, and every time any one comes back from his trap, everyone in the village asks his neighbor, "Well, how many fish did he get?" When ever one in the village reports a little larger catch, than usual, there is a general rejoicing, for every one thinks, that there is chance for them too. If one or more traps are reported not to be catching anything, there is a general discussion, and each one offers a suggestion as to the cause, so that in the end the younger men, learn how to set their fish traps, and how to look after them.

Further up river, at Tuluksak, John also gave a functional explanation of what he observed: "As soon as I arrived, the few Toulksagamut came to greet me. Such a happy go lucky set of folks I never saw. Here they are without food, having already eaten up their fish, and no frozen fish even, still they were all jolly, and eager for a good laugh. This of course is, as it should be, for by this keeping up their spirits they stand a better show of keeping alive." [17]

John attempted, not unsympathetically, to provide a rational interpretation for the actions at Akiak. From a Western point of view the Yupiit exhibited a frivolous disregard for conditions of personal hardship and deprivation. John's description provides a powerful image of a world very different from his own. Although accurate in his explanation for the possible impact of what he saw as a peculiarly optimistic attitude, John misconstrued the origin of such behavior. The Western view of the world focuses on the satisfaction of individual desires, the frustration of which produces discontent. The Yup'ik people, however, were here acting according to a very different cultural logic, whereby the social whole took precedence over individual wants and desires and the expression of solidarity over individual needs. Although John was correct in his observation that the Yupiit sublimated hunger, he was inaccurate in attributing this exclusively to the enhancement of the individual's chances to survive. In fact, the Yupiit experienced hunger as a social as well as an individual fact, reciprocity insuring that either all or none would go hungry.

John's journals for this period are rich in ethnographic observations and commentary referring to activity witnessed as well as oral traditions. One long entry recorded in the fall of 1897, explicitly labeled "Historical notes," included an abbreviated account of the last great battle of the Aglurmiut warriors and the Kuskokwim Eskimos. [18] One explanation for these increasing references to Yup'ik ceremonial and subsistence activity is John's awareness of the possible value of documenting these events and changes for posterity. This may have been heightened by his own sense of transience. Most of his time during this period was spent among the people. No longer having the responsibility of the general management of the mission, John was traveling more than ever before. If he had been more successful as an administrator, his skills as an ethnographer might never have blossomed.

DAMAGE DONE

John's last trip for the season was down to the mouth of the Kuskokwim to the sealing banks located thirty miles below Quinhagak. His task was to obtain meat, oil, and skins as food for the school and supplies for the mission. Though the plan was only moderately successful, netting twenty-five seals, John painted the hunt as work well done and signed his journal "John the sealer."

On this trip, while free from what he experienced as Bethel's stifling atmosphere, John made a rare retrospective digression:

Some way, that is for personal comfort I regret that we did not go to Carmel this summer. Somehow, I feel out of place at Bethel, and more than ever I would like if we could go off to ourselves. Then again, I think, that I ought to stay more at Bethel, and, boldly, yet kindly, try to make missionaries of our co-laborers. It worries me that so much ill feeling is constantly smoldering, on account of temporal things, but no effort is made to get ahead of each other in well doing, and Christian grace. But fear I am not fit or able for such a task tho' I try by, not words so much, as by trying to show how one in our position should live.[19]

Here John reiterated a yearning to be away from the close confines of the mission hub. Even before the call to Carmel, Edith had wished to move away from Bethel and out among the people: "The Quinhagamute [Quinhagak] people have really improved during the past year. . . . Without just being able to say how, I feel that they are no longer indifferent to us and our teachings. They are still heathen, but their fear of us seems to be passed away. . . . I wish we could live here a few years. I am sure we could help these people."[20]

Both John and Edith simultaneously felt repelled by the tension of Bethel and drawn to the periphery of the mission field. On a trip made later that winter to Akiak, John commented to Edith how much he liked the village, feeling that "the people are more open hearted and genuinely kind."[21] There he stayed with his old friend and companion Helper Kawagleg who always kept a bunk ready for him. John's comment is auspicious. Fourteen years later, on his return to the mission after an absence of over ten years, it was Akiak, not Bethel, that he and Edith would make their home.

Though John's confession had cleared the air between himself and Edith, it had permanently muddied their relationship with the Bethel missionaries. Although neither John nor Edith wallowed in their distress, the cumulative effect of erratic and brief comments on small incidents is telling. This is especially true in contrast to past years, when their trials grew from without rather than from within the mission party. John voiced his discomfort in March 1897 while Edith was away at Ougavig visiting the Webers: "I take my meals at the Dr's in spite of what has been written, I feel that we can still live peacably together. Both are as kindly as they can be, but in my heart, I still feel a little 'queer'."[22]

Edith bore the brunt of the unpleasantness in Bethel, where she had grievances both great and small. In August 1897 she wrote that all but Ella and Herman were jealous because they couldn't speak the Yup'ik language. This complaint found damaging expression. In John's absence Edith attempted to translate the services for the native audience, but Brother Helmich forbade her, quoting the biblical proscription against women speaking in public. The result was that in John's absence Bethel had no fluent missionary.

Brother Helmich's overly zealous standards caused conflicts in other areas as well. In September a storm stranded a group of natives in Bethel. Edith wrote, "Brother H. was displeased that they stayed so long and asked for food. He gave them so little fish that they complained of hunger. One funny fellow in the crowd said that if they were kept over another day, they would have 'Helmich for dinner.' The remark brought forth a hearty laugh all around, but the weather cleared and they left for home so the missionary was spared." Edith continued, "It hurts the mission and the people declare that they will not work for Bro. Helmich again."[23] Edith's most perceptive criticism is aimed at the manner, rather than the content, of Helmich's action. As he was an impetuous and abrupt individual, Edith worried that his behavior would alienate mission converts.

For obvious reasons the relationship between Edith and Miss Mack was also strained, and Edith's greatest struggle was to feel forgiving and kind towards her: "I pray daily for grace to be silent this last year under her slights and foundationless accusations." Edith also worried that Miss Mack's venom would wreak havoc on the mission in general: "If she says all that she intends to, to the folks in the east, she will harm the work not a little. There they will not know that she eases her own conscience by trying to drag everybody else into trouble. They will at least think that her word is good."[24]

While feelings ran high within the mission party, the Kilbucks continued to receive support from their native co-workers. The helpers wrote to the mission board on their behalf, and many expressed anxiety that they be permitted to continue to work on the Kuskokwim: "Nobody wants us to go away [to Carmel]. If they knew it, we would far prefer to stay."[25]

During the winter of 1897–1898 John's travel journals generally reflect his good spirits. On a layover in Akiak he wrote, "You will see that I have not been depressed in spirits, but when my work is done, I feel relieved, just about in the same way that colts feel when they kick up their heels and take a run." Later that month, when he accompanied a party of white men to Togiak, his journal voiced his satisfaction in the opportunity provided for camaraderie: "This trip has been quite a picnic, all the way, and I have enjoyed it immensely."[26] In March John accompanied the chief engineer of the steamer *Hamilton* back to the boat's winter quarters on the Yukon near Russian Mission and in April traveled downriver to Quinhagak to visit the newly established reindeer herd. When he pulled into the deer camp, one of the herders cried, "Here comes Jack" (John's well-known lead dog), taking it for granted that the animal's master was along.[27]

While the missionaries along the Kuskokwim struggled to settle their differences and dwell harmoniously, as their doctrine required, events were unfolding four thousand miles away in Bethlehem, Pennsylvania, to again throw them into disarray. Apparently, the particulars concerning John's confession were not fully communicated to the mission board until Weber's return in September 1897. Until then the board had been unaware of Miss Mack's involvement and the extent of John's adulterous relations with native women during Edith's absence. The board was also distressed to learn the extent to which the Bethel missionaries were demoralized, none being willing to continue to work with John who, they felt, had deceived them as well as the mission board by making only a partial confession. Whether this "deception" was real or the product of bitterness and ill will is impossible to gauge. However, the result of this unsettling communication was that the board officially dismissed John from missionary service as well as from church membership and ordered him to return to the States as soon as possible.[28]

Although the mission's two governing bodies, the Society for Propagating the Gospel (SPG) and the Provincial Elders' Conference (PEC), were primarily concerned with the prompt resolution of the situation, they were also anxious that the incident not be publicized. When John's confession was mentioned in the official communication printed in No. 28 of the Herrnhut (German) organ of the Moravian Church, both the SPG and the PEC passed resolutions condemning this disclosure and protesting against any further reference to the case in Moravian church papers. Similarly, in the case of Miss Mack, the PEC deemed it advisable to announce her return as simply a retirement from temporary service and not as a dismissal.[29]

Neither the PEC nor the SPG kept a record of the incoming correspondence concerning any aspect of the Alaska mission for this period. Whether due to negligence or a desire to minimize the negative impact of these controversial years, copies no longer exist of the missionaries' complaints or of the pleas for clemency written by the native helpers on John's behalf. For the governing boards of the Moravian church, perhaps as painful and reprehensible as John's initial error was the overt conflict that it engendered. In any event, due to the value the Moravians placed on both external and internal harmony, published references to this period are to this day either ambiguous or shrouded in mystery.

A DIFFERENT POINT OF VIEW

During the spring of 1898 the board also engaged in a serious reevaluation of other aspects of the Alaska mission. Though not directly causal, John's dismissal was coincident with a general tightening of policies. Board concerns largely focused on the material transactions of the missionaries and their broader repercussions for the work of the mission. These concerns fell roughly into three categories and were all directly aimed at policies that had developed during John's tenure as mission superintendent. Although the board articulated John's dismissal on purely moral grounds, substantial differences also existed between his vision of missionary service and that of his superiors.

The first and perhaps most direct criticism was the SPG board's disapproval of John's decision in 1897 to hire Lewis Gunther to work for the mission. John had asked John Schoechert in Carmel to engage Gunther at a regular yearly salary. Schoechert reported him to be a good fisherman and a good sailor, both practical and energetic. A healthy man and a willing worker, he would be of value to the missionaries, in John's opinion. Nonetheless, no matter how skilled the potential employee, the board could not countenance a missionary asserting such authority. As a result they prohibited the Alaska missionaries from engaging permanent help without board sanction.[30] They wanted more direct control and interpreted John's initiative as dangerously independent.

The mission board's second major concern was trade. At the same meeting in which they expressed disapproval of John's hiring help without board sanction, the SPG informed the PEC that the missionaries could only order goods through the board and not directly acquire them through trade: "The missionaries must remember their duties are those of missionaries, not of trader; no more trade must be entered into with the natives than is really necessary for the conduct of the work."[31]

This pronouncement has been historically difficult to explain, as sparse mention of trade occurs in the formal correspondence of the Bethel mission for that period. In a manuscript letter inserted in his travel journal in December 1897, John expressed his views on the importance of trade and proposed several entrepreneurial enterprises for the mission. It is not clear whether John ever sent this letter or if the board policy that developed the following spring was in direct reaction to it. Nonetheless, the letter evidences the substantial differences that existed between the board's and John's views on the subject and which motivated the board's decisions:

Mr. President [of the PEC]:
. . . I have had the good of the mission in view, and from my experience, I firmly believe that—a) We can supply ourselves with all the fish we need for any sized school, by packing our fish at Quinhagamut [Quinhagak]. . . . The food supply can easily be augmented by seal meat and blubber. . . .
   2) In regard to fuel. I believe that we can supply ourselves in part at least with coal from Kaluyak [*Qaluyaaq*: Nelson Island]. By trading along the coast and at Nunivak it is possible to in part purchase our boot materials at first cost.
   3) More than ever, I am impressed with the importance of establishing a station . . . at Quinhagamut—for the above reasons and also because, I think Quinhagamut would be the best headquarters for the Reindeer Station.[32]

John's vision of the Alaska mission was ambitious, a much more comprehensive cultural conversion than that advocated by the board. This vision was the result of his numerous practical interchanges along the river in which the exchange of goods played an essential part. The following is typical of John's style:

Yesterday . . . we got into Quinhagamut, and we went to work trading at
once. Of all the running, with Kantucks [singular, qantaq: wooden dish],
and grass baskets, and the various little truck, that make up the possessions
of these people. If my passengers paid fares, I would be making money, but
as it is, they only work their passage, to some extent. At Quinhagamut, I left
with Stephen, some trading stuff to buy me dog food, etc., the boiling pots,
to go for either squirrels or sole leather. I also gave them one seal, skin and
all, also the half of the one that I had skinned, also the half of the blubber.[33]

Along with their participation in Petugtaq distributions and their dispensa-
tion of endless small quantities of goods to native friends and parishioners,
over the years both John and Edith had gradually been caught up in an
endless cycle of exchange. To extricate themselves from this process would
have completely undermined the social indebtedness they had achieved at
such cost. Edith had baked cakes for the Christmas distribution, and John
had carried them to the outlying villages. There he had been fed and
housed, perhaps leaving tobacco in exchange for his dogs' board. On his
return to Bethel he might bring Edith a fox pelt or a grass mat as thanks
from a woman for the marriage cap Edith had neatly sewn and sent her the
fall before. John would then travel on to the next place where his host might
treat him royally, sending him home to the mission with a sled full of frozen
fish in exchange for a set quantity of goods.

All through John's tenure in Bethel, goods and services passed between
the people and the missionaries to their mutual satisfaction. In January 1898
John recorded a list of equivalences in the payment of natives for services
rendered and products contributed.[34] The list begins:

Sold 3 cups tea & 1 lb. tallow = 1 sole leather—1.00
4 lbs tallow = 15 king salmon—1.00
2 heads tobacco = 2 mink.—.25

In 1897 John hoped, if anything, to expand the mission's entrepreneurial
activities to include fish packing, coal mining, and reindeer herding. These
enterprises would have increased the role of trade in the life of the mission
as well as the general exchange of goods and services.

When the mission board proscribed the missionaries' "mercenary activity," they failed to see the exchanges in their comprehensive social context, as acts that created value rather than merely transferring it. For the
board, "trade" was a discrete act, where something was given to obtain
something else that more properly should come directly from the board
itself. They misunderstood the fact that these acts of exchange were not
separate, but were part of a larger system of interrelatedness that the Kilbucks, and with them the mission, had successfully entered.

Second, the board underestimated the extent to which material exhanges
were necessary for the work to proceed in Alaska. By their view, spiritual
work could effectively, and should ideally, be separated from the material

exchanges of this world. John, on the other hand, had a practical sense of ways in which trade, gifting, and other acts of material exchange were both expressive and productive of social and spiritual value. He was, however, not unaware of the pitfalls of such a combination. He concluded his letter to the PEC:

> Much vexation of spirit has been manifested, thro' the year [1897], on account of shall I say "mammon" [the false god of riches and avarice]? The Lord recommended, making friends with mammon, but we none of us know how to go about it. Our little pile of stuff is giving us a lot of trouble, much weariness to the flesh, and vexation of spirit. The brother in charge of this department, certainly should claim our forbearance,—from experience I know what it is to try to work and trade at the same time.[35]

Here John was referring to Brother Helmich's notoriously tight fist. Only when he deemed the natives, and sometimes the missionaries, to be in dire straits would he unlock the supply room and dole out what they requested. Though John and Edith certainly had not left the storehouse open to all comers, their sense of what constituted need was more congruent with the Yup'ik point of view. Perhaps they were simply better aware of how and when reciprocation occurred. What Helmich, and with him the board, took to be gratuitous demands, John understood as part of an ongoing exchange.

John had, in fact, come face to face with the practical difficulties attending the confusion of trading and preaching in his mission work. His description of an incident that occurred at Ougavig in January 1898 provides a good example:

> When I entered that place I found that all the men of the village had gathered together, as if for council. . . . It turned out that the principal object of this mass meeting, was to bring complaints against Kapuchluk as trader and helper. The men would like to see him, either just trader, or helper, and not both. . . . After quite a long session, in the Kashima,—we arrived at this decision, that Kapuchluk is to remain, as he is until summer, when he must decide which he shall be, a trader, or a helper, but he cannot be both. This length of time was given him, so that he can collect his debts, in case he decides to give up trading.

John concluded, "After this experience, and lesson, I do not see how I can accept the steward-ship. I can keep the books, but as to trading, I believe that I must absolutely refuse that job, at least so long as I am a preacher."[36]

In a third step, the board tightened mission policy by issuing detailed guidelines for future administration of the work. According to these guidelines, both the income from the services of medical missionaries and the presents received in repayment for entertaining travelers were to be regarded as mission property. Set rates of compensation were to be fixed for the entertainment of travelers and the care of the sick whites nursed for any considerable duration of time. The gratuitous boarding of pupils at the schools was also to be abolished. The missionaries were to encourage native laborers to donate their labor to the mission without charge, and native helpers were not to be salaried unless their appointment necessitated their leaving home. Finally, the congregations were expected to contribute at least three thousand dollars of the nine thousand dollars annually needed to run the mission, now grown to include fifteen missionaries.[37]

Several reasons account for the general concern regarding business practices expressed in the eight-point policy of the SPG. Though partly a reflection of the board's desire to more tightly and directly control the administration of a mission field that they thought had gone astray, the new policies also responded to a more general financial crisis. At the time the Moravian work in Alaska began, the American Moravian Church hoped that it would not lessen the support it would be able to provide for the overall international work of the Moravian missions. By the beginning of the second decade of work in Alaska, however, the American mission was sending substantially less than usual to the Department of Missions in Germany. Finally, the SPG decided that it would make contributions only to the general mission fund after meeting the expenses of the Alaska mission for which they had originally taken full financial responsibility. Although this decision reduced their financial responsibilities, the board found itself pressed to raise the necessary funds. The 1896–1897 costs for the Alaska mission amounted to close to $10,000, in part due to the rising freight costs brought on by the Yukon gold rush. Unfortunately, less than $3,000 was raised in contributions that year, and the SPG was reluctantly thrown back on its own resources. The eight principles established in August 1898 directly reflected the cost-consciousness resulting from these experiences.

The last major policy decision made by the SPG board in response to the condition of the Bethel mission in 1898 was its search for a general superintendent to replace John. Although not immediately successful, the attempt made clear its desire to more tightly control the work of the Alaska mission in the future. Ironically, the qualities they most needed in a leader, including the ability to make decisions and judgments based on conditions in the field, were precisely those the board sought to curtail. These were the qualities which John had demonstrated and which he would later use to advantage in his work for the Bureau of Education.

CRISIS

With the summer of 1898 came the public announcement of the dismissal of two of the Kuskokwim missionaries (John and Miss Mack) on account of "gross moral delinquency." The board readjusted the missionary forces to accommodate the losses, placing Ernest Weber, Dr. Romig, and John Schoechert in charge of the Ougavig, Bethel, and Carmel districts, respectively. In August the board wrote that the mission in Alaska was passing through a "grave crisis,"[38] but they were not referring exclusively to the demoralization and confusion wrought by John's imminent departure. Before their new leadership had a chance to try its wings, the mission's problems were compounded by the tragic drowning of Ernest and Caroline Weber as they attempted to return to the Kuskokwim.

The year's furlough had proved a success and by the spring Caroline Weber was restored to good health. The family traveled overland to San Francisco, sailing from there to Unalaska where they awaited passage to the Kuskokwim. Meanwhile, gold fever had struck the Yukon, and many would-be miners also coveted transportation north. Finally, almost two months after their arrival, a party of prospectors offered them free passage to the Kuskokwim in exchange for their services as guide and interpreter. The Webers agreed, and the party set out by steamer for Goodnews Bay, where they transferred to a small sternwheel river steamer, the *Jessie*.

While the transfer was in progress, Brother Weber made a quick trip by kayak up the Kuskokwim with the precious mail bag. At Quinhagak he was greeted by Edith and her daughter Ruth but left at once to return to the ship. This brief meeting was the last time the missionaries saw Brother Weber. By the time he arrived back at the steamer, the barometer was dropping rapidly; however, the prospectors had already loaded two barges the *Jessie* had in tow, and the party decided to push ahead. They left Goodnews on June 27; almost immediately a storm began to blow. Hoping to be of help, John set out in the *Swan* down the coast toward Goodnews. He ran aground, however, and as the storm was coming on fast, he was forced to return to Quinhagak.

The storm raged strong for three days, with high winds and rain. Although the missionaries waiting back at Quinhagak were hopeful that the *Jessie* had found safe anchorage and had waited out the winds, after the storm had passed, the *Jessie* failed to arrive. Later, bits of wreckage were washed up along the coast. All hands went down with the ship, and the mission lost the couple they had most relied on to fill the Kilbucks' place.

With the Webers' death and the Kilbucks' imminent departure, the mission was in danger of being left, after thirteen years in operation, without anyone fluent in the Yup'ik language or knowledgeable about the area. More important, no one else had achieved standing among the people or demonstrated personal rapport equal to that attained by the Kilbucks and the Webers. With their loss it was feared the mission, like the *Jessie*, would founder and break apart.

In the wake of these troubles the missionaries held a conference on July 25 at which they reassigned and readjusted their forces. Brother Helmich was placed in charge of the Ougavig mission, assisted by the newly arrived Brother and Sister Weinlick. Edith's brother, Herman Romig, remained in charge of the Bethel mission, with Helper Neck residing in nearby Napaskiak and from there ministering to the tundra villages. Then, as news of John's dismissal had arrived too late to allow them time to pack their belongings, it was decided that John and Edith should remain. John was to serve along with Brother Kawagleg at Quinhagak, where he might put his efforts towards work translating the scriptures as well as building projects connected with the new mission station.

Back in Bethlehem, the mission board received the news of their losses with consternation. Along with the details of the Webers' deaths, the mails brought them inquiries from John as to whether or not he should return his ordination certificates or destroy them himself. He also wrote to ask if the mission board forbade him from remaining in any part of Alaska or just the Kuskokwim region and whether or not he was excluded from membership in the Moravian Church. At a session held at the end of August the board answered that he need not destroy his documents, that he was excluded only from the areas in Alaska occupied by the mission, although the board would not pay his way home unless he traveled within the next year, that his membership was forfeited in mission congregations, and that he was to reapply for admission in the home church.

As the situation in Alaska seemed to require extraordinary consideration, in November 1898 the SPG board made a formal plea for John's retention in mission service. Their petition cited a long list of reasons for their request: the peculiar situation in Alaska, where no other missionary was conversant in the Yup'ik language; John's full and humble repentance of a sin committed nearly six years before; the fact that he was providentially compelled to remain in Alaska over the winter; the feeling that he had already been sufficiently punished; the "deplorable" effect his dismissal would have on the native membership and the public in general; the fact that there were many examples of men who had sinned as grievously as he and yet repented and given useful service; and finally, that his "innocent wife" suffered and was punished even more than he, when she could yet be of service in Alaska. As a result of this plea, which the SPG Board unanimously adopted, John was punished even more than he, when she could yet be of service in Alaska. As a result of this plea, which the SPG board unanimously adopted, John a year, to work for the mission in a lay capacity.[39]

Over the winter of 1898–1899 the Alaska mission moved steadily along with no major disturbances. John and Edith continued their work at Quinhagak, on the mission fringe, in a solitude they seemed to find comforting after all the troubles of the past several years. Little record remains of this year. As John was no longer taken up by missionary travels, there was no need or opportunity to exchange journals with a homebound wife. There may also have been more personal reasons why the year left no written record. For a time, silence descended. In the spring of 1899, however, a series of human and natural misfirings again threw the mission into disarray. The ice had been late to leave the river, and the weather was stormy and uncertain at the river mouth; as a result, the supply vessel failed to arrive, leaving the missionaries to spend the summer and fall searching for provisions to last through the coming winter.

Although the missionaries were able to obtain some dry goods from St. Michael before freeze-up, the winter of 1899–1900 proved hard, and food was scarce. The missionaries spent a good deal of time working to supply themselves with fish and game. On one occasion, when out ice fishing in mid-November, John accidently cut his right hand on a rusty fish hook that he had left inside his mitten. Although Dr. Romig treated the wound, blood poisoning set in. Surgery failed to correct the condition. Romig wrote in the mission journal:

> 11/27/1899   As blood poisoning was imminent and the infection extending further up the arm, the hand and forearm being dispared of, Bro. Kilbuck's right arm was amputated today about midway between the elbow and the shoulder joint. The operation took one hour. Dr. Romig performed it. . . .
>   The struggle was hard to loose the arm and for those who had to perform the operation. But as a last hope to save life the operation was performed.[40]

Romig's operation was a medical coup and saved John's life. Also, as the natives had never heard of such a thing, John's stature increased when he successfully came out from under the surgeon's scalpel. To this day, Bethel oral tradition enshrines his ordeal. By some accounts John is said to have cut the arm off himself, and reports both abound and differ in their descriptions of where and how the arm was actually buried.

John's amputation had permanent repercussions in the way the people of the Kuskokwim drainage perceived him, but it only temporarily affected his work. Although his fine right-handed script was a thing of the past, he told Edith that he had no intention of letting his disability handicap him. He was true to his word. Not only did he quickly develop a functional left-handed writing style, but he also learned to shoot a gun and man a boat using his left arm.

As if this incident were not enough personal trauma for one season, "sins of the flesh" again beset the missionaries. The peace reestablished between John and the mission was dramatically and irreparably shattered in December 1899, when Herman Romig wrote in the mission journal, "After the confession of Louisa that the father of her infant son is none other than Mr. J. H. Kilbuck. Mr. Kilbuck admits on inquiry that he is the father of the child. A clear case of adultery with no excuses." Three months later he added, "The mother of Mr. Kilbuck's illegitimate child is very sick and the child will likely be left an orphan for him to care for. He has been informed of these facts and says that he will provide for the child."[41]

Not until spring 1900 did the home boards receive the news of this final act, committed in the spring of the previous year. Their response was immediate and absolute. They at once dismissed John from the service of the Moravian mission in every capacity, and the following August the SPG announced a total disassociation: "The solemn duty has devolved upon us to . . . announce that the former exemplary and valued superintendent, the heroic and once well-nigh idolized John Kilbuck, persistently pursues the course from which we all believed he had turned away . . . and compels our board . . . to give notice that there is now absolutely no connection remaining between Kilbuck and our mission in Alaska."[42]

The SPG and PEC boards bitterly resented John's relapse. Whereas his original crime had been a demonstration of human weakness that, as men, they could understand and as church leaders they could pardon, this second breach of decorum was an unbearable slap in the face. Likely the boards were mortified that they had placed trust and shown forbearance towards a man who still failed to follow the rules.

Also, John's rise within the church had, over the years, come to represent a profound cultural as well as personal triumph for the leadership of the Moravian church. Delaware by birth, he was a child of their missions who they had nurtured and taught and then proudly sent forth as a model of all they hoped a mission might accomplish. With John's fall, this myth of complete conversion also was shattered, and the resentment and bitterness attending its loss were profound.

Finally, the fact that John's affair was consummated with a Yup'ik woman is significant. Although the growth of a relationship beyond the bounds of propriety between John and a fellow missionary could be made comprehensible as the physical expression of a deep spiritual bond, a relationship with a native woman was unforgivable. John had stepped back over the imaginary line separating the world of the native convert and the non-native missionary. As a boy he had chosen to cross the line once and had been idealized for doing so. That he, more than any other, could backslide was unendurable to those who had so carefully raised him. In October 1900 the editor of *The Moravian* requested instructions as to whether he should publish letters of greeting to Edith Kilbuck on her return from Alaska. The board of the PEC instructed him to decline to publish them and to avoid any public reference to the Kilbucks in the future.[43] After this incident, the Kilbucks were not mentioned again in official correspondence for more than ten years.

GOING HOME

In the wake of the disclosures of 1900, John and Edith prepared to leave Alaska. As the Census Bureau had offered John employment again as a temporary agent to gather statistics along the Kuskokwim, John decided that Edith should precede him to the States and that he would follow at the end of the summer. Their farewells in Bethel were brief and subdued. From there they traveled together to Quinhagak, where Edith remained while John traveled down the coast to begin his census enumerations. By the end of May he returned. On July 7 the *Pearl* anchored just below Quinhagak, and the next day John accompanied his family on board. There he said good-bye to Edith, Joe, and "baby" Ruth and returned up the river. His job was to enumerate the living, but as events unfolded, it became a long and dreary naming of the dead.

The journal that John kept for Edith during the summer of 1900 is a stark monument to one of the worst epidemics western Alaska ever experienced. Rivaling in impact the devastation left in the wakes of the smallpox epidemic of 1838–1839 and the influenza pandemic of 1918–1919, the "grippe" or influenza that raged along the river after the arrival of the *Pearl* in 1900 carried away an estimated 50 percent of the population, wiping out the elderly and the sick, the young and the frail, and many in between. Moreover, the speed with which it struck set it apart from epidemics experienced before or after. Within days, whole villages were sick or dying. To this day along the Kuskokwim, elders still reckon events in relation to the "great sickness."[44]

John's journal entries for that summer were unusually terse and unelaborated, the first he wrote in his newly mastered left-handed style. In his first letter to Edith after her departure he wrote, "We arrived at Bethel, the Swan beating us by an hour or so. Everybody of the natives glad to see me. I however, felt like a lost sheep, with you out of the country, I have no pleasure here. . . . Dear Edith, I miss you more than ever, as I never did before. I think of you all the time, and when I think of the children a lump sticks in my throat."[45]

Ten days after John set out from Bethel toward Apokak, he began his journal with brief entries:

> July 25. The Influenza or "gripp" around. . . .
> July 26 . . . Grip is raging above us.
> 28th. I get the grippe.
> July 29th Nearly every body down with the epidemic.[46]

On August 2 he mentioned the first death, an old woman. The next day another woman succumbed. From then on, he alternately worked on the census and helped to bury the dead.

Gradually, John moved past Bethel and on up the Kuskokwim to the Stony River. Rainy and cold weather added to the misery of the people. On his way John listed the names of the dead he and Edith knew: "Oh! but it is some thing dreadful, the way the epidemic mowed down the people." On his arrival in Bethel he wrote, "The measles were out while I was gone up the river and depopulated the country. This summer there were 57 deaths in Bethel alone. I believe the deaths from here up, will soon number 250! Nearly all our loved ones are gone." On September 24 John set off on his final trip downriver as he left for the States. On his way he wrote, "The mortality below Bethel is some thing frightful. Napaxyaxaxamiut [Napakiak] is literally [gone]." At the same time John mentally took leave of the Kuskokwim, many of his Yup'ik friends and converts were also departing.[47]

Back in Bethel Dr. Romig did his best to cope with the sickness and its rapid spread, but he could do little. Perhaps he felt the irony of the situation—the civilization committed to cleanliness had introduced deadly germs that would strike down a defenseless and epidemiologically virgin people. Nor did the Yupiit miss the fact that it was their people, not the whites, who succumbed. Resentment ran deep, and the hostile feelings produced that summer took years to dispel. Prior to 1900 Romig's prestige had grown in proportion to his ability to miraculously cure. The epidemic abruptly curtailed his ascendancy, and he never fully recovered his reputation.[48] Thanks to his timely departure, John's stature remained undiminished.

The Yup'ik association of illness with infraction of taboo probably added to the people's sense of guilt and despair during the summer of 1900. John later described an old man's claim that in trusting the white man's way, the Yupiit had brought the epidemic on themselves.[49] Yet the Yupiit were caught in a vicious cycle. If the sickness was the result of their breach with the past, its effect was to obliterate any chance of returning. The tradition bearers lay dead and dying, and much of the detailed knowledge of Yup'ik oral tradition and ceremony was irretrievably lost with them.

On this cheerless note John set sail toward Dutch Harbor, where he finished his census work while he waited to book passage to Seattle. Not until the end of October did he board the steamer *Newport*. On the slow journey south, John's journal entries begin to expand, and he provided brief pictures of such ports as Karluk, Homer, Seldovia, and Valdez. Also, for the first time, he turned his attention toward future business opportunities: "In regard to my future business, I begin to get some light, but I do not see my way as clearly yet, as we can reasonably expect in this world of uncertainty. There is a party on board, who think of prospecting the Kuskoquim for fish and for that purpose setting up a salting station. I may make use of my knowledge in this line, and get into something better than the fur trade."[50] John wrote that his time at home would be considerably shortened. Even before his arrival in the States his thoughts were turned back toward Alaska.

John handed in his census work on his arrival in Juneau, and the census officer informed him that no less than Governor Brady was anxious to see him: "The Gov.—wants me to go into missionary service for the Presbyterian Church. The Governor knows my position, for Mr. Lyons frankly told me that he heard about and the Governor asked him for verification. Still the Gov. wants to give me work." Though John had no chance to pay the governor a visit, he later wrote Edith, "Well, Hon, I have thot much about this plan of the Governor's. One thing I have decided, and this is I will not *ask for service*, or put myself in the way for it—and then if it comes to me *in spite of everything* else, I will seriously and contientiously consider about accepting it."[51]

As the *Newport* continued down along the coast, John found further opportunities to discuss future business possibilities with his fellow passengers. The question of how to make a living was on his mind, and he attacked the problem with increasing energy. Every plan pivoted on his return to Alaska. He wrote, "You see I am not travelling for nothing, but I am studying business." [52]

As his voyage neared completion, John turned his thoughts from means to ends:

> My dear Edith, there has never been a time in my life, when I tho't more about and, in all my planning, the end and aim has always been your well fare. . . . [O]nce I dreamed of my being about to be wedded to some one else, a total stranger, with you in the room, and you not having any objections. I was so puzzled that I woke up, and was so relieved to find it all a dream, and also that *before* I got married, I was awakened. . . . Well, Hon—I will now stop, before you get too much love (?), and be able to stand a little, when I reach you.

Several pages further, the journal and the journey quietly come to an end: "Goodbye, I your husband—what thinks enough of you to scribble these lines for you. *John.*" [53]

RETURN TO NEW WESTFIELD

When Edith left the Kuskokwim mouth in mid-July, she traveled south to San Francisco and then overland to her old home at the New Westfield Mission in Kansas. There she was met by her father, Joseph Romig, who had returned to Ottawa that spring to serve once more at the mission where Edith was born. Brother Charles Steinfort had been in charge of the New Westfield Mission from 1885 until March 1900, coincident with the Kilbucks' tenure in Alaska. While the Alaska mission had grown and prospered during this time, the Kansas Indian mission had not. By 1899 the mission family had dwindled to sixty-nine people, no longer enough to justify a full-time missionary, let alone a school or other support services. The result was that in 1900 the Moravian Church withdrew official support for the New Westfield Mission. Steinfort departed, and Joseph Romig came out of retirement to assume temporary charge as missionary-without-pay.

Joseph Romig's and the Kilbucks' return to the mission coincided not only with the withdrawal of mission support, but the withdrawal of federal support as well. On November 8, 1900, after Edith's arrival but before John's, the federal government issued patents to the Indians remaining at the mission, formally dissolving their trust relationship. Following an assimilationist policy that would eventually reach all the way to Alaska with the passage of the Alaska Native Claims Settlement Act in 1971, the law required the Indians at New Westfield to trade their aboriginal rights to the land they occupied for a set amount of property and cash. Though the transition from tribal to civil government was rarely easy, the fact that the mission had also withdrawn its support exacerbated the situation of the Indians of New West-field. At the same time that the federal government chose to make Indians citizens and "free men," the mission decided that their diminished numbers could not justify formal church assistance. Virtually overnight, the Indians were left inexperienced and unguided, with taxes to pay and schools to support.

Returning to New Westfield with scant resources and without work, the Romigs and the Kilbucks immediately stepped into the void created by the formal discharge of federal and mission rights and duties. On January 1, 1901, John and Edith bought the mission property, including both the mission residence and the chapel, from the Moravian Church. The house they patched and painted, creating a home they could return to on furloughs when in Alaska. The chapel they deeded as a gift to the people of New Westfield, and the congregation named it Kilbuck Chapel in their honor. There both John and his father-in-law kept the services, independent of the Mission Society.[54]

In retrospect it is difficult to judge the character and quality of the four years that John, Edith, and Joseph Romig spent at New Westfield. As they lived together under one roof, there was no call for the long journals that passed between them and tell us so much about other years. Rather, only a handful of still portraits remain from which to reconstruct their lives.

Perhaps most moving is the picture, painted years later by their daughter Ruth, of their first Christmas at home after so many years. It was December 1900, and John had been back less than a month. All the family gathered in the large woodframe mission house. There was Grandpa Romig, along with Uncle Gene and Uncle Ben, Edith's younger brothers who were attending college at Lawrence, Kansas, at the time and made their home with them. Various other aunts, uncles, and cousins came to welcome John home. Best of all, both Harry and Katie came home from school to be with their family. Ruth was only nine then, and eighty-seven years later she recalled this, out of all her Christmases, as the best she had ever known. This was partly because of the abundance of presents, compared to the small gifts which had made Christmas along the Kuskokwim. What made the day special, however, was the fact that it was the first time since she was a baby that the family had all gathered together in one place at one time. With Katie and Harry going back to school, it was also the last. In thinking over the implications of what she had said, Ruth added, "That was the only time our family, Mother, Father, Joe, Harry, Katie, and I were all together, here, in this world. And you know what? This is the first time I ever thought of it."[55] Although their work in Alaska had pulled and would continue to pull their family physically apart, separation was experienced as a condition of life and not as a deprivation. Ruth found the absence of the separation remarkable, not the separation itself.

Fig. 11.5. Kilbuck family portrait, Ottawa, Kansas, 1900. (Kilbuck family)

Fig. 11.6. The mission house at New Westfield, circa 1900. From left to right, Katie, Edith, Ruth, Joe, and Harry Kilbuck, Herman and Ella Romig, and Joseph Romig, Sr., seated. (Romig Collection, Anchorage Museum of History and Art)

Fig. 11.7. Tableau entitled "The Last of the Mohicans." John Kilbuck and his daughter Katie photographed in the mission yard at New Westfield, September 1903. (Moravian Archives)

Another picture illustrating John and Edith's years at New Westfield shows a summer scene in front of the mission house, where the family was gathered to be photographed. The picture does not show them locked into a tight formal group. Rather, the camera is removed from its subjects, who seem to wander into its view in a scattered, random manner. Edith and Katie sit to one side, while Joseph Romig sits in a chair to the other. Back slightly stands Harry Kilbuck and Herman and Ella Romig. Everyone appears quiet and subdued, as if caught off guard on their way toward some goal not yet in view.

Another photograph from this period is opposite in character. In it John and his elder daughter Katie are dressed in fringed buckskin and surrounded by numerous artifacts brought home from the Kuskokwim. Together they depict a formal tableau entitled "The Last of the Mohicans." The similarity of John's own position with that of the romanticized Indian he portrayed is not past remarking.

John and Edith stayed at New Westfield just under four years. Edith kept house and cared for the children while John farmed the rich bottomlands and helped his father-in-law with the mission and school. All the while, he considered his future work. Although he made inquiries into various business-related schemes, none ever materialized. By the fall of 1903 another plan presented itself, one that would take the Kilbucks back to Alaska and place them in service of a different kind.

On November 21, 1902, at the opening exercises of the new schoolhouse at New Westfield, John gave a short talk entitled "My First Day at School" in which he recalled his entry into the mission school thirty years before.[56] This step had shaped the course of John's entire life. Perhaps remembering his own experience, when a request came from the United States Bureau of Education to return to Alaska as a teacher at the new school in Barrow, John accepted. Though sorry to leave their children, all four of whom stayed behind in school while their parents were gone, both John and Edith were anxious for work. With the purchase of the New Westfield property they had gone into debt for the first time in their lives. A return to Alaska promised financial relief, and once again they made plans to head north.

CHAPTER 12

NEW MISSION

MOVE TO BARROW

John and Edith greeted the invitation to return to Alaska with satisfaction and relief. Although distressed at the prospect of breaking apart their family, in the winter of 1904 their financial resources were virtually exhausted and they had no clear plan to bring themselves out of debt. The job offered by the United States Bureau of Education was a means both to reestablish their footing in the material world and to return to the place where John, especially, wanted to work.

John initially inquired about employment beginning in the summer of 1905; however, the bureau wrote back that if they could ship to Alaska in the spring, they were wanted immediately. The bureau was as glad for the Kilbucks' inquiry as the Kilbucks were for the bureau's enthusiastic response. After a brief and rapid-fire correspondence, John signed a contract with the Bureau of Education to teach among the Inupiat of northern Alaska for a twelve-month period beginning June 1, 1904. The understanding was that he would teach in Barrow through the first winter and move to Wainwright the next summer, where he would oversee the erection of a schoolhouse and hold classes through the following year.

June 1904 found both John and Edith bound for Nome aboard the *St. Paul*. On their arrival John described the character of the philanthropic work he found in progress in the region. Regardless of his statements' accuracy concerning the situation in northern Alaska, they say a great deal about the attitude John brought with him concerning the manner in which cultural conversion should ideally take place.

From my own observation I came to the conclusion that the people who seem to have the interest of the natives at heart, are endeavoring to make the same mistake that was made in the case of the Indians. There is talk about reservations, and government rations etc. This arrangement of course would of necessity create the office of Eskimo Agent, and some business house will be obliged to send in a stock of shop worn goods and musty bacon, all at the price of good goods. Let us hope that such a thing will never come to pass. The Eskimo thus far have been self supporting, and are fully capable to continue to be so, with proper direction. At present the natives who live beyond the reach of gratuitous help, are a much better sight to look upon, with their mark of sturdy independence, than the abject and dirty appearance of the loafer about Nome, expecting to receive grub from some body who thinks he is philanthropic.[1]

On August 10 the Kilbucks landed safely at Point Barrow. John described what they found on coming ashore, a world "white in winter and brown the other part of the year." About two hundred Inupiat inhabited the point. An additional seventy native men lived with their families several miles to the west at the Cape Smyth whaling station. Operated by Charles Brower (a former sailor employed by the Pacific Steam Whaling Company), the station consisted of "several large warehouses, the dwelling—large enough to house several crews of whaling ships—and cabins for the Eskimo. About half a mile from the Whaling Station is the Government school building— erected in 1905,—and the Presbyterian mission, maintained since '98. The rest of the town is strung out for fully a mile down the coast."[2]

In the winter of 1905 John described the natural resources on which the coastal Inupiat depended:

Now I will turn your attention to the sea, the Arctic Ocean. To the Eskimo, the sea is what the farm is to you. Out of the sea, he makes his living, and his wealth. The seal, walrus, polar bear, and the Bowhead whale, are the particular crops that are to be harvested. The Bowhead is the most valuable; his body is large enough to furnish food and oil for a village for an entire winter, and his mouthful of bone will buy anything that the white man brings in his big ship. Seals and bear are to be had at all seasons of the year, if they can be found. The whale is only secured in the early Spring, as he passes here, on his migration eastward. . . . About the 15 of April the shore whalers, move out on the ice, and live there for about six weeks, or until the ice becomes untenable.[3]

Along with the economic and environmental contours of the landscape, John also briefly described the social divisions of the region as he understood them. He distinguished between the inland and coastal-dwelling Inupiat and remarked on the feuding that characterized intergroup relations until just before his arrival: "The present custom of blanket tossing after a successful whaling season is a relic of wartimes. In former days upon the return of a

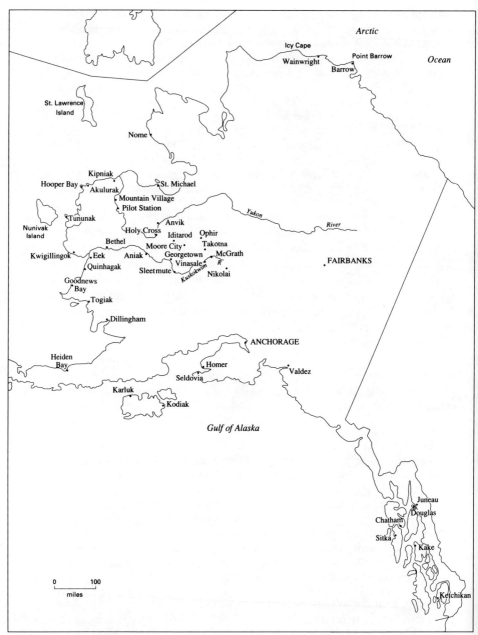

Map 4. *Alaska, 1900*

successful raiding party from the inland, blanket tossing was one of the features of the celebration that usually followed."[4]

John estimated that several hundred Inupiat lived in the interior of the arctic slope region, regularly coming to the coast to trade caribou skins for whale oil and meat; however, he gave no further detail on traditional social divisions. This is understandable, as employment had attracted many inland Eskimos to the coast (primarily Barrow), where the Inupiat had already experienced more than a quarter of a century of direct contact with non-natives before the Kilbucks arrived. Shore whaling had begun at Point Barrow in 1884, the year before the Kilbucks arrived on the Kuskokwim, and by 1893, five hundred Inupiat men and their families were gathered at the whaling station.[5] Whereas the Kilbucks had constituted a major factor in changing the face of life along the Kuskokwim, in northern Alaska they entered a social environment already substantially altered by a commercial enterprise that had passed the Kuskokwim by.

Throughout his descriptions John depicted Point Barrow as perched on the geographic edge of the North American continent on the outskirts of what he termed the "world movement":

> Here we come into daily touch with an age that carries us into the prehistoric times. . . . In the villages, the posts for the caches and racks—are the ribs of whales—and the crotches to hold the cross pieces are the lower jawbones of the polar bear. In every day use are stone lamps, with moss for wicks—flint and bone instruments for tanning hides—flint and steel in place of matches—stone, handled with bone, for maul and hammer.
>
> The arrival of the world movement is evidenced by the stove pipes sticking out of every hut and cabin,—frame cabins scattered thru the village—built of lumber brot in by trading ships and whalers from the states—usually painted red and trimmed with white—stoves—granite ware utensils for kitchen and table—sewing machines—phonographs—flour, sugar, tea, coffee—rice, beans—all these things are to be found in greater or less quantity in every village of the north. . . . Among the new articles requisitioned by one of the wealthy Eskimos is a pedometer—probably to use in his hunting expeditions, or to determine the number of miles he must travel in herding his domesticated Reindeer—of which he has several hundred.[6]

On his arrival John viewed himself as witness to a tremendous cultural transformation already in progress. In his opinion, the balance of the changes had been for the better: "What have the missions and schools done for these people? Viewed from the standpoint of material good, there has been a great advance in the physical condition, approaching the physical features of civilization." However, change was at a cost: "[The people possess] natural honesty [and are] learning to deceive from the methods of the white traders. The idea of getting even, nothing for nothing and very little for five dollars. In changing $10, charge a commission of $2.00."[7]

Into this human landscape John and Edith arrived, armed with strong opinions and bent on using their combined energy and experience to affect the course of the future of the Inupiat people. Neither of the Kilbucks directly compared the Yup'ik Eskimos of western Alaska and the Inupiat Eskimos of the Arctic coast. Early descriptive passages mention gross economic differences, including the Inupiat reliance on sea mammal hunting, specifically whaling, as opposed to the dependence on the salmon fishery that characterized the Kuskokwim Eskimos. They assumed, however, that these Eskimos were a variation on a people they already knew well. Although the timing of the harvest, the species harvested, and the methods of food preservation were different, the Eskimos of northern Alaska shared with their southern relatives a common reliance on the products of the land and sea for food and clothing. Historical and social differences were only parenthetically remarked.

The combined effect of their prior experience along the Kuskokwim and their comforting, albeit distorted, sense of familiarity enabled them to quickly assess the situation. It also gave them the confidence to start to work almost immediately on a program of cultural and economic reform. John's position as school teacher differed considerably in externals from his past role as preacher and spiritual advisor. As a salaried employee of the federal government, he was responsible to a power structure that differed significantly from that of the mission board of the Moravian Church. In the Arctic, however, his basic program of activity remained remarkably similar to what it had been during his last years along the Kuskokwim.

FROM PREACHER TO TEACHER

The Bureau of Education had hired John to teach school, and the classroom became the primary arena of his activity. Alhough not without experience, John had only intermittently held responsibility for the school at Bethel, preferring and excelling in the work of itinerant missionary. As soon as he arrived in Barrow, however, he set to work to clear out the supplies that crowded the small frame chapel that the Presbyterian missionary, Mr. Spriggs, had made available for his use as a schoolhouse that winter. On September 26 he opened its doors, and armed with the *New McGuffey's Reader*, *Rice's Rational Spelling Book*, and *Hall's Arithmetic Primer*, he began to preach the value of English and mathematics.

From the time the school opened, things looked bright. Some young scholars whistled, wiggled, and wandered about physically, but John managed to keep them on track. At the end of the second day of classes he wrote, "For about half an hour today I had my little ones so interested and busy that every tot kept his or her place and never took eyes off their work. I feel encouraged, altho' by [the time] school was out I was as tired as any farmer ever gets walking after a plow."[8]

Over the next four years John successfully communicated basic skills to his young scholars. Through a combination of personal sensitivity and cultural suppression, he was able to effect substantial changes. Although the modern policy of "assertive discipline" had yet to be invented, John was certainly cognizant of its underlying principles. For example, he described his attempt to teach English: "I reduced the school to absolute silence for ten minutes, by giving them permission to talk in the English." Later that year, he required any student that spoke Inupiaq during school hours to stand up: "During the first few days, I had nearly the entire school upon their feet at times. . . . Today I only had a few scholars who were obliged to stand up."[9] John understood the power of peer pressure. In actual practice he relied more often on positive reward: "The greatest freedom is allowed in the school room, about consulting each other about their work, and it is noticable how the pupils keep out of mischief. The rule that all speaking must be in the English is responsible for the quiet that prevails, and the privilege to talk to each other even during school hours, is a great incentive toward the use of the English language."[10]

Just as John's approach to teaching English bore the stamp of his practical comprehension of group dynamics, so did his efforts in the cause of arithmetic. His primary goal was to better fit his students for situations they would face in their future work as householders, herders, whalers, and, in some instances, traders. John designed lessons in addition and subtraction with this in mind. His requisition for his second year of teaching included two sets of tin money of all denominations.[11] After Christmas 1906 the arithmetic hour evolved into "keeping store."

> The blackboard was the store, upon which a list of household articles and provisions, and other articles necessary and otherwise, was plainly written and the prices. Several of the advanced scholars, acted as clerks, selling and making out the bills of sale. The rest of the school was given cardboard money (homemade) with which to purchase any article desired,—the only limit being the amount of money on hand. . . . It is needless to say that this method of learning the use of Arithmetic was popular, for it was intensely so. It also served to give occasion for a word of advice about economy and care in buying. . . .
>
> The school divided up into three distinct kinds or class of buyers.
>
> (1) One class was distinguishedly careful, and their characteristic features were in knowing what was wanted, and in never spending all the money in hand. There were not many in this class. Some of these have gone out of the store without buying—because the articles desired were not to be had.
>
> (2) In this class the buyers were careful enough, buying first of all the necessities of life,—but never stopped until the last penny had been spent. The majority of the school comprised this class.
>
> (3) The members of this class put all their money into useless and extravagant articles—things that showed well, were their hobby. . . . Strange to relate, however, there were but few in this class,—about as many as in the first class.[12]

John's years spent along the Kuskokwim were not in vain, and he was able to use the schoolhouse as an arena in which to communicate the two skills he thought the Inupiat would most need if they were to succeed in their dealings with the outside world—the ability to speak and a rudimentary understanding of the mechanics of monetary exchange. Along with these skills John taught the value of thrift, industry, and economy. Be there no doubt that the third class of buyers was made to know the error of their ways as surely as any sinner.

John was effective as a teacher and cultural translator because of his ability to create meaningful metaphors to better communicate his message. Much like the rhetoric of the Moravian helpers who had trained under him in Bethel, his lectures evoked imagery that worked to connect his message to the Inupiat way of life as a first step in transforming it. In one of his first lectures to the school, John likened learning to hunting as a way of justifying and explaining the etiquette he believed his classroom required. Even the form of his discourse, in which the argument is presented in three different ways before the final point is made, recalls traditional Yup'ik rhetorical structure in which narrative action is organized according to a tripartite scheme.[13]

> The older scholars have been as a rule well behaved, but lately there was a growing tendency to hilarity and much unnecessary talking. . . . I concluded to try an appeal to their reason. . . . In the middle of the afternoon session, I called the school to attention—Then I said: Do you know what it is to hunt? ("Yes" from some of the older scholars.) Here you hunt the bear, the whale, the fox, the seal, and ducks. The whale you hunt, in a boat, a skin boat. How many men are in one boat? (Some one said 8; George said, some more, some less.) Well, say, there are 8 men to a boat. Now, while they hunt, the whale, do they make a noise with their paddles? ("No!")
>
> Do they talk and laugh? ("No.")
>
> If you hunt a fox, and see one, do you make a noise? ("No"). No, of course not, but you try to get near enough to shoot the fox, by go[ing] along with as little noise as possible.
>
> When you are hunting ducks, and you see a flock of ducks flying toward you, do you walk around in plain sight of the ducks? ("No") No! You sit down, or lie down, and are as quiet as possible.
>
> Now when you come to school, you are hunting.
>
> You are hunting for something to put in your mind. You look in your books, and you want to get something out of those books. If you talk and laugh and make wise and walk around—you will not get anything from your books. . . .
>
> Your mind may be quick to learn, and you have good books, still if you make noise, talking and laughing, you will not learn. The men lose the whale, you lose the fox or the duck, and you lose, what you might learn from your books. I don't lose it, but you lose it.
>
> But the men are glad when they get the whale, you are glad when you get

a fox,—so you will be glad when you learn to read, write, and use figures, and what you get will do you good! Now, you may take your books again.[14]

Though John's sympathy for the people among whom he worked greatly facilitated a mutual comprehension, he constantly strove for a total transformation of the Inupiat way of life. The answers he gave to a litany of questions put to him in the spring of 1905 make clear the character of his goals. When asked "What is a medicine-man?" John answered "A worker of lies." When asked if it was wrong to sing a charm song when out hunting, John answered, "Yes, God is the only one to whom we should tell our wants and ask for them from Him." Likewise he advised that floors should not be scrubbed with urine, men should not hunt on Sunday, and dogs could not go to heaven.[15]

As along the Kuskokwim, John was outspoken in his opposition to daily acts grounded in traditional metaphysics and was anxious to replace Inupiat rules of action with his own. Just as he had encouraged industry and thrift in the classroom store, he promoted modern hygiene and Christian prayer. At the conclusion of this barrage, he wrote that "someone who will direct and lead these inquirers is sadly needed."[16] John was ready to fill that role as much as his secularized position would permit.

John assessed the lives of the Inupiat as limited in the extreme: "No one can realize how little of life these people live,—a life such as the foxes held down by ignorance, he nonetheless considered them clear of the greater sin of living "below their abilities and opportunities."[17] As a consequence, they were worth his efforts. He viewed these people as he had viewed the Yupiit—shrouded in darkness—and his responsibility was to bring them into the light. It is unlikely that the Inupiat shared this condescending vision of their presumed inferiority any more than had their Kuskokwim relatives before them.

TALKING, HEALING, TRAVELING

Although the classroom was the focus of John's activity during his years in northern Alaska, both he and Edith also devoted energy towards speaking, healing, and traveling as they had along the Kuskokwim. None of these endeavors received the attention they had in years past or would in the future. Nonetheless, the Kilbucks continued to view them as important aspects of their new mission.

Turning first to learning Inupiaq, John and Edith were under the false impression that the language spoken along the northern coast of Alaska was a dialect of the Central Yup'ik language they had learned to speak along the Kuskokwim, and as such could be easily mastered. The reaction of the Inupiat to their attempts at direct communication reinforced this assumption: "To a limited extent we were able to converse with all the Eskimos we met, and we always received a hearty handshake from them. I think they took us to be Eskimos too, some species they had never seen before."[18]

Although their intentions were good, John and Edith never succeeded in mastering Inupiaq. Unlike their Kuskokwim parishioners, many of the Inupiat with whom they had regular dealings already spoke English, having learned it from the whalers and traders who had worked in the vicinity of Barrow and Wainwright for the previous two decades. The ones that did speak Inupiaq—the children—were the objects of John's pedagogical efforts, and consequently he had little opporunity to converse in Inupiaq in the classroom. Edith's activities focused primarily on her household responsibilities rather than the wider community. Although the visitors she received provided an opportunity for her to learn the native language, she did not put forth effort in that direction. Rather, her thoughts were turned to the life she had left behind and which she hoped to resume after their term in Alaska was done. Both John and Edith had arrived on the Kuskokwim ready to make their lives there. Toward that end, they were open to all that they might absorb from the people and the place. They came to Barrow twenty years later and twenty years older, still willing to work but perhaps not so able to change.

The limited medical ministry John and Edith carried out in Barrow was more successful than their effort to learn the language. They came supplied with a variety of homeopathic medicines, and John's contract with the bureau provided reimbursement for his efforts towards the maintenance of community health. Nevertheless, the soap that they handed out and Edith's persistent battle for better hygiene comprised their biggest contributions.

Despite John and Edith's few resources, the people appreciated what they were able to do. In late summer 1905 John wrote that Edith had been given the first salmon trout taken that season in thanks for medicine she had brought to a sick child. She also regularly visited the sick, bringing hot soup and bread when no medicine was available. John would later write, "The people are certainly grateful, and they frequently express the opinion, that but for the medicine, the tundra would be covered with boxes." [19]

During his years along the Arctic coast, John's travels were also more circumscribed than they had been in western Alaska. As with his mastery of the language, the hours he spent in the classroom constrained his ability to journey over the landscape. Although John's own traveling was limited, especially during his first year in Barrow, he filled his journals with the comings and goings of the Inupiat people in their efforts to draw a living from the land and sea in the vicinity of the Cape Smyth whaling station, the school, and the Presbyterian mission. In February 1905, John wrote to Sheldon Jackson that although the people showed interest in the school, their constant movement played havoc with attendance. [20]

During the year in Barrow John was not only employed at the school but also acted as temporary supervisor for the whaling station in the absence of Charles Brower,[21] while the latter was out on the ice, whaling. As the pulse of the northern Alaska coast quickened with the spring, John's shore duty

Fig. 12.1. Photograph given to the Kilbucks with the inscription "At the whale dance, the women are tossed up in blankets. The height of these women's ambition is to go up and down gracefully and to wear clean, white panties." (Kilbuck family)

set him apart. He was, however, able to make one journey to the whaling camp six miles out on the ice, where he witnessed the rapid retrieval of $8,000 in baleen. Before he left the floe, John feasted on cooked whale-skin: "The saying is current in these waters that who ever eats 'black-skin' will always come back to the arctic. If this be true, I am a candidate for returning."[22]

MOVE TO WAINWRIGHT

John stayed close to home for the remainder of spring. As June approached he made preparations to move to Wainwright to oversee the building of a new schoolhouse and the off-loading of the year's supplies. When the work of establishing the school was completed, he planned to return to Barrow and move with Edith to their new home.

John arrived in Wainwright in June and wrote Edith a brief description of what he found. Being removed from a trading station and having only limited contact with the whaling fleet, the people lacked many of the material comforts found at Point Barrow, where the whaling station had been for a number of years. The people continued to live in sod houses, relying for their livelihood on the "fruits of the sea," including seal, walrus, and several varieties of fish. The cast-iron stoves, clothing, and dry goods enjoyed by the Point Barrow Eskimos were notably absent, and the community's desire for a school was in part motivated by the material benefit it would provide: "The educational advantages do not impress these people, so much as the 'loaves and fishes,' which will be a help in eking out their physical existence." [23]

Just past the middle of July the Wainwright school house was completed, and John made a beeline for Barrow "to fetch my bride." On his arrival, he was welcomed by the long-looked-for letters which he and Edith shared "turn about" as in their Bethel days, each reading their letters to the other.

> On and on we went, until we were so surcharged with the magnetism that flowed into our hearts in a large copious current from the little square white cells, as we broke the seals, that we got up and putting on our wraps we went out into the wide, wide, world, and walked beside the sea. [24]

Suddenly, at the end of July a native messenger arrived with a telegram from home with sad news. Their elder daughter Katie was dead. Because of the impending freeze-up they could not even anticipate hearing the details of her brief illness until the spring. Although John and Edith were together when the news came and lent each other support, this first loss at such a distance and such a time could not have been easy.

Whatever their feelings, John and Edith proceeded with the move to Wainwright. Although ready to work, John early articulated the finite character of that work. With family ties grown deeper, their desire to serve was matched by their desire to be done, and Edith especially filled her letters with the expectation of their return.

ENTERPRISE

Although John saw the Inupiat people as "shrouded in darkness," he also judged them ready and willing to "come into the light." In the past John had concentrated on the spiritual dimension of this enlightenment: He had been mentor and spiritual advisor. Although still committed to working a transformation on the spiritual state of the people, in Wainwright John focused primarily on improvements in their material standard of living. This he believed to be the prelude to meaningful change and the manifestation of Western virtues, such as thrift and industry, that would produce it.

From the beginning one focus of John's activity was coal mining on a small but significant scale. Soon after his arrival at Cape Smyth, he discovered that there was a submarine coal mine along the coast toward Point Franklin and that heavy southwest gales mined the coal in tons, landing it on the beach free of charge. Within a month John had sacked and hauled a half-dozen tons of soft coal for home use. [25] The following year's requisition included a request for one thousand coal sacks. By October 1906, with the help of Inupiat workers, he had mined ten tons of coal for the school. By the following spring he already had grossed $500 from the sale of twenty tons of coal and anticipated that he would be able to make more. Edith cited this lucrative enterprise as a factor in their decision to remain in Wainwright.

Unfortunately for the Kilbucks' personal finances, by 1906 the government ruled against the sale of coal to the schools by bureau employees. This restriction only seemed to intensify John's interest in the enterprise. Previously, he had paid Inupiat laborers with supplies including flour, rice, tea, sugar, and material for clothing. Now, he reasoned, the government could pay the people directly for the work. The people could use the cash to pay for the building of frame houses and the purchase of ammunition as well as other supplies.

John found ready support for this revised program within the Bureau of Education. In 1908 a bill was introduced into Congress to set aside the coal fields at Wainwright and Icy Cape exclusively for exploitation by the Inupiat.[26] Under John's supervision, natives continued to mine coal, pack it in flour sacks, and haul it to neighboring villages by skin boat in summer and by dog team and reindeer sledge in winter. The bureau furnished the people with a market each year for approximately thirty tons of coal for the Wainwright, Barrow, and Icy Cape school buildings. The new arrangement was mutually beneficial as it saved the government a freight bill of $750 and gave the people an opportunity to earn $600 worth of supplies each year.

Not only was John's coal mining scheme successful, but his commitment to enterprise found additional outlets. Just as in Bethel, whenever possible John exchanged goods for services rendered by Inupiat workers. In a letter to Sheldon Jackson written in the spring of 1905, John asked for flour, white drilling, baking powder, rice, and beans to pay natives for longshore work in landing government supplies.[27] On a more modest scale, John and Edith exchanged meals for aid in various building projects.[28] The feeding of large numbers of people was a familiar chore to Edith from her days on the Kuskokwim. During their years in Wainwright it became a regular and sometimes burdensome occupation.

John was committed to transforming the Inupiat manner as well as means of living. Although he fostered coal mining as a money-making enterprise, John also made an effort to introduce stoves for heating. If the people dug the coal, they should also burn it. Before the Kilbucks left Wainwright they had helped a number of families purchase coal-burning stoves. Here as on the Kuskokwim, the enterprise the Kilbucks encouraged created needs which in turn required continued enterprise to supply them.

Along with his efforts at improving the standard of living, John also encouraged the thrifty storage of supplies for the winter. In the fall of 1906 he commented on the snowball effect of his efforts to cut a winter's supply of ice: "Since one man has cut his ice supply for the winter, another has

taken the notion and is preparing to do likewise. We take note of these signs
of thriftiness with pleasure and are influenced to make greater efforts in
showing them how to make the most and best of what they have." [29]

John's development plan also included the establishment of a reindeer
herd at Wainwright. John had been an enthusiastic advocate of the reindeer
industry ever since he observed it in Bethel in 1898. As deer herds were
established in northern Alaska before his arrival, he had opportunities to
investigate the pros and cons of the enterprise. He remained favorably impressed, and in a letter to Sheldon Jackson he championed the people of
Wainwright who had already made repeated requests for deer. In his requisition for 1907 he asked for a hundred deer, convinced that the time was
"most propitious" for such a step. [30] His request was granted.

John and Edith stayed in Wainwright for only three years. There, as on
the Kuskokwim, they studied the needs of the Inupiat, as they understood
them, and endeavored to convert them to Western enterprise without making them overly dependent. By the time the Kilbucks left, they had seen
results of their efforts. Isolated families were gradually moving in from up
and down the coast, attracted by the coal market, reindeer herds, and ice
cellars full of whale, walrus, and seal meat. A foghorn had even been req-
uisitioned to provide direction for homebound hunters. Although attendance at the school continued to fluctuate between three and thirty, depending on the season, the students that did come were pliable and willing. From
the beginning, John encouraged the people to "better their condition," and
his efforts contributed to that end.

While John's Wainwright journals were full of his schemes for progress
among the natives, Edith described their effort to put their own finances in
order. Although the first two years had been profitable, the Kilbucks still
did not straighten all their debts at home. After the government barred
employees from buying fur and selling coal, there was little opportunity for
making any outside money. Edith elaborated plans for their future:

> It will take nearly $500.00 to bring us home. It don't look much like clearing
> the home and getting started, yet we wish to establish the home at once for
> the childrens sake. . . . If it were not for Ruth and Joe we would gladly come
> back. Doors are open to us *every where* in this country, some that would
> benefit us financially, and all with a great opportunity for doing good. . . .
> Dr. Hamilton said last year that we "*must not think of leaving the work*" and
> yet if we could we are planning to do so. [31]

LOOKING HOMEWARD

While John planned for the combined material and moral transformation of
the people of Wainwright, Edith tended to the more immediate needs of
family and friends. As often as not, her thoughts were turned homeward.
Meanwhile, John opened the doors to the schoolhouse for the third time,
offering a course of study including geography, singing, marching, and

arm exercises, as well as the essentials of English and arithmetic. Edith wrote, "Yesterday Papa opened school with sixteen pupils. They could not be prouder or happier if they were in college." [32]

Just before classes started, Edith and John received a visit from William T. Lopp, John's immediate superior in the bureau. Though he had come to inspect the schools, he also spoke to the natives and talked to John about the proposed reindeer herd. Although an infrequent guest, Lopp would become one of the Kilbucks' closest friends and associates over the next decade and would help arrange their eventual return to the Kuskokwim. Lopp had also served as a missionary at Cape Prince of Wales before his employment by the Bureau of Education. He and John had much in common in experience as well as in their vision of what their work entailed, and Lopp played an important role in forming the policy under which John's work prospered. Edith appraised him "a thoroughly good man." [33]

In their journals for this period, John and Edith confirmed their belief in the natural goodness of the people among whom they lived, "unsullied" by either the virtues or the vices of civilization. Although Edith sympathized with the plight of the natives and did not blame them for what she termed their "condition," she did not consider them her equals. Although blameless, like children, these "simple and benighted heathen" were a trial she bore willingly but with effort: "True, I don't have hard work here. . . . but the publicity, the strain of being in a crowd of dirty, ill mannered, inquisitive natives, with nothing elevating or refining in any part of the day and no quiet until we retire at night, is quite a cross sometimes." [34]

Homesickness, perhaps, played a part in this description of her trials. Indeed, life in Wainwright at any season was quieter than life in Barrow, where ice cream parties and evening games of flinch with Charles Brower and Fred Hopson from the nearby whaling station had provided pleasant distractions. Also, the summer found John and the natives busy harvesting, and Edith was left much to herself.

Their second winter in Wainwright proceeded quietly, with circumscribed activity. School closed in April, as young and old alike were pressed into service for the whaling season. With the departure of families for the ice, Edith and John traveled to Barrow to visit their friends the Spriggs. While they were in Barrow a straggling miner delivered letters from home saying that Harry Kilbuck was seriously ill and a telegram announcing his death on March 8 in Salem, North Carolina. Not until months later, after the arrival of the regular mail, did they learn the circumstances surrounding his passing.

However subdued John and Edith were during the year following Harry's death, in ways small and large the people of Wainwright were able to draw them out of themselves and into the work at hand. Although their plans were turned upside down by the death of two children in as many years, they still had their "people." In the evening while they wrote in their journals they were kept company by the two Inupiat girls, Bessie and Nellie. Both were affianced and much occupied with the sewing of their trousseaus, under Edith's direction. The school children of both Barrow and Wainwright also kept them on their toes, constantly writing them letters that must be answered lest the industrious scholars taste disappointment so young. Men and women visited each evening for regular Bible instruction as well as to listen to the phonograph until the magic hour of nine o'clock when it was Edith's habit to let her company depart.

Among their regular visitors during the fall was a young Inupiat woman who had been born in Barrow but who had been taken to the States for ten years to be educated. On her return, she could not speak Inupiaq or readily engage in any of the activities expected of her. Edith listened to her troubles, helped her where she could, and remarked that she doubted that under the circumstances the girl should have returned home at all.[35] Perhaps she should never have been taken away in the first place.

Comments such as these affirm the distance that Edith felt separated the world in which she worked and the one to which she hoped to return. Other entries betray a belief in the underlying brotherhood of humankind. Commenting on Nellie's spooning with her fiancé Bert, Edith wrote, "They are Eskimos, tis true, but they are natural human beings the same as the rest of us, and I am glad that they are." This brotherhood did not always manifest itself where one might expect to find it. For example, Edith proclaimed Wainwright girls to be "just like any others"—based on their common fear of mice:

> A mouse will set the girls of Wainwright to running and screaming, very much as some girls in the States would do, and the boys,—like *other* boys—*will* catch them to scare the girls with. So you see Eskimos are not strange animals, or dreadful creatures, or feelingless people. They are *just* like the rest of mankind; just as human, having the same thoughts and feelings—the same faults and virtues, and they love to romp and laugh as well as anyone. The young people are like all young people; the older ones, perhaps more solemn sometimes.[36]

With the arrival of summer John and Edith prepared to leave. Though they began to watch for the revenue cutter *Thetis* in June, it was two months before they were able to get away. Even then, wind and weather prevented them from boarding at Wainwright. Instead, they were obliged to leave by skin boat on August 21, passing through fields of floating ice to meet the ship which bad weather had detained at Icy Cape, sixty miles to the south. When they arrived, they found eleven ships, including whalers, supply ships, and the *Thetis*, all waiting to go north.[37] The captain subsequently tried to reach Barrow, but within fifty miles he was compelled to turn back and set sail for the home port. By September 3 John and Edith were in Nome. By the nineteenth they arrived in Seattle, and on October 6 they reached Ottawa, where they were met by both "Dody" and the "Garl" (Joe and Ruth).

Although the goal they had striven for was finally in hand, they were not to enjoy it. They had gotten away from Wainwright, but the supply ship had not. On it were furs and ivory they had bought in exchange for their household gear and extra supplies. The profit from these goods was intended to be their support for the year until John got work. Without it, they were forced to forego plans to travel to California and New Mexico to see friends (including the Weinlands) and relatives. To make matters worse, Edith's health continued poor, and her medical expenses were considerable. As soon as he arrived in Ottawa, John wrote to the bureau affirming his interest in continuing work in Alaska, and he was rehired to teach in Douglas, Alaska, as soon as he could find passage.[38] After four years of yearning for Kansas, John's homecoming ended before it had begun.

THE DOUGLAS YEARS

Some time ago I learned the secret of keeping sweet in these words: "If you cannot do what you want to do, try to want to do what you can do."
                                    —*John Kilbuck to Edith Kilbuck, 1910*[39]

The Kilbucks reached Ottawa, Kansas, on October 6, 1908, after an absence of more than four years. There they met their children Joe and Ruth, who had been staying with Edith's brother Ben at Hatch, New Mexico, and the Will Stewart family at Marion, Kansas, respectively. Though the welcome was warm, farewells were already begun. After a stay of only ten days, John and Ruth, now eighteen, boarded the train for their return journey to Seattle. Edith remained at home in the company of Joe, where time and rest would mend her health. On November 11, John and Ruth reached Seattle and booked passage on to Douglas, Alaska, where they arrived on November 28 and immediately took charge of the government school.

Located on an island in southeastern Alaska across Gastineau Channel from Juneau, Douglas presented John with a very different economy and ecology from either the Arctic or sub-Arctic of his past experience. The damp, heavily forested coastline of southeastern Alaska comprised the aboriginal home of the Tlingit Indians. Nearly one hundred years of steady intervention by outside interests had reduced the Douglas Indians to the status of second-class citizens in ways far more overt and pernicious than the Yup'ik Eskimos had yet experienced. The Indian school where John was engaged to teach was located on the flats between the non-native settlement of Douglas and the Treadwell Gold Mine. John described Douglas as all around them, on higher ground, and looking down on them in every sense. In his first letter home to Edith, he wrote that Douglas was the largest field in the district and the worst. This applied to both the condition of the people as well as to the equipment of the school, which was makeshift at best.[40]

John and Ruth's first days in Douglas were spent scrubbing floors and walls and trying to make the school building (which had previously been a dwelling) habitable. They prepared the downstairs rooms as classrooms and set the upstairs aside as their living quarters. While they were at work with soap and water, they received the government doctor as their first visitor. When the man found that John was a full-blooded Delaware, he confided with some embarrassment that his own great-grandmother had been a Sioux. Both surprised and pleased with what he took to be John's singular openness concerning his ancestry, the good man proposed to take John on a tour of the district to exhibit him as a specimen of what education could accomplish.

Although John was more amused than flattered by the proposition, he took heed of Doctor de Vighne's remarks concerning the "backwardness" of the local people. On closer inspection, he concurred, remarking that the two chief ways in which this backwardness was demonstrated were in the unsanitary living conditions and the heavy drinking of the Indians gathered together on the flats of Douglas. John blamed the poor sanitation not on the habits of the people, but on the location of the community. The houses were situated on the tide flats, strung out along one narrow central thoroughfare and built up on pilings. Garbage dumped into the bay from both the Tread-well Mine and white Douglas above them eventually came home to roost under the boardwalk of "Indian Town." While John found that most individual houses were neat and "homelike," the total environment was depressing. To correct the situation, action on the part of the Douglas city government was necessary. During his tenure as teacher, however, John saw little improvement from this quarter.

The second limiting factor to the health and well-being of the Douglas Indian community was the prevalence of strong drink. This was especially true on "black letter day," when the Treadwell Mining Company paid off its native workmen: "The Whiskey peddler begins his deadly business, and I understand does not stop until he gets all the native workingman's ready cash."[41] Long-time Douglas residents informed him that thanks to the efforts of the territorial government and its recent crackdown on gambling and prostitution, the situation was 100 percent better than it had been before he arrived. Still, John never worked, before or after, in an environment so befuddled by drink.

John was no quitter, and even if he were, his stretched personal finances allowed him little choice. He gave three years of service to the school at Douglas, but from the first month of his stay he talked of leaving. No more than a month after his arrival, Dr. de Vighne asked John if he would be interested in a transfer to Kake—"a strictly temperance town. . . . the one village that is very far behind in civilization." John wrote to Edith, "I think the doctor has correctly judged that I would not stay in this hole longer than my contract holds me."[42]

Even before the doctor's suggestion, John was mentally moving back to the Kuskokwim and to his life as an itinerant reformer: "I am still covetous of Herman's place [assistant superintendent on the Kuskokwim], altho I try not to be, but that kind of work is more to my taste, and if I cannot have you with me, I prefer moving about to being established in one place alone. . . . I have now been in every district of Alaska, and if I can keep on in the service, I must be able to command a good position. So far I have been in places where no one wanted to go, and I feel now like choosing where I want to be located."[43]

Perhaps John felt so keenly the limitations of the work at Douglas that first year because of the absence of Edith and the homelife she provided. Ruth proved a capable and willing housekeeper, but John missed his wife. Though he had no particular complaint, he spent the year pining for Edith in much the same manner as he had during their first prolonged separation almost twenty years before. Moreover, the Douglas letters are replete with longing for a retirement that never came. Although this theme periodically marked John's correspondence all through his life, he lived out the rest of his days in harness. His marriage to his work in Alaska was as compelling a force in his life as his marriage to Edith. When Edith was near, his journals were full of his work. When she was far away, his journals were full of her.

During the winter and spring of 1909, John "put in his time scribbling," filling page after page for Edith in a voluminous correspondence. Alternately addressed to "my dearest sweetheart," "dear Susan," "Honeybunch," and "Hon," John was cheered by news of her returning health and old, accustomed spryness. One note held condolences for his toothless "Thuthan" after the dentist had pulled out the last of her upper teeth in preparation for a new plate. Another letter admonished her to enjoy her well-deserved rest: "I have always been ambitious to give you a good time, and in some measure this has happened this year."[44] Yup'ik endearments close several letters, along with testimony to his efforts to live a blameless life for her sake.

John's correspondence also detailed the constrained character of his activities in Douglas compared to years past. In Barrow and Wainwright he had been able to extend his influence to touch the lives of every member of the community; however, the Douglas school acted as one among a number of influences on the Indian community it served, including the Treadwell Mine and the Douglas civil government. Therefore, the broad-based reforms typical of John's previous administrations proved both inappropriate and impossible to implement.

Within his more circumscribed domain John first implemented plans to rechannel the monthly monies set aside by the Bureau of Education as payment for a janitor. Instead of hiring a single individual, John dispersed this money among the older school boys who were willing to help in the maintenance of the building. Although this infusion of government funds into the local economy was modest in comparison to what the coal mines and deer herds had accomplished in the Arctic, the same principle was at work. Just as John had employed paper and tin currency to teach the value of the dollar in Wainwright, he used the small sums paid out to the young Indian students to teach them about the management of money. Also, as in Wainwright, John encouraged the use of the English language through journal writing in the classroom.

Concerning the content of his lessons, John wrote that he always tried to select something bearing on the formation of right principles of living. His emphasis was on order and hard work, backed up by patience rather than punishment: "A great deal of forbearance, and kindliness backed up by firmness have produced better results than strict discipline. The best discipline is work, and it is surprising how quickly the average child takes to work."[45]

As the school term drew to a close, John wrote Edith that she and Joe should plan to join him as soon as she could. As a result, she packed her things once more and by the end of May the family was together again in Douglas. In need of a continuous income, John had applied to teach summer school to the children of the native cannery workers gathered at Chatham, near Sitka at Sitka Bay. No sooner had his family arrived and settled in Douglas than John had to leave them for his summer's work, rejoining them at the end of August.

During the year that followed, Joe worked at the Treadwell Mine at a salary almost equal to that of his father. He was not only able to save money for college but also to give $60 a month toward paying off the remaining mortgage on the family farm in Ottawa. Ruth also contributed $30 a month from her teacher's salary. Edith, who had a horror of debt, registered relief and gratitude. Between John's and her children's earnings, and her management of their living expenses, they were able to save a substantial sum. Their finances were also helped by the sale of their Wainwright furs for over $1,000, which was double what they had anticipated. The year 1910 saw the home place paid for and the family clear of debt after almost a decade of financial uncertainty.

Not only did the family prosper during the following year, but the school was also successful. Attendance doubled, averaging thirty-one students a day out of a total school population of eighty-six. John attributed the decline in absenteeism to small premiums offered as rewards for full attendance. Colored pencils, tablets, combs, neckties for the boys, and hair ribbons for the girls served to attract and hold the children's interest as well as to encourage attention to personal appearance. John also began publicizing the students' progress in the local papers with good results. Finally, he was able to introduce an "industrial" branch to the school, including instruction in fancy stitchery, woodworking, and basketry. All three innovations increased interest and participation.[46]

SEASON OF FREEDOM

> *I myself have not experienced such a season of freedom from care and worry*
> *and such an elation of spirit. Everything conspires to make this summer one*
> *long to be remembered as one of the best stretches in the highway of life. . . .*
> *[I am] on the edge of the woods, the last one on the street. So what else can*
> *you expect but that my pen should talk.*
>
> —*John Kilbuck, 1910*[47]

As John's second year of teaching at Douglas drew to a close, he was again offered employment managing a summer school. This time the bureau assigned him to work at Point Ellis, where a cannery drew workers from Kake, Killisnoo, and Sitka. As Joe was still employed at the mine, they decided that Edith would continue to keep house for the children at Douglas while John was gone. The separation would be brief; John would be home by the end of August.

Whatever the drawbacks of this plan, John succeeded in overcoming them, at least in part through an abundant and high-spirited correspondence with his family. Everything he found at Point Ellis met with his approval, and he put the best of his thoughts on paper. As Point Ellis was linked to Douglas by regular steamship service, John was able to send home mail at least once a week. He received long, cheering letters from Edith just as regularly, and all through the summer his correspondence comprised a rich and immediate source of satisfaction. The unintended result was that for the first, and perhaps only, time in his life John had the requisite time and peace of mind to record some of what he had learned during his years along the Kuskokwim.

Not even the routines of mealtime intruded. Shortly after his arrival at Point Ellis, he embarked on a demanding diet and program of physical exercise restricting him to a single midday meal, which he took at the cannery. A cup of hot water sufficed for breakfast and dinner. With the fervor of a convert, he even suggested that Edith embark on the same regimen. John was feeling fit and fine. With the surfeit of energy resulting from his almost monastic existence, he began to write.

During the summer John filled both sides of 125 pages for Edith and his children. At one point he queried his family, "Don't you begin to feel rather deluged with letters from me?" As if to excuse himself, he continued that his letter always rested "with the pen and ink beside it, so every time I sit down the most natural thing for me to do is to go shoving my pen." Even the placement of the table worked an attraction: "I remember reading in papa's letters . . . about writing with no fire in the house and the door open, and that description fits my case right now."[48] The stage was set, the lights were up, and John was ready to begin.

Of all the thousands of pages John and Edith penned in their lifetimes,

perhaps the most valuable, page for page, were the ethnographic manuscripts John produced during that summer. These manuscripts included
"Something About the Innuit of the Kuskokwim River, Alaska," "Important War Stories, Customs, and History," and "How Fighting Among the
Coast Natives was Begun." The first mention made of his ethnographic
endeavors occurred at the end of June: "I did not write a word in my
'Sketch' today, for I did other writing." Nine days later, he gave an extended
description, indicating what he was about and why:

> About six more pages and then I will be able to send you my first installment
> of my sketch. . . . My primary object is to get all the material down, and
> afterward when put into manuscript form, the subject will be arranged more
> systematically. The task looms up in larger proportions than I anticipated—
> but I mean to go on with it to the end—for I think I owe that much work to
> the Yupiat,—and to the student of ethnology. The literary features of the
> sketch may not be much—but much of the subject matter will be new, and
> all of it will be authentic. I have spent no thot on what I shall do with it, my
> present concern is to get it written.[49]

On July 13 he sent the first copy book off, followed by a brief respite
from writing in which he "freshened up for more later." By the twenty-first
he was back at work and from that time forward made almost daily reference
to his efforts. On the twenty-eighth, he wrote, "I have devoted most of my
time to my sketch, and now a few more sittings will finish the second
book."[50]

John indicated that he intended his summer's work as a beginning of
something more substantial. The more he wrote, the more value he saw in
the fruits of his labors. By the end of the summer he was carefully making
copies of everything he wrote "for future reference, in case I should attempt
something more elaborate." Just before he left Point Ellis, he described to
Edith his plans to extend his ethnographic efforts:

> I am glad you enjoyed my "sketch" and the Tlingit stories. The sketch is only
> in preparatory stage—and later I will try, as did General Grant—to dialate
> it to larger proportions. I did not have the time to get more of the Tlingit
> tales—much to my regret—for they are certainly interesting. Oh! how I
> regret that I did not take down more of the Kuskoquim stories for many of
> them are intensely interesting and some thrillingly so. Since I am developing
> sedentary habits—I am more inclined to writing—and this is the reason I
> have a great drawing for Kuskokwim—for gathering the material that may
> become profitable, if I can develop enough literary merit.[51]

Although not the only factor, John's literary ambitions were both the motivation for as well as an expression of his desire to return to the Kuskokwim.

Although John left Point Ellis with the best intentions to continue his
writing, never again did he have either time or mental space comparable to
that experienced during this summer. The copy books remained unedited,

and John neither polished nor published what he had written. Nonetheless, the manuscripts that he mailed to Edith from Point Ellis remain an invaluable source of information on the Yup'ik Eskimos of the Kuskokwim River.

John wrote less than one hundred pages of ethnographic description during the summer of 1910. The manuscripts are, however, rich in information and cover a variety of topics, including harvesting patterns, household composition, social groupings, as well as intra- and intergroup relations. Although his descriptions of late nineteenth-century ceremonial activity are often superficial and sometimes confusing, he gives us more useful information on these subjects than any writer before him, except Edward Nelson,[52] and many that would follow. His command of the language gives added weight to the Yup'ik terminology that he chose to incorporate into his descriptions, and the names he employed for late nineteenth-century regional groupings are particularly valuable.

Not only is John's work valuable because of its detail, but it also stands out because of the sympathetic voice it commanded. Though other missionaries in western Alaska described the character of the people among whom they worked, few of them wrote with comparable empathy. During his tenure in Alaska, John's friend and colleague William Weinland described the Yup'ik people as "decidedly phlegmatic in temperament. . . . They are dishonest, thievish, and their word can not be trusted. . . . [T]hose living on the low flats towards the mouth of the river . . . are sluggish, dull, and filthy . . . stupid and listless."[53] This description appears harsh when compared with John's more charitable evaluations of the Yup'ik people.

By the middle of August John put away paper and pen and prepared to return to his family in Douglas. His state of mind was comparable to "a ship about ready to begin a voyage, I am now riding with a short anchor line."[54] Two weeks after his return to Douglas, Joe took passage down to Washington, where he planned to study horticulture at Washington State College, in Pullman. The rest of the family remained in Douglas, and for the third year John and Ruth taught together in the government school. Again, this period of domestic contentment left scant written record. Excepting Joe, the family was together, and all we know of the year is from a handful of school reports, along with Edith's letters to her father.

As the school year drew to an uneventful close, the family prepared to leave Douglas. Edith was the first to start, and on April 9, 1911, boarded a steamer for Seattle. Arriving three days later, she stopped overnight at the Lopps'. Mr. Lopp spoke to her concerning plans for the coming year, suggesting that she and John return to Barrow. This she refused point-blank: "I don't want to go, and say so. He also spoke of Akiagmute [Akiak], which sounds better to me."[55]

By the first of May Edith was back home in Kansas, where she received a letter from John announcing his acceptance of Lopp's offer to work at Akiak. Her brother Herman Romig had been advanced to the position of

United States commissioner, leaving the Kuskokwim field vacant at last. Almost at once, Edith made plans to head north. Before she left, however, she boxed and stored John's manuscripts, which she had carried with her from Douglas, along with their small but valuable ethnological collection. These she placed in two small tin cash boxes and three large tin bread boxes in the vault of Ottawa's First National Bank, where they remained until her final return from Alaska in 1922.

Edith arrived back in Seattle by the end of May, and John and Ruth joined her there on the twenty-ninth. The trio stopped at the Arlington Hotel, spending their days shopping, filling out lists of dry goods, and sending off packets of stationery to friends in the Arctic. On his first visit to the bureau's Seattle office, John was informed that his salary was being raised from $100 to $125 per month, putting him nearer the top of the payroll.

Finally, on June 10, Edith and John sailed from Seattle on the gasoline schooner *Abler*, bound for the Kuskokwim. As the flat-bottomed vessel had no keel and was overloaded with cargo and passengers, it rolled in the heavy seas. It had the advantage, however, of being able to take them all the way to Akiak, where they arrived the first week of July. John wrote:

> On the evening of July 5, 1911, the *P. J. Abler*, with the teachers for Akiak on board, slowly steamed past the fishing camp about 3 miles below the village of Akiak, and the pilot, David Hawk Skuviuk, called out to the men to come up and help unload the ship. There were shouts from the shore; in a twinkling canoes were launched and forthwith a chase ensued, wherein the *Abler* had to burn more oil to keep ahead of the pursuers. At 6:10, according to the ship's time, Akiak was reached, and as the water was high the vessel anchored close under the bank, ending her voyage of 24 days from Seattle with all on board in high spirits. In a few minutes I was ashore and was heartily welcomed by the natives, who had arrived as soon as we did.[56]

CHAPTER 13

RETURN TO THE KUSKOKWIM

He says he is here to "Devil-up" (develope) the country. I believe it.
—Edith Kilbuck, 1912 [1]

MUCH HAD CHANGED during the interval between John and Edith's departure from the Kuskokwim in 1900 and their return to Akiak in 1911. Just as John was boarding ship in the fall of 1900, heading towards Seattle, the Kuskokwim sustained its first substantial influx of prospectors. Many of these men had recently been disappointed in Nome and were intent on finding pay dirt along the middle and upper river. With them came traders hoping to make their living, if not their fortune, supplying the prospectors.

Only one significant discovery was made before the Kilbucks' return, that being a strike along the Tuluksak River. During the next ten years only one other was made, on the upper Kwethluk River. As a result few miners and traders came to live and work in the Bethel area. As late as 1915 John wrote that there were at most one hundred whites living along the river, and the majority of those were settled some distance from the major native population centers. Mineral deposits were located generally at the headwaters of tributary creeks and streams, while native villages and camps clustered primarily along the river. Native and non-native segments of the population had little contact. Moreover, traders acted as intermediaries in the exchanges that did take place. Though hundreds of miners used the Kuskokwim as a travel artery during the first two decades of the twentieth century, remarkably few references to Eskimos appear in the books and journals written about the region during this period. Conversely, references to miners and mining in the Kilbucks' massive correspondence are few and far between. [2]

Nevertheless, compared to other parts of Alaska and considering other possible scenarios, the increased access and river traffic that accompanied mineral exploration along the Kuskokwim had a dramatic impact on social

Fig. 13.1. Bethel, 1908, as seen from the top of the Moravian church. The first house is in fore-ground, with the lumber mill behind and to the left. (John Felder, Yugtarvik Regional Museum)

dynamics along the river. While still in Wainwright, John and Edith received "chilling" reports of the negative influences of the miners and gold seekers traveling past Bethel. Sister Helmich wrote to Edith in 1907 concerning the arrival of miners and schooners on the river: "She thinks the mission's best days are over. . . . [When miners come] the innocent and ignorant suffer at the hands of so-called civilization. . . . These acquired evils are harder to fight than the natural ignorance and superstition of a heathen people."[3]

By the time the Kilbucks returned in 1911 the Kuskokwim region was experiencing its first real boom. Riverboats began to ply the Kuskokwim to supply mining camps recently established at Moore City and Ophir. Before 1900 the annual supply ships had off-loaded their supplies at Warehouse Creek at the mouth of the river, from which the goods were laboriously freighted to points upstream. By 1911 John and Edith could ride, bag and baggage, all the way to Akiak. Although the channel remained uncharted until 1916 and even then posed a substantial obstacle, by 1908 schooners with auxiliary gasoline engines had begun sailing directly between San Francisco and Bethel.[4]

By the time the Kilbucks returned, the Northern Commercial Company and the Kuskokwim Commercial Company had brought the riverboats *Lavelle Young* and *Quickstep* over from the Yukon. Both of these sternwheelers were relatively new arrivals on the Kuskokwim, the latter having made her first run up the river in 1907 and the former in 1910. Along with the *Victoria* and the *Nunivak*, which, like the *Quickstep*, had been imported in 1907 to transport goods to villages and gold camps along the Kuskokwim, they worked a dramatic change along the river they supplied. The once-isolated villages of the middle and upper Kuskokwim became annual ports of call for an ever-increasing variety of vessels. The new river steamers not only bore an expanded capacity for men and goods, but required a growing inventory of local products that native people were paid to provide.

First and foremost, the river traffic created an important source of income through the sale of wood to fire their engines. Many local natives spent part of each winter cutting cordwood, which they sold to local traders, who in turn were under contract to supply a given quantity of wood for the summer season. The local market for fish and furs also boomed. The fur trade proved an especially profitable enterprise through the 1920s. Although John complained loud and long that local natives often received far less than market value for their furs, prices remained relatively high. The profits made from the sale of fish, furs, and cordwood gave the natives access to all that money could buy along the Kuskokwim.

Compared to the conscious transformations required by the Moravians, the changes wrought by the gold miners, traders, and riverboat men after the turn of the century were largely indirect and unintentional. Nevertheless, their impact was substantial, especially in the realm of economic opportunity and the exploitation of local resources for sale in a steadily expanding market economy. Conversely, the changes that the Moravian missionaries had worked to accomplish during their first decade along the Kuskokwim had been both directed and explicit.

While the new commercial interests were at work, other forces were also effecting change along the river. With the increased access and the expanded demand for local resources that the Kuskokwim area had experienced, a major shift had also come in increased federal involvement in the area. The United States Bureau of Education's plans to establish a number of schools in the first decade of the twentieth century resulted in a slow but determined effort on the part of a handful of bureau employees to extend federal influence over the natives of the territory of Alaska, drawing them farther along the road to civilization. Two of the most energetic workers in this new secular mission were John and Edith Kilbuck. As they had begun their career as missionaries on the banks of the Kuskokwim, it was appropriate that twenty-six years later this new mission spirit should bring them full circle, back to the Yup'ik people among whom they had first worked.

THE JOY OF HEAVEN

> *The natives are wild with joy at our return. In church the native helper, who gave a talk, likened their joy at meeting us again to the joy of heaven when they would meet all those whom they loved and from whom they had been parted. . . . I am sure the up-river people will also be glad to see us again, but no more so than we will be glad to see them.*
>
> *—Edith Kilbuck to her father, 1911* [5]

While in Douglas, John especially yearned for the Kuskokwim. From what little we know of the hopes of the Yup'ik people, the pining appears to have been mutual. Although they had been gone from the river for over a decade, John and Edith were remembered larger than life. When the Kilbucks' good friend and colleague William T. Lopp, then chief of the Alaska Division of the U.S. Bureau of Education, visited the Kuskokwim in 1909, he inquired in a number of communities about the people's interest in having a school. Not only did villagers endorse a school at a meeting in Akiak, but they named the requisite teachers:

> A number of their men in well-worded speeches asked for a school, pointing out that their nearest and only school on the river was at Bethel, 40 miles down river. I promised the school, but warned them that they would probably have to wait a few years till Congress gave us sufficient money to send a teacher and wife and materials for a school building. They thanked me and then seemed to be discussing the proposed school. Being unfamiliar with the river dialect, I was unable to understand the drift of their discussion. However they soon satisfied my curiosity. Kawagleg called for quiet and through our interpreter, informed me that they would like to select the first teacher,

and named Mr. and Mrs. Kilbuck, and asked if I could send them. When I answered, "Yes, if they can come," a chorus of thanks went up. As the meeting broke up they each shook my hand as they departed and thanked me for the promised school and Kilbucks.[6]

Two years passed before the government was able to fund a school in Akiak. But when the *Abler* pulled up to Akiak in the summer of 1911 and disgorged its load of Kilbucks and cargo, including supplies for a new school, the villagers found Lopp's promise fulfilled to the letter. Months later Edith would describe the personal impact of their arrival: "They like to tell me how glad they are for our return, and nearly everyone gives a graphic account of their surprise and delight when first the news of our arrival reached them. Alice says she got weak all over and had to sit down because she trembled so, that happy she was. Others had palpitation of the heart, or put things away and could not find them again."[7]

John and Edith had little time for writing during their first weeks back along the Kuskokwim. First came the work of unloading and storing their personal supplies as well as those for the new school. They set up housekeeping in a small two-room cabin until the schoolhouse could be completed. Also, as the people were still busy with their summer fishing, John worked to clear the site for the new school and contracted a non-native carpenter, Mr. Hansen, to work on the building.

Hansen proved a sorry choice. He required constant prodding and seemed bent on sloppy work. Edith, who managed the project, found him extremely provoking: "It makes me just about desparate to see him spoil nice material. . . . In most instances good work is as easy as bad. It is either ignorance, or carelessness."[8] Flawed as she found it, by mid-September the school was ready for use, and Edith managed their move into fresh quarters.

During the remainder of the summer the new school was not the only thing completed. Akiak experienced a small-scale building boom, encouraged by the newly arrived tools (including saws, levels, chisels, and planes) and materials the Kilbucks made available to the people. On their arrival, Akiak had no more than five log cabins, out of eleven habitations occupied by a total of nineteen families. After the fishing season was over and the people returned to the village, a number began work either renovating their old homes or building new ones. As each cabin neared completion, the school would furnish scrap lumber for use in the window and doorframes as well as leftover paper, trimmings, and varnishes. The town was then painted red, literally, with a mixture Edith concocted out of left-over red cherry stain, floor oil, turpentine, varnish and coal oil! When a new cabin was ready for occupancy, Edith made up curtains for the windows.

Not only did the Kilbucks encourage the use of their tools and materials, they also made some attempt to control the new village layout. Edith described mixed success along these lines: "I plotted the new end of town and tried to have them build the houses in line, and set them straight. I am not so very proud of my success however. In spite of all my watchfulness, one old Jay set his house off the line and turned it at an angle. I have been pulling up their stakes and starting them right since then."⁹ John had a comparable experience in communicating the cultural requisites of town planning. The following autumn two men were bent on putting outhouses in front of their new cabins, but John successfully convinced them to relocate to the rear.

The Kilbucks gave help and materials for the new houses in the same spirit Edith had shown during the 1880s and 1890s when sharing her precious sewing trimmings, and the results were equally effective. By the end of the summer, six new cabins had been built and five more were nearing completion. Every able householder was working to get logs and begin construction. By spring of 1912 Akiak boasted thirteen cabins, for a total of seventeen dwellings housing ninety people. Though men still used the communal men's house (qasgiq) as a meeting hall and work place, the single-family dwelling and the nuclear family residential pattern it supported were very much in evidence. Edith and John were correct when they noted the importance of the new houses as an object lesson of what "industry and perseverence" could produce up and down the river. The cultural conversion they advocated involved a fundamental change in orientation—the replacement of the circle by the square. By insinuating changes in the habits of everyday life, they paved the way for the incorporation of the geometric grid of Western civilization.

TRAVELLING RESUMED

Even before the building boom commenced, after spending just over a week in Akiak, John began traveling again. As soon as he had safely stored the goods and hired Hansen for work on the school building, he left on a trip up the Kuskokwim to explore the possibility of starting a school farther upriver. On July 15, 1911, he boarded the steamer *Lavelle Young*, which he took as far as Sleetmute. He returned home on the *Quickstep* on July 23.

John wrote Edith a full account of his travels, much like the journals penned before 1900. This particular journal, as well as one written a month later detailing an overland trip to Hooper Bay, is rich in references to the changes that had occurred since he had last traveled in the region. While the journal format, like the natural landscape, was unaltered, the contents were markedly transformed.

John's opening comments concerned the novelty of steamboat travel and the market in cordwood it supported: "We made several stops yesterday for wood. The first was at [Little] Russian Mission. . . . Here Elia was the only one I knew. He had a cord of wood to sell, taking a sack of flour and a pound of $1.00 tea." John also remarked on the introduction of the fishwheel, although he remained skeptical of its merits: "Bettles . . . has set up a novel fish trap—a revolving affair—worked by the current. The affair is continually dipping, working like a water wheel. How successful it is, I do not know, but during the time we were passing it, I did not see that a single fish was caught." [10] In fact, the introduction of the fishwheel had a dramatic effect on the Kuskokwim fishery above Akiak. The increased salmon harvest it produced provided a substantial surplus which the natives then sold or traded to white men living along the river. Hunters used the remainder to support bigger dog teams, with a corresponding increase in their ability to harvest and visit farther afield. This technological innovation was perhaps hardest on the women. [11] Though it made harvesting easier, it substantially increased the job of processing the catch.

The most dramatic transformation John recorded was the meager population of the region, compared to 1900. On passing the once bustling settlement of Kalkak (old Kalskag), he noted only five cabins and hardly half a dozen children. Likewise, he reported Kolmakovskiy as a "very lonely looking place" and the country up the river sparsely inhabited. Napaimute (*Napamiut*), once a powerful and important village, was now only a remnant. The white trader George Hoffman had set up business in a small cabin there. Similarly, the native population of Georgetown was a scant seventeen individuals. John estimated the entire native population from Georgetown upriver to Big Bend at fifty. Though the epidemic of 1900 had not reached this part of the river, John wrote that diphtheria and influenza had later carried off a large number of people. In his official report to the Bureau of Education he noted, "In my trip from Akiak to Slitmiut [Sleetmute] I was impressed with the fact that the native population has decreased at least 50 per cent since 1900. . . . I think the average age of the children would be about 6 or 7 years. The people in general are far from robust, although I met with no actual sickness." [12]

Of his trip to the coast by way of the tundra villages John had little better to report: "Around every village and along the high ways of travel, beside lake and stream, the preponderance of small boxes, tells the pathetic story of the little ones cut off by the hard conditions of primitive life. Also there are but few men and women who could be called old. Truely, these people are like grass, which flourishes today and withers on the morrow." Back in Akiak, Edith also testified to the losses the region had endured. While John was gone to Hooper Bay, she wrote him concerning one woman who had lost her husband and all four children in the epidemic of 1900, adding, "They like to slip in when I'm alone and tell me about that dreadful sickness, and how it wiped out whole families, and even villages. It pleases them that I remember every body and can recall the names and relationships after all these years." [13]

Not everything that John observed during his trip upriver was discouraging. He was pleased that all along the river the log cabin was crowding out the semisubterranean sod house, especially above Aniak. Some of these cabins had a partition, and all had stoves. He also found the people to be better dressed and many spoke English. In a letter to his friend "Chief" Lopp he noted that the ravages of disease in the past eleven years had convinced the present generation to practice something radically new for the preservation of health. Hygiene in general was improved. For example, on his return journey, on reaching Sleetmute, he noted that the burning of the bedding and clothing of a woman who had recently died from tuberculosis was "a good beginning made in the work of stamping out the 'white plague'."[14]

At the same time that John and Edith were deeply moved by the magnitude of the losses the natives had endured since they had last lived along the Kuskokwim, they were equally struck by the changes that accompanied the steady growth of the non-native population. After his visit to Georgetown, John wrote to Lopp describing the boom and bust related to mineral exploration experienced by a single settlement: "It is claimed that there were about 400 whites gathered here during the past winter. These whites stampeded to this place late in the fall and necessity rather than the discovery of gold, compelled them to make shelter for the winter. It has turned out that there is nothing in the vicinity of Georgetown to warrant the population, so there has been an exodus, and the prospects of Georgetown remaining a town are very poor." Eight days after John visited Georgetown, a fire wiped out all but twenty-five of its two hundred cabins.[15]

After his trip upriver John emphasized his concern about the devastation wrought by fires such as the one that destroyed Georgetown. As miners and prospectors never found gold along the Kuskokwim in amounts comparable to strikes made on the Yukon or around Nome, few chose to stay and work along the river. Of those who remained, a handful were careless and even negligent in their relationship to local resources: "Parks related how one of the men who came over with them from Iditarod, willfully let a fire get away." As a result, fires associated with the miners destroyed much more than the several hundred cabins that had made up Georgetown and seriously depleted both game and game habitat: "I personally saw the force of this remark, for this year's fires have covered thousands of acres of timber and moss country both below and above Georgetown. How far back from the river the burnt area extends I was unable to learn."[16]

Based on what he saw and heard from both the native and non-native men and women who called the upper Kuskokwim home, John made a number of recommendations on how best to deal with the situation. First, he advised the gathering of the scattered native population into one or two large native "colonies," each with a school as well as a herd of reindeer:

> The Natives want to live to themselves and are willing to colonize, and keep the white man out of such colonies. There is no one settlement of natives, at Georgetown or vicinity large enough to warrant the establishment of a school. Game and fur bearing animals are rapidly disappearing before the onslaught

of white hunters and trappers, and the destructive fires that rage from time to time and this year in particular.

The natives about Georgetown, 50 in number, have selected a site about 3 miles above the town for a school and colony. The natives of Slitmiut have chosen a location five or six miles below their present place, which will be central for about 90 people.

The natives at Slitmiut and Georgetown are so anxious for deer that they are willing and want the opportunity to buy them. [17]

John recommended the immediate establishment of a school at a site near Sleetmute which would serve the greater number of natives. He judged it more likely that the natives of Georgetown and vicinity would move to Sleetmute than the other way around. This site also had the advantage of being further removed from the deleterious influences of Georgetown: "Although Georgetown may never amount to much as a town still it will be a gathering place for miners for some years. The K.C. [Kuskokwim Commercial] Co. operates a saloon, and this with the miners is a menace to the welfare of the natives. The people now want to move away from Georgetown which they will be loath to do in a few years." Later John added, "Among the natives there is a very evident desire to keep away from the white men. They wish to live by themselves, and they would like to have the whites do the same." John wrote to Edith:

I find that the natives want to get away from the white settlement, and are anxious for a school and for gardening and for deer.

Now that I have succeeded in getting the people willing to colonize, I will urge the Department not to delay in furnishing a school, and placing a herd of deer at this point. The success of my plan here has an important bearing on the efforts I will put forth in gathering other scattered villages upon common ground. [18]

The issues underlying the current debate on tribalism and native separatism have strong historical precedent.

In his report on Georgetown John also proposed that the bureau give the natives a contract for building a log schoolhouse. This would be an added means of encouraging the scattered families to gather into a community in which they participated and took pride. John viewed a direct contract with members of the native community as a positive counter to the established pattern of non-native ownership of the numerous wood yards whose business it was to sell fuel to the river steamers on the Kuskokwim. Before John left the Kuskokwim in 1900, natives often sold wood directly to the steamers. Now white men largely controlled the wood yards and hired natives to cut the wood. Later, John would have more to say on the use of local timber by the people of Akiak. In March 1912 he staked a timber tract just above Akiak for use by the natives for the improvement of their village, thereby successfully subverting the plans of an enterprising white man to establish a wood camp there the following summer. [19]

At the same time that he made a case for local hire in the construction of the new schoolhouse, John recommended that the bureau establish a herd of domesticated reindeer at the site, making it the distributing station for the entire upper Kuskokwim: "The deer are an actual necessity and will draw my people to the school."[20] Finally, he recommended that the government furnish full information regarding aboriginal claims. John's comprehensive plan was farsighted, incorporating elements still considered critical in rural Alaska, including land claims, continued access to renewable resources, adequate education, and local hire.

TRIP TO HOOPER BAY

John returned to Akiak for a handful of days at the end of July 1911; however, summer was a short season and on August 2 he pressed on in the opposite direction to oversee the establishment of a new school at Hooper Bay. His route was down the Kuskokwim to the mouth of the Johnson River, which he ascended, continuing along the interior route by streams and lakes with only one portage to Baird Inlet. From there John traveled to Tununak where he took passage with a native trader who was going to Kipniak (*Qip'ngayaq*: Black River), about seventy miles beyond Hooper Bay, for trade goods. As he journeyed north he noted the abundance of fish, fowl, and fuel in the form of driftwood available in the rich coastal environment. Two days later, on the evening of the twenty-fourth, he and his party arrived at Hooper Bay, the only village that was inhabited year round along that stretch of coast.

On the twenty-seventh the schooner *Bender Brothers* dropped anchor, bringing both the new teachers and the materials for the school. John spent the next three weeks overseeing the construction of the schoolhouse and paving the way for a smoother relationship between the people of Hooper Bay and the new educational enterprise. The natives were less than enthusiastic about the new school due to their unpleasant experiences with traders and census takers who had previously traveled among them:

> A few favored the plan of having a school in their midst, but the majority did not want it. The only use they have for a white man is to get as much out of him as possible, and they prefer *che-cha-kos* [newcomers]. The white man is considered to be indebted to the native for the possession of this country, for which there was an exchange of money, but the natives never saw any of it. Then many of the men have been around St. Michaels and worked on steamers, and they have really exaggerated ideas about the value of their services.[21]

After settling things at Hooper Bay, John headed home down the coast. He briefly described major settlements along the way, the first being Kaialivik (*Kaialivigmiut*). Situated about twenty miles from the mouth of the Kaialivik River, which empties into Hazen Bay on the Nelson Island side,

"This at one time was a populous village, supporting two kashigis, which means that there were from 180 to over 200 people. Today there are only five igloos and one Kashigi."[22]

While at Kaialivik, John met a dozen families and concluded that although they were well disposed toward a school, the lack of a suitable site as well as the migratory habits of the people were prohibitive. Traveling farther south, he endorsed starting a school at Tununak on Nelson Island. Once a good-sized village, Tununak had since dwindled to a handful of white men and a family or two of natives, but the good anchorage and abundant forage for reindeer encouraged John to recommend it as a school site.

John was unable to visit the villages to the south of Nelson Island. He did note their close affinity with the lower Kuskokwim, which the people visited for five months out of the year for sea mammal hunting and fishing. The only place he mentioned as a possible school site along this lower coast was Cal'itmiut, but even that presented deepwater access problems.[23]

PROGRESS ON THE HOME FRONT

While John was gone, Edith managed construction of the new schoolhouse, gathering and chopping of cordwood, and other prewinter chores. Much to the dismay of local traders, the Kilbucks' policy was to pay native workers in goods (including flour, coffee, tea, and lard) rather than cash. The natives were satisfied with the arrangement: "The people are continually saying 'Mr. Lopp is a good man. His flour is *good*, and his calico is not like moskitto net. He sends us things just as though we were white people.'"[24]

The means of paying native workers continued to be an issue into the new year. In November 1912 John wrote to Lopp concerning payment for help in the construction of the schoolhouse: "For [the] reasons that the natives were faithful and the very reasonable cost of the building (cheaper than could be put up by others) I would like to have you favorably consider the request of the workmen. It will cost the gov't no more money, while the gain would be double to the native. I wish you could see the amount of stuff $197.75 represents bought from the Kuskokwim stores." For this as well as other building projects in Akiak, John chose to pay the workers a little more and have them board themselves rather than have Edith cook for them. He also paid by the hour so that those who chose to work longer would be paid a higher wage. John's policies proved effective, albeit controversial, along the river: "Ex-delegate [Frank] Waskey when he passed thru here examined the house critically, and then asked 'How do you manage to get the natives to work?' You know the old song about the natives being unreliable workmen, working only by fits and starts. When I told him that we went to the timber August 2nd to cut the logs, and now Sept 27, the house was finished, he said: 'You are entitled to be proud of what [you] have done in that time.'"[25]

On September 20 Edith opened the newly completed schoolhouse to twenty-seven children. In fact, students were so abundant that she was forced to turn would-be boarders away. The previous year she had written to Lopp, "Nearly all of our school girls and boys have been to visit us. Because we were connected with the Bethel Boarding school, they thought we would take boarders. They brought their children from far and near. It made my heart ache to turn them away. They begged so hard to leave them. Orphans who have been with relatives at a distance are coming back to the village to stay with relatives here and go to school." [26]

By December 1911 John wrote Lopp to request a new schoolroom large enough to accommodate fifty scholars and proposed using the present school-room to teach the "domestic arts," including cooking, baking, sewing, washing, and ironing. Nine months later John announced that the new building neared completion and urged, "I would like you to see it for you would be willing, I think, for us to build another house like it at Eek River. Give us a chance, will you?" [27] John never stopped planning.

Writing to Lopp in January of 1912, Edith spoke enthusiastically about the seeds she had ordered and planned to plant in the garden plots that had been prepared the preceding fall. No sooner had the Kilbucks arrived in Akiak than John had cleared and Edith had sowed a small bed with radishes, turnips, and lettuce: "Everything did well, and our table was furnished with choice radishes and lettuce . . . The turnips did not do so well, for the rabbits ate the tops. The school children got what the rabbits left." [28]

The success of John and Edith's garden promoted a number of villagers to follow suit. Six family plots were spaded up and fenced, as was a quarter acre next to the schoolhouse. The people of Akiak, natives of other villages, and a handful of miners joined the gardener ranks. John predicted that if they succeeded, many more would follow suit. At the end of the summer, he held a small harvest festival to encourage the project: "I got everybody to harvest their gardens. I am to weigh the biggest turnips, potatoes, etc. to find out who raised the record sizes. This will stimulate the people to caring for their crops next year. I will make it a public affair." [29] John even began to make plans for selling the surplus in years to come. His forecast proved accurate. The harvest was rich and varied, and gardening flourished along the river.

The winter of 1911–1912 was marked by simple pleasures. After his return from Hooper Bay, John began teaching in earnest. As in Wainwright and Douglas, he emphasized spoken and written English as well as practice with the ever-popular toy money. He occupied some evenings with talks on personal hygiene and proper ventilation, after which the villagers might be treated to a round of music on the graphonola. The latter proved so popular that the Kilbucks were called in to help orchestrate the purchase of a similar phonograph for the village.

John and Edith hosted constant visitors. Their old friend Kawagleg came to see them almost daily, as he was devoted to John. In December a youth arrived, employed first as an apprentice and later as a chief herder, who John and Edith referred to as "young Kilbuck" or Kilbuck Tsheilgak. Throughout their decade in Akiak, he was an irregular but welcome guest.[30]

As well as receiving visitors, John and Edith paid regular calls on their neighbors. John carefully reported the character of these calls: "In village work our endeavor has been to identify ourselves with the people, taking part in anything that affects their welfare. We visit them in their homes as neighbors, much in the same way as they visit each other. In these visits we never criticize the way they keep house or their personal appearance, but we treat them with the same respect we would a neighbor in the States. We always remember that we are guests, and they are the hosts." In the same report, he noted the villagers' general desire to keep away from white men, a category of person with whom he and Edith were not aligned.[31]

A major problem arose during the winter concerning the management of the deer herds downriver near Kinak,[32] and John's time was occupied with its resolution. The herders complained that the non-native superintendent of the herd, Mr. Lively, was unfairly cutting down their rations so that they could not attend to their work properly. Lively, in turn, maintained that the herders were both intractable and insubordinate. At first John was inclined to view the trouble as deriving from Lively's inefficiency and ineptitude, rather than any overt attempt to cheat the herders out of their due: "Lively is a mighty good name but it is on the wrong man!" John believed that the herders needed firm discipline and respect for the person in charge, which was not the case: "In the presence of other men I heard his own wife say under provocation: 'When I marry another man, I hope it will be one who can do something!' "[33]

Although the allegation was later dismissed, some charged that Lively had been issued the rations irregularly and sold the surplus for profit elsewhere. These accusations and counteraccusations, which flew back and forth between Kinak and Akiak, provide an object lesson in what could occur when non-native supervisors and native employees did not trust one another. After an investigation, District Superintendent Evans concluded:

> The whole affair was unfortunate and unusual. It is caused to a certain extent by the lack of confidence on the part of the natives. The Government has not been in touch with the natives until the last two years and while it seems strange, the natives do not have confidence in the mission that has been operating among them and representing the Bureau of Education during the past 15 or 20 years. The mission has been operating stores for profit and so handling the herds that they might derive all the profit possible. Under the circumstances the native herders immediately concluded that the Government teacher was not dealing fairly with them.[34]

It is difficult to judge whether or not the cause of the breakdown in communications was as Evans assumed. At any rate, Lively proved himself incapable of the kind of leadership John both advocated and embodied and which work along the Kuskokwim required.

The Livily affair underscored all that John believed a leader should not be. A multitude of arbitrations John successfully performed during his first winter back in Akiak portrayed the alternative. Edith described the character of these demands: "John heard them talk over their troubles. A herder shot a miner's dog. Should he pay? A miner's dog bit a herder's deer. Shall he pay? A native woman is hired to sew for the Lapps a year. Can she leave before her time is up."[35] Another time dogs from the Moravian mission killed five deer and injured several more. The mission, however, was reluctant to pay more than $40 per deer, which the natives considered a low rate. It was left to John to go to Bethel to intercede on the herders' behalf.

Among his many hats, John also wore that of itinerant marriage counselor. On one occasion, he remarked to Edith, "A young man here had his wife and children taken away from him by her relatives, who live at Akiak, and connected with herders. I will have to see about her return." Likewise, he acted as amateur social worker. Of singular interest is the solution he worked out to the problem of one particularly insistent local indigent:

> He is foolishly simple and cannot care for himself. He is a slave to his stomach and has no thot but to get something to eat. He begs and steals food at all hours of the day and night. . . . [W]hen the school was established at Akiak, he was sent here because this village was his original home. He would go from house to house putting up a pitiful tale of having had nothing to eat that day, regardless of the fact that he had just eaten at another house. To put a stop to this imposition the following plan was adopted. A card was inscribed on the face of it with his name and on the reverse side was drawn a net with a fish in it. Every morning he came to the school house for the card and was told what family to go to for the day. This family fed him and put him to work, usually at cutting wood, taking the card and returning it to the schoolhouse, in the evening. The next day he would be sent to another family. Thus he was cared for all winter altho the people could not well afford to do so. All the families were instructed to make the man work for his food, and no one should feed him without the card. He at first rebelled and tried to get food without the card or he would demand food without working, after delivering his credential, but all to no purpose, for the people lived up to their instructions.
>
> Once he delivered the card to a family other than the one to which he was sent. The next day he was refused the card and had to do penance by fasting until evening. After this he settled down to be good, and tho his work was not always worth his food, he had to do something. Toward the end of the winter he improved enough to be in demand.[36]

Both innovative and effective, this solution bears the mark of an imported pragmatism simultaneously acceptable yet without precedent in nineteenth-century Yup'ik social life.

John also worked to change the rules by which the local market system operated. One goal during his first year back in Akiak was to help the "deer boys," as he called the herders, out of debt. In a letter to Lopp, he described his success along these lines:

> Upon looking over the situation, I found that the mission had the monopoly of the meat market. Dr. Shlaben had already started to break up this monopoly and I amplified this beginning by telling the boys that they must sell where they get the best prices and treatment. One of the K.C. [Kuskokwim Commercial] firm came charging up to Akiak New Years day, and wanted to know if I had anything to do with their not being able to get meat from the boys. I told him I was working for an open market, and the boys were instructed to sell to whom so ever gave them fair prices and fair treatment. A day or so afterward one of the missionaries dropped in on me and he was loaded up. I got the drop on him, and when I got thru with him—he acknowledged storing a carcas that was intended for the K.C. Co. and was very anxious to help get the boys in shape so that they could pay their debts.
>
> Today there is an open market and besides the boys can get cash, either in part or all—from the K.C. Co., and from the N.C. Co. The mission hesitates to give cash and the result is they have no meat to sell.[37]

Along with his role as intermediary, John was an active agent of change. By the close of his first year in Akiak he had begun myriad projects. Not only was the school established and flourishing, but John taught English and mathematics to the deer herders to facilitate their record keeping. He and Edith also helped villagers with orders for major trade goods, including the ever popular phonographs, rocking chairs, shoes, sheep bells, and steel ranges.

Spurred on by the progress he perceived in the peoples' desire to make and furnish their own homes, John also wrote Lopp concerning a plan to start a stock company village store comparable to modern cooperatives. In a letter to P. Claxton three years later, John's plan evoked a rationale similar to that behind Alaska Native Claims Settlement Act village corporation legislation enacted almost seventy years later:

> The introduction of a store with sufficient supplies to meet the demands of the natives on this river located at some convenient point like Bethel, would, I think, follow out your idea. . . . After the business is well established there will be no trouble to dispose of it by the sale of shares to the natives. With a competent man at the head, with necessary assistants, the enterprise would become a business college at the same time, and in this way the natives would soon be able to run the concern themselves. A branch store could be established at every village where there was a school, which should get its supplies from the central store.[38]

John also favored a post office for Akiak, as the village increasingly functioned as the center for a number of mining camps. He strongly recommended that an officer of the law, specifically a U.S. commissioner, visit Akiak or Bethel annually to hold court and provide more effective legal oversight along the river.[39] Beyond health, education, and welfare, John's planning included the introduction of American political institutions. He toyed with the idea of asking for a windmill to supply running water to Akiak for convenience, improved sanitation, and irrigation as well as an incentive for people to locate in Akiak. The range of his vision was immense.

By stressing the incorporation by the Yup'ik people of the everyday forms of Western economy and society, including the reorganization of space and the transformation of time into labor that could be bought and sold, John presented a direct challenge to the traditional Yup'ik way of being in the world and habits of daily life. Unlike federal Indian agents in the continental United States, John's influence never involved brute force or material dispossession. His subtle brand of colonization of indigenous modes of perception and practice was nonetheless effective and never more so than during his tenure in Akiak.

In as much as the Yupiit internalized his point of view, John left his real mark. Even more than during his early days working on the mission's behalf, his efforts to "improve" Akiak and its surrounds were decisive in restructuring the Yup'ik conceptual universe, and in laying the base for their introduction, insofar as they were willing, into industrial capitalist society. New homes fitted up with Western goods attached their owners to the commodity market. The weekly schedule and annual calendar of church and school activities increasingly ordered everyday life. The sale of cordwood began the objectification of time and the alienation of labor. The process of cultural conversion along the Kuskokwim cannot be viewed as the all-or-nothing commitment to the Protestant ethic, but rather as the gradual appropriation of Western conceptions of time, space, and personhood. Though they ran John's projects and proposals through the filter of their own culture, the influence on their ways of seeing and being in the world was immense.

EMPTY NEST

The summer of 1912 found John at work on the new schoolhouse and Edith engaged in an even mix of visiting and gardening. Even so, at the close of their first year back along the Kuskokwim River, she began feeling the strain. To make matters worse, that fall Edith was startled by the appearance of a sore on her breast. To obtain a clear diagnosis she made the long trip over the portage to the Yukon and down the river to St. Michael, where an army surgeon pronounced her trouble to be an abscess rather than cancer. Much relieved, she headed home, where she arrived November 27 after almost three months absence. John wrote Edith concerning his efforts to keep up his spirits while she was gone:

> I have succeeded in evolving two John Kilbucks, as it were, something like two brothers. One of them is like the little fellow who must have mamma,

and as the natives say, "natshigluni" [*nacigluni:* literally, not wanting to be left behind]—while the other one, like a big brother, is trying to comfort and console—saying "mamma will soon be back." He keeps up a stiff upper lip, and ploughs into what must be, with a determination to be equal to the demands of the situation.

Later that month John remarked lacking only his "chum" for full comfort and even so, that they continued united in spirit. When at the end of September a group of natives invited him to stake a gold claim, he solemnly named his share the "Honeybunch."[40]

Though Edith returned in fair shape, she remained weak and run-down throughout the winter. John, who had been homebound all fall managing the school, continued to keep busy in and around Akiak. Edith maintained that but for the draw on her heartstrings exerted by her children, she would be content to live and work in Akiak forever. This caveat, however, loomed large. As they entered young adulthood and approached the decisions that John and Edith considered so important for their future happiness and well-being, the desire to be closer to them, to guide their steps, proved difficult to resist. The upshot was not Edith's flight to her children's side. Rather both came to Alaska for one last year with their parents before beginning their own lives.

Ruth and Joe had always been as different as they had been close. Joe appeared content to work quietly and retire to himself at the end of the day, while Ruth was more spirited and lively. Oddly enough, Edith equated Joe's retiring character with her husband's attentiveness, whereas it is in Ruth's energy and curiosity that the outsider can read the father's mark: "That is one of your traits that I have been so thankful for, all my life. When your work was done you were *sure* to come right home, and I loved to watch for you. That is what I'm doing these days."[41] True, John never dawdled after work. At the same time, his work was never done.

After her parents returned to Akiak, Ruth had gone to Winston-Salem, where she worked toward a teaching certificate which she received in the spring of 1913. One month later she sailed back to the Kuskokwim, where she had been born twenty-two years before. It was well that Edith had Ruth as a companion during the winter of 1913–1914, as management of the expanding reindeer industry required John to spend increasing amounts of time away from home. He lived the winter on the trail as in years gone by, while Ruth took over the classroom in his absence. In February, traveling alone, he visited all the deer camps and schools from Akiak to Goodnews Bay. After a two-day respite, he left again to visit the Lapp camps, not returning to Akiak until early March.

The year sped by. When home, John helped in the school, worked over reports and correspondence, and held a winter convention of deer men to encourage the reindeer industry. In the middle of January Edith wrote, "We now can take a rest, the first since Thanksgiving. Inventories, requisitions,

Fig. 13.2. Akiak Church, 1913. (F. Drebert, Moravian Archives)

reports and other writing have taken all our time since the Holidays and convention. We are quite tired out, all of us."[42] They had reason to be tired, as just after Christmas over three hundred people had descended on Akiak for the second annual Reindeer Fair. Races and competitive events commanding substantial prizes as well as lectures and discussions on the business of herding attracted fifty deer men from up and down the river. This convention was John's idea, introduced on an experimental basis the year before. It had proved a tremendous success and continued to be an annual highlight for the remainder of his tenure in Akiak.

Along with his work for the bureau, John also resumed his role as unofficial preacher in Akiak's new chapel. This he always did in the Yup'ik language, accompanied by his friend and co-worker Kawagleg. As Kawagleg became increasingly involved in missionary travelling over the tundra, more often than not he left John in charge of the Sunday services at Akiak.

Even with all the activity associated with the school, the reindeer industry, and the church, the villagers of Akiak still had time to attend a Bladder Festival celebrated in near-by Akiachak in early February.[43] Although the church had long stood firmly against the annual masked dance (Kelek) and the Great Feast for the Dead (Elriq), both the Bladder Festival (Nakaciuq) and the Messenger Feast (Kevgiq) remained. Although the former was still considered harmless, the latter came under attack after John's return to Akiak. He conceived both the reindeer fair and the expanded church services in part as replacements for these "pernicious" traditional displays.

Spring breakup found the family reunited, as John's traveling temporarily slowed. The mail arrived in early May and found John, Ruth, and Edith together to share it. The largest portion comprised letters from their friends in northern Alaska, with whom both Edith and John kept up as lively a correspondence as that written in their early days working for the mission. One letter especially cheered Edith. In it Joe talked of coming up to join his parents for a year. This was timely as summer approached and Ruth grew anxious to return to the fiance she had left behind.

In June John steered his new skiff, powered by his first Evinrude motor, down to Bethel to see Ruth off. An old friend, the captain of the *Ruby*, was glad to take Ruth on board, proclaiming her father "the straightest man that ever wore shoes."[44] The "dear garl" arrived in Seattle on July 11, where she was married that same day to Van Patterson. The Lopps were at the wedding as well as brother Joe. As icing on the cake, the letter bearing the news of Ruth's safe arrival and marriage announced Joe's definite plans to join his parents in September.

While he was in Akiak, Joe worked in the school, where he was in charge of the primary department, consisting of the four-year-olds and older children not yet ready to enter the first grade. He also had time to hunt and fish with his father. Edith was kept company by a native youngster named Lily, whom she and John had boarded since the summer when her mother was taken into custody as mentally ill. The child's presence did as much to help Edith as the other way around.

The year was a hard one for the village. Though the price for goods remained about the same, the villagers' ability to obtain supplies was curtailed by World War I and the subsequent drop in fur prices from 50 to 75 percent below the previous year. Bad weather cut down the garden crops,

Fig. 13.3. John and Joe Kilbuck, wearing parkas made by Edith, standing by their house in Akiak, 1915. (Kilbuck family)

Fig. 13.4. John, Edith, and Lily standing in front of their house at Akiak. (Kilbuck family)

especially potatoes, to one-half of the past year's harvest. Villagers found it hard to purchase such staples as soap, cloth, flour, sugar, and tea. That same year, however, the annual Reindeer Fair featured a collection for the relief of widows and orphans created by the European War, indicating that along with soap and flour, the Christian concept of charity was already taking hold.

Fig. 13.5. Akiak school children performing "Little Christmas Pictures." (Kilbuck family)

Austerity did not detract from holiday festivities. The entire village gathered for a communal Thanksgiving dinner, already a fixed affair, and again a collection was raised for the destitute at home. At Christmas the school children gathered greens and trees to decorate the church. At the services on Christmas Eve, 225 sacks of cakes, candy, nuts, and popcorn were given out, and Edith described the village as looking as nice as any country congregation at home. Joe's homecoming did not pass without comment, and at Christmas Yup'ik friends brought him special gifts, including a fur parka collar presented by none other than the Mountain Boy.[45]

During the spring Joe talked a good deal about the family's returning to the old farm in Ottawa. Edith wrote that although there were disadvantages to the plan, at least "it would be home, we *own* the place and it would support us." They might still return, she reasoned, and buy a herd of deer while Joe got started outside, perhaps building on the homestead that John had staked that spring just across from Akiak. When John had made the claim, Edith had been "elated over our prospective home"; however that was the year before, when Ruth was still with them and with the prospect of Joe's coming up. Now Ruth was already gone, and Joe was soon to follow. Edith was as much feeling the pull of her children as the push of needed rest and retirement.[46]

After Joe's departure Edith lived in a state of expectation that as soon as possible she and John would follow. Even if she had not been anxious to join her children, the year would have been a hard one. In the fall the nonarrival of the vessel *Abler*, combined with the late arrival of the *Bender Brothers*, meant the Kuskokwim Commercial Company's river steamer *Quickstep* would not make her annual upriver journey. Supplies were short all along the river.

As if the shortage were not enough, the assistant teacher that John had expected to help him failed to materialize. The result was a heavy burden at the school, which started late and ended early. Enrollment was down from the past year, as John could not handle such a large school on his own. Edith pitched in and took charge of the sewing for the school and the village, the latter consisting of making patterns and suggestions. She also attended to most of the medical work. As there was a good deal of sickness during the year, including a half dozen fatal cases of meningitis, this was not easy.

By May Edith had worn herself out and took to her bed. For three weeks, she lay seriously ill. By the first of June, however, she had recovered enough to oversee John in the packing of their last box. On the ninth she wrote, "Sad as the parting was with our people, it was not prolonged, for we left so very unexpectedly. Some were not even at home to see us off. Kawagleg came with us. . . . He wants to be near us as long as possible. Many of our old neighbors here have called on us."[47]

The *Kuskokwim River* arrived on July 15, and on the twenty-second both John and Edith once more waved goodbye to friends along the Kuskokwim who came to bid them farewell. Lily stood on the dock, solemn and sad. Confused at the breaking up of the home she had known over the past year, Edith described her as looking as though the sun would never shine in her life again. Little did the girl think that, far from a final leavetaking, her "papa John" would be back before the first frost and Edith not long after.

CHAPTER 14

SAVING THEM FROM THEMSELVES

To the man in the field the extreme need of saving these native peoples from themselves and the adverse conditions surrounding them is vividly apparent.
                    —*John Kilbuck to P. Clayton, 1915*[1]

FORWARD STRIDES

After years of constant movement and separation, John and Edith's first half decade in Akiak was typified by an uncharacteristic regularity and peace. Especially after Edith's return from the Yukon and the arrival of first Ruth and then Joe, their home life returned to normal in ways unprecedented either before or after. Normalcy, however, was never synonymous with the quiet acceptance of conditions as they were. The Kilbucks were always busy "improving" things. Although the changes during this period appeared incremental written into daily diaries and journals, the cumulative effect was enormous.

In one particularly detailed letter written to her father in the spring of 1913, Edith reflected on the marked changes she had witnessed during the first years after her return to the Kuskokwim. From her perspective, the people had not been, nor were they now being, "torn away" from their own practices, but rather were being "shown a better way." Insofar as their efforts were "rewarded with success," the old ways were dying a "natural death" without "bitterness and strife."

> I would like to see any one come into *this* village and suggest a return to the former ways of living, to the wasteful potlatch, the simple, ridiculous dances and plays. Our people have too much else to think of and do. They are . . . too busy bettering their condition to think of the past. . . .
>
> The children of today ask their parents "what is a Shamman? What did

288

they do that they were criticized so?" And when they are told, they laugh and wish they could see the ridiculous performance "just for fun."[2]

The above gives a hint at the magnitude of the transformation experienced by the people along the river in a single generation. Of the ninety men and women living in Akiak in 1913, more than half had been born since the Kilbucks came to Alaska in 1885. Those who had then been children had since grown to adulthood and, if they lived, were now raising their own children in a social environment substantially different from that known in their own youth.

In her letter to her father, Edith described the external markers of this transformation. First she listed changes in the diet: "This year the table of native families contained plenty of bread, some butter, tea, coffee, canned milk often, sugar; and turnips, rutabagas, a little cabbage, and venison, fish and other game. The food is well prepared. The bread is good. Dishes have been washed too." Edith favorably compared this "wholesome diet" to a meal of frozen fish traditionally served up to an entire family in one large communal dish. She also remarked on the fact that "decayed fish is a thing of the past," replaced by salt-cured salmon in many instances. Likewise, seal oil had been replaced by lard and tallow and "kerosine lamps are used by all."[3] Little did Edith suspect that the long-term consequences of such dietary changes would eventually include varicose veins, heart disease, and diabetes.

The recently introduced gardens were in part responsible for the change in diet. Edith described their efforts in that direction:

Over in the new school house which is forty feet long, and has glass on the south side nearly the whole length, we have our garden boxes. Cabbage, cauliflower and other plants, including some flowers, are growing nicely. This week we put several bushels of potatoes in boxes to sprout. The more ambitious natives bought from one to two dollars worth of seed at ten cents a pound. . . . The Natives are enthusiastically working with and watching their boxes. They observe *everything* I do with ours. . . . One man at least, intends making a cold frame.[4]

As lessons were over for the year, the schoolhouse doubled as a hothouse for the entire community.

Along with changes in their diet, the people of Akiak, more so perhaps than any other group along the Kuskokwim, had experienced a transformation in their general standard of living: "They all live in houses and have stoves and good dishes, that is, granite wear dishes. The women wear dresses instead of the old style shirt-like garment. In Summer they have shoes and stockings." The Kilbucks helped facilitate these changes.

The people are now to that point where they *desire* to live better. They *want* to improve their homes. . . . [T]o make their few dollars go as far as possible

Fig. 14.1. Mr. Nose, putting a Best Flour sack to use, Akiak. (F. Drebert, Kilbuck family)

we have sent direct to Seattle for many things with their money. . . . Including the orders of the Lapp families we have ordered more than a thousand dollars worth of things and the money went with the order. . . .

This order includes flour, sugar, tea, coffee, milk, clothing, shoes, chairs, bed springs, sewing machines (4), steel ranges (2), tools, phonographs, and many other things.

Edith often found a way to supply "useful" goods people did not think to buy, giving a pair of flat irons to the woman who tried to keep her children's clothing looking neat and clothespins to the one who was faithful at washing.[5]

Edith also remarked changes in habits of personal hygiene. Villagers had dug outhouses and carefully ventilated the new houses. John's lectures against spitting and urinating in public had been heeded. He noted that more soap was in use, more people wore clean garments, bathed regularly, and scrubbed floors weekly, and on fair days bedding could be seen flapping in the wind.[6] All these efforts did something to counter the spread of introduced diseases, which were also more prevalent.

Even with so much already under way, both Edith and John had concrete goals for the future. John advocated the establishment of a hospital along the river, viewing Akiak with its large school and growing population as the logical location. To facilitate continued growth, he also lobbied for a sawmill. Once this was in place, he reasoned, it would be no big step to the construction of a new church, a village bath house, and a workshop. Moreover, he hoped to encourage individual families to dig cellars for their homes, to build boardwalks, and garden fences. Plans for these developments grew out of his first year's work in Akiak. Within half a dozen years, all would be realized.

Though both John and Edith hoped the village might achieve changes in material well-being, they also recognized the need for a continuing economic base to support improvements in the standard of living. As early as his annual report for 1912, John remarked that work on the schoolhouse and the sale of wood to the school provided important opportunities for villagers to earn flour, tea, and sugar right at home. From the early 1900s the village economy reflected a reliance on government subsidy.

John believed it was the government's duty to provide, among other things, sources of income sufficient to "raise up the conditions of the native peoples in Alaska": "The problem of extricating the Natives of Alaska from the narrow confines of primitive life and placing them in the higher and broader sphere of the world life, without question is one that is not easily solved. It is a question that should command the earnest attention of not only our educators but our legislators."[7] John considered the bureau's policies in Alaska as an advancement over those practiced on his own people in Kansas. In comments directed to Commissioner of Education P. Claxton concerning the modification of educational policy in Alaska, John approved the plan of bringing natives together in villages of four hundred to six hundred: "It seems that the gathering of the people into villages is the only way to reach any number of individuals with schools."[8] He immediately pointed out, however, the impossibility of such a gathering unless residents could develop an economic base to sustain it. By 1915 he had identified a critical factor in regional development, one that to this day threatens to undercut state and federal attempts to support population concentration and to facilitate health care and education. Schools did draw people together and, in fact, had to do so for the bureau to carry out its mission. Yet with nothing to sustain those new-formed communities, their future was in jeopardy.

Among the possible candidates for the support of native communities along the Kuskokwim, John gave serious consideration to fishing, fur trapping, and reindeer herding. The first he dismissed out of hand, as several concerns from outside Alaska had already tried packing plants along the lower river but had been forced to give them up after several seasons. The subsistence fishery had undergone substantial growth with the introduction of the fishwheel above Akiak, and some natives were able to make a profit

Fig. 14.2. Girls' industrial class scrubbing church floor. (Kilbuck family)

Fig. 14.3. "Wheels of industry sometimes slide at Bethel." (Kilbuck family)

marketing their annual surplus to local whites. Nevertheless, the relatively small local demand and the complexities of marketing further afield precluded salmon fishing as a viable economic base in the near future.

Fur trapping, on the other hand, held out somewhat brighter prospects for the immediate future, as it was already well established and connected to a wider, nonlocal market. John believed that for native trappers to increase their profits, a system would have to be developed whereby they could get market value for their furs. Although there was no question that natives produced the bulk of the furs shipped from the river, middlemen profits prevented this industry from benefiting the people. The temporary fall in prices connected with the outbreak of World War I also demonstrated the unreliability of the fur market.

John identified two critical elements in village economy as it was beginning to develop in 1916: "The two big forward strides that these people have taken are animal husbandry and tilling the soil."[9] His views reflect the nineteenth-century belief that the movement from hunting to husbandry represented a forward step on the road to civilization. As social evolution was thought to require gradual domestication of the natural environment, progress along the Kuskokwim was ideologically linked to reindeer herds and gardens.

"TEN TONS OF SALABLE TUBERS"

From a contemporary standpoint the contention that agriculture could ever financially benefit the Kuskokwim Eskimos seems far-fetched; however, in the early days of the Kilbucks' experiment in culture change in Akiak, gardening proved profitable. Describing their fifth harvest, John wrote:

> The returns in money from the gardens for vegetables sold were—$50.00 for one year, $150.00 for the next and $750.00 for this year. The price of potatoes was $200.00 per ton until this year when it was lowered to $140.00. This village had the distinction of being able to supply the potato demand for this section of the Kuskokwim valley, disposing of at least 5 tons. The "Abler" failing to arrive with the winter's supply of potatoes for the river, was a fair wind to potato growers, and Akiak had its share. Ten dollars was the lowest realized on the last crop by an individual and the highest was $240.00. There were 14 sellers of vegetables, and these averaged $53.57 a piece. The quality of the vegetables, especially potatoes, has improved from year to year. The buyers, principally miners and prospectors, were well pleased to be able to get new potatoes of such good quality.[10]

John viewed gardening as the means of transforming the region from one inhabited by mere consumers to a community of "virtuous producers."

> The present conditions the world over have intruded themselves into this country, and the conditions are such that the natives must be taught to adjust

Fig. 14.4. Kawagleg and wife, son, and daughter in their garden of potatoes, turnips, and other vegetables. Edith noted, "He sold $182.00 worth of vegetables from this garden and had all they could eat for themselves all winter." (Kilbuck family)

themselves to them. We, certainly, took time by the forelock when we got the natives to take up gardening. They are now that much farther along toward self support and to being producers, and [not] simply consumers. Producers are what are in demand now, and they are the ones who make the backbone of this mighty strife of arms. I have already preached on economy, and return to depending on the products of the country, rather than depending on the things imported from the out side. Flour will be five dollars a sack and other articles in proportion. Fish will be in great demand, so we all must do our best to get every able bodied man to put up all the fish he can. It takes much talking to get the people started at anything new, or is irksome."[11]

John was not alone in valuing gardening as a source of food, a source of income, and last, but not least, a source of moral fortitude and vigor. Were not the cultivators of the soil the salt of the earth itself? Surely Christian values stood a better chance among a people committed to the settled life of the farmer over against the migratory habits of their "heathen" ancestors? So John reasoned, and in the Bureau of Education he found ready support. Lopp backed him to the letter, going so far as to forward a prize turnip and potato that John sent down the Kuskokwim by way of the *Bender Brothers* to the commissioner of education in Washington, D.C., as proof of what agriculture could accomplish along the Kuskokwim.

Fig. 14.5. Reindeer herders at Bethel, around 1910. (Yugtarvik Regional Museum)

Although John continued to preach the moral, dietary, and financial rewards of agriculture throughout his tenure in Akiak, he was even more enthusiastic about the reindeer industry. Contrary to local mythology, John did not bring herding to the Kuskokwim. Herding, introduced to the region a decade before his return, was part of a general plan for regional economic self-sufficiency and growth laid out under Commissioner of Education Sheldon Jackson.

The Kuskokwim reindeer industry was relatively unimportant in Alaska as a whole. Yet for more than forty years it played an important role in delta life. In 1892 Sheldon Jackson introduced reindeer herding to northern Alaska. In his overtly assimilationist policies, Jackson believed herding to be the ideal means of giving the natives an industrial education and practical lessons in the Christian work ethic, turning them from uncivilized hunters and fishers into "civilized" herders and teamsters.[12] Herding also was presented as a viable solution to native destitution, though resource depletion such as had occurred around Nome during the gold rush was not a factor on the Kuskokwim, as no sharp increase in the population with a consequent increase in the demand for meat had occurred. It has been argued that the presentation of the reindeer industry as a solution for scarce resources was merely a cover for federal support of missionary activity.

The Bethel missionaries, including John, enthusiastically had requested deer in 1896: "We feel the need of a more civilized mode of life for these Eskimo, and these deer seem our only hope."[13] In 1901, the federal government consigned 176 animals to the Moravian mission. By 1904 the delta supported 1,046 reindeer, and by 1915 the industry appeared firmly established.

In Akiak in 1912 John noted that six families were directly involved with the reindeer industry through either a son who was a herder or an apprentice or through a daughter married to a deer man.[14] Of a total population of fewer than one hundred, this was already significant. In 1915 John described Akiak as headquarters for nine different herds of reindeer under the care of thirty-eight men. By then John's commitment to reindeer herding was complete: "The Kuskokwim district is large and thickly populated with natives who urgently need the benefits of the reindeer industry, and, from an economic standpoint, there is no other industry to which these natives could turn to save themselves as a people."[15]

John viewed formal education as a prerequisite to successful herding: "The step from the present habit of each individual doing what he pleases and just as he pleases to the requirements of the reindeer industry is a long one and only an exceptional native can successfully make it. The school is the natural stepping stone between these two modes of living and makes it possible to extend the reindeer industry to a greater number of individuals." The supply of educated natives considered necessary to the success of the deer industry was, however, already running low, as "the rapid increase of the deer has outstripped the supply of dependable apprentices." [16]

John urgently requested more schools. In June 1916 he reiterated a plea which remained his rallying cry for the remainder of the decade: "More schools on the Kuskokwim River and on the west coast. The work accomplished at Akiak could be duplicated in other villages, if Congress would give the Alaska Division of the Bureau of Education the necessary funds." [17] Finally he called for the appointment of a district superintendent of reindeer, whose principal duties would be the active oversight of the industry. The bureau never acted upon this recommendation, and after John's retirement no comparable guidance for the reindeer industry was ever provided.

During his first half decade in Akiak John spent as much energy monitoring the reindeer industry as he did teaching school. Although both jobs came under the umbrella of his bureau appointment, they often worked against each other. To teach, John needed to stay put in Akiak. To manage the deer, he needed to seek out the herds as they moved back and forth across their tundra home.

Perhaps John's most successful and satisfying work with the deer men occurred during the winter of 1914, when Ruth's presence in Akiak allowed him to leave for a month at a time to investigate the condition of the government herds. The travel journals that he wrote for Edith during these trips rival the quality of any that he wrote during his years as itinerant missionary. His descriptions of the dynamics of herding are particularly revealing. Twenty years later, what was then a new and intriguing industry in which everything seemed possible, failed on the delta for reasons still difficult to judge. During his travels John witnessed both the potential strengths and inherent weaknesses of the enterprise as they were played out during the industry's most successful decade.

John left Akiak on January 24, heading downriver in a sled pulled by deer. Traveling southwest, he worked his way between herding stations, carrying out informal inspections along the way. Each camp consisted of half-a-dozen tent frames and cabins. The wives and children of the chief herders were often present, while the apprentices usually bunked together in a single dwelling. These camps varied and so did the herds. Some John found in good condition, and some he judged poorly cared for. He often laid the blame for poor herd management on inexperienced or unqualified herders. The descriptions of individual herders formed an important part of his observations. He wrote, "Tommy has proven to be a good deer man, and an excellent chief herder. His men are loyal to him, and obey him implicitly. The spirit in this camp is very good. The deer are also in good condition, improving in size." On the other hand, farther down the coast,

John met and described the herder Karl whom he judged as knowing "how to handle deer, if only he were more successful with men." [18]

John's evaluations of herds and herders focused on the ability of men and animals to play by the rules, like miniature armies. He considered the ability to give and follow orders along a definite chain of command, from the chief herder to the deer themselves, as the critical factor for success. John urged the herders to "spend all your spare time breaking deer to harness. You can not have too many trained deer." Where firm discipline was not present, such as the lower coast, John doubted if the industry could take hold: "We remained in camp all morning, waiting for the herd. . . . I finished reading Wassili's Journal, and from it I glean the fact that these lower people are difficult to get to take to the reindeer industry with its necessary discipline. From [what] Wassili tells me, I think, it will be difficult to get apprentices to remain in the herd." [19]

Two years later John's fears were confirmed: "Since the establishment of the Kinak herd, in 1910, only three boys have finished their apprenticeship, the fourth being on trial for another year. This camp has made more trouble than all the others combined." [20] John's predictions proved accurate on two counts. As anticipated, the lack of formal education in the tundra villages and along the lower coast meant that the population remained "uncivilized" and "undisciplined" relative to their upriver counterparts. Without the requisite discipline, herding failed. Thus, the apparently disparate facets of John's practical mission worked to reinforce each other. Along with gardening and the general reconstruction of village space, the reindeer herds and bureau day schools depended on each other, regrouping on Yup'ik soil to form an analogue to Western culture.

Just as John viewed discipline and order as indispensable to the success of herding, he believed his primary responsibility to the herders was helping to adjudicate the conflicts that threatened to disrupt the relationship both between herding groups and within them. Along with evaluative observations, endless arbitration characterized John's trips to the herds. For example, on his way downriver during the winter of 1914 John received the report that three deer that had strayed to the Kinak side of the Kuskokwim had been killed by two natives from Kwigillingok. He immediately determined to locate and confront the guilty parties on his way home from Goodnews Bay, giving them the choice of paying for the deer or going to jail. On a second trip that winter he was called to decide the case of a miner who had unharnessed his dogs on the creek in front of his house, inadvertently allowing one to run to the nearby herd, where it caused one female to be killed in the crush as well as injuring a number of other deer.

The man had to pay $40.00—which I tho't sufficient. He thinks the charge was excessive, but he said nothing to me, and he paid the price.

The man thot that he should be shown clemency, for he claims that he did not know the deer were so close—since we had not told him. He however knows that he is in a deer country, and further more at a deer camp, besides he is on the highway—where deer teams travel, so his own judgment should have prevented him from taking the slightest risk. I am sure he will be more careful about turning his dogs loose in the future.[21]

During that same winter John also investigated the use of poison for taking game by a local non-native trapper. Several dogs owned by herders died as a result and, as in the case of the miner, through John the herders asked the trapper for compensation. As in his work with the deer men, John required adherence to the rules by the river's entire population.

John's view of the relationship between the herders and their deer as a hierarchically ordered chain of command contrasts in significant respects with the Yup'ik view of the relationship between men and animals as a reciprocal exchange between human and nonhuman persons. The discipline he required of his herders, however, both in relation to the deer and in relation to each other, produced decisions compatible with the requirements of mutual respect and care prescribed by the traditional system. John viewed the deer as an objective resource that could be counted and owned, not as nonhuman persons with whom the herders had a relationship, and he communicated this point of view to his apprentices. His management continued to be successful, insofar as both the Western and Yup'ik points of view required the same solution in situations of conflict—just compensation for damage done.

Along with the resolution of disputes between herders and nonherders, John also played the role of jury and judge in the adjudication of conflicts between herders. For example, on his second trip a deer man consulted John concerning his obligations to the owner of the herd and the wages he might rightfully claim. In another case John commented on the moral lessons both required by and learned in the course of herding:

The Nukluk boys saw the practical effect of untruthfulness and it was a good lesson. Mr. Spein had traded a bull to them sometime in the early summer. Since then another bull similar in appearance and of about the same size came into the Nukluk herd along with others. The stray again left the herd. When Mr. Spein saw the bull with his mark, he asked the boys if it was not his—the one that strayed into their herd. They said it was not, but it was the one he had traded to them. Mr. Spein was inclined to doubt the boys' word. He said the bull he lost had been haltered and would "follow the line" i.e. lead, and he wanted to test this one. The animal was caught—and haltered. The test proved that the bull would follow the line,—and it was quite tame. There was however another test—and that was to have the animal identified by Spein's brother—who had taken the one the boys got to their camp. He was called—and after a brief examination, said the animal belonged to the boys.

Mr. Spein was satisfied. The boys felt relieved. Mr. Spein said that if the boys had not lied—he would have taken their word when they claimed the deer.[22]

As well as providing a view of the value and scope of his role as arbitrator in the management of the reindeer industry, John's journals also picture the camaraderie of herding. Near the end of the downriver journey during the winter of 1914, he described a day spent corraling and counting a single herd, recalling the excitement that attended the deers' attempts to escape: "How the boys did enjoy the action, when a large bunch of wild deer were to be handled. Sometimes the boys laughed so hard that they could hardly stand up. The way to handle deer is the same that applies to any other animal—and that is never give way. I stood guard a number of times at the exit, and the way a bunch of deer would come charging—was enough to make me wish to be somewhere else,—but by sticking to my post, no deer ever got by me."[23]

John enjoyed the excitement of the corral work as much as the herders did. As always, his eyes were open to potential improvements in the status quo. For example, reindeer management was complicated by an elaborate system of cuts on the deer's ears to establish ownership and identification. Two years after his experience counting the herd, John lectured the herders on the use of aluminum buttons as ear marks to facilitate the enumeration process, making it more accurate and systematic.[24] John reasoned that not only could the metal tags help in the easy identification of the exact age of living deer, but if perchance a deer died and was not found until animals had picked the carcass clean, the button could always prove the owner.

Along with his work with the herders in the field and at the annual fair, John wrote enthusiastically about the state of development of the reindeer industry along the Kuskokwim. He attributed the success of the industry to the ability of individual herders to own deer:

> Up to our advent only men who went thru the required term of apprentice-ship were in possession of deer. The privilege of any native of good standing to acquire reindeer had been given by the gov't some years before our coming to Akiak, but no one had taken advantage of it. Now in this village, there are 14 individuals who have acquired deer thru purchase either with cash or labor. They own from 2 to 50 deer each, aggregating something like 127 head.

Furthermore, the government protected the individual owner's possession of his deer, including the proper disposition of the herd after his death. John viewed this as a major factor in creating and maintaining interest in purchasing and owning deer. Here he made a critical observation, one that signaled the beginning of a dramatic change in attitude toward personal property and the rights and duties of the individual within the community:

Fig. 14.6. John chopping wood at Akiak, around 1915. (Moravian Archives)

"The present owners do not expect to get such a great benefit from the few deer they are able to purchase, but they look upon the transaction as a provision for their children. Before this, a native may be ever so rich, but his wealth, great or small, upon his decease, went mostly to outsiders, while his own immediate family usually soon became destitute."[25]

John's concern for the success of the industry went beyond the material well-being that it guaranteed to the value transformation that it simultaneously required and made possible. His view of property directly challenged the nineteenth-century Yup'ik view of the world whereby an individual's material possessions were not considered assets of the nuclear family. Rather, the goods of the deceased and his family were the means of celebrating an essential continuity by hosting his spiritual rebirth with ceremonies such as Elriq following his death. John's strategy directly challenged this expression of generational continuity in the human spirit world, replacing it with continuity in the man-object relationship. As in the Yup'ik understanding of land ownership, John sought to replace a relational view of property rights with a possessive one.

John's effort to inspire people to be "beforehanded instead of behindhanded" was manifest beyond the deer industry. He wrote:

This year we had one notable instance of forehandedness. Rob't Egsack who was employed by the Moravian Mission as an itinerant missionary, collected firewood in the summer, in sufficient quantity to provide fuel for his own and father-in-law's families, for the entire winter, and still has a good supply on hand. He also hired a man to saw and split stove wood for his family while he was away from home. It is safe to say that this is the first case of this kind among the natives of the entire Kuskokwim river.[26]

John gave credit for this dramatic transformation to the successful suppression of the "potlatch" (probably Kevgiq). Though previously considered the most benign of the traditional ceremonies, it had come to embody all that was wasteful and harmful in traditional patterns of exchange: "Our work was not to get the purchase money, nor the privilege of buying deer, not to convince him that he ought to try to make provision for his family's welfare, in the future, for there is hardly a parent who does not think of this himself, but it was to break away from an ancient custom—the potlatch."[27]

John embraced reindeer ownership not only for its economic advantages, but as a moral alternative to the traditional rules of reciprocity and exchange, which he viewed as both contrary to and incompatible with the concept of individual ownership fundamental to Christian family and community life. Only when the "potlatch" was abandoned would individual ownership be secure, and only with individual ownership secure could the people move forward on the road to "civilization":

> With the potlatch out of the way, home comforts engaged the attention of the people. The women and children at once began to be better dressed, the wife was given a sewing machine, a better stove, and ample supply of kitchen and table ware, and food the year round. The men were able to keep their best dogs, a good gun, a full supply of steel traps and a good boat, without having to give up these things on demand as in the days of the potlatch. By a little practice of economy and self denial, a savings bank account was possible, in the form of reindeer, which is the very best bank for the Alaskan native. Debt, the bane of the Eskimo's life, has been less and less with each succeeding year.[28]

At the same time that John came out strongly against the potlatch, he was equally forceful in the creation of what he viewed as a viable and morally acceptable alternative. His introduction of the deermen's fair, held annually at Akiak until his retirement in 1921, rivaled his role as arbitrator. Comparable to his policy of assertive discipline in the classroom in Barrow, John conceived the deermen's fair as providing the incentive necessary to help the herders rise above themselves in their efforts with the deer. Whereas his arbitrations dealt primarily with instances of rule breaking, the fair was intended to reward adherence to a new rule, the Protestant work ethic.

One of the most successful fairs took place between December 22 and 30, 1916, and included both field events and indoor deliberations. The fair

Fig. 14.7. Deermen attending the second annual convention at Akiak, January 1914. (Kilbuck family)

opened on a wide plain near Akiak. The herders had established a temporary camp, complete with a round tent thirty feet in diameter used as an assembly hall. There thirty-three herders and apprentices gathered from eight camps to await the arrival of the deer: "As the deer came plunging down a gulch, and spread out fan shape on the lake, a sight to stir the emotions of a lover of animal life, an old herder remarked: 'A short while since, we had nothing, but now look at that herd, our own, our wealth.'"[29]

The fair featured a variety of events, including a demonstration of butchering techniques, competitions in lassoing wild bulls, driving untrained bulls, and rifle shooting. While the herders tested their skills against one another among the deer, the "deer women" were judged in a massive bread-baking and parka-sewing competition. Foot races, a sled show, and pulling contest followed. After outdoor events were completed, the herders adjourned to Akiak proper, where they attended church services and a Christmas program given by the children.

The fair concluded with meetings in the schoolhouse, during which John and the bureau superintendent for the western district, Walter Johnson, instructed the herders in their work. These lectures articulated the values that John believed must be inculcated into the herders for the industry to succeed. John quoted Johnson's advice, as follows:

The deer work is like running an intricate machine. You must learn how every part is put together and what it is for, if you expect to learn how to run it. Then by experimenting and watching what the expert does, you will learn what each part of the engine will do and so know what to expect. Apprentices should do their work with the same vim and put as much care and thought into their work as they do with the work at the Fair when they are trying for prizes.[30]

The next topic discussed was the watch and, as in John's comments in the field, the importance of strict discipline: "For if each man on watch does as he thinks best, regardless of his orders, nothing will be accomplished and the work will not progress, as it will if one man is in charge and his orders followed. This would be like a stream that is very crooked. . . . But where the leader of the camp is followed, and all work together harmoniously it is like following a straight stream."[31]

Though the fair focused on the positive inculcation and reward of the values successful herding required, disputes also were settled. John played the role of prosecuting attorney, Johnson presided as judge, and the chief herders were impaneled as the jury. Most of the offenses involved failure to attend the deer properly or to follow the orders of a chief herder. If guilty, the accused would either be reprimanded, docked a certain number of deer, or, if the breach was serious, forbidden from continuing to work with the deer men.

The same emphasis on discipline and obedience that John had demonstrated during his field trips was the focus of these public deliberations. As in the disputes John had mediated in the field, the public exposure and reprimand of the slack or careless worker proved an acceptable and effective means of problem-solving within the larger organization. Public shaming through ridicule songs performed during Kevgiq had been used as a means of social control in the past, and in the deermen's court it found a viable replacement.

Herding failed to become the economic panacea and moral force that John envisioned. Over the years the deer gradually became concentrated in the hands of white businessmen and Lapp herders, who had originally come to instruct the Eskimos in reindeer husbandry. Local Yupiit were employed as hired herders, and native-owned herds were consolidated with mission herds. Although after 1908 the post-Jackson government policy put the deer under native control, the reindeer industry remained tied to mission activity. Missionaries continued to play the role of overseers and supervisors, and herding helped subsidize missionary activity and support the mission stations.

In the early 1930s some forty-three thousand reindeer were grazing along the river system. In the late 1930s the number was approximately the same, with herds at Akiachak, Kalskag, and Kwethluk. Yet in the early 1940s the

Fig. 14.8. Lapp herders arriving at Akiak, March 1915. Note the boat-shaped sled used by the Lapps. Each sled holds about 200 pounds, and one man usually handles seven sled deer. (Kilbuck family)

herds declined so rapidly that they were almost nonexistent by about 1946. At that time only six hundred reindeer were reported for a single herd in Akiak, along with a government herd on Nunivak Island and one at Hooper Bay. By 1949 the Akiak herd had strayed, and the Hooper Bay herd had decreased markedly because the people were not sufficiently interested and had tried to hold the herd near the village where the ranges were depleted. By the 1950s the only deer remaining in the delta were on predator-free Nunivak Island.[32]

The natives of the Kuskokwim were asked in the summer of 1948 what they thought had led to the decrease in the deer. Predation by wolves, starvation, poor herding and management, excessive butchering, and mixing with caribou were some of the reasons given. To this list were later added disease, marketing problems, and vacillating government policies. The reindeer industry also may have failed because of conflicts with traditional social norms: "The Eskimo herded when they were young and free from familial obligation, but very few viewed herding as a lifelong occupation. The Kuskokwim Eskimo were accustomed to sedentary village life. They were gregarious and regarded the physical and social isolation of camp life as disagreeable."[33]

Although there is some controversy as to the weight that should be given this one factor, the Yup'ik people are in fact a shore-dwelling people, accustomed to seasonal migrations but not to the constant nomadic existence close herding required. They also enjoyed large winter social gatherings that the lonely life of the herder precluded. During John's tenure the annual deermen's fair could replace some of the intervillage feasting the herders were forced to forego. The last deermen's fair was held in Akiak in 1920, after which John retired from bureau service. Had this form of recognition, encouragement, and training continued, the deer industry might have stood a better chance of success.

Already in 1915 even the best herders had a typically short tenure and used their profits in deer to purchase a house in Akiak or Bethel, where their family awaited their early retirement. Herding conflicted with the centralized trends it was introduced to support. Ironically, the very natives who did the herding were both those most interested in and those precluded from taking advantage of the formal education the mission stations and gov ernment schools were beginning to make available, as they were away at reindeer camps for the better part of the winter.

From the beginning the requirement that herders forego the social and educational advantages of village life hampered the reindeer industry. Perhaps a more severe test, however, was the inability of the industry to provide a viable replacement to traditional subsistence pursuits. Fishing and fur trapping had the advantage of providing a relatively dependable means of support. On the other hand, even a hard working young herder could not support his family exclusively through herding.

At the same time, the requirements of close herding made it extremely difficult for deer men to engage in traditional subsistence pursuits. During the summer fishing season the needs of the deer kept the men away from the river; therefore, they were unable to take advantage of the valuable summer salmon runs. In the pattern that developed, a young man worked as a herder while his family remained at home to harvest the fish, supported in part by his income. Along with the other sacrifices, apprentices found themselves economically disadvantaged as well.

Although John never expected that herding would totally replace hunting and fishing, he believed it could provide stability to an economy liable to dangerous fluctuations and relieve the seasonal food shortages that plagued river life. In fact, although food shortages were relatively common, death from starvation was both infrequent and localized. Nonetheless, John felt the situation merited strong and immediate remedy. In the spring of 1916 he wrote, "The year just closed has been a trying one for this entire river. . . . At least a traveller in the upper country reported the natives so hungry as to become wolfish . . . This report stirred up considerable comment and suggestions of ways and means to save the Kuskokwim Eskimo from extinction thru starvation. In the end it was considered to be the Govt's duty to come to the rescue thru its Bureau of Education." [34]

John looked at herding as a way to instill the long-term approach to life that he felt the people desperately needed and that herding required. However, not only was there no strong economic motivation to abandon the immediate rewards of fishing and trapping, there was decided economic pressure for herders to continue active in traditional subsistence pursuits. This combination of herding and subsistence harvesting proved possible given the division of labor within the extended family. It was not always an easy one, however, and only those closely influenced by either the Kilbucks or the mission were willing to commit to herding on a long-term basis.

Another factor contributing to the decline of herding in the 1920s and 1930s was the formation of reindeer associations in which ownership was vested in the group rather than the individual. Because it tended to diffuse authority and responsibility, this last difficulty is particularly significant in light of John's equation of the long-term success of the enterprise with individual ownership. This mandate was ignored in later years, a factor which probably contributed substantially to the decline of herding.

Finally, it is worth noting a recently recorded native explanation of the deer's demise: "Later on people didn't take care of the meat any more. They threw it around to the dogs. Then one time the wolves came up and the reindeer were gone." This brief statement suggests two different explanations for the deers' decline. First, there is the possibility that the Yupiit treated the deer poorly because they did not regard them as they did other animals, as nonhuman persons worthy of respect. Rather they objectified them as "our own, our wealth." [35] Viewing them as objects that could be counted rather than subjects with whom they had an ongoing reciprocal relationship, they lacked a sense of obligation to attend them. They ignored the deers' needs, and the wolves did the rest.

The connection of the destruction of the deer with the hunter's neglect of the hunted also suggests an opposite interpretation and evidence that traditional subsistence ideology still governed the Yup'ik understanding of their relationship with the deer. Yup'ik hunters traditionally viewed animals as an infinitely renewable resource possessing both an immortal soul and an awareness comparable to that of humans. According to Robert Brightman, human activity was instrumental only insofar as it influenced reactive decisions in the animal and spirit worlds. Animals would continue to allow themselves to be taken only if they were shown proper respect. Hunters could not affect animal abundance, only their accessibility.

The value traditionally placed on individual responsibility was reinforced during John's tenure by his constant emphasis on self-discipline and personal integrity. A list of suggestions for herders that he wrote in Wainwright and later used on the Kuskokwim sound as Yup'ik as they do Protestant: "Learn to be QUICK. . . . Get up early. Keep busy and you will not be lonesome. . . . Make your sleds, harness, and snowshoes before you need them. Get plenty of bootgrass every summer." [36] These standards were compatible with the nineteenth-century Yup'ik code for conduct. Had like-minded managers continued in charge of the enterprise, the successful marriage of Yup'ik personal integrity and Western individualism that John saw embodied in the deer industry might have been accomplished.

CHAPTER 15

ASSISTANT SUPERINTENDENT OF THE WESTERN DISTRICT

I can see that the year will be a busy one for me and here is where I will find my peace and joy. I will have the satisfaction of placing our record of service in this land on a basis that will out last our natural lives. I will ever keep in mind the fact that this is your work as well as mine, and I will work for you just the same as tho you were right at my elbow.
—John Kilbuck to Edith Kilbuck, 1917[1]

RETURN AND RECONCILIATION

John and Edith left Akiak in June 1916 after five full years back on the river. Edith never intended to return. Her health was broken to the point where she had to be carried aboard ship on their departure. The couple reached Seattle on the morning of August 12. That evening, Edith wrote the following journal entry:

> Mr. Lopp at once requests John to go back to Alaska for the winter as a Hospital will be erected at Akiak and new teachers are to be installed as well as a Doctor and nurse. This was not atall in our plans. I thought I never would consent to his returning but the need is pressing and if I am better again he will go. . . . It is hard to have him go back alone, and I need him when I am sick, but I believe I am getting better so His will be done, and His cause be furthered. I don't wish to return but I would go with him if I were able.[2]

Thus, within less than a day, new and larger responsibilities threw over John's planned respite from work along the river. Just as in 1908 on his return from Wainwright, the bureau, in the person of Lopp, stepped between John and anticipated retirement with plans that spoke to the heart of his work in Alaska. Lopp not only asked John to return but to do so in the capacity of assistant superintendent of the western (Kuskokwim) district, rather than as local teacher and bureau representative.

Certainly, the increased scope of work must have appealed to John, especially as his oversight of the reindeer industry had already allowed him to expand his work within the district. During his years in Akiak, he had developed strong opinions on the direction bureau work must take for it to

310

benefit the region as a whole. Lopp's proposal must have held the irresistible appeal of giving John the power to enact some of the many programs he envisioned. Also, after the death of his father, the only motivation for a return to the hills in Kansas was Edith's need for rest. Kansas held John's history but no longer his home.

For the next dozen days Edith and John stayed at the Seward Hotel as John prepared to leave for the Kuskokwim with a party of new bureau employees. His plan was to take passage on the return trip of the vessel by which he and Edith had just come down. While in Seattle they took in the sights, including the Mary Pickford play *Hulda from Holland*. On the twenty-fourth John set sail on the *Umatilla* for Nome and St. Michael. Edith wrote, "It was *hard* to see him go. I am getting better of course, or he would not have left me, yet I feel so helpless without him. . . . His going is like a dream."[3] Eight years ago, John's departure for Douglas had been hard to reconcile, even with the knowledge of imminent reunion. This time Edith bade John good-bye, convinced that although his work was in Alaska, she would probably never be able to follow him there again.

After John set sail, Edith immediately headed east for Ottawa, arriving September 1. Joe and his wife Novello met her at the station and took her back to the home place. Within a week Joseph Romig, Sr., joined them, coming north from Independence to make his home with them. Edith divided the weeks between unpacking and consultations with the doctor: "Dr. Lawrence . . . says I should never return to Alaska again. The work and responsibilities would soon break me down again."[4] A month later, she had all her lower teeth taken out so that by the end of the year she might be fitted with a second plate. During the interval she stayed with Joe and Novello, awaiting the birth of the couple's first child.

Edith worked in the community of Ottawa as well as at home. After the first of the year she was appointed president of all the canning clubs in the county and traveled occasionally from one to the other giving lecture demonstrations. In January she visited Ruth, Van, and baby Van Doran in Durham, North Carolina. She moved on to nearby Winston-Salem, later traveling north to Philadelphia, Bethlehem, and a number of other communities with Moravian congregations, where she gave talks about Alaska to encourage the mission work. She especially advocated a boarding and training school on the Kuskokwim, which could also serve as an orphanage. John later took up the same crusade, and in part thanks to their effort the Moravians established an orphanage along the Kwethluk River in 1925.[5]

Although John had ministered informally to congregations in Kansas, Wainwright, Douglas, and Akiak over the last dozen years, Edith's lecture tour marked the first public reference to her husband's work officially sanctioned by the Moravian Church since John's expulsion in 1898. From 1900 to 1910 the church had nothing to say to him. After his return to the Kuskokwim in 1911, however, the Provincial Elders' Conference (PEC) went on record in favor of his readmission to mission service. In part, the shortage of missionaries along the Kuskokwim prompted this request. In the fall of 1911, just as John and Edith arrived in Akiak, Brother Stecker was prevented from returning to Alaska as intended. At the same time Brother Schoechert left the Kuskokwim on furlough.

Beyond their practical need for his services, the PEC believed that John's continued dedication to the Alaska field merited reconsideration: "Bro. Kilbuck, we are convinced, is again truly consecrated in the Lord's service, stands well with the government, has manifested a very brotherly and Christian disposition toward our missionaries, and because of his knowledge of the language, and long residence and work among the Eskimos, has great influence with the people." In view of both the mission's needs and John's capacity to fill them, the conference voted to restore John to the ranks of the ministry. Although the board was willing that John should be welcomed as a member of the mission church and asked to assist as a lay worker, they declined to allow him to resume ordained missionary status. During the next five years, though not officially working within their ranks, John remained on friendly terms with the missionaries at Bethel. In 1913 the PEC went so far as to extend a welcome and a promise of support in his seminary studies should Joe Kilbuck decide to enter mission service.[6]

Finally, just before he left Akiak in the spring of 1916, a special conference of the mission board in Bethlehem formally reinstated John as a missionary of the Moravian Church.[7] Although gratified by the request, John declined to forego his work for the bureau. Instead of returning to the Kuskokwim for mission work, he chose to return as a representative of the federal government. His view of service had expanded into secular domains normally outside the purview of missionary work. Although he remained friendly to the Moravian Church, John Kilbuck chose to champion the bureau's cause.

MANAGING THE KINGDOM

> *I have met a number of natives who have seen me before somewhere on the Kuskokwim. They just laugh all over themselves to hear me talk the native language. . . . They invited me to their kashim this evening to witness one of their dances, but I have more important things to do.*
>
> —*John Kilbuck, 1916*[8]

On September 4 John arrived in St. Michael, where he booked passage on the SS *Susie*, heading upriver to Russian Mission. From there he planned to portage over to the Kuskokwim and down to Akiak, where his duties would begin.

> Mr. Lopp has laid out a pretty heavy program for my year's work. I will have, of course, the hospital and the supervision of the Akiak school and village. He wants me to spend at least a week at Goodnews Bay and also visit Togiak and Kulukak. Then I am to look at the coal on Nelson Island and on

Fig. 15.1. Government schoolhouse at Russian Mission. Orthodox church in background. (Kilbuck family)

Eek River, make a report and send out samples. Mr. Lopp does not expect [District Superintendent] Johnson on the Kuskokwim this winter . . . so I will have a little kingdom of my own.[9]

In Russian Mission John attended the local Orthodox church. Though cool to some of what he saw, his observations lacked the denominational fire of his youth. The service he judged to hold "a real gospel message." Although not completely won over, he was impressed with the degree of support the church simultaneously drew from within the community and lacked from without: "He [probably Father Amkan] . . . has received no salary for two years. At that time he had received orders from his Bishop to go to St. Paul Island, but the people did not like to have him go, so they petitioned the bishop to allow him to stay. . . . The people give him all the support that he has, although that is not sufficient." In the end, John voiced qualified approval of the church he had held in such disrepute during his first years as a missionary: "It is too bad that there is so much of the immaterial connected with the worship of this church, because in the main she teaches salvation thru Jesus by the cross. If there were no other church, I would be a Greek Catholic, rather than a pagan."[10]

The first week in October John traveled over the portage and down the Kuskokwim to Akiak, where he was warmly welcomed: "The news of my return was known up and down the river long before my arrival. Never-the-less my arrival was a surprise and it was a big and happy one." Although John did not elaborate, he viewed his return as timely, serving to shore up the community's new-won, still tentative, "moral progress." In his brief absence, some had already fallen away: "The people must have thrown their good behavior to the winds and become wild; there seemed to be no respect left for other people's right of property."[11]

As soon as John arrived he took off down the river on a brief school inspection. Though he had promised Edith that he would pull out his pen for love letters, his faithful Corona (John's first typewriter) accompanied him for that purpose. He also carried a photo of his first grandson, Van Doran, which he proudly displayed to the cackles and comments of Yup'ik friends along the river.

On his return to Akiak, John found himself confronted by the formidable Mrs. Lulu Evans (soon to be Heron), the newly arrived nurse for the hospital. A middle-aged woman whose husband had been a Presbyterian minister, the energetic widow promptly assumed the reins of the Akiak household. By then a single roof sheltered the trio of local bureau employees, including John as district manager, the mild-mannered Miss May Wynne as school teacher, and Mrs. Evans in charge of the medical work.[12] John gave Edith a description of the new arrivals.

> Mrs. Evans at once set the natives off to themselves. I can see that I am to see many things done that I am not accustomed to and that really go against me. Mrs. Evans is a trained social worker and her methods are of the machine-made kind that appeal to the intellect and take little account of sentiment. She seems to be in great earnest and is going into clarifying the entire atmosphere of the village with a terrible rush, that, for the time at least is carrying the people off their feet. . . . She is a live wire, and my concern is that she does not consume herself. . . . As to Miss Wynne, I can only say that she is altogether after my notion for this work. She is steady in all her ways, and she is so sensible.[13]

Though Mrs. Evans was up to the mark in her work, her character made for a rocky home life. She was averse to natives visiting in the house and made the people that came to see John less than welcome. Although this inevitably caused friction, John's journals do not dwell on whatever domestic discord may have resulted. Instead, he spent his time preparing for a winter of traveling.

On November 18 John started upriver to inspect the deer. His first stop was Wassili's camp, where he mentioned one child, Katie, who was afraid of him and another, Harry, who was just learning to run around. Where he had lost his own children, Yup'ik rules of cosmological rebirth found them alive again in an upriver fish camp. Yup'ik children had also been named for John's mother, Sarah, and John honored the relationship accordingly: "I shot a very large snipe, and gave it to my mother, Sarah Percy. She was so pleased to get it. . . . She is about the size of [Joe Kilbuck's daughter] Katherine. When they ask her to point out her son's house, she points out this way. She does not talk yet."[14]

Although John traveled to oversee the deer industry, as in years past the people brought up a multitude of questions for settlement. On this particular trip the majority concerned marriage problems. As a missionary, John had often preached against the sin of adultery. As a government representative, his diatribes focused on the legal dimensions of the breach. The moral crime of living together in sin had become the civil crime of unlawful cohabitation. While in Tuluksak, villagers called John to consider the case of an unmarried couple: "I informed them that they had broken the law of the land and disobeyed the teachings of the church by living together without being legally married. By so doing they had placed themselves in position to be prosecuted by the Gov't. The best thing that they could do now was to lose no time in getting married. If they did not get married I would have to report them to the Commissioner as living together unlawfully." [15] At the same session, John advised one married man that if he wanted to leave his legal wife, he must travel to the court at Iditarod to apply for a divorce. John also undertook to legalize adoptions.

Perhaps the most intriguing example of John's efforts toward injecting Euro-American notions of legality into Yup'ik life was his response to the plight of a Yup'ik healer:

> We stopped at Makagwaliks for our tea. Ozivilingouk came in and I greeted him as Dr. Ozivilingouk, to his confusion. As I was preparing to leave he called me into his cabin and told me this: Some years ago as we were coming home from our spring camp while I was carrying my canoe over a portage I came across the skelton of a frog, standing on the edge of a frost crack in the earth. Putting down my burden I, according to instructions that I have heard, went up to the skelton and placing my hand spread out with the palm down, down close to the skelton, and said, "Give me power to heal bruises." Then I went on my way and when I returned the skelton was gone. Ever since just by rubbing my bare hand over a bruise the blood will come out without puncturing the skin and there is no trick connected with it such as pricking my own hand with any instrument. Since then when people came to him he had been able to draw the bad blood from their wounds with out lancing, simply by rubbing his hand over the bruise. He has been paid something for his services. He then asked me if he should continue to exercise his power.

In his past incarnation as missionary, John would probably have advised the man to stop his practice on the grounds that it was heathen sorcery. His current response was not so much concerned with moral as with regulatory order:

> I told him that he must get a license to practice the same as any other doctor. He would have to appear before some doctors who would give him a paper allowing him to practice as a regular doctor and get his fees. Otherwise he was liable to be prosecuted for practicing without a license and collecting pay for it. He wants me to tell the in-coming doctor about him, and in the mean time he would refuse to treat any more cases that were brought to him. [16]

Arriving back in Akiak at the end of November, John immediately left in the direction of Goodnews Bay. The distance between camps proved more than the deer could travel in a single day, and he spent the night on the trail. Arriving at Eek the next day, he was warmly greeted by the woman Janey, whom he had called alternately "sister" and Tokogluk (probably *tukurliq*: host, wealthy person) from his first years in Bethel. "My Tokogluk was very glad to see me and she did what she could to make my stay comfortable. . . . She says that she will have a pair of sealskin boots ready for me by my return." At Christmas that year, John would fulfill the obligation he had incurred by giving her a dress and a bottle of perfume. John's relationship with Janey was more than a formality accompanied by a material exchange and represented an enduring friendship. On a future visit, he wrote to Edith that the two had sat talking until late into the night, exchanging stories about their lives' doings. [17]

On his arrival in Goodnews Bay, John reached both the end of his journey and the beginning of his work when he was called upon to arbitrate between the government teacher, Mr. Anderson, and the people of the village. Although Anderson was hard-working and had high expectations for his students, John reported that he had tried to force things, using violence in his dealings with recalcitrant scholars. He had also accused the people of "persistent thievery" when they took lumber and coal from the school, while the people likely viewed their acts as borrowing from the abundant supplies the stingy teacher was hoarding. The combination of high standards and aggressive methods had inflamed the villagers, leading to their formal request for the teacher's removal.

John's tack was to listen to the natives' complaints, carefully writing down all they said. After that he confronted Mr. Anderson, who at first raged at him for taking sides with the people against him. After a day and a night of talk, Anderson eventually admitted to being at fault and promised to do better. The last step was for John to gather the people together again and admonish them to try to live at peace with their teacher. John advised them that although it might be easy to get the government to close the school and take away the teacher, it would not be nearly so simple to get them to open it again thereafter. [18]

Although John left Goodnews Bay with promises on both sides to make a new start, the cease-fire was temporary. Less than two months later he received a letter from Anderson detailing continued problems. Among the incidents he related was a violent confrontation with a truant schoolboy whom Anderson grabbed by the hand to bring him to heel. According to Anderson, "The boy scratched like a wild cat. I gave him one on the side of the head and took him out by force. His grandfather was very angry, and I had a time to get him away from the door so I could get out." [19]

Several days later, Anderson burnt his arm in another violent struggle with a distraught villager. He noted that although John's visit had temporarily cleared the air, he was convinced that it was a "waste of money to try to keep this place going."[20] Though admitting his own failings, he ultimately laid the blame on the antagonistic attitude and unruly behavior of the people of Goodnews Bay. Unaware that his propensity to physical and verbal abuse rendered him largely unsuitable for bureau work, he closed by suggesting that with his "experience" he might best be transferred to Bethel or Akiak!

Anderson's peculiar personality, given to meticulous housekeeping one moment and fits of temper the next, proved incompatible with village life. Nevertheless, John believed that Anderson's good qualities outweighed his bad and that it was worth the time to try to work the problems through. He tried to create an opportunity for the crisis to be resolved, but in the end the solution to the Goodnews-Anderson conflict was Anderson's removal. This case illustrates John's main frustration with his position as regional monitor for bureau activities—observing what was present, having an opinion on what was needed, being unable to provide it.

Arriving back in Akiak, Brother Arthur Butzin caught John up on national news.[21] The war was nearing an end, President Wilson had been reelected, and, "also very acceptable," Alaska had gone dry. Akiak was full of holiday doings and visitors. Altogether 235 people, including the entire local white population, crowded the church for the annual Christmas services. John remarked his pleasure at being a spectator to the event. Even so, he was called upon to take a small part, reading scripture and offering a prayer. Christmas dinner at the house included an unprecedented eight white men and five white women.

Though Christmas proved a busy season, the weeks immediately following were even busier. By the second week in January, John orchestrated the annual deermen's fair, which was well attended, with spectators coming from as far away as Iditarod. The storeowners across the river in "White Akiak" donated a long list of prizes for the competitive events, including a phonograph. A new feature of the fair was an examination of the apprentices on the care of the herd. Of the twenty questions that John put to the group, the best paper had fourteen correct answers, followed by thirteen, ten, and all the way down to one. The upshot was John's introduction of a standardized course for the apprentices the following year.

After the fair John made plans for another trip downriver as far as Togiak. Dispelling any doubt, if that were ever possible, about his preference for travel, John wrote, "As this is a long trip I will have plenty of time to rest up from the close confining work that I have passed thru this month." Later he added, "I would like to be on the trail all the time!"[22]

By the end of the winter, John had traveled a total of 1,690 miles (330 by motor boat, 175 by dog team, and 1,185 by deer). He had visited all of the four district schools two or more times, including those at Goodnews Bay, Quinhagak, Bethel, and Akiak. He also inspected nine reindeer camps, established one new herd, and combined the herd at Kinak with that at Kalskag.[23]

LOVE AND DUTY

Soon after his return to Akiak, John wrote Lopp a long, detailed letter concerning his plans and recommendations for the coming year. Due to retirements and transfers, new teachers were called for at Quinhagak, Goodnews Bay, and Kinak. At the same time, he requested additional teachers as well as expanded facilities for Akiak and Bethel. Concerning his personal plans, John wrote:

> I do not know anything definite now. I of course expect to remain long enough to finish the work of installing the Hospital among the natives and the new workers. If you want me to stay longer than this year, I suggest that you give me an appointment for the year, with the understanding that I can quit at any time without hurting your feelings. If I possibly can I want to catch the last fall boats either via Bethel or St. Michael. My wife needs me, and if I had the money I would go to her sooner, but I must at least stay long enough to earn my transportation. I hope you can open your heart and hand to the extent of giving me one hundred 50 dollars per month, at least. I place no limit above that figure, that is up to you.[24]

In closing, John told his chief that although he "wanted to live and die in Alaska," he had "duties nearer home" and must go. To Edith, on the other hand, he had claimed his work in Alaska a duty he could not dismiss, while his heart was with her in Kansas. The apparent contradiction was explained in a letter to Edith later that year in which he described how he conceived these different and conflicting "duties."

> My own desire is to come to you, and do whatever I can to cheer and sustain you in these trying times. . . . The natives at large need me, and this I say not for my vanity's sake, but it is a fact, which you probably know even better than I do, that my presence on this river helps the native to get better treatment from the whites. The whites hesitate to be hard on the people, unjustly, because they think that my influence, both with the natives and the department, is too great not to be reckoned with.[25]

John had but one duty—his commitment to the Yup'ik people of the Kuskokwim—but two loves: Edith and traveling. Although spatially the two opposed each other, his devotion to each one seemed to empower rather than detract from his love of the other.

John's love for Edith and his work in Alaska filled his days. Over and over again the journals he wrote during his travels spoke of his dreams of Edith. Some of these dreams were worrisome, others depicted her as in real life and left him happy and satisfied. One of the most striking pictured her as close to engaging in profanity as she probably ever came: "In one of my naps last night . . . I distinctly saw you sitting on a TABLE and you were talking with a man, who was sitting across the room from you. As I made my way toward you, in a loud clear voice, I heard you say 'GEE WHIZ.' I stood stock still, and the shock woke me up." [26]

With the approach of summer, John's oversight of the district schools and bureau herds came to a temporary end. As the river opened up and the large sternwheelers began to move upriver, he detailed the new industry that the Kuskokwim had come to support. By the summer of 1917 Bethel harbored close to fifty craft of all sizes, shapes, and colors, with plank boats out-numbering those made out of skin. [27] This was a remarkable technological transformation.

A new fish plant had also been established at the mouth of the Eek River, where native workers could earn $2.00 a day. Local fishermen sold king salmon for $.25 a pound and small salmon at $.05, some men taking home almost $50 after the runs subsided. At the end of August John remarked that thanks to the heavy run of salmon, the Eek Saltery had been able to process one thousand silvers a day. He viewed this expanded fishery with mixed emotions, however, detailing his concerns regarding a Mr. Joaquin's intention to set up a line cannery the following year at Bethel: "I am not sure that canneries are permissible in fresh water, i.e. for the canning of salmon. I will have this looked up, for I am not in favor of a cannery so far up the river, and especially right in the fishing grounds of a village of natives. There has been some trouble already, I am told thru the removal of a set net belonging to Zachariah." [28]

Although peripherally interested in the expansion of commerce along the Kuskokwim, John's great task over the summer was overseeing the construc-tion of the new hospital. Most of the materials had arrived in the fall of 1916, but the carpenters and doctor had not. Therefore, the summer of 1917 was devoted to work in Akiak. Before beginning, John made one more trip downriver to Goodnews Bay to oversee the landing of the supplies and coal for the local school as well as to get workers for the hospital. After stopping at Goodnews Bay he decided to make the round trip, continuing on to Nushagak and the peninsula, which he expected to be quicker than taking a small craft home from Goodnews Bay to Akiak.

Stormy weather drew the trip out to more than a month's duration and caused John no end of anxiety concerning his responsibilities back in Akiak. On the positive side, John felt that the sea voyage had "braced him up" after the winter's work and worry, as his job as assistant superintendent was be-ginning to prove trying.

Another thing I have found out, and that is that I would just keep on going south, if I would not be leaving the Department in a lurch. I have no han-kering, whatever, for going back to the Kuskokwim. . . . However, I am going back, from a sense of duty. I will grit my teeth together, with the determination to do my best, and give the best of me to the work. Then when

I leave, it will be with the satisfaction of knowing that I did not quit, because it was hard.[29]

Whatever the drawbacks of John's inadvertent coastal excursion it exemplified his effective intervention on behalf of the Yup'ik people of the Kuskokwim. On his arrival at Port Heiden, John met natives from the Kuskokwim who had come down earlier in the summer on the vessel *Breaker*, which had gone to the river in June for workmen for the local cannery: "The natives were glad to see me, and they thot that their troubles were over. They asked me right away if they could get home, and when I answered them in the affirmative, they heaved a mighty sigh of relief."[30]

A group of thirty natives from the Pacific side of the peninsula were in a similar situation: "This year about thirty of these Aleuts were brot around the pass on one of the cannery ships, with the understanding that they would be taken home in the same way, so the natives claim. The Cannery Supt. claims to have never made any such promises, and refuses to give them transportation, only to the head of Herendun [Heiden] Bay." John noted that the natives usually came as far as the portage in large skin boats (bidarkas). The fact that these thirty did not was further evidence that there had been some misunderstanding: "I instructed Mr. Culver [the cannery foreman] to wire the situation to Mr. Lopp. A delegation of these natives waited on me, and I explained to them what was being done to get them to their homes."[31]

After looking into the situation, John concluded that the poor run of fish that summer and small size of the pack put up by the canneries had contributed to the cannery superintendent's uncooperative disposition. Whatever the superintendent's rationale, John needed more than diplomacy to win his point:

> The superintendent positively refused to give transportation home to 30 Aleuts. I had had a quiet talk with him about the treatment of natives in general. Mr. Culver, later again brot up the question of transporting the natives but the Supt. only agreed to take all the natives to the head of Herendun [Heiden] Bay, but would not furnish them transportation on the Pacific side. I prepared a telegram about the situation, to Mr. Lopp and instructed Mr. Culver to send it. This morning Mr. Culver told me that when he presented the telegram for the supt's O.K. (this being required)—the Sup't refused to pass it, telling Mr. Culver that it was none of his business—but after storming a bit—he cooled down and said that he would see to it that the natives got home. This is another point scored in my favor. Mr. Culver is rather a thorn to Supt. Amundsen, and that is probably why there was a hitch about the affair. Mr. Amundsen does not want it known in Gov't circles outside that his Company had left the natives in a lurch.[32]

Along with arranging transportation for the natives, it was also left to John to help the Kuskokwim natives home. On the return of the *Eunice* he saw that they had their accounts settled and were promptly gotten on board, as the captain was anxious to leave. In the process he made pointed observation of what the natives had gotten for their summer's trouble:

> I found that all the boys had over drawn their accounts. The boss Chinaman did the employing of the natives while the Co's store looked after getting back all they earned. Expecting that the natives would earn at least $100.00 for the season, the Co. did not hesitate to advance as much as $60.00 to some of them. None of the boys, it would seem, earned enough money to pay off these store bills, so there was nothing coming to them. All they have for their summer, is some clothing, and a lot of experience which will prove of interest, when related to the stay-at-homes.[33]

RETURN TO AKIAK

After more than a month's absence, John returned to Akiak on August 4, bringing the young Yup'ik girl Lily back with him. On his visit to Quinhagak the previous fall he had seen her for the first time since his return to Alaska. Although Lily seemed contented with her foster parents, John wrote that she appeared dazed when she saw him, just as when they had last seen her: "Her eyes glistened and her lips quivered as with strong emotion. There was a lump in my own throat." Later that spring he tried to find another place for the child, as the growth of her foster family meant that she was being neglected. He was reluctant to suggest that Mrs. Thorton, of Flat, who apparently wanted to adopt a child, take her, as it had never been his intention to send Lily away from her own people altogether.[34]

John determined to bring Lily home with him to Akiak on his return in August, confiding to Edith that in his heart she filled the same place as a child of his own. He wrote Edith a number of times concerning his wish to bring the girl home to Kansas with him on his return, but he seemed convinced that it could never be. Lily remained first John's and later Edith's close companion during the remainder of their years in Akiak, in part filling the space created by the departure of their own children.

Back in Akiak, John resumed work on the endless administrative tasks. The carpenter, Mr. Scott, had arrived to take charge of the construction of the new hospital, and John helped him hire a work crew and get started. John had been appointed weather observer and by the end of August had received and housed the new instruments. From then on John's journal entries to Edith included daily minimum and maximum temperatures as well as river ice conditions. Although the outfit for the new post office had not yet arrived, John expected it any day, at which time he would assume the duties of postmaster as well.

In mid-August John was joined by Dr. Frank Lamb, who had come over from Nulato to take charge of the hospital. To acquaint the new doctor with the territory, John gave his outboard motor a quick overhaul and took Dr. Lamb on a brief tour of the villages. The year before Nurse Evans had examined more than six hundred individuals and concluded that of these at least one-third had tubercular histories or active symptoms. Half the remainder she judged normal, the other half below normal.[35] These statistics were not taken lightly, and Dr. Lamb set to work to evaluate the situation and formulate a response.

At the same time that John's cycle of work increased, he faced his tasks "more wholeheartedly" than earlier in the summer.

> I see a lot of work of the kind I like ahead of me, right up to the time when I shall get on board of some ship that will bear me homeward. I will do traveling right up to freezing, and then as soon as the ice is safe, I will be on the go again, and about the only time that I will be at Akiak will be during the fair. Dr. Lamb [and I] . . . will be inseparable, for I find him to be [the] kind of man who can be chummed with. . . . I intend to have Dr. Lamb fully posted as to the work in all its detail, so that he can take right a hold. I have no doubt that my mantle will fall on him.[36]

The fall that had appeared promising dragged. School was not opened until the end of October, as John was occupied with medical work, weather instruments, and postal regulations. John wrote to Edith, "It's not work that makes me tired, it's not having things go as they should. It will be the greatest pleasure to hoe my own potatoe hill."[37] Writing in the same vein, he noted that he never planned to be away so long in the beginning and never intended to be parted so long again. In fact, this was the last season of work in Alaska in which the distance of a continent separated them.

As a respite from his work in Akiak, John visited the Moravian mission in Bethel, which he experienced as "an oasis in the desert": "It was so peaceful and restful. I did not have to watch every word that comes out of my mouth, lest something would be twisted to mean a hurt."[38] The expansion of the non-native workforce at Akiak and the complexity of the secular concerns for which it was responsible had increased interpersonal turmoil. As a result, Akiak began to experience some of the same growing pains that the mission at Bethel had undergone with the growth of its force beginning in 1893, and John experienced some of the same discomfort. Ironically, it was at the mission that John found relief from his present stress.

John elicited a warm reception on his visits. He wrote Edith that her name came up often and that she was remembered with affection: "The missionaries all think so much of you, so much in fact that they would like to have us come back and work with them."[39] The missionaries still hoped that John might rejoin them in the spring, and in November 1917 he was invited to hold Sunday service at the mission once more. There he preached his first English service in years to a full house.

Along with entertaining requests for his return, John also received encouragement concerning his ethnographic interests: "I had told Mrs. Schwalbe about my intention to collect child stories of the Eskimo, and she has shown her interest by getting one for me from Emma, about the porcupine. She thinks that such a book would be readily accepted by the public." Brother Butzin had remarked the previous spring on the value of John's prodigious correspondence, which even in his lifetime was legendary: "He remarked that if it were not that I had heirs for my letters, he would like to have me will them to him. They are however not of the character to interest any other person but our own family."[40] Both comments reflected John's literary enterprise, and both underestimated the value of his labors. At the same time that John demonstrated his interest in Yup'ik oral tradition, he restricted his inquiry to what he mistakenly perceived as no more than "child stories." He believed his personal correspondence had no worth beyond his immediate family. On the contrary, from the point of view of both regional history and ethnography, what he recorded was invaluable.

THE KILBUCK POINT OF VIEW

Although John may have underestimated the value for posterity of his "endless scribblings," he was fully convinced of the importance of his presence along the river. This was especially true with the steady growth of nonnative influences, both positive and negative. John was troubled over the dancing and drinking that the traders and miners had introduced in Bethel and Akiak and spoke loud and long against such "pernicious distractions." In a typical aside to Edith, he wrote:

> The dancing still continues and the results from these gatherings are not of the best. The teachers are doing what they can to combat the evil. . . . I understand that some liquor has been given to native women. I am going to speak to Mr. Felder about this, with the hope that he will take warning. In a couple more months he will have to quit handling the stuff or else get deported, for every government employee is under obligation to help stop the liquor business.[41]

Though John remained hopeful that drinking might be curtailed, he feared the deleterious effects of the evening "socials" that were increasingly a part of life along the river: "The teachers at Bethel had to contend against the white man's dance. This form of amusement has taken strong hold of the natives; the white men foster it and do everything to encourage it. The natives do not realize as yet that they are paying dearly for the pleasure they get out of these dances."[42] The dancing craze had just arrived in Akiak, and John hoped that the sentiment among the older people against it was strong enough to prevent it from taking hold. He believed the natives' success in "resisting temptation" was in large measure contingent on the ability of teachers and missionaries to furnish "harmless amusements" to lessen its appeal.

Although the increase in non-native activity along the river brought "temptations," it also brought benefits. A major advantage, from John's point of view, was increased access to Western goods. On a visit to Goodnews Bay in February 1918 he gave a "practical talk" to the residents concerning their future:

> The prospective presence of a great number of miners in this immediate vicinity will present many favorable opportunities for bettering their condition materially. There will be chances to work, there will be more demand for whatever the natives usually get from themselves, as fish and fur clothing. Now will be their time to get and be doing, with the view of getting things they have been doing without, first and foremost being better houses. Besides fish, the miners will be glad to be able to buy vegetables. . . . I urged them to depend on the teachers for guidance, who are especially instructed to look out for them. While there are good men among the miners, still . . . the miners as a whole respect the natives as long as they cannot lead them into doing what is not right, but just as soon as they can lead them astray just that quick they have no respect for them.[43]

In Akiak, too, development in the non-native sector influenced the material circumstances of community members, much as local capital development projects do today. John described the situation of two industrious hospital employees: "[Henry] has been working off and on at the Hospital ever since the building began, so he has been able to keep his folks well provided. . . . Manutuli has been steadily at work on the hospital from the beginning and he has kept his folks in flour and tea, besides clothing all of his brothers and sister, as well as his mother."[44] John remarked on the "advancement" such employment made possible: "Robert has been adding improvements to his house. Both rooms are neatly papered, his china closet is also papered and the contents are well arranged. He showed us a wash stand he had made today, and proudly showed two basins, the one, with white lining is for morning when the face is washed, and the other a commoner looking one is for the day when the hands only are washed."[45] At the same time, John noted with satisfaction the increased willingness of white men to legally bind themselves to their native wives. Commenting on one such groom, he wrote, "The white man is evidently not of the same way of thinking as the one who said, 'What, me marry a native? No, for I do not want my blood to be running around here eating stinky fish.'"[46]

Not only were natives increasingly able to live like whites and with whites, John was gratified to note that they were also inclined to give like whites: "I presented the call of the Red Cross service. I gave a good half hour talk . . . and then appealed to the people to give as much as they could to this noble cause. . . . The cause appeals to them and so far all the adults have been giving a dollar apiece, and the larger children, fifty cents and the rest even the babies a quarter each child."[47]

Through their charity Yup'ik donors expressed their status as Christian citizens possessing duties as well as rights. Whereas their initial "civilization" was regarded as a gift necessary for individual survival, membership in a Christian community entailed obligations to the world at large. To John, this extension of their capacities as civilized persons implied their efforts toward conformity with the nineteenth-century "moral majority" and their progress toward membership in a homogeneous Christian nation. John played a central role as catalyst in this transformation, urging the people on in his characteristically pragmatic style. He was forever on the lookout for ways to help the natives help themselves. Although reluctant to trade away the lumber left over from the construction of the hospital, which he had earmarked for use in building a wash house, he was anxious to encourage local industry.

> Waska fixed up Percy's house by putting down flooring he bought from Felder. . . . I did so want to help them out for they have been so industrious so finally thought of a way to encourage them. I told them that I was willing to exchange lumber with them, they to bring me the lumber next spring from the mission for what they would get from me. In this way I will not be any worse off for lumber, and it will be a great accommodation to them.[48]

At the same time that John watched out for opportunities to help "advance" the Yup'ik people, he took a strong stand against misuse of the government's helping hand.

> Last evening I had a meeting with the men to determine the price of wood for this coming year. The men wanted $8.00 for standing timber per cord, and $7.00 for drift wood. I gave them a talk after these bids were in, drawing their attention to the fact that they were asking more of the Govt. for wood than of any one else, and more than I had to pay at Bethel. . . . I told them that if wood was so high here, altho we lived in a timbered country the Govt. would take to shipping in coal, and then the means of earning some extra money would be gone for them. I told them to go home and think this matter over, and let me know on the morrow what they concluded to do. . . . At the meeting this evening, the men decided that they would sell cord wood at the rate of $6.00 for green wood and $5.00 for drift, which is a whole lot more reasonable.[49]

Juxtaposed to these encouraging signs of the natives' growing commitment to Western thrift and industry, John also recorded the "moral laxity" he felt inhered in the vestiges of the traditional Yup'ik ceremonial round. The physical and moral dangers that John believed were associated with traditional redistributive mechanisms were exemplified in the midwinter dance held at Kwigillingok in the winter of 1918 and in the period of destitution and starvation that followed. In John's annual report for 1918 he gave a highly prejudicial description of the traditional Kevgiq, or Messenger Feast:

There is another dance that must be taken into serious consideration, and that is the native dance called Kuvgagyagak, a dance in the nature of a potlatch. The more advanced of the natives are giving up this dance, but it is doubtful if it will become obsolete in the near future. One village invites one or more of the other villages to its dance, and besides entertaining the visitors, it will, as requested by the visitors, turn over to them any piece of personal property they request. Usually the hosts not only dance to the limit of their wealth, but draw on their credit as well. It is supposed that the visitors will give away stuff to equal or even excel the value of what they received from their hosts, but this seldom happens.[50]

John described the situation at Kwigillingok, where harvests had been abundant the previous summer and fall. The people chose this opportunity to make their reputation and invited several villages for Kevgig: "Each individual wanted to outdo some rival in giving. The visitors went away well off, taking even the guns and traps of the hunter. Before the play was over a storm set in and lasted a long time. During all this time the hosts fed their guests and their dogs." Food began to run short before the end of the winter. All might have come out well if the spring sealing season had been timely and abundant. However, the season was backward, and by mid-April reports reached Akiak that the people along the coast were starving. The slow spring meant that food was short up and down the river, although there was no immediate danger of starvation. To be on the safe side, John decided to send supplies to the coast: "I have made up my mind to get up a relief expedition, and drive some deer down to the sufferers and see if I cannot help them to get strong enough to help themselves. I will take deer from Young Kilbuck, which I am sure the Govt. will replace. I will take as many as he can spare, ten or fifteen at least."[51]

On his birthday, May 15, John was pleased by the safe return of the relief party: "Percy says that he learned that there have been ten deaths, probably all from starvation or its effects. . . . The principal danger facing the people is that of over eating, after their long fast. This is the best birthday present I can expect, to have the relief expedition I set afoot under the most unfavorable conditions of trail and weather, succeed and to know that it was a godsend in timeliness."[52]

John traveled to Kwigillingok in mid-June, bringing additional supplies. Although many people had left the village for summer camp, thirty-two of the most impoverished remained. John noted that the situation was in every respect grimmer than he had heard:

It is reported that children were allowed to starve, which may be true, for people become dehumanized by hunger. . . . Up to the time of my visit 23 had died at Quigillingok [Kwigillingok] and 18 in the surrounding villages as a direct result from the shortage of food. Since then, I learned, 5 or 6 more have died. Quigillingok had a population of 300, and another village,

Tshalin [Cal'itmiut], had 200. Food conditions were unusually bad in the entire Kuskokwim Valley, but these two villages suffered the most.[53]

Although periods of starvation probably only rarely followed Kevgiq, John drew a moral from the incidents of that spring: "The lesson of the whole matter is this: There is no occasion for this starvation; it was brought about by that play. Other people who did not have so great a supply of food weathered the adverse conditions of the spring in good shape. . . . This is a good time for either the Territorial or the Federal Government to prohibit these potlatches."[54]

John's view of the importance of frugality makes his position comprehensible. What is surprising, however, is that he so far had missed the significance of the midwinter give-aways. According to Robert Brightman, an inverse relationship existed between giving and starving. They viewed fish and game as infinitely renewable resources, their availability increasing in proportion to their use. Though a display of status was part and parcel of Kevgiq, it sought to accomplish the revitalization and validation, through massive gifting, of the people's relationship to the fish and game on which they depended. Only if what they had acquired was totally consumed could they expect to successfully harvest in the future. Far from a virtue, hoarding one's harvest for personal consumption was a cultural impossibility, given the social character of the relationship between harvesters as well as between hunter and hunted. From the Yup'ik point of view, if people failed to give what they had been given it would not be given them in the future.

On John's return from Kwigillingok he preached a strong sermon against ceremonial distributions and their detrimental after effects:

> I began with Cain's remark, "Am I my brother's keeper?" and led up to Paul's statement, "Wherefore, if meat make my brother to offend, I will eat no flesh while the world standeth, lest I make my brother to offend." Having just returned from the scene of starvation and having there seen how selfishness works, for I saw a woman who was abandoned by her brother and sister to perish, without food, without water, unable to move, I had an excellent illustration of the spirit of Cain's answer and question. I know I made a strong impression.

Certainly the exigencies of scarcity might undercut concern for one's fellow villagers. Ironically, however, the dance distribution to which John attributed the problem was believed by the Yupiit to guarantee, through the ritual consumption and hosting of the spirits of the game, that such scarcity would never occur.[55]

At the same time that John decried the improvidence inherent in traditional distributions, he also delivered a lecture in Bethel deploring the wastefulness of the younger Yup'ik generation who had "fallen away" from the admirable example of their elders: "The subject of food saving is one that the present generation is sadly neglecting, being the fault mostly of the parents in not heeding the teachings of their forebearers. Food and other things are much more abundant than in former times, so the people in general have been careless and the children do not know what it is to restrain their appetites." In fact, the practices that John deemed "wasteful" and "unrestrained" may not have been as recent in origin as he thought. John was correct that careful treatment of animals was traditionally required, as people's offenses were said to come back to them. But this careful treatment was not necessarily synonymous with frugality as he defined it, as the Yupiit viewed animals as infinitely renewable resources. John interpreted the traditional Yupiit as natural conservationists, bent from time immemorial on careful, waste-free management of a finite resource. On the contrary, only the availability of animals, not their existence, was within the range of human influence. The basic assumption underlying John's understanding of the Yup'ik relationship between humans and animals was that the obligation to limit kills and avoid waste was an aspect of traditional "respect culture." This was, however, a partial and incomplete understanding of the Yup'ik point of view.[56]

Throughout their tenure in Alaska, John and Edith were confounded by the combination of care and apparent extravagance by which the Yup'ik people dealt with animals. On his trip to Hooper Bay in 1911, John remarked on a successful beluga drive, after which the natives harvested only select cuts of meat. He was appalled by what he perceived as the natives' improvidence, remarking, "Here they are acting according to their time honored custom that the more they kill, the more whales will return the following year. Such carelessness will cost them dear the following spring." John remonstrated against this same carelessness in his complaints against Kevgiq distributions in which the Yup'ik people "acted as if there would be no tomorrow." He was accurately observing the practical consequences of the idea that one's future hunting luck was partially dependent on the complete use of stores from the previous year. This practice played an important part in showing the animals that the people respected them. John concluded that the exigencies of primitive methods of meat preservation accounted for this practice. More than a functional means of disposing of excess, these feasts continued to be held as the prerequisite for a successful harvest in the coming year and, as such, were deemed essential sacred acts, whatever their social cost.[57]

John misconstrued the meaning of Yup'ik actions in important respects. In practice, however, his position often coincided with ideal Yup'ik behavioral norms. For example, that same spring he preached on the need to be pure in thought and word as well as deed, virtues common to both Christian and traditional Yup'ik ideology. As John observed, however, a discrepancy existed between the Yup'ik admonition not to injure another's mind through hurtful speech and the practical use of gossip and ridicule (for example, indirect verbal attack) as a preferred means of social control: "I spoke on the uses of the tongue, my remarks being based on the verses in the third chapter of James. My aim was to have the people be more careful of their gossiping and talebearing. *Yuliunak* [acting in an iritating manner] is altogether too lightly regarded by these people and yet it is just thru this talking about each other that gives rise to so much bitterness, and heart burnings." [58]

John's recollections of another successful sermon reflected a second parallel that worked to his advantage: "Without knowing it I had . . . laid a good foundation for this sermon on the Holy Spirit, when I preached about the temptation and fall of Adam and Eve, in the Garden of Eden. After dwelling on the hardness of the human heart, and the price required to change it, my sermon narrowed down to the Flesh and Spirit. . . . I do believe the Spirit inspired me, for my thoughts flowed connectedly, and the words were not wanting to express those thoughts." [59] Although he did not detail what was said, his sense of accomplishment indicates that his advice concerning the hardness of the human heart rang true to Yup'ik listeners who brought to the sermon a belief in the power and fragility of the human mind.

The Yup'ik definition of laziness, as recorded in a letter to Edith, also bears a marked relationship to John's own standards: "Kawagleg says that Dr. Lamb has won his good opinion because he is not lazy, i.e. that he never puts off attending to patients to a more convenient time." [60] These resemblances are striking and perhaps reflect John's increased internalization of a Yup'ik point of view, at least in what he chose to recall from his own background. Like his views of Kevgiq, however, remarks such as that concerning the "immorality" of gossip indicate that a large gap still separated John's point of view from that of the Yup'ik people among whom he lived. Whatever the depth of the exchange, in the spring of 1918 John's oratory was bent on the redirection of the Yup'ik people, body and soul. He might draw on their traditional values to make his case, but he did not intend to reproduce them.

WHO WILL BE KILBUCK?

Along with managing the work at the hospital and monitoring the situation at Kwigillingok, John's spring was a busy one. In late February he traveled to Goodnews Bay, where he visited the local teachers, the Gwynns: "Mrs. Gwynn says that the natives seem to like me very much, and she is fond of repeating what Dennis, one of the deer men had said. He was speaking of my going away, and he shook his head and said, 'Who will be Kilbuck?'" [61] Although historians may not subscribe to the great man theory of history, some Yup'ik Eskimos did.

Returning to Akiak a month later, John wrote Edith, "I made a stir with my white mustache. The children crowded around me and looked at me

Fig. 15.2. John Kilbuck, 1918. (Moravian Archives)

Fig. 15.3. Akiak Hospital. (Yugtarvik Regional Museum)

with wide open eyes and mouths. People seemed to realize for the first time that I was old."[62] Home in Akiak, John saw the hospital through to completion and settled down to work on reports and correspondence until breakup would free him to return to Kansas. His annual report as assistant superintendent of the western district came to an optimistic conclusion. Lauding the value of the newly completed hospital, John wrote:

> And now what do we need more on the Kuskokwim? First and always more money, to put up modern school houses at Bethel, Akiak, Quinhagak and Eek, and to establish new schools; and there should be buildings for gymnasiums to go with every school. The biggest task we have on our hands is to save a worthy people from the ravages of tuberculosis. We now have the school and the Hospital, all that is needed is the Gymnasium. The hospital was a long time coming, but it came, but we hope that the Gym will come quicker.[63]

In fact, a school gymnasium did not materialize for more than fifty years, and Bethel and Akiak remain without public gym facilities today.

Busy with his work, John experienced fewer and fewer bouts of homesickness. During the course of the year, however, he became increasingly frustrated with his position as regional monitor for bureau activities. He wrote to Edith that although he observed what was present and knew what was needed, he was more often than not unable to provide better:

> It is a relief to realize that in the near future I shall be free. For some reason I have so many things brought up that require my attention, as for example: "I regret that it is necessary to bother you with the details connected with the making and shipping this shelter [for weather instruments] but you seem to be the hub of the Kuskokwim wheel and we know of no one else to whom we can turn for help." Hub I am, but I am your Hub, and that is all the hub I want to be.[64]

Just as the character of the Bethel mission had changed with the growth of its staff in the 1890s, Akiak had changed with the completion of the hospital and the arrival of the new doctor and nurse as well as a new school teacher. A distinction also began to develop between native Akiak and its white counterpart clumped around the trading post on the opposite bank of the river. The backbiting and squabbling that attended this division wore on John's patience and wherewithal to continue work in Akiak.

In the beginning the bureau had provided support for the transformation John sought to implement among the Yup'ik people. As bureau work focused on the material improvements of life along the river, John increasingly used the pulpit as the staging ground for this dialogue. Perhaps he was already considering rejoining the Bethel missionaries in their work. Brother Butzin was wooing him to take charge of a helpers' school, a theological seminary for native brethren: "Everybody is predicting that we will be back in a year or two. Even strangers say we will be missed very much, and think that we are a necessity on this river. The missionaries are of course just hoping with all their might that we will come back, and cast our lot in with them." [65]

Not only the missionaries sought to claim John's talents. A California businessman named Skidmore made John a handsome proposal. In exchange for his help in setting up a private reindeer business along the Kuskokwim, Skidmore promised John the presidency of the company as well as a substantial share of the profits. John confided to his friend Dr. Lamb at Akiak, "I told him that if I returned to Alaska it would not be because I wanted to make money, and if I did return, it would be to continue my work with the natives, either with the Bureau of Education, or the mission. He said that he was told by the missionaries that they would grab me quick, if I wanted to throw in my lot with them." [66] As the hour of his departure approached, John as usual was contemplating the form of his return.

Following breakup, John put his work in order, and on July 2 he left Akiak for Quinhagak via Bethel. Returning to Bethel and boarding the schooner *Ruby*, he noted that "Capt. Knaflich, when he was collecting fares from the passengers, asked me if the Govt. was paying my expenses, and when I said that I was paying my own way he said, 'You will not pay me anything. You are the best friend I have on the river, and so you are going free on my boat.'" On July 18 John finally set sail: "How do I feel? I really feel just like a log. Everything and everybody seem so far away, out of reach, while I am just going, somewhere. I think this is the result of the long waiting over the delays." [67]

John arrived in Seattle on August 6 and spent a week at the Stevens' Hotel. While he was there, he worked at the bureau's office with Lopp on school requisitions and teacher appointments. He stopped in at the optician's to get his glasses fixed before boarding a Union Pacific sleeper bound for Kansas City. By the beginning of September he was back home with Edith on the family farm for the first time in more than a decade.

CHAPTER 16

AKIAK WORK RESUMED

Little is known about John and Edith's time together in Ottawa. Joseph Romig's journal reveals that Ruth and Van Doran, Jr., visited the family farm at the end of September. John and Edith traveled to Independence, Kansas, in January where John addressed a church group and talked about his experiences in Alaska. Somewhere between these two dates the couple decided to return to Alaska, although it remained unclear what form their work would take.

In November John wrote to the Provincial Elders' Conference in Bethlehem that he and Edith were contemplating a return to the Kuskokwim to round out their active service. He told them that he had seriously considered Brother Butzin's suggestion that he take charge of a native helpers' school. Though the mission board was willing, he held back, hoping that the bureau would establish the Kuskokwim valley as a separate district and offer the superintendent's position to him. They did, and John prepared to return to an expanded district including the lower Yukon drainage, the lower and middle Kuskokwim, and the Togiak and Nushagak river drainages. At the same time that the bureau made John's appointment official, they hired Edith as matron of the new Akiak hospital.[1]

When John left Akiak in the summer of 1918, the community had finally attained the trio of services for which he and Edith had worked so hard—the church, the school, and the hospital. The satisfaction that he felt in 1918 may have been particularly gratifying contrasted to the trauma and dismay of his first leave-taking, which came on the heels of the death and disruption of the epidemic of 1900. However, the outbreak of influenza in the continental United States in 1918 undercut John's sense of accomplishment. By the winter of 1918 the disease had become pandemic and was working its way towards Alaska. By Christmas influenza had already reached Nome, where it took the lives of 65 percent of the native population. From there it worked its way down the coast and ravaged the Yukon. John's friend and colleague Dr. Lamb crossed the portage to give what help he could, contracted the disease, and died. A quarantine was established north of Nelson Island, in hope that the Kuskokwim could be spared.

While still in Kansas, John wrote an article for *The Proceedings* describing the plight of orphans along the Kuskokwim and making a plea for the establishment of an orphanage and training school. His article was partly motivated by his fear that the number of orphans would markedly increase as a result of the influenza epidemic then in progress. Whereas the epidemic of 1900 had affected all ages, the influenza epidemic concentrated on the old and middle-aged, leaving many children parentless in its wake.

In his article John described the plight of the "'legak" (*elliraq*), or orphan. Parenthetically he noted that the term "'legak" was also used for a person who had not a single relative or a wife or a husband left. He then opposed their ideal and actual plight: "In the oft told tales the Eskimo storyteller goes at great length to depict the final enviable success of the 'legak in attaining the headship of a community through this prowess as a hunter and a man of sense. In actual fact the life of a 'legak is minus of everything that makes life attractive, and how any of them survive is a mystery."[2] John went on to describe the marginal position of the orphan in Yup'ik society and, for young men, their role as errand boys for the entire men's house. He also noted what contemporary Yup'ik elders still recognize as a social verity—the desirability of taking an orphan as a son- or daughter-in-law, given the absence of demanding and interfering in-laws.

The apparent discrepancy between Yup'ik ideal and practice that John described had its own cultural logic. The eventual success achieved by and recognition given to an originally hapless orphan in the oral traditions was a rhetorical instance of the power of inner discipline and selfless behavior to achieve success against all odds (that is, being left without relatives). Many orphan tales recount the friendship and kinlike relationship that develops between the orphan and the human elders or animal mentors they serve. This relationship is achieved by virtue of the orphan's strong mind and careful action. Success within the oral tradition was marked not only by what heights people achieved, but by what obstacles they conquered. An orphan, by definition, had everything to gain and much to overcome. Also, in the context of Yup'ik cosmology, a tension existed between the biological possibility of orphans and their social impossibility.[3] The paradoxical rise to power of the orphan in the oral tradition was an attempt to resolve this contradiction.

The existence of the worst possible case of the abandoned child and qasgiq slave may have been less frequent in the eighteenth century than it was after the introduction of epidemic disease to the epidemiologically virgin population of western Alaska in the early nineteenth century. When the Kilbucks arrived on the Kuskokwim in 1885, they were witness to extreme social disruption directly related to the population decline dating from the small-pox epidemic of 1838–1839. It is impossible to know how the Yupiit dealt with biological orphanage prior to the epidemic and whether they treated such children as socially destitute. Whatever the traditional patterns, on their arrival in western Alaska the Kilbucks found unwanted children—children who gave them their first foothold by filling the mission school with the human remnants of a people deeply affected by introduced disease.

Within a decade these same orphans took on the role of native helpers, beginning the work of evangelism from within. John dubbed these children their chief help in establishing the future mission. In giving the Kilbucks their orphans, the Yup'ik people had given them the key to unraveling their culture from the inside. Had there been no epidemiological disruption, perhaps there would have been no orphans to shelter and convert. Along the isolated coast of western Alaska, where the effects of epidemic disease were not as far-reaching, conversion was a much slower process. Ironically, the existence of needy orphans was both the motivation for the Kilbucks' return to their work along the Kuskokwim as well as a critical element in their past success.

On May 6 Edith and John left Ottawa for Alaska, traveling overland by way of Colorado and Hatch, New Mexico. They weathered a train wreck in eastern Colorado but were not injured. Finally, on June 19 they set sail from Seattle on the *Ozmo*, reaching Akiak on July 20, 1919. They found that the epidemic had not reached the Kuskokwim after all. It had, however, succeeded in motivating John and Edith's return.

SUPERINTENDENT KILBUCK

On July 21 John boarded the *Tana* to survey the needs of his new district. The bureau had scheduled the establishment of new schools at Kwigillingok and Eek on the coast, one in the tundra villages west of Bethel, and two upriver from Akiak. His first trip took him to McGrath to peruse proposed school sites and make arrangements for taking the census. He traveled all the way up to Takotna, a town brought into existence by the discovery of placer gold on the surrounding creeks. There he counted fifty cabins, each with a garden. The upper Kuskokwim also boasted a number of roadhouses, dredging concerns, potato gardens, and a varied assortment of non-natives who had settled along the river.[4]

Returning from Takotna, John traveled on to Nikolai on the south fork of the Kuskokwim. There he met with the local Indian population to discuss a plan to bring them together in one place and establish a school. He concluded that such a plan was premature and instead suggested that the bureau establish schools at Napaimute and Sleetmute on the middle Kuskokwim. He found that the upper section of the river numbered just sixty souls scattered in eight settlements on five different streams, with the Kuskokwim as a connecting highway for summer travel. The distance of the nearest settlement to Nikolai was 69 miles by water and nine miles by trail, while the farthest was 250 by water and 50 miles by trail. John concluded, "It is not to be expected that they will make as radical a change as we are asking upon short notice. They require time."[5]

Arriving back in McGrath, John reboarded the Steamer *Tana*, on its return to Akiak. Though scenic, the trip was prolonged. Before John reached home, he was already planning to continue down to Bethel to meet the incoming supplies for the new school at Kwigillingok as well as over to Holy Cross to send a telegram to Lopp at the local wireless station. From bulletins he had received while still aboard the *Tana*, he learned of President Wilson's veto of the Civil Sundry Bill in the latter part of July. The immediate implication for John's work was a back seat for school plans for the coming year. John regretted the delay, hating to lose any time in the establishment of new schools in his "sadly neglected" district. The object of John's ire was clear: "The Government men who have the Alaska school work in hand are not to blame for the halting progress of education in that land, but the Government at Washington. We cannot establish schools with words or good intentions, but must have funds, and these Congress refuses to furnish."[6]

After only three days back in Akiak, John visited the tundra village of Nunatschak, a gathering of 113 people, to look over the site for a new school. From there he continued on to Quinhagak, over to Goodnews Bay, and back up the coast and home to Akiak by the end of September. Just after Thanksgiving he was off again to the Yukon to conduct school inspections, attend to census work, and investigate the condition of the reindeer herds. He arrived at Pimiut on November 29 and Holy Cross on December 2. There, many of the natives came to let John know that he was no stranger to them. One man showed John his son, introducing the boy as John's "ilogatsungak" (*iluracungaq*: little male cross-cousin of a male). At Holy Cross a woman who had met John on the Kuskokwim years ago pulled him into a house: "And so it has been going since my arrival on the Yukon, many folks seem to have seen me sometime and remember me, while I did not recognize any of them."[7]

Traveling up the Yukon as far as Anvik, John had his first opportunity to visit the Episcopal mission located there and to meet the Reverend John W. Chapman, who had been in Alaska almost as long as John. While not overtly hostile to each other, the two missionaries did not see eye to eye. Chapman disapproved of John's ecumenical tendencies, while John found Chapman's missionary ideal superficial.[8]

From Anvik, John returned to Holy Cross, where he visited the Catholic mission and conducted a brief inspection of their school. He was ill at ease with the formality of the institution and wrote home, "The Catholics surely know how to flatter. I feel that I am getting real proud of myself, everyone around me is so awfully deferential."[9] In both places, John met with the local natives. The Anvik contingent requested that the federal government staff their newly constructed infirmary. The men from Holy Cross asked that a territorial school be established there as an alternative to the mission.

At the end of his stay in Holy Cross, John wrote to Edith concerning the "uneven success" of the Yukon missions:

> You know that Holy Cross and Anvik were mission centers almost as long as Bethel. I find that superstitious beliefs and practices still are in open evidence. There are still Shamans, and they are still strong, and the masquerade [Kelek] is still observed. Materially the people have improved . . . but the light of the soul seems strangely dim. Probably as I get to know the people better, my opinion will change for the better. The natives themselves have complained to me that the missionaries are asking them to give up what they had been accustomed to do all their lives, referring to the heathen rites practiced in the mask festival, saying that they cannot give it up all of a sudden. This would lead one to suppose that the missions are just now turning their attention to the abolishing of these heathen practices.[10]

From Holy Cross John traveled down the Yukon to Mountain Village, where his first impression of the government teachers was that they were inveterate "knockers," intent on downgrading everybody but themselves: "Before I went to bed I knew the principal bad qualities of every white man of any prominence from St. Michael to Anvik."[11] John was also surprised that the school's Christmas program consisted of a fish pond and nothing more. However, he was impressed by the teachers' dedication and talents and encouraged them to stay on in bureau service.

John's work on the Yukon kept him away from home into the new year. Along with school inspections, perhaps his most important function was smoothing over differences that had arisen between the representatives of the native and non-native interests in each community. A good example of this aspect of his work concerned the resolution of a dispute between a Yukon native and a new teacher.

> Mr. Sullivan was driving him and the other natives from him by his quick temper, and by his never, or not always doing as he promised. That was about all there was to the complaint. Mr. Sullivan asked me in the presence of one of the herders who understood English, what Henry [the disgruntled native] had to say. I passed on the information in a general way and gave instances where similar complaints had been made, notably against myself, when a native once asked me why I lied so much etc. In a general way also I tried to get him to see the situation from the view point of the native. I rather think

that the shoe pinched pretty hard, for his face turned red, and the native with us watched him closely to see what effect my words would have.

Several days later John recorded another instance of the coincidence of Yup'ik and Kilbuck parsimony:

There was one fellow, about as fat as a porker ready for market, who put up a hard luck story about not having grub, and that even now he and his family have to go to bed supperless, quite frequently, and so he would like to have the Govt. help him out with grub. I told him that I would let him know later what would be done. By inquiry I found out, as I expected, that he is the lazy man of the village, and that his own nearest relatives will not give him help, altho well able to do so.[12]

On the trail over the portage and back to Akiak, John recalled his own history and the longevity on which his ability to act as a go-between was based: "Twenty years ago I traveled this same trail with Dr. Romig, Mr. Lind and Mr. Crow, the engineer who overhauled the sawmill at Bethel. Then I had a fine team of dogs. Twenty years more and I might be using an airplane here or elsewhere."[13]

THE SALVE BOX

Throughout John's fall traveling, he kept Edith posted in long descriptive letters, full of observations concerning the native people he met as well as those of Scandinavian, Russian, German, American, and even Turkish extraction. These letters he typed out, single-spaced, on a new portable Remington that accompanied him on the trail. The letters have a full-bodied, newsy style and only rarely lament or belabor the separations. Aside from hugs sent to Lily ("Tell her I think of her every day, and know that she is helping you.") and periodic reports on the progress of the war he was waging with "tobaccoitis," he rarely referenced a wish to be other than where or what he was.

The journal that Edith kept for John was equally chatty and vivid, full of the details of daily life in both native and non-native Akiak. As far as the natives were concerned, Edith described with mild amusement many a small step on the road to "civilization," as she understood it. Responding to a young man's request for help getting together the goods necessary for him to marry, she wrote, "I gave him . . . 25.00 and he left, all smiles, to buy his outfit, which will likely be, a striped ticking dress, deer skin boots, squirrel skins for a parka and some flour, tea and sugar. He will be a rather dirty and shabby groom, but if the girl don't object, why should I. When he returns, I'll give him a bar of soap."[14]

At the same time, Edith was prone to long tirades concerning the damage done "our Natives" by the growth of the local non-native population. Speaking of the marriage of native women to white men she wrote, "Native girls

Fig. 16.1. Moravian congregation in front of the Akiak church. (Kilbuck family)

who marry white men seldom continue to be happy after a few years. . . . If the man is poor, they suffer greater hardships than if they had a good native husband. If he become rich, he usually loses his desire for a native wife . . . and if he cares anything for his children he takes them with him to the states, and the woman is desolate and forever bitter and unhappy." Over the years, Edith consistently worked against these marriages: "These trifling white men think it is an honor to marry *them* rather than a native, but we have this delusion pretty well trained out of the girls' heads." [15]

Edith's duties in Akiak were light, relative to years past. In John's absence she monitored the arrival of the year's freight. Beyond the regular inventory of dry goods this included a cow and chickens, a piano, and the equipment for the new weather bureau, wireless station, and electric light plant. As in the old days at Bethel, she had her hands full delegating the work of the federal "mission": "I don't have to do any of it of course, but I must manage every bit of the work." Management, however, proved no easy task, especially for a woman with Edith's perfectionist bent: "I'd rather do the work any time than keep after others to do it right." [16]

As the hospital was equipped with a full-time cook and maintenance man, Edith happily found herself with time on her hands to sew and visit. Because of a knee condition, she got out very little that fall. She was regularly visited, however, by innumerable natives and non-natives, friend and foe alike, all come to tell her their troubles and their joys: "They have no fear that what they say will go any further, and sometimes I can advise or comfort them by knowing what their troubles are." [17]

Apparently the troubles she mediated far outstripped the pleasures recounted. As the year progressed, the situation seemed to get worse. The new doctor proved to be rough and bigoted: "I was giving quite a long talk to them [in Yup'ik] on the Doctor's instructions. . . . The Doctor also was taking in the conversation and his face was a study. At the close he remarked, addressing me, 'I'd like to try you on a bunch of apes. I believe you could make them understand. Such a jargon I never heard before.' Was that a complement or otherwise!" Edith was also distressed to see "her people" backsliding and running around with "a certain class of whitemen": "It seems that during our absence they had no direction or restraint, and now they prefer that life, and shun us because we cannot approve of what they do; and they were nice girls, our hope and pride in the early day. The white men, some of them resent my being 'mother confessor' to the entire village, and boast that *some* of the girls will not tell even me what goes on." [18]

Although partially comforted by John's contention that without their presence in Akiak things would be even worse, Edith fretted, "More white men means more temptation and some are bound to fall, but, O, it hurts me to see a single one of them go wrong." The friction at the hospital did not help: "I must be pouring oil on the troubled waters constantly or there would be more storms than we have." As the year wore on, Edith increasingly described herself as a "huge salve box" to the troubles of the community, as someone was always "wanting to be rubbed, smoothed, sympathized with, praised, flattered, approved of and even advised on all subjects."[19]

Bickering and petty jealousies characterized life at the hospital, and both sides of each issue inevitably came seeking the Kilbucks' support: "I seem to need to be here in my own room a good deal. It is a haven for so many people who feel blue, or imposed on or nervous." At the same time, Edith felt herself distanced from the immediate strife: "It all makes my head swim. There was a time when I was in the midst of everything, helping to plan and make things *go*, but I can't do it anymore. I am too nervous and too forgetful. Anyway, it is not my work at all, yet of course I like to hear about it and am interested in its success, because I am interested in the people for whose benefit it is planned."[20]

On the bright side, the growth in Akiak's non-native population provided unprecedented opportunity for Edith to socialize with other white women. On one occasion she hosted eight women for tea: "It will be the first time in my Kuskoquim experience that so many white women were near me at one time." The years that followed continued to be characterized by an even mix of companionship and interpersonal stress. Had she been younger, she would have preferred the work of teaching in one of the newer schools to the constant diplomacy required in the growing metropolis of Akiak: "I must shut my eyes to so *many* things that it gives me a feeling of being a party to things I don't approve of. . . . In so public a work we must see and pass by a great deal, but it hurts, when it affects our people and we have no way to interfere. . . . We were better off when no white men were near us, and the Natives were better off if they only knew it."[21]

Though life in Akiak proved trying, especially during the year following their return, John and Edith's personal life prospered. Edith wrote home that she was "all puffed up" with pride at the news of the birth of her third grandchild. At the same time both John and she were relieved by Joe's offer to buy the family farm for $15,000. It was now clear to both of them that John would never work the land. Work in Alaska would always take precedence over the Kansas bottomlands. It had been hard to think that the house in which Edith and all her sisters and brothers were born might go out of the family altogether. Joe's offer was welcome and readily accepted.

Finally, the relationship between John and Edith had both mellowed and deepened with time. Far from the sometimes volatile romance of their first decade or the sober character of their middle years marked by an unsettled career and long periods of grieving, during their final years together in Akiak they might be characterized as "best pals." Although Edith would still complain (probably justifiably) when left alone to shoulder the Akiak work at Christmas or on their anniversary, more often she appeared content and without the chafing of years past. Both wrote funny glimpses of rather intimate encounters in letters to the children after their return. Edith described John's efforts at verse:

He is not a poet, although he has on several occasions tried his hand on me, I much prefer that he should express his affection in common everyday prose. It is much more suitable to two old geese like we are. His last attempt was this, "Hon I'm just crazy about you, etc." Now that is what I call *fine*. I know just what he means, and how he feels. It satisfies both of us and don't take near the effort.[22]

Edith also wrote the children a playful account of John's somewhat unusual nocturnal activities: "He still has terrible nightmares when he sleeps, and worse than ever. Why any one so mild and kindly in his waking hours can be so belligerent in his sleep is hard to understand. I am obliged to sleep with one eye open so that I can duck under the covers when he begins to perform. If he is fighting a man, why, *I'm* the man. If he chastises a school boy, I'm the boy, if he is killing snakes, I'm the snake and when he kicks a dog, I'm the dog."[23] Later, Edith recorded the grand finale to John's night-time calisthenics: "Father had a nightmare. . . . Last night he kicked a dog, but it happened to be the *wall*. He was so surprised, and pretty badly hurt. . . . When I asked him what was wrong he said a dog was getting his *pie* and he kicked it. It was a whole pie too. No wonder he made such a vigorous protest. He don't often get that much pie at one time."[24]

During these last years John and Edith continued to speak to and about each other with dry understatement and affectionate humor. On the occasion of a wedding anniversary spent apart, John wrote, "My dear wife:—On this anniversary of our wedding, allow me to congratulate you for being able to live with me for thirty-six years, and still survive. As for me I have to think of Olson's remark, 'How did such a nice woman get such a mean man?' "[25]

WORK AMONG THE PEOPLE

At the same time that John and Edith's relationship to each other had mellowed and deepened over the years, so had their relationship with the people of the Kuskokwim. On a visit to Bethel, Edith wrote, "The natives call on us. Some of the older ones were young with us in the first years of our labors here. We compare gray hairs and rheumatic knees, and talk over old times. These people will always be loyal to us."[26]

Returning to Akiak with the new year, John began at once to "unwind a lot of Government red tape" and get out the January mail, including the inventory, annual requisition, monthly report, and quarterly and semi-annual reports, all of which came due at the same time. Edith lamented, "Already I can see the figures like little imps dancing before my eyes and refusing to become reconciled."[27]

With the paper work well under way, John began meetings with forty reindeer men gathered in Akiak to plan for the coming year. Although some things had become tangled during the year they had been away, John was largely satisfied with the state of affairs. The issues brought up for discussion in January included planning for a reindeer convention the following year and talking up a cooperative store that John hoped native capital could underwrite. Shares were set at $10 each, and pledges were taken to the value of more than $270, mostly by the deer owners. The store was to supplement the sawmill already in operation, and the enterprise was dubbed the Kuskoquim Lumber and Trading Company. Although it was too late in the season for an order to get out that year, under the direction of the government school teacher the plans could be realized the following year.

With the Akiak work in shape by the end of January, John set out downriver to complete the full circuit of his district before spring. His first stop was Napaskiak, where the entire Bethel native population had gathered to attend the "old masquerade or shaman dance" (probably Kelek). Although the masks and much of the accompanying paraphernalia had been discarded, the ceremonial form remained intact.

Earlier in the fall, Edith had also noted continuity in elements of the traditional ceremonial cycle at Akiak: "The village is expecting to be invited to Akiachak to a berry festival [probably Ingulaq] and he is busy making a song. . . . The village is full of people, Akiachak having been invited up for a dance and feast." The following summer, she gave slightly more detail on the same series of events:

> Akiak has been having its annual funfest and dance. First they attended the one at Tuluksak. Upon their return they went right down to Akiachak to theirs and two days ago these two villages were Akiaks guests. Mr. Forrest [the government teacher] thinks Akiak must have given out $2,000 worth of goods, but I doubt it. Today they are all off to Quichluk [Kwethluk], which will end the season of frolic, and *then* everybody will turn to their work again for another year.[28]

In a letter written home to Ruth and Joe, John confirmed that the traditional fall ceremonial, Qaariitaaq, had survived into the 1920s:

> The children of the village gather together after lamp-lighting time, and go to every dwelling and standing close together in a circle, facing each other, they start a low murmuring noise, with mouths tight shut, the sound growing more intense and louder until it explodes into a yell. This is done three times. Sometimes they are invited into the house, and given a treat of cakes, cookies or something considered dainty and nice. The evening is spent going the rounds of the entire village, every house being given a chance to treat the boys, for this is purely a boys stunt. It might be considered the Eskimo boy's Hallow-een.[29]

As in years past, John and Edith held the traditional ceremonial round culpable on two counts—the worship of pagan images and the wasteful squandering of a person's worldly goods. On the first count, the Kilbucks, viewed the ceremonial forms that had been retained as happily devoid of the idolatry of years past. Where gift-giving was retained, as in the Kwigillingok Kevgiq of the winter of 1917–1918, the Kilbucks continued both to misconstrue and object to the character of the traditional Yup'ik attitude toward the source and use of material wealth.

Edith predicted the rapid demise of what remained of traditional ritual distribution along the river. On the occasion of a dance and distribution at Akiak the following spring she wrote:

> Yesterday, the two visiting villages stayed most of the day. Each one carried home a load of deerskins and other gifts. Waskas donated more than all the others put together I think in the name of their beloved daughter who makes this her "coming out" and can now think of suiters and perhaps a husband. It is a strange way to celebrate the coming to maturity of a young girl, but it is custom and they are proud to have the means to give her so fine an introduction into society. She herself is rather embarrassed over the publicity and might prefer to remain a *girl* a while longer. Schooling changes the viewpoint of this present generation. It will be but a few years until these old customs will all be done away with, as the many others that have already passed, never to return.

Though Edith was correct that dance distributions would soon disappear along the Kuskokwim, Kevgiq still takes place annually in contemporary Yup'ik communities from the mouth of the Yukon River down to and including Nelson Island along the coast. Also, since 1983 Bethel has hosted a number of large intervillage dance celebrations that in many ways reflect the spirit of their traditional counterparts.[30]

Not only did the Kilbucks object to the excesses of formal gifting, they also sought to undercut the more generalized notion of a man's duty to share his material wealth among his relatives. In one instance John worked to preserve the capital of a native who had made a small fortune ($7,000) through the sale of a coastal mining claim. Eventually, it was decided that the monied native would have to be physically removed from his home village and should become a deer man "in order that there will not be so many to help him eat up his provisions."[31]

The Kilbucks' attempts to redirect the Yup'ik willingness to share was as significant as their objections to traditional exchange practices. In effect they tried to replace Kevgiq distributions directed towards and hosted in the name of particular men and women with the notion of charity towards nameless others. For example, during John's winter travels downriver he spent a part of his energy encouraging the local Kuskokwim natives to send a sledload of footgear to destitute school children at Nushagak. In the same letter in which he commented on the attenuated "masquerade" taking place at Napaskiak, John wrote describing his efforts toward the inculcation of Christian charity: "I am going to make an appeal to the Bethel natives and try to get them to do something for their fellow people." In fact, John worked to replace the Yup'ik notion that tied gifting to the realization of particular human relationships with the Western Christian notion of charity directed to anonymous others. As in his plea for donations to the Red Cross, he must have had some success, as Edith happily noted "a sled load of boots, 11 dogs, and a kind hearted whiteman leaving Bethel on a trip of 250 miles." [32]

GOVERNMENT WORK: FROM BAD TO WORSE

When John returned to Akiak at the end of April, he was sorry to learn that the situation at the hospital had deteriorated in his absence. There was constant trouble between the doctor, the nurses, and the native help. Edith wrote, "The Doctor swears at the patients, even the ladies, the cook gets the sulks and sets up poor meals, the butcher shows up with fresh meat two weeks late and we live on bacon and salt salmon, the new teachers run down our beloved people and ridicule them when *we* love them. Lily even had to be spanked." Soon after John's return, he and Edith moved out of the hospital. Edith was relieved: "We moved over here, to Alice's and Robert's house, where it is so clean and quiet and comfortable. . . . The floors are all covered with inlaid linoleum. The range is as bright as new although four years old. . . . I don't know how I stood the public life of the past year." [33]

Though the work continued to frustrate, the summer provided unprecedented material luxury. Not only had Edith acquired a 1/4-horsepower electric washer ("I don't know how I ever got along without it"), but by midsummer John had put down $800 on an "Alaska Automobile"—a new skiff and Evinrude motor. Yup'ik friends in Akiak were also experiencing a moderate boom as the price of furs continued to climb: "Jackson brought back 100 muskrats valued at 2.50 each. Waskas have 264. Others have less, but none are without the means to pay off debts and put in a supply of provisions for the fishing season." On one occasion, at least, this new-won affluence found expression in a small token of appreciation. In the early years the Kilbucks could not have bought marriages had they tried. Thirty-five years later, "Ben . . . paid father a five dollar bill after the ceremony. That is his *first* native fee for performing the marriage ceremony and of course he gave it to me. He gives me all fees of that kind. They have never amounted to much up here, but I have my lovely furs from fees paid by white couples." [34]

At the same time that John occasionally performed both marriages and funerals, he also preached regularly in the church at Akiak in Yup'ik. When the government teachers began to attend regularly, he preceded his remarks with a brief recitation in English. By the early fall John and Edith had made the decision to rejoin mission work the following summer. Edith wrote happily of the house that the mission had agreed to build for them:

They are indeed happy to have us join their numbers—especially just now when they are so short of men to preach and teach the people—in their own language. I am glad to go into the service again. We find the Government work most discouraging, with lack of money to push the things we want to do and some very discouraging people to work with. We had hoped to benefit the Mission by seconding their long cherished desires for good schools in their district and having suitable buildings erected at the various Mission Stations. . . . We have failed to help them as we had planned, so now we will work with them and do what we can to make their burdens lighter.[35]

Though in part a product of their frustration with government work, the Kilbucks' decision to rejoin the mission was also an expression of their perception that mission converts already suffered from the "evil influences" of the greater white society: "To combat this will require the best that is in all of us. Even now some have been drawn into sin, and stay away from church, or if they go they are hard and inapproachable, because the conscience condemns them whether they are openly accused or not. We want to save the young, but it is the young these vile white men seek to ruin." In a more forgiving moment Edith admitted that it was wrong to say that all white men were bad. She belied this charitable remark by contending that "the majority are far from elevating."

And now there is a prospect of *big* mines opening up above us. The prediction is for 2000 people rushing in before a year is over with Bethel the end of ocean navigation and a big town there—and larger ones right at the mines. All this means work aplenty, money, luxuries, temptations and vice. Already a company is talking of building a moving picture hall at Bethel, and from what we know of these better educated pleasure loving natives, they will surely squander many of their dollars there. Even this is not the worst evil in view. There will be gambling and wide open dance halls. Perhaps even liquor in some form or disguise will be handled, and then goodbye to the virtue of the women.[36]

From a contemporary perspective, Edith's worry that movie houses and recreational dancing might threaten feminine virtue appears both conservative and naïve. These views, however, mirrored the asceticism and otherworldly standards of the Moravians of her day. In fact, her worst fears were realized in the half-century that followed. However convenient it might be to dismiss her point of view as evangelical rhetoric, the subsequent history of the Kuskokwim was plagued by problems she identified in 1920.

The Kilbucks enthusiastically reentered missionary service, committed to using what the years had taught them to carry on the "good fight" along the Kuskokwim. Edith wrote:

This advantage we have. The people love us. They have confidence in us and in the end many will return after they have found the new pleasures carry a sting. . . . The Missionaries are faithfully doing their best. There are now on this river four who are a great power in the work, because they all speak the language. These are Bro. Stecker, Bro. Butzin, Bro. Hintz, and Bro. Drebert, but there should be many more. John will have the instructing of Native Missionaries as his particular work. We will take the five upper villages: Ougavig, Tuluksak, Akiak, Akiachak and Quichluk [Kwethluk] as our special field, with the Reindeer camps in the Mountains in addition. It will keep us busy too. I almost wish we might begin right now instead of next year.[37]

A year remained between their decision to rejoin the mission and the expiration of their contract with the bureau. In prospect the time looked as though it would fly. John planned to begin a busy season of traveling as soon after freeze-up as possible. No new work would be taken up due to a combination of shortness of funds and high prices. Both John and Edith found these constraints discouraging, as they had planned a number of new schools and general improvements for the entire district, none of which could be realized. Even with these projects laid aside, John would need to spend much of the winter abroad to have his district in good shape for the new superintendent, Mr. Forrest.

At the same time that John began to make plans for his last season traveling for the bureau, life in Akiak promised to improve, with the forced resignation of Dr. Ventners. Edith commented dryly that his parting words might be taken as a compliment or otherwise: "He said to Father: 'You have never liked me, we have never liked each other but this I do say, you have been square and fair with me, so here's my hand. . . . Mrs. Kilbuck is the only damn christian in the bunch.'"[38]

With the doctor's departure, John and Edith moved back into the hospital quarters where they could be more comfortable. As the winter closed in, however, it became apparent that the year was not to be peaceful and spite-free. Mr. Forrest took up residence in the new power house, and much to Edith's dismay it became the social center of Akiak: "Father and I have been invited to a dance for tomorrow evening. Think of it! The teachers are having it and we are sorry. It is hard to keep the natives away from dances when the white people go. They will surely feel justified now, for Government Employees are supposed to set them an example of what is right." Commenting on the teachers' Sunday card parties, she wrote, "Each year [the natives] see more and more of the dark side of civilization."[39]

Edith later commented on the habits of one of the Akiak teachers, whom she otherwise found blameless: "I noticed however that Miss Cairns does knitting on Sunday and plays cards, dances and skis and skates. This is not a complaint. I am only telling things as they are." In the context of such stiff standards, Edith was above reproof: "Up in this country, everybody plays cards. Mr. Gieske asked her [the new teacher] yesterday if she had succeeded in teaching me to play. She said, 'No, she couldn't even get me to say 'darn it' no matter what the provocation might be.'"[40] Other problems were more troublesome than the increase of "moral laxness" in the white community; Edith's worst fears for the Yupiit began to be realized: "Bethel is a vice center and I fear our young people here are not untouched by such things. Sure it is, I have never known in years past of so much slander, backbiting, lying, and deviltry of all kinds. I don't know who to trust any more."[41]

In reading Edith's commentary on her last years in Akiak, some allowance should be made for the selectivity of memory. For instance, in commenting on the current missionary efforts she wrote, "[The native helper] was asked to denounce his own people for not wanting to work when they were asked, yet the accusation was only half true, and there are two sides to the matter. *We* never found the people unwilling to do things for us, *I* could get them to work now if it was my place to attend to such matters." When they finally did resort to positive discipline, she wrote, "I believe these social gatherings will be more apt to win the children than so much whipping. The Forrests have whipped more children in the few months they have been here than we have in thirty five years, and their discipline is not as good as ours was."[42]

At the same time she found fault with current workers, Edith dramatized the overall progress Akiak had made when she compared its situation in 1920 to that in Bethel thirty-five years before:

> I sometimes think of our first years of teaching, with the poor filthy little boys and girls who so reluctantly came to school, frightened, half fed, half clothed, and O, so dull. It took real grace to stay in the same room with them for half a day. Night often found us with a head ache from the intolerable odor of their food, and unwashed steaming bodies. Until we could induce them to bathe and change their garments at least once in a while, it was far from pleasant working with them.
>
> How different it is now. When the bell rings the children troop past my window, smiling and eager! The girls wear shoes and stockings, good underclothes, dresses and apron. Almost every girl has a nice coat as well as her fur garments, and a big bow of ribbon on her hair—not little narrow ribbon—but real hair ribbons tied nicely on well combed hair, bobbed in the latest style.
>
> The boys are well clothed, but parents stop at that. They don't have any extras, and some of these are years too young for the garments they wear. Never-the-less they are happy, and full of fun. The meek, quiet boys of early days are a thing of the past. They are coming into their own and are *real boys* even to being rough and boisterous at times.[43]

Edith's juxtaposition of the unwashed past and the beribboned children of thunder communicated her pleasure in the present. Although life was never perfect, the winter continued full. The doctor never arrived, but plenty of natives came to the hospital for care. Edith's own health was remarkably good, and she showed her old energy. In the fall she wrote the children, "To me *work*, is one of my best blessings. I enjoy every kind of

work and am unhappy when I *must* be idle for any length of time." During
that fall Edith was busy and therefore happy. Secure in the present, she
eulogized the past.

> Two weeks ago today you arrived and what a happy two weeks it has
> been. . . . Personally I have liked nothing better than when we were clearing
> land, digging out stumps and having delightfully big bonfires . . . but I was
> with you and that was a joy. . . . Of course we are older and slower now. We
> have also learned to do *without* many things we once thought necessary to our
> happiness. But we have so *much*. Never have we lacked anything that we
> really needed, and every gift of God has been a real luxury, because our
> childhood days were so full of privation. We learned to appreciate his smallest
> gifts to the full.[44]

While Edith managed the hospital work, John commenced his winter
traveling as planned. After a brief respite in February, he made a coastal
circuit on his last official trip as government superintendent. Heading
downriver to Napaskiak, he stopped briefly to visit with Young Kilbuck.
From there he ran as far as Apokak, which he found deserted, as the men
of the village had all gone to Eek to attend the closing of what John labeled
a "bladder festival." Finally, on March 21, John arrived at Kolukak by way
of Goodnews Bay and Togiak. All along the coast he was dismayed that the
natives had failed to take part in the "general advancement" occurring along
the river.

> The natives of this coast and Togiak river are very poor, probably the poorest
> in my district, and they are an unwashed lot. They usually have enough to
> eat, which is the main concern with them. . . .
>   The coast country seems to be very suitable for reindeer, and there is room
> for many herds. In a faint way the natives think the deer a very desirable
> possession, but they do not have the energy required to become a pastoral
> people.[45]

In the same letter John remarked the lack of non-native food. Although
valuable fur-bearing animals were close at hand, the natives did not pursue
them: "The trouble is the natives do not seem to have the get-up in them,
having probably over-exerted themselves at the play they held this winter."
John surmised that the rich coastal environment and satisfying local economy contributed to the natives' disinclination toward the Christian work
ethic embodied in trapping and herding:

> Another reason why it has been hard to keep apprentices at the camp, is the
> fact when spring comes along with the lure of easy and lazy times on the ice
> and water, the young men and boys cannot withstand the call, just as the hobo,
> leaves any job he may be holding down during the winter, but when spring
> comes he must go on the road. The deer camp is a good place to "hole
> up" for the winter, so think the youth of Goodnews and the surrounding
> villages.[46]

Although John was less than impressed with the distance the coastal Yupiit had come toward incorporating the Protestant ethic, he did what he could to reinforce local industry and commerce. In one passage he described counting out ninety-five silver dollars as payment to a native for a cross fox skin the man had given John to sell for him the year before. Men and women filled the room for the occasion, and the neatly piled coins impressed them with the rewards of industry as well as with the reliability of the one-armed man doing the counting.

Before returning home, John made one last quick trip down river and over to Kwigillingok, where he was able to help the resident Moravian Brother Hinz out of a misunderstanding with the local people. The natives called John to a meeting to hear their complaints concerning Hinz' heavy-handed treatment. Although John declined to intercede, reminding them that he was not responsible for the missionary part of the work, he counseled them to try to see the situation from the missionary's perspective. At the same time he spoke to Brother Hinz, advising him to be more tolerant and forgiving in his dealings with natives that did not share his views. John was also displeased to note a number of plural marriages within the community and did what he could to dissuade the offenders from their present path. He left with the goodwill of the community, a neat trick for a man certainly as opinionated as any of his missionary brethren.

However unimpressed John may have been with the conditions of coastal life, he did not leave without kinsmen: "Again I have found a relative in this village. She came to me upon my arrival and let me know that she is a relative of mine since we came from the same family. I suppose she still believes I am descendant of the Apokak man who drifted to sea on the ice years and years ago."[47] On that note of familial recognition, John headed home to Akiak and Edith.

CHAPTER 17

END OF AN ERA

REJOINING THE MISSION AND GOING HOME

Yes, he was faithful, and with his dying breath, he told us how to live.
—Yup'ik parishioner to Edith Kilbuck, 1922[1]

During the winter of 1921 John's travels went well, and Edith wrote home describing Easter week spent with friends in Bethel. Even so, Edith likened the arrival of breakup to "opening prison doors to set you free." The hospital and school personnel had gotten on no better during the winter of 1920–1921 than they had during the previous year: "Each one would like *our* sympathy and support. Of course we have mental leanings, but refuse to show them, and absolutely refuse to discuss the unpleasant differences between them. They justly fear a scandal. . . . This is almost as unpleasant as last year."[2]

At the end of June, John and Edith took leave of the hospital and moved into a small cabin: "We leave quietly, with the good will of everyone, and we will be happy and content with less pay, for our work is a work of love. That is its own reward."[3] Less than two weeks later, on July 1, John reported to Bethel, where Brother Butzin assigned him to the new Akiak district of the Moravian mission, including the villages upriver from Bethel with Akiak as its center.

After their departure from government service, the Kilbucks watched in dismay as the new doctor, who had arrived in June, proved himself even less suited to bureau work than his predecessor. Their old friend Lopp visited that fall and sorted out the immediate trouble, sending the unfit doctor packing. After this last episode, however, neither Edith nor John

352

ever referred at length to bureau personnel or activities in their private journals or letters home. Their new work with the mission filled its place.

During the rest of the summer John laid out plans for what was to be the new mission house in Akiak. Edith wrote, "It seems natural to be starting a new work, that is, building the necessary houses and making a home. This we have done so many times up here, but now it is harder, for we are older and not so able to do the hard work any more. However we manage to work up quite an enthusiasm, no matter if it is mainly talk as yet. When we can move out of this crowded little cabin into our own house we will rejoice."[4]

Besides their living quarters, the new thirty- by forty-foot residence would be large enough for a classroom and office for the native helpers' school that was to be John's special charge. There, qualified Yup'ik brethren would receive training and Bible instruction. At the same time Edith would tutor their wives in homemaking so that the women could assist their husbands in the work of Christianizing and "civilizing" the people. In his last official letter to the PEC, dated December 12, 1921, John spoke enthusiastically concerning his plans to train the native catechists, who he hoped would take his place when he was gone.

The lines for the new building were laid out at the end of the summer, and several rafts of logs were purchased and made ready for the sawmill the following spring. He sent a requisition to the PEC requesting the necessary building materials and contributing $500 of their savings for furnishing the new mission station. John spent a busy fall visiting his new district to reacquaint himself with the people. Among other things, he successfully encouraged the people to support their own churches. He also tried to promote increased intervillage visiting associated with church activities. He preached the virtues of traveling, which had figured so strongly in his own life:

> This coming Wednesday Father will conduct Communion services [in Akiachak] and I hope to go with him again. We want to take some of our people with us. It is seldom they get together, these Christians from the different villages. They can go for a berry feast or native dance. Why not go for a days church services and Communion? Father is in hopes that this may be the means of awakening a deeper interest in things Spiritual and indeed our people need all the encouragement they can get.[5]

In October, however, John became seriously ill: "Father . . . has indeed been very sick. . . . Severe pains in the stomach and distress in the region of the liver led us to believe there was perhaps a stoppage in the bile duct." Perhaps because of John's illness, Edith reflected on their advancing years: "Now Owen (the old school boy) is the father of a large family and even a grandfather, so surely *we* must be growing old, only we don't stop to think about it."[6]

Although older, John had no intention of slowing down. After he was on the mend at the end of October, Edith commented on his crowded schedule:

Fig. 17.1. Helpers' class at Akiak. Upper row, from left to right: Wassili of Akiachak, Robert Egsak, Kawagleg of Akiak, Rev. John Kilbuck, John Lomack of Akiachak, Jerry of Tuluksak; lower row, Neck of Eek, Rev. Arthur Butzin, and Uloagtluk of Akiak. (Moravian Archives)

"It keeps father studying each evening to prepare for so many church services a week." Thanksgiving that year was particularly busy and well-attended, including an English service at 10 a.m. and a Yup'ik service that evening. After holding the morning service, John and Edith had coffee with the native congregation in the church and then at 3 p.m. joined the white population for dinner at the hospital. On this occasion there were a total of twelve white men and nine white women present, the biggest white gathering Akiak had ever known, save transients. Edith would later expand upon the character of the guests: "Five of the ladies are foreigners, three trained nurses, and not one ignorant person in the lot. We have never been so fortunate in our associates."[7]

John continued active until Christmas. On that day he and Edith visited every house in Akiak to see the decorated trees of their long-time friends and parishioners. On the twenty-seventh he headed downriver to Bethel, both to meet with Brother Butzin and to give communion in the surrounding villages. As his return was delayed, Edith spent a quiet New Year's alone. John arrived the next day but left immediately for Tuluksak to conduct a funeral. After that, he began preparations for holding a week of prayer and giving communion in the three larger villages in the new upriver district—Akiak, Akiachak, and Tuluksak.

On January 23 John returned to Akiak tired and sick from a month of steady traveling. During his absence he had held services each evening as well as in the daytime. He also had conducted numerous private interviews with members of the congregations. In his first and last annual report for the new Akiak mission, he wrote with pleasure concerning the success of his vigorous inquiry: "The encouraging feature of the work in this district, is the fact that one can distinguish those who are for Christ, those who are lukewarm, and those who are deliberately doing as they please."[8] His efforts, however, had worn him out, and immediately on his return he was forced to take to his bed.

John's fever and fatigue did not abate after his return home. Instead, by January 29 he was seriously ill with a combination of pneumonia and typhoid fever. By then he was delirious, speaking almost entirely in Yup'ik. During the next three days he came in and out of consciousness, calling on the people to live and die in Christ. Although he had the best attention that the hospital could provide, by the thirty-first he was very low and Edith hurriedly sent for Brother Butzin. On that day, she wrote, "The entire village is stricken with grief and all are praying that he may yet be spared."[9]

Brother Butzin arrived late in the afternoon on February 1, having driven eighty miles from the tundra villages with only a brief stop in Bethel to change dogs. By the time he arrived, John had regained consciousness. Although he recognized Edith and his friends, he did not speak. Early on the morning of the second, Edith wrote, "Just before leaving us he said to me 'Tonight you shall gather the people together and talk to them. Tell them that it is not enough to be Christians on Sunday, Christians at church, but they must be Christians in the home, Christians as families, teaching their children, holding family prayers. Then they too will be workers for Jesus, helpers to the Missionaries and native assistants. Tell them this.'"[10]

At 3 a.m., February 2, 1922, at the age of sixty, John Henry Kilbuck died. His last words were a compelling valuation of his own life: "Now that I have come to the end, it is not as hard as I expected it to be." In her journal Edith wrote, "Without a struggle, without a sigh, he fell asleep in Jesus and his end was perfect peace."[11]

His funeral, held that same evening, drew people from up and down the river. Brother Butzin repeated John's dying words to the sad gathering. The next morning Edith accompanied his body to Bethel, where she buried him beside Brother Torgersen, close to the spot where they had begun their work so many years ago. The sleds pulled slowly out of Akiak. A white friend drove the first sled, bearing the coffin, while Edith followed in Robert Egsak's sled: "As we passed Akiachak the chapel bell rang. Someone came out and asked us to drive near the shore and halt. The entire village gathered around the flag which was at half mast and sang three Easter hymns of the resurrection, after which our teams were swung out into the trail again and we proceeded on our way."[12] The hymns that were sung included "We Shall Sleep But Not Forever," "Blest Be The Tie That Binds," and "Nearer My God, To Thee." Yup'ik Moravians sang the hymns in their own language, a tribute to John who had helped with their translation.

Arriving in Bethel, the Butzins took Edith in and showed her every kindness. The funeral was held Saturday, February 4, the service delivered in both Yup'ik and English. Whites as well as natives attended, and Brother Butzin repeated John's parting message. Brother Butzin also preached on the text that John had been given on his ordination years ago: "Be ye faithful onto death and I shall give you the crown of life" (Revelation 2:10). Of this text, Edith wrote, "I think it will be remembered by all the people, coming as it does . . . after his going home, for they say, 'Yes, he was faithful, and with his dying breath he told us how to live.'"[13]

The Russian Orthodox people of Kwethluk, whose parents and grandparents had forcibly expelled John years ago, attended the funeral. Along with them came their priest, who was visiting at the time to give communion: "Although Greek Catholics they were friends to the departed and truly mourn his loss."[14] As a tribute, the Kwethluk Orthodox helper brought a large wooden cross which he planted at the foot of John's grave. The cross was carved in the Protestant rather than the Orthodox style. This to the man they had once exorcised as the devil incarnate.

The Kuskokwim region mourned John's death, and memorial services were held in all the villages. People spoke of themselves as "fatherless orphans" in their bereavement, a fitting yet ironic testimonial given John's special concern for that category of person. With John's death crumbled plans for the immediate establishment of the helper's school. In fact, the Yup'ik brethren met with Brother Butzin soon after the funeral and asked that the mission send Joe Kilbuck to take his father's place in the mission work. Although the helpers' plea was impossible, it expressed the loyalty John retained in death. John's old friend Kawagleg followed him to the grave before June.

Within a week Edith returned to Akiak where she remained busy with church work. March found her preparing to return to the States with the first boat in June, and she occupied herself breaking up her home, packing her personal things, and disposing of her supplies. Although she was nervous and capable of little work herself, she was not bowed down with grief: "I don't look *back* and grieve, but ahead and trust."[15]

In April Edith moved with Lily to Bethel, where she remained until her final farewells in June. From the time of her arrival there until practically the moment of her departure, she and Brother Neck ("so enthusiastic and zealous") worked on translations, a task John would have undertaken had he lived: "I am giving the story and the *meaning* rather than an exact translation of words. It takes time. We discuss the meaning after reading over the passage and then the most understandable way to express it in Native. He then takes it down word for word in his own method of writing." The two continued their work together into the spring: "Neck and I nearly finished one whole chapter this forenoon. Lately I have been unable to sleep. All night long I am trying to put English into understandable native and yet not change the meaning of the original text. It is difficult at all times and often next to impossible to make a perfect translation." Edith wrote in June, "Neck and I are working hard on the translations. We are going to get the children of Israel out of Egypt before I leave, if the ship has to wait for me. We will then leave them with Moses for the present. Neck is chafing because we can not go on—all the way to the Holy land, but I don't feel very well. . . . I think I won't undertake so long a journey at this time."[16]

Although friends made her life comfortable, the spring found Edith restless and lonely: "It seems that Father just must come and take me home. Spring always meant geese and gardens and sewing and house cleaning. I miss him so." Ill health added to Edith's troubles and her longing for a home of her own continued to grow; however, it was hard to imagine a home without John: "I long for just one hour with him . . . to talk things over and plan a little. . . . If I were only strong I would miss him less. He saved me at every turn, and now I must do without these dear attentions and learn to live alone."[17]

Edith remained in Bethel through the spring, dividing her time between reading and resting so she would be strong when the ship arrived. By the end of May she was feeling well enough to write, "I think of many things I will do. To revise our manuscript will take me at least one year. Perhaps I can have some sketches published later on."[18]

By June 1 the river was open, and everything was hurry and bustle in preparation for the *Admiral Goodrich* which would take Edith and other passengers home. On the twenty-second, she bade her old friends Brother Neck and David Hawk good-bye. Although glad to go, she wrote that it hurt her to leave. On the twenty-third, the *Goodrich* left Bethel. A news bulletin was announced just after they boarded ship, and she remarked the advent of the wireless along the Kuskokwim: "It seems so wonderful that my *last* days in Alaska should see this come to pass, even here, on the very edge of the world."[19]

The voyage was hard, its only bright spot the companionship of Lily, who accompanied her home. Of the decision, Edith wrote, "We took the child when she was three years old so she knows no other home or parents and in our hearts she was as much ours as an own child. It would be like another funeral in the family to give her up. Besides she needs me."[20] From the time she left the Kuskokwim the little girl was called Mary to avoid the ironic contrast between her dark skin and her white name. This companion-

Fig. 17.2. Mary Lily, Ottawa, Kansas, 1922.
(Kilbuck family)

Fig. 17.3. Edith Kilbuck, 1918. (Moravian Archives)

ship was not to last, however, as three years later Mary Lily died of tuberculosis.

Finally, on July 7, they landed safely in Seattle, and on August 12 Edith and Lily arrived in Independence. During the years that followed, Edith made her home with Joe and Novello, first in Ottawa and subsequently moving with them to Hood River, Oregon.

One might think that on her return home Edith's writing days were done. On the contrary, although she never attempted the manuscript revisions that she had mentioned after John's death, Edith kept up a lively Alaska correspondence from the family home at Hood River during the years that followed. In this way she continued to provide encouragement for another decade to men and women interested in Alaska. A half dozen years after her return, she composed a circular describing the bedding and clothing needs of the Moravian Children's Home. Ever practical, her article included instructions on how best to construct comforters and quilts, pillowslips ("A muslin pillow case feels about as warm as sheet iron"), dresses and aprons, and boys' shirts and pants to meet Alaska specifications.[21]

Edith spent the last years of her life with her daughter Ruth in Charlotte, North Carolina, and in the Moravian Home in nearby Winston-Salem. During that year alone, she gave more than forty talks in local Moravian churches, busy to the end telling of her and John's "life work." She died on December 21, 1933, at the age of sixty-eight and was buried beyond the wide cedar avenue in God's Acre in Winston-Salem.

MISSIONARY AND MISSIONIZED: FULL CIRCLE

With John's passing and Edith's departure came the end of one of the most dramatic periods in the history of the Kuskokwim drainage. From their arrival in 1885 until Edith's final farewells in 1922, the people of the Kuskokwim had experienced changes as substantial as any experienced before or since. They had also managed to retain a uniquely Yup'ik view of the world and one which many of John and Edith's actions supported, if not always consciously. How precisely had the Yup'ik people of the Kuskokwim changed and how remained the same between their first hesitant encounters with John and Edith in Bethel in 1885 and their tearful farewell two score years later? How great was the discrepancy, if any, between what the Kilbucks had spoken, what the Yupiit had ultimately heard, and what the native converts would in turn preach to their descendants?

When John and Edith arrived in western Alaska in June 1885 they found a people already devastated by the onslaught of epidemic disease associated with the arrival of the Russians earlier in the century. As much as one-third of the delta population had died in the smallpox epidemic of 1838–1839. These unprecedented losses had changed the character of intergroup relations, most significantly putting an end to interregional warfare. Moreover, these losses helped pave the way for the transformation of the day-to-day life of the people the Kilbucks encountered on their arrival. The Yup'ik people had also made infrequent contacts with Russian traders and priests since the establishment of Russian Mission in 1845 and Kolmakovskiy in 1841. Although both traditional subsistence and ceremonial life remained intact in significant respects, Russian trade goods had been introduced, and some Yupiit had received baptism at the hands of an Orthodox priest.

During their first years along the Kuskokwim, the Kilbucks employed an intense five-fold strategy of building, speaking, teaching, healing, and traveling to further undercut traditional ways of being and to provide appropriate "civilized" Christian alternatives. They helped to establish a mission station characterized by a regular round of activities which effectively modeled both the Moravian doctrine of a lived faith as well as the Protestant work ethic. From this vantage point, they worked to replace belief in the power of the local religious leaders, the shamans, with faith in the Almighty. The homeopathic remedies that formed an indispensable part of the missionaries' conversion kit directly challenged the shamans' powers both to cure the sick and to intercede on behalf of the living. Likewise, Moravian prayer meetings, Bible instruction, and an elaborate round of church activities provided alternatives to Yup'ik ritual and ceremonial activity. The missionaries also denigrated traditional social norms and sexual mores while consistently invoking the social and moral superiority of the nuclear family.

By 1895 the persistence of the Kilbucks and their colleagues was beginning to pay off. In and around the major centers of Moravian activity, a combination of their words and deeds began to bring changes. Modern medicine consistently showed itself superior to the amulets and incantations of the shamans. Likewise, the missionaries' technology, including their sawmill, boats, methods of food preservation, and printed language worked to attract converts. The power of their goods proved the "truth" of their religion.[22] Where the Yupiit accepted John and Edith, however, it was not so much because they viewed them as having unique and superior power. On the contrary, they viewed them as having power as traditionally defined.

For both the nineteenth-century Yup'ik people and the Moravians, the connection between thought and deed was fundamental. Thus, the Moravian admonition that belief in Christ must be supported by daily acts in his behalf found a comprehending audience among a people for whom right thought and efficacious action were inseparable. In the same way, John's contention that the prayer of a sinner would find direct heavenly response was interpreted in the light of traditional Yup'ik sympathetic hunting magic. Familiar with the use of ritual performance to insure the success of future action, John's Yup'ik audience was already primed for what amounted to his creative reformation of an accustomed form. Although both the Moravians and the Yupitt possessed religious specialists—the church hierarchy on the one hand and the shamans on the other—both laid primary emphasis on the person as the one responsible for his or her own actions and fate. This, too, helped facilitate the transformation underway.

In part as a result of these contiguities, the Kilbucks and their fellow missionaries were able to insinuate themselves and their view of the world into Kuskokwim life. More important, by 1895 they had mobilized the support of a handful of Yup'ik men and women both to translate and to preach the Moravian "New Way." Especially after John and Edith's departure in 1900, it fell to these native helpers to continue the process of converting their own people.

As the Kilbucks prepared to leave western Alaska after fifteen years of proselytizing, they came away convinced that they had helped to lay the groundwork for the successful conversion of the entire region. However, even before John boarded ship in the fall of 1900, influenza arrived on the Kuskokwim and within a season seriously undermined what he and Edith had helped to build. John estimated that as much as half the adult population died during that summer from the combined effects of influenza, measles, and later in the fall, pneumonia: "The population now consists of the young generation—like the second growth of timber—with here and there a middle aged person."[23] This human disaster served to further undercut the authority of the traditional shamans, who not only showed themselves unable to save their followers but in most cases their own lives as well. Although their inadequacy can help us understand their demise, it is not sufficient to explain the form of their replacement. For that we must look to what came after them.

When John and Edith returned to the Kuskokwim in 1911, they confronted a world greatly altered from the one they had left a decade before. Not only were many of their friends and co-workers gone, but a number of new influences had arrived along the river. Following the Klondike gold strike in 1896 and the rich Nome strike three years later, prospectors had come to the Kuskokwim to seek their fortune. Though no major mineral deposits were discovered, a number of small and moderately productive claims substantially increased the non-native population along the river. Unlike the missionaries who had preceded them, neither the miners, traders, nor steamboat crews came with the intent to change the Yup'ik people among whom they lived. Moreover, the direct contacts between the Yupiit and the non-native entrepreneurs were infrequent and largely economic in character. Nonetheless, life along the river was profoundly affected. More trade goods were available and more opportunities existed to earn money to acquire them. The growth of the cash economy directly challenged traditional reciprocity and concepts of ownership.

The Kilbucks worked in Akiak in the aftermath of the epidemic devastation of the nineteenth century and on the eve of the postwar pattern of government dependency. Because of the economic expansion along the river and their new role as federal representatives, the Kilbucks accomplished as much in the material as in the spiritual realm during their ten years in Akiak. Under their direction the people built new houses, dug gardens, expanded reindeer herding, and gained access to an unprecedented array of trade goods and new technological developments. In 1916 John described the transformation of the domestic economy:

> This village, upon our arrival five years ago occupied less than an acre of ground space, consisting of four cabins above ground—2 half underground and 4 huts altogether underground, beaver style—ten habitations for about 115 people. Today the village is spread over a space of no less than five acres, upon which are erected three rows of dwellings, 24 in number, not including the school house, teacher's dwelling and the church. These 24 cabins are as a rule occupied by one family—are well lighted with from two to four windows, and have means of ventilation without opening the door. Eleven of these cabins have cellars under them—and one under the school house—that is 32' × 16' × 6 1/2'. There are also eleven private water closets. In 1911 there were no ranges—and only one sewing machine. Now there are five ranges, 19 stoves, 18 sewing machines and six phonographs. Such furniture as chairs, rocking chairs, and bed springs from the great Outside are to be found in these homes.[24]

The Kilbucks' impact had been in the transformation of the ordinary as well as the extraordinary aspects of Yup'ik society, forming an analogue to Western culture along the Kuskokwim. Preaching the value of time, money, and the written word, their practical mission engendered a novel perception of the world and the "Real People's" place within it. Their friend and superior William Lopp later eulogized, "Akiak, with its gardens, its thousands of reindeer, its sawmill, its post-office, its school, its hospital, its church and its people elevated from hovels to homes, seemed, at the time of Mr. Kilbuck's passing, to be the crowning work of his career . . . the outstanding accomplishment of their helpful lives."[25]

Although the people of Akiak increasingly spoke English, lived within four walls, worked for wages, and attended church, they remained independent, their lives focused on extended family relations and the pursuit of the fish and game on which they had relied for centuries. Animal husbandry and tilling the soil had been embraced by an energetic minority, but the people ultimately ignored these eminently "civilized" activities when they conflicted with traditional subsistence and settlement patterns. Though much had changed, much also remained of the Yup'ik Eskimos' traditional view of the world. Most important, they continued, for the time being, masters of their own lives.

If the journals of John and Edith are to be believed, their years in Akiak produced relatively easy acceptance of the often devastating circumstances, especially the high death rate, associated with a period of rapid social change. This positive experience, in turn, may in part be attributed to the

Fig. 17.4. John standing with the Akiak school children. (Moravian Archives)

Kilbucks' efforts towards change of a specific character. Throughout their years on the Kuskokwim, they sought to replace Yup'ik animism with the form and content of the Moravian faith. The discipline and order they preached appealed to the Yupiit as a novel spiritual solution for an unprecedented social crisis. Combining their traditional sensitivity to the spirit world with the discipline of the Protestant work ethic, the people of the Kuskokwim found it possible to become fervent Christians without ceasing to be Yup'ik Eskimos.

Although they worked to effect a profound transformation in the material circumstances of the people who remained after the epidemic of 1900, the Kilbucks required the people to internalize their aspirations. Rather than experiencing changes as imposed from without, their policy of "helping the natives to help themselves" allowed the people of Akiak to retain a sense of control of the circumstances that were shaping their lives. At the time, the Yup'ik residents of Akiak probably did not experience irreconcilable conflict in core cultural concepts, such as the definition of personhood or the notion of cosmological recycling. Whereas the material and social circumstances of life had been greatly altered, fundamental aspects of Yup'ik ideology remained intact. Edith spoke more truly than she imagined when she wrote that the people did not feel "torn," as what had been introduced was accepted as distinct from and not in conflict with the cultural concepts the Kilbucks thought they were replacing.

Today, when the people of the Kuskokwim hearken back to a golden past, most envision the state of affairs that existed in the region in the early 1900s. Some scholars believe that by this point what remained of the traditional Yup'ik way of being can be termed no more than a "remnant culture," as traditional religion, social organization, technology, and political organization had been largely displaced by Western alternatives. Certainly, the nineteenth-century ceremonial round was no longer practiced in its original intricate detail. Also, with the demise of the men's house, the residential separation of the sexes was all but eliminated. At the same time, the deaths of so many people before and after 1900 meant that the traditional socialization process was substantially disrupted, in both form and content.

Although the external circumstances of life had dramatically changed, the men and women of the middle Kuskokwim possessed a distinctive language and value system, certainly altered from the time of their grandfathers but still retaining many vital continuities. Rather than remnant, the period during which the Kilbucks worked in Akiak might better be characterized as a renaissance. Far from being experienced as a lessening, the second decade of the twentieth century was probably a very exciting period, with an abundance of new ideas and skills adding to, rather than subtracting from, the quality of family and village life.

In the end, Western Christianity, in the form of Moravianism, interacted with, but failed to supplant, Yup'ik ideology and action along the Kuskokwim in a number of important ways. Although the traditional residential division of the sexes was abandoned, in part through John and Edith's tireless efforts on behalf of the single-family dwelling, a pronounced sexual division in daily life, especially harvesting and food processing activities, continued. In the same way, a number of young men, whom John judged the hope of their people, enthusiastically embraced herding and gardening. However, this usually occured only insofar as these activities did not conflict with traditional harvesting activities. Where such conflicts existed, herding and gardening were abandoned.

Along with the sexual division of labor, the constitution and significance of extended family relations remained largely intact. Though disease and subsequent dislocation wrought temporary havoc among the people, the Yup'ik relational system, epitomized in the belief in the perpetual cycling and essential continuity of living things, continued and helped to make intellectual as well as social structural sense of the situation. Through a complex of so-called "fictive" and adoptive processes (including the rebirth of John's own mother and children), orphans and widows were reintegrated into the larger social group. Continuity in the traditional naming system, as well as the use of kinship terms of reference and address, provided the Yup'ik men and women of the Kuskokwim with tools to help them reconstitute themselves socially in the face of the population swings of the early twentieth century.

The Yup'ik language, which was the necessary prerequisite of the above, also continued a vital force in daily life. John remained convinced that children needed to master English in the schoolroom as preparation for the encounters with non-natives which would be an important part of their adult lives. At the same time, John continued to speak and to preach to the people in their own language, which they in turn continued to employ in both domestic and public arenas. Beyond the words spoken, many of the traditional patterns and functions of speech remained into the twentieth century, including a vital oral tradition, cultural prescriptions and admonitions directing social action, and sociolinguistic functions such as teasing, gossiping, and ostracism (nonspeech). The positive implications of the undiminished and ubiquitous character of village gossip noted by Edith are worth recalling.

The cultural role and value placed on oral performance is also tied directly to the vitality of the Yup'ik language. Less than ten years after John first preached in the men's house, native brethren followed in his footsteps to preach to their own people. This use of the public forum by native men and women to witness for Christ was tremendously important. The less confrontational tactics of the native brethren helped the Moravians to gain entrance into this arena and allowed the audience to make sense of the message. In the same way that discourse in the men's house figured as a major element in the traditional Yup'ik educational process, the Moravians preached that the Word of God could only be received if continually and publicly restated.

Although the traditional ceremonial round had been dismantled by the beginning of the twentieth century, gifting and reciprocity retained important functions in everyday life. Traditional attitudes toward objects, involving a reciprocal rather than a possessive relationship, continued to dominate peoples' ideas concerning the use and ownership of material goods. Though John and Edith were in many ways successful in suppressing the traditional cycling of goods which they judged excessive, they remained caught up in less elaborate, yet nonetheless significant, ongoing reciprocal exchanges.

Finally, Yup'ik cosmology placed fundamental importance on the power of the human mind, and it was in terms of this concept that the Yupiit were subsequently able to restate and understand the Moravian message of Christian responsibility and accountability. In the same way, though the concept of original sin was new, the Christian emphasis on salvation and life eternal corresponded at least in part with the traditional belief in rebirth made possible by proper action in life. Many Yup'ik people were successful in resolving the contradiction between the Christian theological emphasis on individual salvation and the social emphasis of nineteenth-century Yup'ik daily life. This they did by practicing Christianity in a way that deemphasized individual salvation while simultaneously harnessing divine help in improving the condition of the community of believers.

The emergence of the modern church and state along the Kuskokwim was a dialectical process, an interaction between the missionary (both federal and Christian) and the Yup'ik consciousness. During the Kilbucks' tenure it is inaccurate to say that Western Christian ideology "won out" because of perceived superior power. Rather, it interacted with and was in part changed by the Yup'ik ideology and action it came to transform. Though John and Edith succeeded in many dimensions of their work, their success did not constitute acculturation or unidirectional modernization. On the contrary, the Yup'ik encounter with Christianity in general and with John and Edith Kilbuck in particular was a complex and creative process, leading to the emergence of new cultural forms.

The Kilbucks' last year along the river provides testimony to this process. Frustrated with work involving federal oversight in the Western secular domain, John and Edith returned to the more holistic enterprise of missionary work among the people, especially the native helpers. They saw that the circumstances of life along the river were increasingly fluid and subject to a number of powerful external influences and that the "good life" that they strove for must now, more than ever, be sought from within. John's first and last sermon ("Be ye faithful onto death and I shall give you the crown of life") was given to the people in their own language after his passing, and to this day the passage marks his grave. This was a powerful message, given both the circumstances of his own life and the meaning this concept had grown to encompass in his lifetime. In the months after John's death and before her departure, Edith learned of at least two baby Johns and one newborn Henry. Also after John's death, the native helpers asked in their own tradition of generational continuity that John and Edith's son Joe come to take his father's place. With Edith's help, Brother Neck continued his work translating the Bible into his own powerful pictographs until the time of her departure. Real people had internalized John and Edith's vision of life eternal in Yup'ik terms.

A CONSENTING UNION

The lives of John and Edith Kilbuck illuminate the process of cultural conversion along the Kuskokwim. Reading between the lines of their intent, we catch a glimpse of the aspirations and understandings of the Yup'ik people whom they sought to convert. In the process of viewing their life work, macrohistory postulating the growing hegemony of Christianity over local ideology is found wanting. As an alternative, John and Edith's journals and letters make possible the beginnings of a dialectical reading of Kuskokwim history.

Analysts of and participants in native-missionary encounter in the Arctic have often portrayed conversion as an all-or-nothing process in which the native culture is alternately totally transformed or left virtually intact. Missionary encounter is not presented as a dialogue, but in terms of relative failure or success. For example, the easy acceptance of Moravian ideology along the Kuskokwim has been explained by reference to an inherent weakness in the traditional nineteenth-century Yup'ik value system.[26] On the other hand, many descendants of that encounter, modern natives and non-native clergy alike, maintain that Christianity simply gave new form to what they had before, that in effect there has been no change.[27]

The result of viewing the native-missionary encounter as either pure oppression or enlightenment is that missionaries are alternately criticized as tyrannical colonizers ruining noble natives and reified as noble reformers saving savage souls. As an alternative, the preceding pages have presented the interaction between the Kilbucks and the Yup'ik people as an encounter between different systems of meaning. In western Alaska, this encounter resulted in neither total commitment nor total rejection of one by the other. Instead, a subtle internalization of selected cultural categories took place, through both deliberate and unintentional negotiation. People made conscious choices based on perceived congruities between Yup'ik and Christian systems of meaning.

As stated in the introduction, the native-missionary encounter cannot be viewed as a series of cultural rapes, but rather as legitimate, fruitful "consenting unions."[28] The relationship between the Yupiit and the Kilbucks was one such union. The story of their encounter is especially instructive, as it combines missionary and government influences. The Kilbucks accomplished their missionary work during the first years of an enterprise when individuals could make their greatest impact. Ironically, as evangelists—the least flexible members of Victorian society—they arrived armed with a spiritual integrity that provided a powerful model for the people among whom they worked. As the mission became more fully established, difficulties increased within the mission itself. Also, complications arose as other whites, including miners and traders, settled in the region.

The situation gradually changed, and so did the Kilbucks' perception of their "mission." Whereas originally committed to a far-reaching program of cultural assimilation, toward the end of their careers they sought to use reservations to "preserve" the Yupiit from the "bad elements" of white society. Whereas in the lower forty-eight states, desire for aboriginal lands had pushed Indians onto reservations to clear the way for white settlement, United States Bureau of Education employees working in Alaska at the turn of the century, including the Kilbucks, sought to "buy time with space" by segregating the natives from encroaching whites so that they might "learn at a measured pace."[29] Although the Kilbucks' paternalistic perception of the Yupiit as "their people" was grounded in false assumptions of cultural superiority, their actions effectively provided at least some Yupiit with a new arena in which to express their cultural identity. In western Alaska, the means of domination and assimilation turned out to be a mechanism for creative self-representation.

Especially during their last two decades in Alaska, the Kilbucks were motivated by a desire both to "protect" native people and to give them a choice, rather than attempting to restrict their options. Throughout their tenure in the north and southeast, as well as along the Kuskokwim, the Kilbuck's challenged natives to *selectively* incorporate the accouterments of Western civilization. They not only attempted to shield natives from "no-account" whites, but provided alternatives, some of which the natives accepted and some of which they did not. The Kilbucks made only limited progress in their efforts to transform the Yupiit into laborers in the larger society. Their mission had an undeniable impact, but the Yupiit ultimately dictated the terms of their success.

The Kilbucks' dual project of Christianization and Americanization was comparable in many respects to that advocated by other Christian reformers of their day. Government officials working within the Anglo-Protestant tradition also shared these goals and made John's transition from preacher to teacher both practicable and personally successful. In Alaska as in the Lower Forty-eight, both missionaries and Bureau of Education employees conspired for the cultural domination of indigenous peoples. As the careers of the Kilbucks and their associates, including Romig and Lopp, make abundantly clear, the separation between church and state was not a deeply held tenet during this period in American history. During the nineteenth and early twentieth century, Protestant missionaries conspired with the United

States government to accomplish the twin goals of "civilizing" and Christianizing America's aboriginal population.[30]

Although the Kilbucks shared goals common to the other Christian reformers of their times, their proselytizing for the American way was selective and conditional rather than blanket condemnation. Whereas many Protestants strove for nothing less than the obliteration of Native American culture, including language, religion, ceremonies, and social patterns, in many ways the Kilbucks—both consciously and unconsciously—accommodated themselves to the Yup'ik point of view insofar as it did not constitute a direct obstacle to their view of a Christian life. Thus, although the Kilbucks preached the value of English as a necessary survival tool in a changing world, they carried out their own work in Yup'ik, translating their message into the native language instead of the other way around. In the same way, although they rigorously suppressed what they viewed as "heathen idolotry," they were active participants in elaborate social and ritual exchanges. Although they opposed the traditional shamans at every turn, their goal was to transfer responsibility and authority to a native clergy as soon as possible. As a result, they were able to provide alternatives worth considering in a situation of rapid social change, which the Yupiit were able to selectively appropriate according to their own practical purposes.

The strength of the Kilbucks' mission lay in the degree it allowed converts an opportunity to simultaneously change and not change during a period of dramatic population fluctuation and unprecedented outside intervention. Native Americans have been much more motivated to preserve what they can of their traditional cosmologies in their reactions to missionaries and white agents of change in general than has been appreciated, and the Yupiit are no exception. Their conversion to Christianity during the late nineteenth and early twentieth centuries did not comprise a blanket denial or retreat from the old ways. Such a reading of history represents the colonial ideal, not the complex reality of cultural change, simultaneously involving appropriation, resistance, and translation. Rather, conversion in western Alaska appears to have been the productive interpenetration of Christian and Yup'ik sources—a consenting union.

Throughout the Kilbucks' tenure in Alaska, the Yupiit were active participants rather than passive objects in the conversion process. Ethnocentric factors channeled agreement and disagreement on both sides of the exchange. As demonstrated in the 1890 execution of Brother Hooker, and less dramatically in their qualified acceptance of herding and gardening twenty years later, the Yupiit had just as strong opinions about what was right and wrong as had the Kilbucks, opinions which both organized their reactions to specific events and oriented each to the other.

As historian Francis Paul Prucha points out, the Anglo-Protestants began to lose their hegemony in American life and culture as the twentieth century developed. Their effort to create a "Christian nation" to include all inhabitants of the United States subsided to the point where today the colonial aspects of that goal are points of guilt and embarrassment. By the 1920s, in Alaska as well as the lower forty-eight states, science and technology began to replace religion as the means of salvation.[31]

The era of missionary activity as the chief locus of cross-cultural encounter had drawn to a close. The experiences of John and Edith Kilbuck had spanned the years of missionary dominance, bridging the gap between spiritual and secular missions. Never again would a single institution have such a sustained impact on the Yup'ik people, nor would the details of one couple's life work reveal so much about the history of the people they sought to transform.

NOTES

Abbreviations

ARCA   Alaskan Russian Church Archives
AROCA   Archives of the Russian Orthodox Church in Alaska
KC   Kilbuck Collection, Moravian Archives, Bethlehem, Pennsylvania
PEC   Provincial Elders' Conference
RBIA   Records of the Bureau of Indian Affairs
SPG   Society for Propagating the Gospel

Chapter 1. Anthropologists, Missionaries, and Natives

1. John Henry Kilbuck, Journal to Edith, January 16, 1892. Kilbuck Collection (hereafter cited as KC).
2. Ivan Karp, "Review of *Colonial Evangelism*, by T. O. Beidelman," *American Ethnologist* 4:215; T. O. Beidelman, *Colonial Evangelism*, 51
3. John Webster Grant, *Moon in Wintertime: Missionaries and the Indians of Canada in Encounter Since 1534*, 258.
4. R. Lechat, "Evangelism and Colonialism," *Eskimo* 33:3.
5. Grant, *Moon in Wintertime*, 205; Robert F. Berkhofer, Jr., *Salvation and the Savage*.
6. Marshall Sahlins, *Culture and Practical Reason*; James Clifford and George E. Marcus, *Writing Culture: The Poetics and Politics of Ethnography*; George E. Marcus and Michael Fischer, *Anthropology as Cultural Critique*.
7. Jane Schneider and Shirley Lindenbaum, "Frontiers of Christian Evangelism: Essays in Honor of Joyce Riegelhaupt," *American Ethnologist* 14:1–2; Claude E. Stipe, "Anthropologists Versus Missionaries: The Influence of Presuppositions," *Current Anthropology* 21:165–79.
8. Stipe, "Anthropologists Versus Missionaries," 166.
9. Ibid., 168.
10. Ronald J. Burwell, "Comment on Stipe: Anthropologists Versus Missionaries," *American Ethnologist* 21:169; Roger M. Keesing, *Cultural Anthropology: A Contemporary Perspective*, 459, cited in Stipe, "Anthropologists Versus Missionaries," 165.
11. Frank A. Salamone, "Anthropologists and Missionaries: Competition or Reciprocity?" *Human Organization* 36:409.

12. Mary Taylor Huber, *The Bishop's Progress: A Historical Ethnography of Catholic Missionary Experience*, 9.

13. Kenneth M. Morrison, "Discourse and the Accommodation of Values: Toward a Revision of Mission History," *Journal of the American Academy of Religion* 53:365.

14. Grant, *Moon in Wintertime*, 2, 58.

15. Beidelman, *Colonial Evangelism*; Huber, *The Bishop's Progress*.

16. Jean Comaroff and John Comaroff, "Christianity and Colonialism in South Africa," *American Ethnologist* 13:1.

17. Huber, *The Bishop's Progress*, 213.

18. Lechat, "Evangelism and Colonialism," 7.

19. The term Creole is used to designate a person of mixed Alaska-native (Aleut or Eskimo) and Russian ancestry. During the Russian American period in Alaska, Creole was a heritable status in the male line with one putative Russian ancestor.

20. Bethel was established seventy miles upriver just downstream and across the river from the native village and trading post of Mumtreglak (*Mamterilleq*).

21. Grant, *Moon in Wintertime*, 216.

22. Lydia Black, "Ivan Pan'kov—An Architect of Aleut Literacy," *Arctic Anthropology* 14:94−107; Lydia Black, *Iakov Netsvetov: The Yukon Years 1845−1863*; Wendell H. Oswalt, *Mission of Change in Alaska: Eskimos and Moravians on the Kuskokwim*; James W. Van Stone, "Some Aspects of Religious Change Among Native Inhabitants in West Alaska and Northwest Territories," *Arctic Anthropology* 2:21−24.

23. Sergei Kan, ed., "Native Cultures and Christianity in Northern North America: Selected Papers from a Symposium," *Arctic Anthropology* 24:1−66; Calvin Martin, *Keepers of the Game: Indian-Animal Relationships and the Fur Trade*; Adrian Tanner, *Bringing Home Animals: Religious Ideology and Mode of Production of the Mistassini Memorial Cree Hunters*.

24. James W. Henkelman and Kurt H. Vitt, *The History of the Alaska Moravian Church 1885−1985: Harmonious to Dwell*; Barbara S. Smith, *Russian Orthodoxy in Alaska*.

25. Henry Warner Bowden, *American Indians and Christian Missions: Studies in Cultural Conflict*.

26. See Kenneth M. Morrison, "Discourse and Accommodation of Values," 365.

27. Kenneth O. L. Burridge, "Missionary Occasions," in *Mission, Church, and Sect in Oceania*, ed. J. A. Boutilier, D. T. Hughes, and S. W. Tiffany, 1−30.

28. Rene Maunier, *The Sociology of Colonies*, 168; Beidelman, *Colonial Evangelism*, 4.

29. L. A. Coser, *Greedy Institutions*, 67−68.

30. James W. Fernandez, "The Sound of Bells in a Christian Country," in *The Massachusetts Review*, Spring 1964, 588.

31. Beidelman, *Colonial Evangelism*.

32. See Comaroff and Comaroff, "Christianity and Colonialism in South Africa," 7−11 on the career of John Mackenzie, a missionary who shared John's goals but lacked his power to realize them.

33. Marshall Sahlins, *Islands of History*, ix.

34. Beidelman, *Colonial Evangelism*, 30.

35. Mikhail Bakhtin, "Discourse in the Novel," in *The Dialogical Imagination*, ed. Michael Holquist, 259−442; James Clifford, "On Ethnographic Authority," *Representations* 1:118−46.

36. Sahlins, *Islands of History*.

37. See Schneider and Lindenbaum, "Frontiers of Christian Evangelism," 1−8.

38. See Susan F. Harding, "Convicted by the Holy Spirit: The Rhetoric of Fundamental Baptist Conversion," *American Ethnologist* 14:167−81.

39. See Huber, *The Bishop's Progress*, on conversion in the ironic mode.

Chapter 2. The Kilbucks and the Moravians

1. S. H. Gapp, *Kolerat Pitsiulret or True Stories of the Early Days of the Moravian Mission on the Kuskokwim*, 3.

2. J. Taylor Hamilton and Kenneth Gardner Hamilton, *History of the Moravian Church, 1722–1957*, 281.

3. Francis C. Huebner, *Charles Kilbuck: An Indian's Story of the Border Wars of the American Revolution*, 1.

4. While John and Edith gave their children the middle name Henry, their children and children's children gradually dropped its usage. Their great-grandchildren, however, have begun to revive the tradition. One recent Kilbuck descendant was named Elliot Henry Kilbuck Asbury, while the parents of another went one step further back in time and gave their son Gelelemend as a middle name.

5. David Zeisberger, American Province Baptismal Records for 1789, Moravian Archives (hereafter cited as MA).

6. Edmund de Schweinitz, *The Life and Times of David Zeisberger*, 694.

7. Huebner, *Charles Kilbuck*, 2.

8. Rev. Harry E. Stocker, "The Moravian Church and Its Mission Work," *The Moravian* 66:30 (hereafter cited as *Moravian*).

9. Hamilton and Hamilton, *History of the Moravian Church*, 42.

10. Elma E. Gray, *Wilderness Christians: The Moravian Mission to the Delaware Indians*.

11. Hamilton and Hamilton, *History of the Moravian Church*, 158.

12. Adelaide L. Fries, *Customs and Practices of the Moravian Church*, 49.

13. Ibid., 50–52.

14. Edith M. Kilbuck, "John Henry Kilbuck," 1930, KC.

15. John Kilbuck to Edith, July, 1910, KC.

16. Edith Kilbuck, "John Henry Kilbuck," KC.

17. Joseph Romig, "Sketch of the Indian Mission Work," Romig Papers, 75.

18. Ibid., 4–5.

19. Letter to Mr. Schwenitz, 1874, New Westfield Mission Records, Moravian Archives.

20. Edith Kilbuck, "John Henry Kilbuck," KC.

21. John Kilbuck to the children, January 1, 1908, KC.

22. Hamilton and Hamilton, *History of the Moravian Church*, 221.

23. John Kilbuck, letter, January 13, 1905, Box 6:3, KC.

24. John Kilbuck to Edith, 1910, Box 8(3):6, KC.

25. Gapp, *Kolerat Pitsiulret*, 13.

26. See William N. Schwarze, *History of the Moravian College and Theological Seminary*, 20, 145–66, for a detailed discussion of the necessity for and development of the seminary, class and faculty composition, as well as the scholars' course of study.

27. John Kilbuck to Edith, June 8, 1910, KC.

28. Bethlehem Church Diary, 1884, 275, MA; Society for Propagating the Gospel (SPG), Minutes, April 16, 1884.

29. The full title is: The Society of the United Brethren for Propagating the Gospel Among the Heathen.

30. SPG, Minutes, August 25, 1884.

31. Gapp, *Kolerat Pitsiulret*, 14.

32. Romig, "Sketch of the Indian Mission Work," 6.

33. Edith Kilbuck, Journal, February 22, 1921, Box 4:16, KC.

34. Edith Kilbuck, letter, October 10, 1898, KC.

35. Joseph Romig, "A Sketch of Mrs. J. H. Kilbuck," Box 7(2):21, KC.

36. Ibid.

37. Edith Kilbuck, letter, January 1, 1886, KC.

38. Ibid.

39. John Kilbuck, "Letter to Bishop E. de Schweinitz, June 21, 1885," *The Moravian* 30(45):713.

40. The name refers to the biblical text, Exodus 28:10–13, 19: "And behold, the Lord stood above it, and said I am the Lord God of Abraham thy father, and the God of Isaac; the land whereon thou liest, to thee will I give it, and to thy seed. . . . and he called the name of that place Bethel."

41. The Alaska Commercial Company built a warehouse at the mouth of the Kuskokwim for the storage of goods pending their transport up the river. As the unloading place for the yearly supplies was such an important point in the area, it became known as "Warehouse" on Warehouse Creek.

42. John Kilbuck to family, November 18, 1885, KC.

43. Edith Kilbuck, Journal, March 14, 1886, KC.

Chapter 3. Something about the Yup'ik Eskimos

1. Ann Fienup-Riordan, ed., *The Yup'ik Eskimos as Described in the Travel Journals and Ethnographic Accounts of John and Edith Kilbuck, 1885–1900*, 1–28.

2. Steven A. Jacobson, *Yup'ik Eskimo Dictionary*, 28.

3. Fienup-Riordan, *The Yup'ik Eskimos*, 3.

4. Yup'ik (plural Yupiit) may also be rendered as Yupik (plural Yupiks) in English, omitting the apostrophe which standard orthography uses to signify a geminated consonant. The native spelling has been retained in this text.

5. Don Dumond, *The Eskimos and Aleuts*, 154–59.

6. Ibid.; Robert D. Shaw, "The Expansion and Survival of the Norton Tradition on the Yukon-Kuskokwim Delta," *Arctic Anthropology* 19:59–73.

7. Wendell H. Oswalt, "The Kuskowagamiut," in *This Land Was Theirs*, 125.

8. Fienup-Riordan, *The Yup'ik Eskimos*, 9.

9. Ibid., 10.

10. Henry Michael, ed., *Lieutenant Zagoskin's Travels in Russian America, 1842–1844*, 254; Edward W. Nelson, "A Sledge Journey in the Delta of the Yukon, Northern Alaska," *Proceedings of the Royal Geographical Society*, n. s., 4:669–70; Wendell H. Oswalt, *Alaskan Eskimos*, 24–26; James W. VanStone, "V. S. Kromchenko's Coastal Explorations in Southwestern Alaska, 1822, *Fieldiana* 64:33.

11. Michael, *Lieutenant Zagoskin's Travels*; E. W. Nelson, *The Eskimo about Bering Strait*, *Eighteenth Annual Report of the Bureau of American Ethnology*, 1896–1897, Part 1; Oswalt, *Alaskan Eskimos*.

12. Ann Fienup-Riordan, "Regional Groups on the Yukon-Kuskokwim Delta," in *The Central Yupik Eskimos*, Supplementary Issue, ed. Ernest S. Burch, Jr., *Études/Inuit/Studies* 8:63–93.

13. Fienup-Riordan, *The Yup'ik Eskimos*, 4–5.

14. Ibid., 12.

15. Ibid., 43–50, 390–92.

16. Nelson, *The Eskimo about Bering Strait*, 264, 327–30; Michael, *Lieutenant Zagoskin's Travels*, 281.

17. Michael, *Lieutenant Zagoskin's Travels*, 92, 204, 281, 308.

18. Wendell H. Oswalt, *Bashful No Longer: An Alaskan Eskimo Ethnohistory, 1778–1988*, 51.

19. Fienup-Riordan, *The Yup'ik Eskimos*, 217–18.

20. Michael, *Lieutenant Zagoskin's Travels*, 30, 281.

21. Wendell H. Oswalt, "Ethnicity or Ethnocide: An Alaskan Eskimo Case Study," 5.20, 4.19.

22. Oswalt, *Bashful No Longer*, 62.

23. Fienup-Riordan, *The Yup'ik Eskimos*, 13–14, 36.

24. Ibid., 19.

25. Ernest S. Burch, Jr., "Traditional Eskimo Societies in Northwest Alaska," *Senri Ethnological Studies* 4:267.

26. Fienup-Riordan, *The Yup'ik Eskimos*, 34.

27. Ibid., 19–20.

28. Fienup-Riordan, *The Nelson Island Eskimo*, 178.

29. Ibid., 213–28.

30. For instance, upon waking each morning, the pregnant woman had to quickly rise and exit from the house before she did anything else, so that her child's exit from the womb would be a speedy one. Similarly, she had to be careful not to hesitate in the performance of any task or put off any contemplated action, but had to always move quickly and with assurance so that her child likewise would be born expeditiously.

31. Fienup-Riordan, *The Nelson Island Eskimo*, 219.

32. Nelson, *The Eskimo about Bering Strait*, 515; Fienup-Riordan, *The Yup'ik Eskimos*, 81.

33. Fienup-Riordan, *The Nelson Island Eskimo*, 153–58.

34. Fienup-Riordan, *The Yup'ik Eskimos*, 17.

35. Fienup-Riordan, *The Nelson Island Eskimo*, 218.

36. Ibid., 218, 222–23; Nelson, *The Eskimo about Bering Strait*, 425.

37. Fienup-Riordan, "Regional Groups on the Yukon-Kuskokwim Delta," 63–93.

38. For example, in the intervillage Messenger Feast (Kevgiq), the movement of the guests toward their hosts was accompanied by the constant attentions of messengers from the host village whose primary function was to act as go-between during the period of approach.

39. Nelson, *The Eskimo about Bering Strait*, 426.

40. Ibid., 497–98.

41. Ibid., 494–97.

42. Fienup-Riordan, "The Mask: The Eye of the Dance," *Arctic Anthropology* 24:40–55.

43. *Ella* or *Ellam yua* (literally "the person of the universe or weather") is the Yup'ik counterpart of *Sila* or *Silap inua* described for the Inuit. According to Edward M. Weyer, *The Eskimos*, 389, this spirit possesses less fixed and definite traits and functions than those ascribed to other supernatural entities.

44. Fienup-Riordan, *The Yup'ik Eskimos*, 38–39. On Nelson Island the women's performance imitates the mating dances of birds, providing a strong image of the complementarity between the production of game and the reproduction of life.

45. Fienup-Riordan, *The Nelson Island Eskimo*, 229–35; Margaret Lantis, "The Social Culture of the Nunivak Eskimo," *Transactions of the American Philosophical Society* 35:182–87; Elsie Mather, *Cauyarnariuq* (A time for drumming), 31–104; Nelson, *The Eskimo about Bering Strait*, 392–393.

46. Fienup-Riordan, *The Yup'ik Eskimos*, 25–26.

47. When later missionaries more clearly understood the Bladder Festival, they suppressed it to the point where contemporary elders have been, until very recently, reluctant even to talk about it.

48. Fienup-Riordan, *The Nelson Island Eskimo*, 209, 222; Mather, *Cauyarnariuq*, 105–51; Nelson, *The Eskimo about Bering Strait*, 363.

49. Fienup-Riordan, *The Yup'ik Eskimos*, 40.

50. Phyllis Morrow, "It is Time for Drumming: A Summary of Recent Research on Yup'ik Ceremonialism," in *The Central Yupik Eskimos*, Supplementary Issue, ed. Ernest S. Burch, Jr., in *Études/Inuit/Studies* 8:136.

51. Fienup-Riordan, *The Yup'ik Eskimos*, 38.

52. Lantis, "The Social Culture of the Nunivak Eskimo," 87; Morrow, "It Is Time for Drumming," 115; Nelson, *The Eskimo about Bering Strait*, 359.

53. Jacobson, *Yup'ik Eskimo Dictionary*, 268, 384.

54. Edith Kilbuck, Journal, November 8, 1887, KC.

55. Lantis, "The Social Culture of the Nunivak Eskimo," 188; Mather, *Cauyarnariuq*, 159–85; Nelson, *The Eskimo about Bering Strait*, 361–63.

56. A simplified version of the traditional Kevgiq continues to be practiced in parts of western Alaska to this day (Ann Fienup-Riordan, *When Our Bad Season Comes*, 191–203). At least in some areas Kevgiq retains an impressive array of social functions, including social control through ridicule, punishment in the form of ostracism, the expression of social differences, and the celebration and recognition of a young person's coming of age (Eskimo Heritage Project, The Stebbins Potlatch).

Chapter 4. Gospel of Service

1. Provincial Elders' Conference (PEC), "Rules and Regulations of the Moravian Mission in Alaska, June 2, 1927," Moravian Archives.

2. Beverly Prior Smaby, *The Transformation of Moravian Bethlehem: From Communal Mission to Family Economy*, 239–43.

3. Edith Kilbuck, "Do Missions Pay?" 1918, Box 7(3):23, KC.

4. Ibid., 1.

5. Ibid., 9.

6. Ibid., 5–6.

7. John Kilbuck, "Second Annual Report of the Mission in Alaska, May 31, 1887," *Moravian* 33(31):487.

8. John Kilbuck, "Letters from Bro. Kilbuck," in Fienup-Riordan, *The Yup'ik Eskimos*, 172.

9. The first mission house was renovated as part of the Moravians' centennial celebration in Bethel in 1985. It can also be seen to commemorate the beginning of the restructuring of space in western Alaska according to a Western model now taken for granted. Although the contemporary dwellings of Bethel and the surrounding villages are square, true to traditional spatial concepts, municipal plans are far from gridlike.

10. Edith Kilbuck, "Do Missions Pay?" 4.

11. As early as 1768 the Moravian John Ettwein railed against missionaries who possessed an inadequate knowledge of the language of the people among whom they worked (Kenneth Gardner Hamilton, "John Ettwein and the Moravian Church During the Revolutionary Period," in *The Transactions of the Moravian Historical Society*, 195).

12. John Kilbuck, "Annual Report of the Mission in Alaska from June, 1885 to June, 1886," *Moravian* 31(30):473; Edith Kilbuck, "Letter from Bethel to the Women's Mission Society of the M. E. Church of Independence, Kansas, July 13, 1886 (Concluded)," *Moravian* 33(9):133.

13. Edith Kilbuck, Journal to her father, December 4, 1885, KC. Based in part on these word lists, a brief grammar and vocabulary were prepared by Augustus Schultze in 1889 and revised and published in 1894.

14. John Kilbuck, "The Early History of the Mission in Alaska," Box 7:5, KC.

15. Edith Kilbuck, Journal to her father, August 3, 1886, KC.

16. John Kilbuck, "Second Annual Report of the Mission in Alaska," *Moravian* 33(31):487.

17. Ibid.

18. Edith Kilbuck, "Journal to her Father, July 14, 1888," *Moravian* 33(49):781.

19. Edith Kilbuck, "Letter from Bethel, July 13, 1886," *Moravian* 33(9):132.

20. Edith Kilbuck, "Journal to her Father, December 3, 1886," *Moravian* 33(6):88.

21. Edith Kilbuck, "Do Missions Pay?" 2.

22. Edith Kilbuck, "Journal to My Dear Father, Joseph Romig, September 8, 1886," *Moravian* 33(4):52; Edith Kilbuck, "Journal, August 27, 1887," *Moravian* 33(37):585.

23. John Kilbuck, "Letter to Bishop de Schweinitz from Bethel. August 3, 1887," *Moravian* 32(42):658.

24. John Kilbuck, "Letter. July 19, 1889," *Moravian* 34(40):627.

25. John Kilbuck, "Letter to Bishop de Schweinitz from Bethel. August 3, 1887," *Moravian* 32(42):659.

26. Edith Kilbuck, Journal to her father, August 11, 1887, KC.

27. Edith Kilbuck to Papa, February 21, 1888, Box 9:1, KC.

28. Reverend Frank E. Wolff established the Carmel Mission at Nushagak in the summer of 1886 in an effort to solidify the work begun in Alaska the previous year, simultaneously expanding the mission field as well as helping to provide better communication and transmission of supplies to the Bethel mission.

29. Edith Kilbuck, Journal to her father, February 23−26, 1886, KC.

30. Edith Kilbuck, Journal to her father, August 3, 1886, KC.

31. John Kilbuck, "Letter to Weinland from Bethel. July 26, 1887," *Moravian* 32(46):727−28.

32. Edith Kilbuck to Papa, January 25, 1888, KC.

33. John Kilbuck, "Letter to the PEC. June 2, 1888," *Moravian* 33(32):497.

34. Edith Kilbuck, Journal to her father, November 20, December 22, 1887, KC.

35. Edith Kilbuck, Journal to her father, November 17, 1889, KC.

36. Edith Kilbuck to Papa, February 21, 1888, Box 9:1, KC.

37. John Kilbuck, "Letter to Rev. E. de Schweinitz, December 1888," *Moravian* 34(33):520.

38. Edith Kilbuck, "Letter from Bethel. March 20, 1889," *Moravian* 34(34):532.

39. Edith Kilbuck to John, April 26, 1896, KC.

40. John Kilbuck, Journal to Edith, February 7, 1889, KC.

41. Edith Kilbuck, Journal to her father, June 8, 1887, KC.

42. Edith Kilbuck to her father, June 12, 1888, Box 1:10, KC.

43. Edith Kilbuck, Journal to her father, June 19, 1889, Box 1:17, KC; ibid., February 21, 1888.

44. Ibid., June 26−27, 1886.

45. Edith Kilbuck, "Journal to My Dear Father, Joseph Romig. Extracts. Concluded. May 21, 1887," *Moravian* 33(9):133; Edith Kilbuck, "Journal to her Father, Joseph Romig, June 12, 1888," *Moravian* 33(48):765.

Chapter 5. Work in Earnest

1. Ernest L. Weber, "A Trip to Kolmokovsky and Beyond. Extracts from Bro. Weber's Diary. May 17, 1890," *Moravian* 35(41):648.

2. John Kilbuck, "Letter to the PEC. June 2, 1888," *Moravian* 33(32):497−98.

3. Ibid., 497.

4. Ibid.

5. Ibid., 498.

6. Edith Kilbuck, "Journal to her Father, Joseph Romig. June 12, 1888," *Moravian* 33(48):765.

7. Ibid.

8. Edith Kilbuck, "Journal to her Father, Joseph Romig. July 14, 1888," *Moravian* 33(49):781.

9. Edith Kilbuck to Papa, February 21, 1888, Box 9:1A, KC.

10. Edith Kilbuck, "Journal to her Father, Joseph Romig. July 14, 1888," *Moravian* 33(49):781.

11. John Kilbuck, "Second Annual Report of the Mission in Alaska. May 31, 1887," *Moravian* 33(31):487.

12. Edith Kilbuck, Journal to her father, February 1888, Box 1:9, KC; ibid., March 26, 1888.

13. John Kilbuck, "Letter to Rev. E. de Schweinitz, December, 1888," *Moravian* 34(33):520.

14. Edith Kilbuck, Journal to her father, November 10, 1888, Box 1:11, KC; ibid., October 6, 1888.

15. Ibid., January 11, 1889.

16. Edith Kilbuck, Journal for John, 1888–1889, Box 1:12, KC; Edith Kilbuck, Journal to her father, 1888–1889, Box l:13, KC; Edith Kilbuck, "Letter from Bethel. April 23, 1889," *Moravian* 34(34):530–33.

17. Edith Kilbuck, "Letter from Bethel, April 23, 1889," *Moravian* 34(34):530.

18. Edith Kilbuck, Journal to John, December 15, 1888, Box 1:12, KC; ibid., January 5, 1889.

19. Ibid.

20. Edith Kilbuck, Journal to her father, January 15, 1889, KC.

21. Edith Kilbuck, "Letter from Bethel. March 20, 1889," *Moravian* 34(34):532.

22. Edith Kilbuck, Journal to John, January, 1889, KC; ibid., February 1, 1889; ibid.

23. Ibid., February 2–7, 1889.

24. Edith Kilbuck, Private Journal, February 15, 1889, Box 1:13, KC.

25. John Kilbuck, "Letter to the PEC," *Moravian* 34(33):520.

26. Edith Kilbuck, Private Journal, February 16, 1889, KC.

27. Ibid.

28. John Kilbuck, "Letter from Bethel to Bro. Bachman. July 22, 1889," *Moravian* 34(41):648.

29. Caroline Detterer, "Journal," in *The Proceedings of the United Brethren for Propagating the Gospel among the Heathen*, 65.

30. Ibid., 57, 64; Edith Kilbuck to her father, November 22, 1889, KC.

31. John Kilbuck, "Letter from Bethel. December 26, 1889," *Moravian* 35(29):449; Edith Kilbuck, Journal to her father, December 12, 1889, Box 1:21, KC.

32. Edith Kilbuck, "Letter from Bethel. March 20, 1889," *Moravian* 34(34):533.

33. John Kilbuck, "Report to the PEC. May 30, 1889," *Moravian* 34(33):519–21.

34. John Kilbuck, "Report to the PEC. May 29, 1890," *Moravian* 35(35):553.

35. John Kilbuck, "Letter. January 16, 1890," *Moravian* 35(29):449; ibid., "December 26, 1889," *Moravian* 35(29):449.

36. John Kilbuck, "Letter. January 16, 1890," *Moravian* 35(29):449.

37. Ibid.

38. Ibid.

39. John Kilbuck, "Report to the PEC. May 29, 1890," 553.

40. Ibid., 551.

41. Ibid.

Chapter 6. The Real People and the Children of Thunder

1. Marshall Sahlins, "Social Science," 12; Robert Brightman, 1983.

2. Fienup-Riordan, *The Nelson Island Eskimo*, 179.

3. Paul John described a distinct category of person who, on hearing something, talks back or answers right away. One who acts in such a way is considered reprehensible because that person bounces pain and anger back to the speaker without regard for the effect of such rash verbalization. On the contrary, one should carefully weigh in one's mind what has occurred before responding to a situation with either an act or a word.

4. According to Paul John of Toksook Bay:

But the other side of it
when it is included in the *alerquun* [instruction],
if he is dealt back with kindness and compassion
it might be beneficial
at the time he is having a hard time and he does not feel
he is considered something good by the other.

Breaking his mind,
thinking to pay him back,
it is not good to do that.

They used to say in those days,
even if he did or said things to people,
we were not to follow his mind and be unkind to him.

5. When discussing indirection, one should bear in mind that what appears to one person as indirect may be very explicit for another.

6. This idea of awareness is antithetical to the state of drunkenness.

7. Roy Wagner, *The Invention of Culture*, 21.

8. Fienup-Riordan, "Regional Groups on the Yukon-Kuskokwim Delta," 76.

9. John Kilbuck, Journal, April 16, 1918, KC.

10. Ibid., May 9, 1918. This controlled use of language carried into the twentieth century. One of the Kilbucks' grandchildren described running out the back door, yelling "Shut!" as it closed behind her, followed by "up" under her breath, as her own small rebellion against her parents' strict control of her speech.

11. Fienup-Riordan, *The Yup'ik Eskimos*, 255.

12. Hamilton and Hamilton, *History of the Moravian Church*, 45.

13. Ann Fienup-Riordan, Transcripts and Translations of Interviews with Yup'ik Elders, Tape 57, 1983.

14. John Kilbuck, Journal, April 14, 1918, KC.

15. Ibid., June 2, 1918.

16. Bob Aloysius, "Ordination Commentary," *Tundra Drums*, May 8, 1986, 17.

17. Edith Kilbuck, Journal to her father, December 5, 1888, KC.

18. Edith Kilbuck, "Letter from Bethel. March 20, 1889," *Moravian* 34 (34):533.

19. Edith Kilbuck, letter, March 20, 1888, KC.

20. Fienup-Riordan, *The Yup'ik Eskimos*, 19.

21. Edith Kilbuck, letter, March 20, 1888, KC.

22. Ibid.

23. Ibid.

24. Ibid.

25. To this day the Yupiit, as well as other Alaska natives, are the subject of negative stereotyping deriving from culturally specific differences in communication styles and concepts of appropriate interpersonal interaction (see Ronald Scollon and Suzanne Scollon, *Interethnic Communication*).

26. The nineteenth-century Yupiit carefully controlled cutting of any kind, particularly during ritually dangerous times, as when the spirits of the animal and human dead were entering or exiting the human world. Ironically, John's own father, William Kilbuck, wore his hair long (see figure 2.2).

27. Edith Kilbuck to her father, August 14, 1888, KC.

28. Ibid., May 12, 1889.

29. Fienup-Riordan, *The Yup'ik Eskimos*, 15; see also Nelson, *The Eskimo about Bering Strait*, 292.

30. Fienup-Riordan, *The Nelson Island Eskimo*, 28.

31. Robert A. Brightman, "Animal and Human in Rock Cree Religion and Subsistence."

32. John Kilbuck, "Annual Report of the Mission in Alaska from June, 1885 to June, 1886," *Moravian* 31(30):473.

33. John Kilbuck, Journal, 1895, Box 5:13, KC.

34. John Kilbuck, "Journal. December 5 to 28, 1888," *Moravian* 35(4):56-57.

35. John Kilbuck, Journal to Edith, December 12, 1888, KC.

36. Edith Kilbuck, Journal to her father, October 1, 1895, KC; ibid., February 1, 1895.

37. Ibid., February 8, 1888; ibid., December, 1889.

38. This name may be a Yup'ik derivation from the Russian word for play or performance (*igra*). It may also have originated as the Russianized variant of the Yup'ik word *Itrukar(aq)*, designating a small gift brought to get into a dance or feast (Steven Jacobson, *Yup'ik Eskimo Dictionary*, 178). Over the years the Kilbucks used it to refer to a number of distinct events, including Petugtaq, Kevgiq, and Ingulaq.

39. John Kilbuck, "Annual Report of the Mission in Alaska from June, 1885 to June, 1886," *Moravian* 31(30):473.

40. John Kilbuck, Journal to Edith, August 30, 1897, KC.

41. Edith Kilbuck, Journal to her father, February, 1889, KC.

42. The twentieth-century Kilbuck family tradition of never letting guests depart empty-handed and encouraging them to eat heartily at their table looks suspiciously like this nineteenth-century Yup'ik pattern.

43. Edith Kilbuck, Journal to her father, July, 1890, KC.

44. John Kilbuck, Journal to Edith, January 16, 1892, KC.

45. Edith Kilbuck, Journal to her father, August 29, 1893, KC.

46. Edith Kilbuck to her father, March, 1890, KC.

47. Caroline Weber, "Diary, December 10, 1890," *Moravian* 36:787.

Chapter 7. The Testing

1. John Kilbuck, January 2, 1891, Box 5:8, KC.

2. Edith Kilbuck, Journal, November 10, 1888, Box 1:11, KC.

3. John Kilbuck to Edith, January 24, 1890, KC; Edith Kilbuck, Journal, February 25, 1890, KC.

4. William H. Weinland, "Report of the Missionary Exploration Expedition to Alaska. (Part I). 1884," *Moravian* 30(1):5-6.

5. Edith Kilbuck to her father, December 15, 1889, KC.

6. Iakov Korchinskii, "Iz Putevykh Zametok Pravoslavnago Kvikpakhsko-Kuskokvimskago Missionera Sviashchennika Ioanna Korchinskago" (From the travel notes of the Orthodox missionary priest, Iakov Korchinskii of the Kvikhpak-Kuskokwim Mission, 1896), *Russian Orthodox American Messenger* 2:654.

7. Iakov Netsvetov was an Aleut priest who served at Russian Mission from 1845 to 1863. Zakharii Bel'kov was Netsvetov's successor as the major representative of Russian Orthodoxy in western Alaska. Bel'kov was born in 1838, the son of a Creole from St. Paul Island, and moved with his parents to Russian Mission in 1845. After 1868, at the age of thirty, Bel'kov continued the mission's work at Russian Mission and was ordained a priest in 1876.

8. Iakov Korchinskii, "Nekrolog" (Obituary), *Russian Orthodox American Messenger* 3:629-30.

9. Lydia Black, *Iakov Netsvetov: The Yukon Years 1845-1863*, ix-xx; Barbara S. Smith, *Russian Orthodoxy in Alaska*, 5-6; Journal of Worship Services, Fr. Zakharii Bel'kov, Kvikhpak Mission Records, Archives of the Russian Orthodox Church in Alaska, Microfilm 59, Reel 3 (hereafter cited as AROCA).

10. William H. Weinland, Kuskokwim Diary, 1884, Box 8(3), Alaska Materials.

11. Hamilton and Hamilton, *History of the Moravian Church*, 188.

12. Grant, *Moon in Wintertime*, 228.

13. Veniaminov served the Orthodox Church in Alaska from 1824 to 1858, first as a priest working in the Aleutians and later as a bishop. He is remembered for his ethnographic and linguistic studies as well as for his missionary work. In 1979, one hundred years after his death, the Orthodox Church canonized him a saint (Smith, *Russian Orthodoxy in Alaska*, 5).

14. Ioann Veniaminov, "Instructions of Bishop Innocent to Priests under his Jurisdiction, Reiterated by Bishop Tikhon, 1899. Part Second: Special Directions Concerning Instructions, Public Worship, and Treatment of Natives, etc.," *Russian Orthodox American Messenger* 3(20):534–43, 3(21):564–74.

15. Ibid.

16. Ernst Benz, *The Eastern Orthodox Church*, 6.

17. Edith Kilbuck, Journal, January 20, 1891, KC; Edith Kilbuck, "Journal. April 1, 1891," *Moravian* 37(29):456.

18. Edith Kilbuck, Journal to her husband, August 9, 1896, Box 2:8, KC. Whereas the Russian Orthodox were the chief thorn in the sides of the Moravians, after the founding of Holy Cross Mission on the Yukon in 1888, the Catholics became the chief adversary of the Russian Orthodox. Although the Russian Orthodox still considered the Moravian "schismatics" a serious threat, the historical animosity between the Russian Orthodox and the Catholic "heretics" combined with their proximity, transforming them into the major adversary.

19. William H. Weinland, "Letter from Bethel. March 10, 1886. (Concluded)," *Moravian* 31(46):724.

20. Diocese Administration, Fr. Zakharii Bel'kov, Kvikhpak Mission Records, Alaskan Russian Church Archives, Microfilm 139, Reel 152, Frames 145–46 (hereafter cited as ARCA); Annual Report of Fr. Ioann Orlov, Kuskokwim Mission Parish Records, ARCA, Microfilm 139, Reel 171, Frame 80.

21. Annual Accounting Report, by Fr. Ioann Orlov, Kuskokwim Mission Parish Records, ARCA, Microfilm 139, Reel 171, Frame 83.

22. Travel Reports of Fr. Zakharii Bel'kov, Kvikhpak Mission Records, ARCA, Microfilm 139, Reel 169, Frames 650, 655, 657.

23. Iakov Korchinskii, "Iz Putevykh Zametok Pravoslavnago [Travel Notes]," 658.

24. John Kilbuck, "The Hindrances," in Fienup-Riordan, *The Yup'ik Eskimos*, 72.

25. John Kilbuck, "Report to the PEC. May 30, 1889," *Moravian* 34(33):520; Edith Kilbuck, Journal to her father, January 17, 1890, KC.

26. John Kilbuck, "Hindrances," 72.

27. Travel Records of Fr. Zakharii Bel'kov, December, 1888, Kvikhpak Mission Records, ARCA, Microfilm 139, Reel 169, Frames 247–48.

28. Edith Kilbuck, Journal to her father, December 24, 1888, KC.

29. John Kilbuck, "Report to the PEC. May 30, 1889," 520.

30. Edith Kilbuck, letter, February 24, 1889, Box 1:13, KC.

31. Edith Kilbuck to John, January 25, 1895, Box 2:5, KC.

32. Chugapolik Travel Journal of Fr. Ioann Orlov, December 9, 1895, Kuskokwim Mission Parish Records, ARCA, Microfilm 139, Reel 171, Frame 167.

33. Edith Kilbuck, Journal to her father, March 7, 1895, KC; ibid., January 20, 1895.

34. John Kilbuck, Journal to Edith, January 16, 1892, KC.

35. Journal of Worship Service of Fr. Iakov Korchinskii, December 15, 1896, Kvikhpak Mission Records, ARCA, Microfilm 139, Reel 168, Frames 261–62.

36. Ibid.

37. Journal of Worship Services, July 27, 1897, Kvikhpak Mission Records, AROCA,

Microfilm 59, Reel 3, page 22; Kvikhpak Mission Records, ARCA, Microfilm 139, Reel 168, Frames 264–65.

38. Journal of Worship Services, Fr. Iakov Korchinskii, August 22, 1898, Kvikhpak Mission Records, AROCA, Microfilm 59, Reel 3, Page 36.

39. Edith Kilbuck, Journal to her father, March 3, 1895, KC.

40. Smith, *Russian Orthodoxy in Alaska*, 11:12.

41. John Kilbuck, "Report of the Missionaries at Bethel on the Kuskokwim, May 29, 1890," in Fienup-Riordan, *The Yup'ik Eskimos*, 179.

42. John Kilbuck, "Hindrances," 71.

Chapter 8. The Insanity Epidemic and the "Martyrdom" of Brother Hooker

1. Edith Kilbuck, Journal to her father, April 15, 1890, KC.

2. John Kilbuck, "Hindrances," 73.

3. John's published report to the PEC for 1890 provides the most detailed account (John Kilbuck, "Report of the Missionaries at Bethel on the Kuskokwim, May 29, 1890," in Fienup-Riordan, *The Yup'ik Eskimos*, 173–78). John also chose to retell it as part of a general historical account written ten years later (John Kilbuck, "The Hindrances," in Fienup-Riordan, *The Yup'ik Eskimos*, 73–77). Both of these accounts differ substantially in tone from the more intimate description of the event written by Edith in her journal to her father on April 15, 1890 (Box 1, KC). Although Edith's telling relates the same factual sequence, it betrays the distress and emotional upset that were the immediate aftermath of the events. Her husband's unpublished narrative, in which he refers to himself as "the missionary," is much more philosophical and distant.

4. Edith Kilbuck, Journal to her father, March 6, 1890, Box 1:14, KC.

5. Ibid.

6. John Kilbuck, "Report to the Provincial Elders' Conference. May 29, 1890," *Moravian* 35(35):552.

7. Ibid.

8. Morrow, "It is Time for Drumming," 136.

9. Ibid., 136–39; Nelson, *The Eskimo about Bering Strait*, 358–59.

10. John Kilbuck, "Report, May 29, 1890," 551.

11. Journal of Worship Service, Fr. Zakharii Bel'kov, Kvikhpak Mission Records, AROCA, Microfilm 59, Reel 3.

12. John Kilbuck, "Hindrances," 73.

13. Edith Kilbuck, Journal to her father, April 1, 1890, Box 1:14, KC.

14. Ibid., April 15, 1890.

15. Ibid.

16. John Kilbuck, "Report, May 29, 1890," 551; Edith Kilbuck, Journal to her father, April 15, 1890, KC.

17. Edith Kilbuck, Journal to her father, April 15, 1890, KC.

18. Ibid.

19. Oswalt, *Mission of Change in Alaska*, 98.

20. Margaret Lantis, "Folk Medicine and Hygiene, Lower Kuskokwim and Nunivak-Nelson Island Area," *Anthropological Papers of the University of Alaska* 8(1):26.

21. Edith Kilbuck, Journal to her father, April 15, 1890, KC.

22. This man had been married by John that winter. Edith wrote that he was "cast out by his people" as a result of this incident (Edith Kilbuck, Journal to her father, August 10, 1890, KC).

23. John Kilbuck, "Report, May 29, 1890," 551; Edith Kilbuck, Journal to her father, April 15, 1890, KC.

24. Edith Kilbuck, Journal to her father, April 15, 1890, KC.

25. Ibid.

26. Ibid. According to Gapp, *Kolerat Pitsiulret*, 15, the woman's name was Masska, and she was a shaman. The Kilbuck journals contain no further reference to her.

27. Journal of Worship Service, Fr. Zakharii Bel'kov, 1884, Kvikhpak Mission Records, AROCA, Microfilm 59, Reel 3; Travel Records of Fr. Zakharii Bel'kov, 1888, Kvikhpak Mission Records, ARCA, Microfilm 139, Reel 169, Frame 650.

28. John Kilbuck, Journal to Edith, January 12, 1898, KC.

29. Edith Kilbuck, Journal to her father, April 15, 1890, KC.

30. John Kilbuck, "Report, May 29, 1890," 552.

31. Hamilton and Hamilton, *History of the Moravian Church*, 42.

32. Morrow, "It is Time for Drumming," 137.

33. In *Islands of History*, Marshall Sahlins describes a historical event, the murder of Captain James Cook, as prefigured by a mythical reality, the Hawaiians' understanding of Cook's arrival as the appearance of the God Lono. As in the case of Captain Cook, it is possible that Kwethluk natives viewed Hooker as a man possessed by evil influences who must be executed in order that the community endure.

34. Sahlins makes a similar point in *Islands of History*, 108.

35. Margaret Lantis, "The Religion of the Eskimos" in *Forgotten Religions*, ed. Virgilius Ferm, 328.

36. John Kilbuck, "Hindrances," 76.

37. John Kilbuck, "Report, May 29, 1890," 552.

38. Edith Kilbuck, "Journal. September 19, 1890," *Moravian* 37(17):264.

39. John Kilbuck, Journal to Edith, December 6, 1892, KC.

40. Edith Kilbuck, Journal to her father, January 8, 1894, KC.

41. Ibid., October 8, 1894.

42. Robert Fortuine, letter to author, January 19, 1988; Barbara Doak and Barbara Nachmann, personal communication with author, March, 1987.

43. John Kilbuck, "Hindrances," 77. Kilbuck is likening the missionaries' confrontation with the shamans in western Alaska to that of the Apostle Paul in Ephesus with the followers of Diana, the Greek goddess of the moon and of hunting, who feared he would put an end to their idol worship (The Book of Acts, Chapter 19).

44. Ethnohistorians have largely taken John's explanation at face value, mirroring the propensity of mission historians in generl to focus on the causal relationship of facts rather than the form of the encounter between missionary and missionized. Wendell Oswalt (*Mission of Change*, 98) describes the act as murder committed by the Kwethluk Eskimos. As an alternative, the attempt here has been to apply anthropological concepts concerning the creative power of ritual action to the archival material. The issue is not solely why Hooker was killed, but why he was killed *in a particular way*. The goal is to understand why the general phenomenon of culture change and religious conversion takes specific form because of the particular histories of the people involved. It is the specificity of the event, not its generality, that is of interest and what it says about the form and meaning of a particular culture. Only after we understand such specificity can we hope to comprehend the complex phenomena of change.

45. Korchinskii, "Is Putevykh Zametok Pravoslavnago [Travel Notes]," 654. In fact, the Mountain Boy did not die early but lived until sometime after 1915.

46. Both Russian Orthodox and Moravian leaders have discreetly avoided extended discussion of the incident in print.

47. Joshua Phillip, interview with author, Akiachak, Alaska, March 20, 1988, Fienup-Riordan, Alaska Mission History.

48. Missionaries at Bethel, "Report of Bethel for the Year 1890 to 1891. June l, 1891," *Moravian* 36(32):503.

49. Edith Kilbuck, Journal to her father, April 15, 1890, KC.

50. Ibid.

51. Ibid., May 12, 1890.

52. Ibid., August 28, 1890, Box 1:21A.

53. Edith Kilbuck, "Journal. October 15, 1890," *Moravian* 37(18):280.

54. Edith Kilbuck, Journal to her father, February 15, 1890, Box 1:22, KC; Missionaries at Bethel, "Report of Bethel for the Year 1890 to 1891," 503; Edith Kilbuck, Journal to her father, August 28, 1890, Box 1:21A, KC.

55. Edith Kilbuck, Journal to her father, August 6, 1890, Box 1:21A, KC; Edith Kilbuck, Journal, January 20, 1891, Box 1:22, KC.

56. Edith Kilbuck, Journal, April 2, 1895, Box 2:2, KC; John Kilbuck, Journal, August 24, 1893, KC; John Kilbuck, Journal, March 20, 1894, KC.

57. The majority of Yup'ik Eskimos living along the lower Kuskokwim eventually converted to Moravianism, but pockets of Orthodoxy are sprinkled throughout the region. The village of Kwethluk is one of a handful of communities in which Russian Orthodoxy continues to dominate.

58. Edith Kilbuck, "Journal. January 5, 1891," *Moravian* 37(21):326.

59. John Kilbuck, "The Report of Bethel for 1892. June 7, 1892," *Moravian* 37(33):515.

Chapter 9. An Established Work

1. Missionaries at Bethel, "Report for the Year 1890 to 1891," 503. Although this report was signed "The Bethel Missionaries," the wording, including continual reference to himself as "I," indicates that John was the author.

2. Richard Pierce, "New Light on Ivan Petroff, Historian of Alaska," *Pacific Northwest Quarterly* 59:1-10.

3. John Kilbuck, "Letter from Bethel. July 14, 1890," *Moravian* 35(51):808. Although Brother Weber made a journey overland to gather statistics along the coast during the winter, John did all of the traveling on the Kuskokwim.

4. Vinasale was a trading station originally founded as a subsidiary to Kolmakovskiy Redoubt. The station had no permanent native population, contrary to the population figure of 140 published in the census of 1890, which actually represents the total surrounding population (Robert Porter, *Report on the Population and Resources of Alaska at the Eleventh Census, 1890*).

5. John Kilbuck, Journal to Edith, July 27, 1890, KC.

6. Ernest Weber experienced the same reluctance to be counted during his census trip the following winter: "As we were about to enter the fourth [sod house] we found a man standing at the door and he would not let us enter it. . . . They said they were afraid that they should die if I counted them" (Ernest Weber, "Diary," *Moravian* 36(37):583).

7. John Kilbuck, Journal to Edith, July 27, 1890, KC.

8. Ibid., August 17, 1890.

9. Fienup-Riordan, *The Yup'ik Eskimos*, Table 2.

10. Missionaries at Bethel, "Report for the Year 1890 to 1891," 503.

11. Edith Kilbuck, "Journal to her Father, Joseph Romig. July 11, 1890," *Moravian* 35(53):840.

12. Edith Kilbuck to Sister Bachman, September 3, 1890, KC.

13. Edith Kilbuck, "Journal. January 5, 1891," *Moravian* 37(21):327.

14. Edith Kilbuck to Sister Bachman, December 26, 1890, KC.

15. Edith Kilbuck, "Journal. June 14, 1891," *Moravian* 37(31):489.

16. John Kilbuck, "Letter from Bethel to Rev. Prof. A. Schultz. July 3, 1891," *Moravian* 36(37):583.

17. Henkelman and Vitt, *History of the Alaska Moravian Church*, 128.

18. Henry T. Bachman, "Account of Alaska Journey," in *The Proceedings*, 49-52.

19. Ibid., 55.

20. Edith Kilbuck, Journal to John, August 10, 1891, KC.

21. Ibid., August 11, 1891.

22. John Kilbuck, Journal to Edith, January 26, 1892, KC.

23. Missionaries at Bethel, "Report for the Year 1890 to 1891," 503.

24. Edith Kilbuck, Journal to John, January 19, 1892, KC.

25. Ibid., January 16, 1892.

26. John Kilbuck, Journal to Edith, July 3, 1892, KC.

27. Announcement, *Moravian* 37(9):129.

28. John Kilbuck, "Letter from on board the steamer 'Dora' to Bro. Bachman. June 29, 1892," *Moravian* 37(34):532.

29. John Kilbuck, Journal to Edith, July 1, 1892, KC; ibid., July 31, 1892.

30. Ibid., July 3, 1892.

31. Ibid., July 4, 1892.

32. Ibid., July 8, 1892.

33. Edith Kilbuck, "Letter to her Father, Joseph Romig. Extracts. August 5, 1893," *Moravian* 39(9):137.

34. John Kilbuck, Journal to Edith, July 30, 1892, KC.

35. Ibid., October 13, 1892.

36. Ibid., December 2, 1892; ibid., July 16, 1892.

37. Ibid., November 20, 1892.

38. Edith Kilbuck, Journal to John, November 11, 1892, KC.

39. Edith Kilbuck, "Journal. April 1, 1891," *Moravian* 37(29):456.

40. Edith Kilbuck to Rev. Klose, May 12, 1893, KC.

41. Edith Kilbuck, Journal, March 12, 1918, Box 7:3, KC.

42. Edith Kilbuck, Journal to her father, July, 1893, KC.

43. John Kilbuck, "Letter to the Brethren. July 3, 1893," *Moravian* 38(35):547; ibid., 548.

44. Edith Kilbuck, Journal to her father, September 20, 1893, KC.

45. Ibid., February 16, 1894.

46. Ibid.

47. Ibid., March 20, 1894.

48. PEC, "Official Instructions for the Moravian Missionaries in Alaska, given April 1894," 4, Alaska Materials.

49. Edith Kilbuck, Journal, March 31, 1894, KC.

50. Edith Kilbuck, Private Journal, August 1894, KC.

51. Edith Kilbuck, Journal to John, January 29, 1890, KC.

52. Ibid.

53. Edith Kilbuck, "Letter to Brother de Schweinitz. June 5, 1894," *Moravian* 39(44):696.

54. John Kilbuck, Journal to Edith, December, 1893, KC.

55. Ibid., December 27, 1893; ibid, January 1, 1894.

56. While fidelity was considered a "natural state" for a woman, it was not so for a man, who had to fight against his natural instincts to succeed in being faithful.

57. Edith Kilbuck, Journal to her father, March 20, 1894, KC.

58. Edith Kilbuck, Journal, March, 1895, KC; ibid., January 5, 1895.

59. Edith Kilbuck, Private Journal, September 4, 1895, KC; ibid., September 5, 1895.

60. Ibid., November 11, 15, 1895.

61. PEC, Minutes, May 15, 1896, Alaska Materials, 101.

62. Ibid., November 24, 1896; ibid., April 2, 1897.

63. Edith Kilbuck, Journal to her father, November 15, 1895, KC.

Chapter 10. Barriers Continue to Weaken

1. Edith Kilbuck, Journal to her father, February 6, 1894, KC.
2. Edith Kilbuck, "Letter to her Father, Joseph Romig. Extracts. August 5, 1893," *Moravian* 39(9):137.
3. Edith Kilbuck, "Journal Extracts. Bethel, Alaska. August 8, 1893," *The Proceedings*, 51.
4. Ibid.
5. John Kilbuck, "Letter from Bethel to the PEC. August 4, 1893," *Moravian* 38(44):696.
6. Edith Kilbuck, Journal to her father, October 5, 1893, KC.
7. Ibid., December 28, 1893.
8. Ibid., September 5, 1893.
9. John Kilbuck, "Journal. Extracts. During the Winter of 1893–1894. December 8, 1893," *Moravian* 40(2):20; Edith Kilbuck, Journal to John, December 7, 1896, KC.
10. Ernest L. Weber, Ogavik Journal, February 28, 1893, Alaska Materials.
11. John Kilbuck, "Journal. Extracts. December 9, 1893," *Moravian* 40(3):35.
12. Ibid. Kwigogluck was an early center of trade on the Kuskokwim and had a population of 314 in 1880 (Ivan Petroff, *Report on the Population, Industries, and Resources of Alaska, Tenth Census of the United States*, 16–17). It subsequently declined in importance, and by 1906 only a few families remained (Wendell Oswalt, *Historic Settlements Along the Kuskokwim River, Alaska*, 51). Napaimute (*Napamiut*) had a small population in the late 1800s. During their exploratory reconnaissance of 1884, Hartmann and Weinland noted a number of abandoned dwellings indicating that previously the area had been more densely populated.
13. John Kilbuck, "Journal. Extracts. December 28, 1893," *Moravian* 40(5):67.
14. Ibid., 68.
15. Edith Kilbuck, Journal, February 5, 1894, KC; see also Missionaries at Bethel, "Report of Bethel for the Year 1893–1894," in *The Proceedings*, 27.
16. Edith Kilbuck, Journal to her father, December 28, 1893, KC.
17. Ibid., October 5, 1893.
18. Missionaries at Bethel, "Report of Bethel for the Year 1893–1894," 26.
19. Edith Kilbuck, "Journal. Extracts. Bethel, Alaska. December 28, 1893," *The Proceedings*, 59–60.
20. Ibid.
21. Ibid., February 22, 1894, 62.
22. Ibid., May 22, 1894, 65.
23. Ibid., January 8, 1894, 61.
24. Missionaries at Bethel, "Report of Bethel for the Year 1890 to 1891. June 1, 1891," 502; John Kilbuck, Journal to Edith, March 27, 1894, KC.
25. Edith Kilbuck to Papa, February 21, 1888, Box 9:1A, KC.
26. Missionaries at Bethel, "Letter to the Rev. E. T. Kluge, President of P.E.C., January 13, 1896," *Moravian* 41(19):294.
27. John Kilbuck, Journal, November 20, 1893, KC.
28. Edith Kilbuck, "Journal. Extracts. Bethel, Alaska. January 8, 1894," *The Proceedings*, 60.
29. Edith Kilbuck, Journal, February 28, 1895, KC.
30. Edith Kilbuck, Journal to her father, February 1, 1890, KC.
31. Helper Neck, "Letter," *The Proceedings*, 1921, 83.
32. PEC, "Official Instructions for the Moravian Missionaries," Alaska Materials.
33. John Kilbuck, Journal, February 21, 1898, KC.
34. Edith Kilbuck, Journal, September, 1894, KC.
35. "This evening John began a regular course of instruction for a class of young men

preparatory to doing missionary work, most likely to hold the out-stations or to travel from village to village and preach to and teach their own people. Wassili and Eddie are the two beginners. Robert is to join the class later on, he being with his father" (Edith Kilbuck, Journal, October 8, 1894, KC).

36. Edith Kilbuck, Journal to her father, December 16, 1894, KC.

37. Missionaries at Bethel, "Report of the Mission at Bethel, 1894–95. June 1895," *Moravian* 40(39):606–607; 40(40):623–624.

38. Edith Kilbuck, Journal, February 23, 1895, KC.

39. Ibid., January 13, 1895.

40. John Kilbuck, "Missionary Trip", January 31, 1895, KC.

41. Ibid.

42. Ibid., February 16, 1895.

43. Ibid., February 25, 1895. Kamexmute (*Qemirmiut*: bluff village, from *gemiq*: hill, bluff) was probably the camp located just above Bethel that Kilbuck reported abandoned in 1898 (Orth, *Dictionary of Alaska Place Names*, 491; Oswalt, *Historic Settlements*, 44).

44. John Kilbuck, Missionary Trip, February 25, 1895. Note in Chapter 3 the ritual significance of the numbers four, five, and twenty (four groups of five). The latter translates literally as "a complete person," and the number twenty-one signifies more than a person.

45. Edith Kilbuck, Journal to her father, February 28, 1895, KC.

46. John Kilbuck, Journal, March 9, 1895, KC.

47. John Kilbuck, Journal to Edith, February 7, 1894, KC.

48. John Kilbuck, Journal, January 31, 1896, KC. Apokak (*Apruka'ar*) was located on the south bank of the lower Kuskokwim and may have functioned as a seasonal gathering point for salmon fishing and/or trading. Petroff (*Report on the Population of Alaska*, 16) listed it as having a population of ninety-four in 1880.

49. Henkelman and Vitt, *History of the Alaska Moravian Church*, 391.

50. John Kilbuck, "Letter to Bishop de Schweinitz from Bethel, August 3, 1887," *Moravian* 32(42):658.

51. Dr. Herman Joseph Romig, Obituary, KC.

52. John Kilbuck, Journal, February 4, 1894, in Fienup-Riordan, *The Yup'ik Eskimos*, 321.

53. John Kilbuck, "Letter to the PEC. June 2, 1888," *Moravian* 33(32):497. The ubiquitous expression Quyana ("I am thankful") in western Alaska today may represent a traditional verbal response reinforced rather than replaced by the Moravian understanding of the power of prayerful thanks.

54. John Kilbuck, December 1888, in Fienup-Riordan, *The Yup'ik Eskimos*, 134; see also John Kilbuck, Journal, February 1, 1894, in Fienup-Riordan, *The Yup'ik Eskimos*, 310.

55. Harvey Feit, "Hunting and the Quest for Power: The James Bay Cree and White-men in the Twentieth Century," in *Native Peoples: The Canadian Experience*, ed. R. Bruce Morrison and C. Roderick Wilson, 178.

56. Robin Ridington, "From Hunt Chief to Prophet: Beaver Indian Dreamers and Christianity," *Arctic Anthropology* 24:9.

57. Marshall Sahlins, "Social Science; or the Tragic Western Sense of Human Imperfections," 38.

58. Edith Kilbuck, Journal, March 11, 1895, KC.

59. Journal Report of Neck and Sumpka, February, 1897, KC.

60. John Kilbuck, Journal, February 16, 1895, KC.

Chapter 11. Changing of the Guard

1. Edith Kilbuck, Journal to John, August 21, 1896, KC.

2. Although tobacco was not regularly traded into Alaska until after 1800 (Dorothy

Jean Ray, *The Eskimos of Bering Strait, 1650−1898*, 101−102), by the time the Kilbucks arrived leaf tobacco was a ubiquitous trade good along the Kuskokwim. People of all ages still regularly enjoy it mixed with willow ash and held in the side of the mouth.

3. John Kilbuck, Journal to Edith, August 17−18, 1896, in Fienup-Riordan, *The Yup'ik Eskimos*, 342, 343−44.

4. Ibid., August 26, 28, 1896, 346, 347.

5. Edith Kilbuck, Journal to her father, September 20, 1896, KC. From September 20, 1896, Edith announced that a single journal would be addressed to John when he was traveling and to her father when John was at home, as she no longer had time to keep two journals.

6. John Kilbuck, Journal to Edith, January, 1897, KC.

7. Edith Kilbuck, Journal, January 26, 1897, KC.

8. John Kilbuck, Journal to Edith, January, 1897, KC.

9. Edith Kilbuck, Journal to her father, July 10, 1897, KC.

10. John Kilbuck, Journal to Edith, August 16−18, 1897, in Fienup-Riordan, *The Yup'ik Eskimos*, 376, 377.

11. Ibid., August 19, 1897, 377.

12. Ibid.

13. Ibid., August 22, 1897, 381−83.

14. Ibid., September 4, 1897, 386−87.

15. William Weinland, "Letter from Bethel. Letter Third. (Part 2 of 2). January 20, 1887," *Moravian* 32(36):569.

16. Missionaries at Bethel, "Report of Bethel for the Year 1890 to 1891," 503.

17. John Kilbuck, Journal to Edith, November 22, 1897, in Fienup-Riordan, *The Yup'ik Eskimos*, 404−405.

18. Ibid., September 13, 1897, 389−92.

19. Ibid., September 22, 1897, 395.

20. Edith Kilbuck, Journal to her father, June 27, 1897, KC.

21. Ibid., November 22, 1897.

22. John Kilbuck, Journal to Edith, March, 1897, KC.

23. Edith Kilbuck, Journal to her father, September 24, 1897, KC.

24. Edith Kilbuck, Journal to John, September 24, 1897, KC; see also January 19, 1898.

25. Ibid., August 29, 1897.

26. John Kilbuck, Journal to Edith, January 9, 1898, KC; ibid., January 19, 1898.

27. Ibid., April, 1899.

28. PEC, Minutes, March 25, 1898.

29. SPG, Minutes, August 10, 1897; PEC, Minutes, January 4, 1898.

30. SPG, Minutes, May 10, 1898, 234.

31. Ibid.

32. John Kilbuck to PEC, 1897, KC.

33. John Kilbuck, Journal to Edith, September 26, 1897, in Fienup-Riordan, *The Yup'ik Eskimos*, 399−400.

34. Ibid., January 12, 1898, 417.

35. John Kilbuck to PEC, 1897, KC.

36. John Kilbuck, Journal to Edith, January 9−12, 1898, in Fienup-Riordan, *The Yup'ik Eskimos*, 413−15.

37. SPG, Minutes, August 25, 1898.

38. Ibid., 5.

39. Ibid., November 8, 1898, 218−19; PEC, Minutes, November 15, 1898.

40. Dr. Herman Romig, Mission Journal, November 25−27, 1899, Alaska Materials.

41. Ibid., December 18, 1899; ibid., March 21, 1900.

42. PEC, Minutes, March 23, 1900; SPG, Minutes, August 16, 1900, 13.

43. PEC, Minutes, October 18, 1900, 227.

44. John Kilbuck, "1900 Census Trip: Story of Epidemic and Fearful Mortality," in Fienup-Riordan, *The Yup'ik Eskimos*, 436–43; Anna B. Schwalbe, *Dayspring on the Kuskokwim*, 84. The influenza epidemic of 1900 was accompanied by measles, smallpox, and pneumonia. Virtually no coastal community from Atka to Wales was spared from the pestilence, which overall caused the death of a quarter to a third of the entire native population. No one knows the full extent of the deaths, but official estimates run as high as two thousand (Robert Fortuine, "Epidemics II: Western and Northern Alaska," 11, 26). As a result of the epidemic a number of villages along the Kuskokwim were abandoned (Robert Wolfe, "Alaska's Great Sickness, 1900: An Epidemic of Measles and Influenza in a Virgin Soil Population," *Proceedings of the American Philosophical Society* 126(2):114).

45. John Kilbuck to Edith, July 4, 1900, KC.

46. John Kilbuck, Journal to Edith, July 25, 1900, in Fienup-Riordan, *The Yup'ik Eskimos*, 438.

47. Ibid., September 6, 1900, 442; ibid., September 19, 1900, 442–43; ibid., September 24, 1900, 443.

48. Eva G. Anderson, *Dog Team Doctor*, 198–200.

49. John Kilbuck to William T. Lopp, July 25, 1911, KC.

50. John Kilbuck to Edith, November 1, 1900, in Fienup-Riordan, *The Yup'ik Eskimos*, 446.

51. Ibid., November 7, 1900, 449–50.

52. Ibid., November 8, 1900, 451.

53. Ibid., November 9–10, 1900, 451.

54. Romig, "Sketch of the Indian Mission Work," Romig Papers.

55. Ruth Kilbuck Patterson, interview with author, December 4, 1985, Winston-Salem, North Carolina, Ann Fienup-Riordan, Alaska Mission History.

56. Romig, "Sketch of the Indian Mission Work," Romig Papers.

Chapter 12. New Mission

1. John Kilbuck, letter, 1904, Part IV:6–7, Box 7:1, KC.

2. John Kilbuck, Journal, 1905, Box 7(2):9, 122, KC; John Kilbuck, Journal, Box 7(2):14, KC.

3. John Kilbuck, letter, 1905.

4. John Kilbuck, Journal, 1905, Box 7(2):9, 121, 123, KC.

5. John R. Bockstoce, *Whales, Ice, and Men: The History of Whaling in the Western Arctic*, 233, 238.

6. John Kilbuck, Journal, Box 7(2):14, KC.

7. Ibid.

8. John Kilbuck, Journal, September 27, 1904, KC.

9. Ibid., October 11, 1904; ibid., April 10, 1905.

10. John Kilbuck, Annual Report, July 2, 1907, General Correspondence of the Alaska Division of the Office of Education, 1903–1935, Box 21:10710, Records of the Bureau of Indian Affairs, Record Group 75, National Archives (hereafter cited as RBIA for originals consulted at the National Archives and RBIA(M) for microfilm consulted in Anchorage).

11. John Kilbuck, Annual Report, November 3, 1906, RBIA, Box 21:10710.

12. John Kilbuck, Annual Report, July 2, 1907, RBIA, Box 21:10710, 6–7.

13. See Anthony Woodbury, "Rhetorical Structure in Central Alaskan Yup'ik Eskimo Traditional Narrative," *Native American Discourse*, 176–239.

14. John Kilbuck, Journal, November 11, 1904, Box 6(3):2, 7–9, KC.

15. John Kilbuck, Journal, March 19, 1905, Box 6(4), 37–38, KC.

16. Ibid.

17. John Kilbuck to Ruth, July 14, 1905, Box 6, 2–3, KC.

18. John Kilbuck, letter, 1904, Part IV:7, Box 7:1.

19. John Kilbuck, Journal, July 28, 1905, KC; John Kilbuck, Annual Report of the U. S. Public School at Wainwright, July 2, 1907, RBIA, Box 21:10710.

20. John Kilbuck to Sheldon Jackson, February 25, 1905, RBIA, Box 21.

21. Charles Brower was as important in the history of Point Barrow as the Kilbucks were along the Kuskokwim. He was instrumental in introducing shore whaling in north Alaska and was in charge of the Cape Smyth Whaling Company, established in 1893 and active in commercial whaling until 1908 (Bockstoce, *Whales, Ice and Men*, 233–39).

22. John Kilbuck, Journal, May 7, 1905, KC.

23. Ibid., June 27, 1905.

24. Ibid., July 22, 1905; ibid., July 28, 1905.

25. Ibid., September 12, 1904.

26. Harlan Updegraff to John Kilbuck, April 6, 1908, Akiak School File, RBIA(M), Reel 26:347.

27. John Kilbuck to Sheldon Jackson, June 25, 1905, RBIA, Box 21.

28. John Kilbuck, Journal, November 5, 1905, KC.

29. Ibid., October 12, 1906.

30. John Kilbuck to Sheldon Jackson, September 3, 1906, RBIA, Box 21.

31. Edith Kilbuck to her father, September 9, 1906, Box 6:6, KC.

32. Edith Kilbuck, Journal to her father, August 23, 1906, KC.

33. Ibid., August 26, 1906.

34. Edith Kilbuck, Journal, August, 1906, Box 3:1, 11–12, KC.

35. Edith Kilbuck, Journal, September 9, 1907, KC.

36. Ibid., March 27, 1907, 100; ibid., 32.

37. The Kilbucks' departure coincided with the collapse of both the market in whale bone and the whaling industry as a whole. At the end of 1908 the leading whale operators laid up their vessels, and in 1909 the market was so low that only three ships returned to the Arctic (Bockstoce, *Whales, Ice and Men*, 336–37). Ironically, the price of bone had climbed so high that the corset industry was forced to find a replacement in the production of the fashionable stays on which the whaling industry partially based its success. The value of bone fell to nothing, and the whaling industry came to an end.

38. John Kilbuck to Harlan Updegraff, October 7, 1908, RBIA(M), Reel 26:342.

39. John Kilbuck to Edith and the children, July 14, 1910, KC.

40. John Kilbuck to Edith, December 1, 1908, Box 8:10, KC.

41. John Kilbuck to Edith, December 15, 1908, Box 8:12, KC.

42. John Kilbuck to Edith, December 4, 1908, KC.

43. John Kilbuck to Edith, December 2, 1908, KC.

44. John Kilbuck to Edith, April 13, 1909, Box 8:8, KC.

45. John Kilbuck, Annual Report of the Government School at Douglas, May 8, 1910, KC.

46. Ibid., 2, 8–9

47. John Kilbuck, Journal to Edith and the children, July 15, 1910, KC.

48. Ibid., July 3, 1910; ibid., July 23, 1910.

49. Fienup-Riordan, *The Yup'ik Eskimos*, 1–45; John Kilbuck, Journal to Edith and the children, June 30, 1910, KC; ibid., July 8, 1910.

50. John Kilbuck, Journal to Edith and the children, July 17, 1910, KC; ibid., July 28, 1910.

51. Ibid., August 16, 1910, Box 8(3):14; ibid, August 23, 1910, Box 8(3):16. Al-

though John put most of his efforts during the summer of 1910 toward recording the details of life along the Kuskokwim, he also made a brief foray into recording Tlingit oral tradition. The local policeman, Charles Gunnuck, of Kake, told him one story (July 30, 1910, Box 7(2):20), and he was given a second shorter tale by Henry Allen (Box 7(2):15). He made no further recordings that we know of.

52. Nelson, *The Eskimo about Bering Strait*.

53. William Weinland, "Letter from Bethel. Letter Second, January 20, 1887," *Moravian* 32(34):536–37.

54. John Kilbuck, Journal to Edith and the children, August 19, 1910, Box 8(3): 14, KC.

55. Edith Kilbuck, Journal, April 12, 1911, KC.

56. John Kilbuck, Annual Report, 1912, 19, RBIA, Box 21.

Chapter 13. Return to the Kuskokwim

1. Edith Kilbuck, Private Journal, January 10, 1912, Box 3:15, KC.

2. Oswalt, *Bashful No Longer*, 104–105; John Kilbuck to P. Claxton, July 31, 1915, RBIA(M), Reel 1.

3. Edith Kilbuck to her father, February 6, 1907, KC.

4. Oswalt, *Bashful No Longer*, 95

5. Edith Kilbuck to her father, July 5, 1911, KC.

6. William T. Lopp, February 7, 1930, in Gapp, *Kolerat Pitsiulret*, 19–20.

7. Edith Kilbuck, Journal to John, October 2, 1911, Box 3:14, KC.

8. Ibid., August 2, 1911, Box 3:10.

9. Edith Kilbuck to William Lopp, September 28, 1911, 2, KC.

10. John Kilbuck, Journal to Edith, July 16, 1911, Box 8:3, KC. This is one of the earliest, if not the earliest, written references to fish wheels in the history of the Kuskokwim. Contrary to John's opinion, they changed the face of the upriver fishery.

11. Oswalt, *Bashful No Longer*, 114.

12. John Kilbuck, Journal to Edith, July 16, 1911, Box 8:3, 7, KC; John Kilbuck, "Annual Report of the United States Public School at Akiak, a Remote Village on the Kuskokwim River, Hitherto Without a School," in *Report of the Work of the Bureau of Education for the Natives of Alaska, 1911 1912, 22*.

13. John Kilbuck, Hooper Bay Report, 1911, Box 7:2, 6, KC; Edith Kilbuck, Journal to John, September 16, 1911, Box 3:13, KC.

14. John Kilbuck, "Annual Report of . . . Akiak," in *Report, 1911–1912*, 22; John Kilbuck to William Lopp, July 25, 1911, 3, Lopp Collection; John Kilbuck to Edith, July 23, 1911, Box 8:4, 7, KC.

15. John Kilbuck to William Lopp, July 25, 1911, Lopp Collection; John Kilbuck, Journal to Edith, July 16, 1911, 9, KC; ibid., July 24, 1911, 9–10.

16. John Kilbuck, Journal to Edith, July 21, 1911, Box 8:4, 2, KC; John Kilbuck to William Lopp, July 25, 1911, 4, Lopp Collection.

17. John Kilbuck, Georgetown Report, 1911, 9, Akiak School Files, RBIA(M), Reel 1.

18. Ibid., page 11; John Kilbuck, "Annual Report of . . . Akiak," in *Report, 1911–1912*, 22; John Kilbuck, Journal to Edith, July 18, 1911, 12, KC.

19. Andrew Evans, letter from the Superintendent of the Northwest District to the Commissioner of Education, July 6 and July 9, 1912, Akiak School Files, RBIA(M), Reel 1.

20. John Kilbuck, Georgetown Report, 1911, 11, Akiak School Files, RBIA(M), Reel 1.

21. John Kilbuck, Hooper Bay Report, 1911, 8, KC.

22. Ibid., 9.

23. Ibid., 10.

24. Edith Kilbuck, Journal to John, August 5, 1911, Box 3:10, KC.
25. John Kilbuck to William Lopp, November 8, 1912, 2, RBIA(M), Reel 1.
26. Edith Kilbuck to William Lopp, September 28, 1911, RBIA(M), Reel 1.
27. John Kilbuck to William Lopp, December 9, 1911, RBIA(M), Reel 1; Edith Kilbuck to William Lopp, January 19, 1912, RBIA(M), Reel 1; John Kilbuck to William Lopp, September 24, 1912, RBIA(M), Reel 1.
28. John Kilbuck, "Annual Report of . . . Akiak," in *Report, 1911–1912*, 20.
29. John Kilbuck, Journal to Edith, September 15, 1912, 15, KC.
30. Young Kilbuck was possibly John's son born out of wedlock around 1899. In 1987 Young Kilbuck's grandchildren continued to reside in Bethel and claimed John Kilbuck as their grandfather.
31. John Kilbuck, "Annual Report of . . . Akiak," in *Report, 1911–1912*, 21.
32. Kinak (*Qinaq*) was one of the largest and best known villages along the lower Kuskokwim during the early nineteenth century. It was abandoned in 1945 when the village relocated two and one-half miles upstream to the modern community of Tuntutuliak.
33. John Kilbuck to William Lopp, November 6, 1911, RBIA(M), Reel 1.
34. Andrew Evans, Letter from the Superintendent of the Northwest District, July 6, 1912, 3, Akiak School Files, RBIA(M), Reel 1.
35. Edith Kilbuck, Private Journal, March 23, 1912, KC.
36. John Kilbuck, Journal to Edith, July 21, 1911, Box 8:4, 6, KC; John Kilbuck to William Lopp, September 28, 1911, 13–14, RBIA, Box 21.
37. John Kilbuck to William Lopp, RBIA(M), Reel 1.
38. John Kilbuck to P. Claxton, July 31, 1915, 4, RBIA(M), Reel 37:497.
39. John Kilbuck, Fifth Annual Report, July 30, 1916, Box 7:4, KC.
40. John Kilbuck, Journal to Edith, September 3, 1912, Box 8:5, 4, KC; ibid., September 27, 1912.
41. Edith Kilbuck, Journal to John, September 20, 1911, Box 3:12, KC.
42. Edith Kilbuck, Diary, January 13, 1914, Box 4:2, KC.
43. Ibid., February 4, 1914.
44. Ibid., June 19, 1914.
45. Ibid., December 24, 1914.
46. Ibid., February 20, 1915; ibid., February 4, 1915; ibid., May 25, 1914.
47. Ibid., June 9, 1916.

Chapter 14. Saving Them From Themselves

1. John Kilbuck to P. Claxton, July 31, 1915, 1, RBIA(M), Reel 37:497.
2. Edith Kilbuck to her father, 1913, 4, KC.
3. Ibid., 4, 5.
4. Ibid., 3.
5. Ibid., 5–7.
6. John Kilbuck, "Annual Report of . . . Akiak," in *Report, 1911–1912*, 21.
7. John Kilbuck to P. Claxton, July 31, 1915, RBIA(M), Reel 37:497.
8. Ibid., 5.
9. John Kilbuck, Fifth Annual Report, June 30, 1916, 4, Box 7:4, KC.
10. Ibid., 7–8.
11. John Kilbuck, Journal, June 14, 1917, KC.
12. Schwalbe, *Dayspring on the Kuskokwim*, 128.
13. Sheldon Jackson, *U. S. Bureau of Education Report on the Introduction of Domesticated Reindeer in Alaska*, 131–33.
14. An individual worked with the herders for a number of years as an apprentice, to learn deer management before he was permitted to own deer. After successfully completing his apprenticeship he was given a set number of deer as payment for his time.
15. John Kilbuck "[Annual] Report of the United States Public School at Akiak, on the

Kuskokwim River, in Western Alaska," in *Report of the Work of the Bureau of Education for the Natives of Alaska, 1914–1915*, 64–65.

16. Ibid.

17. John Kilbuck, Fifth Annual Report, June 30, 1916, 16, Box 7:4, KC.

18. John Kilbuck, Journal to Edith, January 30, 1914, 11, KC; ibid., February 1, 1914, 13.

19. John Kilbuck, "Suggestions for Reindeer Herders," June 15, 1905, RBIA, Box 21; John Kilbuck, Journal to Edith, February 6, 1914, 21, KC.

20. John Kilbuck, Fifth Annual Report, June 30, 1916, 14, Box 7:4, KC.

21. John Kilbuck, Journal to Edith, March 1, 1914, 44, KC.

22. Ibid., February 28, 1914, 41–42; ibid., March 3, 1914, 45.

23. Ibid., March 26, 1914, 57–59. John might well have used the word "person" in place of "animal" in his discussion, as his view of the rules governing human-human interaction was essentially the same.

24. John Kilbuck, "The Deer-men's Fair, December 22–23 and 27–30, 1916, Akiak, Alaska," in "Report to the Bureau of Education," 67, RBIA(M), Reel 1.

25. John Kilbuck, Fifth Annual Report, June 30, 1916, 4–5, Box 7:4, KC.

26. Ibid., 9.

27. Ibid., 5–6.

28. Ibid., 6.

29. John Kilbuck, The Deer-men's Fair," 1.

30. Ibid., 6.

31. Ibid.

32. H. Dewey Anderson and Walter C. Eells, *Alaska Natives: A Survey of Their Sociological and Educational Status*, 197; Oswalt, *Mission of Change in Alaska*, 46.

33. Margaret Lantis, "The Reindeer Industry in Alaska," *Arctic* 3:36, 47.

34. John Kilbuck, Fifth Annual Report, June 30, 1916, 1–2, KC.

35. Community of Bethel, Reflection on Trapping and Reindeer Herding, Education History Series, Tape 2; John Kilbuck, "The Deer-men's Fair," 1.

36. John Kilbuck, "Suggestions for Reindeer Herders."

Chapter 15. Assistant Superintendent of the Western District

1. John Kilbuck to Edith, February 27, 1917, KC.

2. Edith Kilbuck, Journal, August 12, 1916, KC.

3. Ibid., August 23, 1916.

4. Ibid., September 23, 1916.

5. John Kilbuck, "Proposed Orphanage and Training School on the Kuskokwim," in *The Proceedings*, 62–67.

6. PEC, Minutes, October 24, 1911, 219; ibid., November 28, 1911, 237; ibid., June 15, 1913.

7. Ibid., April 18, 1916.

8. John Kilbuck, Journal to Edith, September 4, 1916, Box 8:9, KC.

9. Ibid., August 26, 1916.

10. Ibid., September 17, 1916, Box 8:14; ibid., September 23, 1916, Box 8:17. Father Nikifor Amkan, a native-born priest from Nushagak, served at Russian Mission from 1906 to 1917. Prior to that he was a reader at Little Russian Mission on the Kuskokwim.

11. John Kilbuck, Journal to Edith, October 7, 1916, KC.

12. Mrs. Evans would, over the next two score years, become a legend in her own right up and down the river for her work in the transformation of regional health care. May Wynne's experiences during her years in Akiak have recently been published as *Life in Alaska: The Reminiscences of a Kansas Woman, 1916–1919*, ed. Dorothy Zimmerman.

13. John Kilbuck, Journal to Edith, October 21, 1916, 9–10, Box 8:19, KC.

14. Ibid., May 9, 1917.

15. Ibid., November 18, 1916, Box 8:22.

16. Ibid., November 26, 1916, Box 8:24.

17. Ibid., December 12, 1916, Box 8:25; ibid., March 23, 1918, Box 8:9.

18. Ibid., December 29, 1916, Box 8:26.

19. Anderson to John Kilbuck, February 25, 1917, Box 10, KC.

20. Ibid.

21. Reverend Arthur Butzin and his wife, Elsie, served the Moravian mission in Alaska from 1910 until 1931. On his arrival, Butzin took over the position of superintendent of the Alaska Moravian Mission, a position which he held throughout the Kilbucks' tenure in Akiak.

22. John Kilbuck, Journal to Edith, January 12, 1917, KC; ibid., February 23, 1917.

23. John Kilbuck, Annual Report of the Assistant Superintendent of the Western District, 1918, RBIA(M), Reel 37:252-58.

24. John Kilbuck to William Lopp, February 7, 1917, KC.

25. John Kilbuck, Journal to Edith, June 14, 1917, 6, KC.

26. Ibid., September 25, 1916; ibid, January 18, 1917; ibid., November 11, 1916, Box 8:21.

27. Ibid., September 14, 1917.

28. Ibid., August 19, 1917, Box 8:26; ibid., June 24, 1917, Box 8:17.

29. Ibid., July 27, 1917, 12, Box 8:25.

30. Ibid., July 23, 1917, 6.

31. Ibid., 7.

32. Ibid., July 28, 1917, Box 8:24.

33. Ibid., July 31, 1917, 3.

34. Ibid., November 18, 1916, 7, Box 8:9; ibid., April 20, 1917.

35. John Kilbuck, Annual Report, 1918, 27.

36. John Kilbuck, Journal to Edith, August 25, 1917, Box 8:27, KC.

37. Ibid., October 25, 1917.

38. Ibid., September 15, 1917, Box 8:33.

39. Ibid., February 12, 1918, 5.

40. Ibid., October 18, 1917; ibid., April 22, 1917, Box 8:13.

41. Ibid., November 5, 1917.

42. John Kilbuck, Annual Report, 1918, 22.

43. John Kilbuck to Edith, February 26, 1918, KC.

44. John Kilbuck, Journal to Edith, October 24, 1917, Box 8(7):1, KC.

45. Ibid., October 29, 1917.

46. Ibid., February 20, 1918, Box 8:6.

47. Ibid., June 24, 1918, Box 8:26.

48. Ibid., November 9, 1917, Box 8(7):4.

49. Ibid., October 7, 1917.

50. John Kilbuck, "Report of John H. Kilbuck, Assistant Superintendent of the Schools in the Western District," *Report of the Work of the Bureau of Education for the Natives of Alaska, 1917-1918*, 22.

51. Ibid., 23; John Kilbuck to Edith, April 26, 1918, 19, KC.

52. John Kilbuck to Edith, May 15, 1918, KC.

53. John Kilbuck, "Report of the Assistant Superintendent," in *Report, 1917-1918*, 23.

54. Ibid., 23-24.

55. John Kilbuck to Edith, June 24, 1918, Box 8:23, KC. Brightman, 1983.

56. John Kilbuck to Edith, February 11, 1918, 5, Box 8:7, KC. Brightman, 1983.

57. John Kilbuck to William Lopp, August 12, 1911, KC. Brightman, 1983, 446-50.

58. John Kilbuck to Edith, May 9, 1918, Box 8:21, KC.

59. John Kilbuck to Edith, June 2, 1918, Box 8:22, KC.
60. John Kilbuck to Edith, April 16, 1918, Box 8:18, KC.
61. John Kilbuck to Edith, February 24, 1918, KC.
62. John Kilbuck, March 26, 1918, Box 8:10, KC.
63. John Kilbuck, Annual Report, 1918, .
64. John Kilbuck to Edith, April 25, 1918, Box 8, KC.
65. John Kilbuck to Edith, July 6, 1918, Box 8, KC.
66. Ibid.
67. John Kilbuck to Edith, July 18, 1918, Box 8:25, KC.

Chapter 16. Akiak Work Resumed

1. *Proceedings of the Society of the United Brethren for Propagating the Gospel Among the Heathen*, September 24, 1919, 15.
2. John Kilbuck, "Proposed Orphanage," 63.
3. Fienup-Riordan, *The Nelson Island Eskimo*, 163–72.
4. John Kilbuck to Edith, August 4, 1919, Box 8, KC.
5. John Kilbuck to Edith, August 8, 1919, Box 8:30, KC.
6. John Kilbuck, "Proposed Orphanage," 67.
7. John Kilbuck to Edith, December 2, 1919, Box 8:32, KC.
8. John Kilbuck to Edith, December 10, 1919, Box 8:32, KC.
9. Ibid.
10. Ibid.
11. John Kilbuck to Edith, December 24, 1919, KC.
12. John Kilbuck to Edith, December 30, 1919, KC; John Kilbuck to Edith, January 1, 1920, KC.
13. John Kilbuck to Edith, January 2, 1920, KC.
14. Edith Kilbuck, Journal to John, July 25, 1919, Box 4:4, KC.
15. Ibid., August 19, 1919; ibid., August 9, 1920, Box 4:13.
16. Ibid., October 28, 1919; ibid., October 16, 1919.
17. Ibid., August 28, 1919, Box 4:5.
18. Ibid., October 1, 1919, Box 4:6; ibid., November 9, 1919.
19. Ibid., November 9, 1919; ibid., December 16, 1919; ibid., December 18, 1919, Box 4:7.
20. Edith Kilbuck, Diary, March 28, 1920, Box 4:10, KC; ibid., January 22, 1920.
21. Ibid., March 23, 1920; Edith Kilbuck, Journal to John, October 21, 1919, KC.
22. Edith Kilbuck to the children, February 10, 1920, Box 4:8, KC.
23. Edith Kilbuck to the children, October 13, 1919, Box 4:8, KC.
24. Edith Kilbuck to the children, July 1920, Box 4:12, KC.
25. John Kilbuck, Journal to Edith, March 14, 1921, Box 8:53, KC.
26. Edith Kilbuck, Diary, April 22, 1920, Box 4:11, KC.
27. Ibid., January 1, 1920, Box 4:8.
28. Ibid., August 15, 1919, September 8, 1919; ibid., June 16, 1920, Box 4:9.
29. John Kilbuck to the children, October 1921, Box 8:58, KC.
30. Edith Kilbuck, Diary, March 4, 1921, Box 4:16, KC; Fienup-Riordan, "Nick Charles, Sr.: Worker in Wood," *The Artist Behind the Work*, 45–54.
31. John Kilbuck, Journal to Edith, March 14, 1921, Box 8:53, KC.
32. Ibid., January 29, 1920; Edith Kilbuck, Diary, February 11, 1920, KC.
33. Edith Kilbuck, Diary, March 25, 1920, Box 4:10, KC; ibid., July 8, 1920.
34. Ibid., February 7, 1920, Box 4:8; ibid., May 31, 1920; ibid., July 4, 1920.
35. Ibid., September 5, 1920, Box 4:13.
36. Ibid. A show hall was opened in Bethel in 1924.
37. Ibid.

38. Edith Kilbuck to the children, August 25, 1920, Box 4:13, KC.

39. Edith Kilbuck to the children, November 11, 1920, Box 4:14, KC; Edith Kilbuck to John, December 12, 1920, Box 4:15, KC.

40. Edith Kilbuck to John, December 18, 1920, KC; Edith Kilbuck to the children, April 26, 1921, Box 4:17, KC.

41. Edith Kilbuck to John, March 24, 1921, Box 4:16, KC.

42. Edith Kilbuck, Diary, December 14, 1919, KC; Edith Kilbuck to the children, March 17, 1920, Box 4:10, KC.

43. Edith Kilbuck to the children, October 18, 1920, Box 4:14, KC.

44. Edith Kilbuck to the children, August 9, 1920, Box 4:13, KC; Edith Kilbuck to John, February 22, 1921, Box 4:16, KC.

45. John Kilbuck to Edith, March 21, 1921, Box 8:54, KC.

46. John Kilbuck to Edith, March 14, 1921, KC; John Kilbuck to Edith, March 21, 1921, KC.

47. John Kilbuck to Edith, March 23, 1921, KC.

Chapter 17. End of an Era

1. Edith Kilbuck, Diary, April 17, 1922, Box 4:21, KC.

2. Edith Kilbuck to the children, May 18, 1921, KC; Edith Kilbuck to the children, May 3, 1921, KC.

3. Edith Kilbuck to the children, June 19, 1921, KC.

4. Edith Kilbuck, Journal, August 7, 1921, Box 4:18, KC.

5. Ibid.

6. Edith Kilbuck, Diary, October 17, 1921, KC.

7. Edith Kilbuck, Journal, November 18, 1921, Box 4:20, KC; Edith Kilbuck, Mission Journal, November 24, 1921, KC; ibid., December 3, 1921.

8. John and Edith Kilbuck, "Semi-Annual Report of Akiak," July, 1921 to January, 1922," *The Proceedings*, 47.

9. Edith Kilbuck, Journal, January 31, 1922, KC.

10. Ibid., February 2, 1922.

11. Ibid.

12. Ibid., February 3, 1922.

13. Edith Kilbuck, Diary, April 17, 1922, Box 4:21, KC.

14. Ibid., February 4, 1922.

15. Ibid., March 20, 1922.

16. Ibid., May 19, 1922; ibid., May 29, 1922; Edith Kilbuck, Diary, June 6, 1922, Box 4:22, KC.

17. Edith Kilbuck, Diary, April 23, 1922, Box 4:21, KC.

18. Edith Kilbuck, Journal, May, 1922, KC.

19. Ibid., June 24, 1922.

20. Edith Kilbuck, Diary, April 28, 1922, Box 4:21, KC.

21. Edith Kilbuck, "Our Eskimo Orphanage and School: Needs That Can Be Supplied by Sewing Societies or Individuals," 7, Box 11:26, KC.

22. "So the Fijian chief said to the Methodist missionary: 'True—everything is true that comes from the white man's country; muskets and gunpowder are true, and your religion must be true'" (Marshall Sahlins, *Islands of History*, 38).

23. John Kilbuck, "Annual Report of . . . Akiak," in *Report, 1911–1912*, 22.

24. John Kilbuck, Annual Report, June 30, 1916, Box 7:4, KC.

25. William Lopp, February 7, 1939, in Gapp, *Kolerat Pitsiulret*, 20.

26. Wendell Oswalt, *Mission of Change in Alaska*. Oswalt has since revised this position in his most recent monograph, *Bashful No Longer*.

27. Aloysius, "Ordination Commentary," 17.

28. Lechat, "Evangelism and Colonialism," 7.

29. James Ducker, "Out of Harm's Way," 1.

30. Francis P. Prucha, "Two Roads to Conversion: Protestant and Catholic Missionaries in the Pacific Northwest," *Pacific Northwest Quarterly* 79:132.

31. Ibid., 136.

REFERENCES

Alaska Materials, Moravian Archives, Bethlehem, Pa.

Alaskan Russian Church Archives. St. Michael-Ikogmiut-Kolmakov and Yukon-Kuskokwim. Washington, D.C.: Manuscript Division, Library of Congress. Microfilm 139.

Aloysius, Bob. "Ordination Commentary." *Tundra Drums*, May 8, 1986, 17.

Amkan, Fr. Nikifor. "O sostoianii del v kvikhpakhskoi missii [On the condition of the Kvikhpak Mission]." *The American Messenger* 20 (1916): 556–57.

Anderson, Eva G. *Dog Team Doctor*. Caldwell, Idaho: Caxton, 1940.

Anderson, H. Dewey, and Walter C. Eells. *Alaska Natives: A Survey of Their Sociological and Educational Status*. Stanford, Calif.: Stanford University Press, 1935.

Archives of the Russian Orthodox Church in Alaska. Parish Records: Kvikhpak Mission. Juneau, Alaska: Alaska State Library. Microfilm 59. From original manuscripts located at St. Herman's Seminary, Kodiak, Alaska.

Bachman, Henry, T. "Account of Alaska Journey." In *The Proceedings of the Society of the United Brethren for Propagating the Gospel among the Heathen*. Bethlehem, Pa.: S.P.G., 1891.

Bakhtin, Mikhail. "Discourse in the Novel." In *The Dialogical Imagination*, edited by Michael Holquist. Austin: University of Texas Press, 1981.

Beidelman, T. O. *Colonial Evangelism*. Bloomington: Indiana University Press, 1982.

Benz, Ernst. *The Eastern Orthodox Church*. Garden City, N.Y.: Anchor Books, 1963.

Berkhofer, Robert F., Jr. *Salvation and the Savage*. Lexington, Ky: University of Kentucky Press, 1965.

Bethlehem Church. Diary, 1884. Moravian Archives, Bethlehem, Pa.

Black, Lydia. *Iakov Netsvetov: The Yukon Years 1845–1863*. Kingston, Ont.: Limestone Press, 1984.

————. "Ivan Pan'kov—An Architect of Aleut Literacy." *Arctic Anthropology* 14 (1977): 94–107.

Bockstoce, John R. *Whales, Ice and Men: The History of Whaling in the Western Arctic*. Seattle: University of Washington Press, 1986.

Bowden, Henry Warner. *American Indians and Christian Missions: Studies in Cultural Conflict*. Chicago: University of Chicago Press, 1981.

Brightman, Robert A. "Animal and Human in Rock Cree Religion and Subsistence." Ph.D. diss., University of Chicago, 1983.

Burch, Ernest S., Jr. "Traditional Eskimo Societies in Northwest Alaska." *Senri Ethnological Studies* 4 (1980): 253–304.

Burridge, Kenneth O. L. "Missionary Occasions." In *Mission, Church and Sect in Oceania*. Edited by J. A. Boutilier, D. T. Hughes, and S. W. Tiffany. Ann Arbor: University of Michigan Press, 1978.

Burwell, Ronald J. "Comment on Stipe: Anthropologists Versus Missionaries." *American Ethnologist* 21 (1980): 169.

Clifford, James. "On Ethnographic Authority." *Representations* 1 (1983): 118–46.

Clifford, James, and George E. Marcus. *Writing Culture: The Poetics and Politics of Ethnography*. Berkeley: University of California Press, 1986.

Comaroff, Jean, and John Comaroff. "Christianity and Colonialism in South Africa." *American Ethnologist* 13 (1986): 1–22.

Community of Bethel. Education History Series. Tape 2. Reflection on Trapping and Reindeer Herding. 1979. Untranscribed. Kuskokwim Community College, Bethel, Alaska.

Coser, L. A. *Greedy Institutions*. New York: Free Press, 1974.

de Schweinitz, Edmund. *The History of the Church Known as Unitas Fratrum or the Unity of the Brethren*. Bethlehem, Pa.: Moravian, 1901.

————. *The Life and Times of David Zeisberger*. Philadelphia: J. B. Lippincott and Company, 1870.

Detterer, Caroline. "Journal." In *The Proceedings of the Society of the United Brethren for Propagating the Gospel Among the Heathen*. Bethlehem, Pa.: S.P.G., 1889.

Documents Relative to the History of Alaska, 1936–1938, Alaska History Research Project. Alaska Church Collection, Vol. 1 and 2. Russian Orthodox Greek Catholic Church, Vol. 4. Russian-American Company Archives, Department of State Historical Archives, University of Alaska, Fairbanks.

Ducker, James. "Out of Harm's Way." Manuscript. 1989. Anchorage, Alaska.

Dumond, Don E. *The Eskimos and the Aleuts*. London: Thames and Hudson, 1977.

Dumont, Louis. *Homo Hierarchicus: The Caste System and Its Implications*. Translated by George Weidenfeld and Nicholson, Ltd. Chicago: University of Chicago Press, 1970.

Eskimo Heritage Project. The Stebbins Potlatch. Kawerak, Inc., Nome, Alaska, 1985.

Feit, Harvey. "Hunting and the Quest for Power: The James Bay Cree and Whitemen in the Twentieth Century." In *Native Peoples: The Canadian Experience*, edited by R. Bruce Morrison and C. Roderick Wilson. Toronto: McClelland and Stewart, 1986.

Fernandez, James W. "The Sound of Bells in a Christian Country: In Quest of the Historical Schweitzer." *Massachusetts Review*, Spring 1964, 357–62.

Fienup-Riordan, Ann. Alaska Mission History. Transcripts of Translations of Interviews with the Author, 1985–1990. Anchorage, Alaska. Prepared with the support of the National Endowment for the Humanities.

———. "The Mask: The Eye of the Dance." *Arctic Anthropology* 24 (1987): 40–55.

———. *The Nelson Island Eskimo*. Anchorage: Alaska Pacific University Press, 1983.

———. "Nick Charles, Sr.: Worker in Wood." In *The Artist Behind the Work*. Fairbanks, Alaska: University of Alaska Museum, 1986.

———. "Regional Groups on the Yukon-Kuskokwim Delta." In *The Central Yupik Eskimos*. Supplementary issue edited by Ernest S. Burch, Jr. *Études/Inuit/Studies* 8 (1984): 63–93.

———. Transcripts and Translations of Interviews with Yup'ik Elders, 1977–1987. Tapes 1–99. Unpublished manuscripts compiled for the Nelson Island Oral History Project. Prepared with the support of the Alaska Humanities Forum, Anchorage, Alaska.

———. *When Our Bad Season Comes: A Cultural Account of Subsistence Harvesting and Harvest Disruption on the Yukon Delta*. Aurora 1. Alaska Anthropological Association, 1986.

———, ed. *The Yup'ik Eskimos as Described in the Travel Journals and Ethnographic Accounts of John and Edith Kilbuck, 1885–1900*. Kingston, Ont: Limestone Press, 1988.

Fortuine, Robert. "Epidemics II: Western and Northern Alaska." Manuscript. 1988. Anchorage, Alaska.

Friday, Joe. Interview (interviewer unknown). Translated by Louise Leonard. San Francisco: Lansburg Productions.

Fries, Adelaide L. *Customs and Practices of the Moravian Church*. Bethlehem, Pa.: Commenius Press, 1949.

Gapp, S. H. *Kolerat Pitsiulret or True Stories of the Early Days of the Moravian Mission on the Kuskokwim*. Bethlehem, Pa.: Commenius Press, 1936.

Gittings, Robert. *The Nature of Biography*. Seattle: University of Washington Press, 1978.

Grant, John Webster. *Moon in Wintertime: Missionaries and the Indians of Canada in Encounter Since 1534*. Toronto: University of Toronto Press, 1984.

Gray, Elma E. *Wilderness Christians: The Moravian Mission to the Delaware Indians*. Ithaca, N.Y.: Cornell University Press, 1956.

Hamilton, J. Taylor, and Kenneth Gardner Hamilton. *History of the Moravian Church, 1722–1957*. Bethlehem, Pa.: Moravian, 1967.

Hamilton, Kenneth Gardner. *John Ettwein and the Moravian Church During the Revolutionary Period*. In *Transactions of the Moravian Historical Society* 12, part 4. Bethlehem, Pa.: Times Publishing Co., 1940.

Harding, Susan F. "Convicted by the Holy Spirit: The Rhetoric of Fundamental Baptist Conversion." *American Ethnologist* 14 (1987): 167–81.

Henkelman, James W., and Kurt H. Vitt. *The History of the Alaska Moravian Church 1885–1985: Harmonious to Dwell*. Bethel, Alaska: Moravian Seminary and Archives, 1985.

Huber, Mary Taylor. *The Bishop's Progress: A Historical Ethnography of Catholic Missionary Experience.* Washington and London: Smithsonian Institution Press, 1988.
Huebner, Francis C. *Charles Kilbuck: An Indian's Story of the Border Wars of the American Revolution.* Washington, D.C.: Herbert Publications Co., 1902.
Jackson, Sheldon. *U.S. Bureau of Education Report on the Introduction of Domesticated Reindeer in Alaska.* Vol. 6. Washington, D.C.: G.P.O., 1896.
Jacobson, Steven A. *Yup'ik Eskimo Dictionary.* Fairbanks, Alaska: University of Alaska, Alaska Native Language Center, 1984.
Kan, Sergei, ed. "Native Cultures and Christianity in Northern North America: Selected Papers from a Symposium." *Arctic Anthropology* 24 (1987): 1–66.
Karp, Ivan. "Review of *Colonial Evangelism,* by T. O. Beidelman." *American Ethnologist* 4 (1984): 215–16.
Keesing, Roger M. *Cultural Anthropology: A Contemporary Perspective.* New York, N.Y.: Holt, Rinehart, and Winston, 1976.
Khlebnikov, K. T. *Russkaia Amerika v Neopublikovannykh Zapiskakh. K. T. Khlebnikov* (Russian America in unpublished notes of K. T. Khlebnikov). Edited by R. G. Liapunova and S. G. Fedorova. Leningrad: Nauka, 1979.
Kilbuck, Edith M. "Journal. August 11, 1887 to September 19, 1887." *The Moravian* 33, no. 37 (1888): 584–85.
———. "Journal. September 21, 1887 to June 8, 1888." *The Moravian* 33, no. 38 (1888): 598–601.
———. "Journal. September 3, 1890 to September 15, 1890. (Part 1)." *The Moravian* 37, no. 16 (1892): 248–49.
———. "Journal. September 15, 1890 to October 5, 1890. (Part 2)." *The Moravian* 37, no. 17 (1892): 264–65.
———. "Journal. October 8, 1890 to October 15, 1890. (Part 3)." *The Moravian* 37, no. 18 (1892): 280.
———. "Journal. October 15, 1890 to November 27, 1890. (Part 4)." *The Moravian* 37, no. 19 (1892): 295–96.
———. "Journal. January 5, 1891. (Part 5)." *The Moravian* 37, no. 21 (1892): 326–28.
———. "Journal. January 10, 1891 to February 1, 1891." *The Moravian* 37, no. 22 (1892): 343–44.
———. "Journal. February 1, 1891 to February 12, 1891. (Part 6)." *The Moravian* 37, no. 23 (1892): 360.
———. "Journal. February 16, 1891 to March 9, 1891. (Part 7)." *The Moravian* 37, no. 24 (1892): 375–76.
———. "Journal. March 11, 1891 to March 21, 1891. (Part 8)." *The Moravian* 37, no. 27 (1892): 424.
———. "Journal. March 24, 1891 to March 29, 1891. (Part 9)." *The Moravian* 37, no. 28 (1892): 441.
———. "Journal. April 1, 1891 to April 11, 1891. (Part 10)." *The Moravian* 37, no. 29 (1892): 456–57.
———. "Journal. April 15, 1891 to June 18, 1891. (Part 11)." *The Moravian* 37, no. 31 (1892): 488–89.
———. "Journal. June 21, 1891 to July 4, 1891. (Part 12)." *The Moravian* 37, no. 32 (1892): 503.

———. "Journal. July 6, 1891 to July 13, 1891. (Part 13)." *The Moravian* 37, no. 33 (1892): 520.

———. "Journal. Extracts. Bethel, Alaska. August 8, 1893 to June 16, 1894." *The Proceedings of the Society of the United Brethren for Propagating the Gospel Among the Heathen*. Bethlehem, Pa.: S.P.G., 1894.

———. "Journal to her Father, Joseph Romig. June 12, 1888 to July 4, 1888." *The Moravian* 33, no. 48 (1888): 765.

———. "Journal to her Father, Joseph Romig. July 13, 1888 to July 28, 1888." *The Moravian* 33, no. 49 (1888): 781.

———. "Journal to her Father, Joseph Romig. July 3, 1890 to July 10, 1890. (Part 1)." *The Moravian* 35, no. 52 (1890): 824–25.

———. "Journal to her Father, Joseph Romig. July 11, 1890 to July 17, 1890. (Concluded)." *The Moravian* 35, no. 53 (1890): 840.

———. "Journal to My Dear Father, Joseph Romig. Extracts. August 2, 1886 to August 22, 1886." *The Moravian* 33, no. 3 (1888): 35–36.

———. "Journal to My Dear Father, Joseph Romig. Extracts. August 24, 1886 to September 13, 1886." *The Moravian* 33, no. 4 (1888): 52.

———. "Journal to My Dear Father, Joseph Romig. Extracts. September 15 to November 30, 1886." *The Moravian* 33, no. 5 (1888): 72–73.

———. "Journal to My Dear Father, Joseph Romig. Extracts. December 3, 1886 to January 23, 1887." *The Moravian* 33, no. 6 (1888): 88–89.

———. "Journal to My Dear Father, Joseph Romig. Extracts. January 30, 1887 to April 1, 1887." *The Moravian* 33, no. 7 (1888): 100–101.

———. "Journal to My Dear Father, Joseph Romig. Extracts. April 3, 1887 to April 28, 1887." *The Moravian* 33, no. 8 (1888): 117.

———. "Journal to My Dear Father, Joseph Romig. Extracts. Concluded. May 2, 1887 to June 4, 1887." *The Moravian* 33, no. 9 (1888): 133.

———. "Letter from Bethel. January 23, 1897." *The Moravian* 42, no. 21 (1897): 328.

———. "Letter from Bethel. March 20 to April 23, 1889." *The Moravian* 34, no. 34 (1889): 530–33.

———. "Letter from Bethel. Extracts. May 23, 1889." *The Moravian* 34, no. 32 (1889): 498.

———. "Letter from Bethel to Miss Amanda Jones, of Bethlehem, Pa. July 21, 1887." *The Moravian* 32, no. 47 (1887): 45.

———. "Letter from Bethel to unidentified Brother. February 14, 1895." *The Moravian* 40, no. 26 (1895): 400.

———. "Letter from Bethel to unidentified Brother. July 24, 1894." *The Moravian* 40, no 5 (1895): 71.

———. "Letter from Bethel to [the] Women's Foreign Mission Society of the M. E. Church at Independence, Kansas. July 13, 1886. (Part 1)." *The Moravian* 32, no. 8 (1887): 116–17.

———. "Letter from Bethel to the Women's Mission Society of the M. E. Church of Independence, Kansas. July 13, 1886. (Concluded)." *The Moravian* 33, no. 9 (1887): 132–33.

———. "Letter from Unalaska. June 23, 1893." *The Moravian* 38, no. 31 (1893): 488.

————. "Letter to the Brethren. July 3, 1893." *The Moravian* 38, no. 35 (1893): 547.

————. "Letter to Brother de Schweinitz. June 5, 1894." *The Moravian* 39, no. 44 (1894): 695–96.

————. "Letter to her Father, Joseph Romig. Extracts. August 5, 1893." *The Moravian* 39, no. 9 (1894): 137.

————. "Letters to her Father, Mr. Joseph Romig. August 22, 1885 to August 31, 1885." *The Moravian* 33, no. 24 (1887): 371–72.

Kilbuck, John Henry. "Annual Report of the Mission in Alaska from June, 1885 to June, 1886." *The Moravian* 31, no. 30 (1886): 472–73.

————. "The Annual Report of the Mission at Bethel, Alaska, 1893." *The Moravian* 38, no. 35 (1893): 547–48.

————. "[Annual] Report of the United States Public School at Akiak, on the Kuskokwim River, in Western Alaska." In *Report of the Work of the Bureau of Education for the Natives of Alaska. 1914–1915*. U.S. Bureau of Education, Dept. of the Interior, Bulletin no. 47. Washington, D.C.: G.P.O., 1916.

————. "Annual Report of the United States Public School at Akiak, on the Kuskokwim River, in Western Alaska." In *Report of the Work of the Bureau of Education for the Natives of Alaska. 1915–1916*. U.S. Bureau of Education, Dept. of the Interior, Bulletin no. 32. Washington, D.C.: G.P.O., 1917.

————. "Annual Report of the United States Public School at Akiak, a Remote Village on the Kuskokwim River, Hitherto Without a School." In *Report of the Work of the Bureau of Education for the Natives of Alaska. 1911–1912*. U.S. Bureau of Education, Dept. of the Interior, Bulletin no. 36. Washington, D.C.: G.P.O., 1913.

————. "Journal. December 5 to 28, 1888." *The Moravian* 35, no. 4 (1890): 56–57.

————. "Journal. January 10 to 21, 1889." *The Moravian* 35, no. 6 (1890): 88–89.

————. "Journal. January 25 to February 1, 1889." *The Moravian* 35, no. 7 (1890): 104.

————. "Journal. February 4 to 12, 1889." *The Moravian* 35, no. 8 (1890): 120.

————. "Journal. Extracts. During the winter of 1893–94. November 17 to December 8, 1893. Over the Tundra to Buy Frozen Fish." *The Moravian* 40, no. 2 (1895): 19–20.

————. "Journal. Extracts. During the winter of 1893–94. (cont.) December 6 to December 10, 1893." *The Moravian* 40, no. 3 (1895): 35.

————. "Journal. Extracts. During the winter of 1893–94. (cont.) December 11, 1893 to January 11, 1894." *The Moravian* 40, no. 5 (1895): 67–68.

————. "Journal. Extracts. During the winter of 1893–94. (cont.) January 31 to February 3, 1894." *The Moravian* 40, no. 6 (1895): 84–85.

————. "Journal. Extracts. During the winter of 1893–94. (cont.) February 4 to May 6, 1894." *The Moravian* 40, no. 7 (1895): 99–100.

————. "Journal. Trip From Bethel to Viniesahle. July 26, 1890 to July 30, 1890." *The Moravian* 36, no. 34 (1891): 535–36.

————. "Journal. [Trip] From Bethel to Viniesahle in a Bidarka. Concluded. August 9, 1890 to August 21, 1890." *The Moravian* 36, no. 36 (1891): 566–67.

————. "Letter. July 19, 1889." *The Moravian* 34, no. 40 (1889): 627–28.

————. "Letter. January 16, 1890." *The Moravian* 35, no. 29 (1890): 449.

————. "Letter from Bethel. December 26, 1889." *The Moravian* 35, no. 29 (1890): 449.

————. "Letter from Bethel. July 14, 1890." *The Moravian* 35, no. 51 (1890): 808.

————. "Letter from Bethel to Brother Bachman. July 22, 1889." *The Moravian* 34, no. 41 (1889): 648.

————. "Letter from Bethel to Brother De Schweinitz. June, 1891." *The Moravian* 36, no. 33 (1891): 520–21.

————. "Letter from Bethel to the Provincial Elders' Conference. August 4, 1893." *The Moravian* 38, no. 44 (1893): 696.

————. "Letter from Bethel to Rev. Prof. A. Schultz. July 3, 1891." *The Moravian* 36, no. 37 (1891): 583.

————. "Letter from on board steamer 'Dora' to Brethren of the Moravian Church. July 3, 1893." *The Moravian* 38, no 35 (1893): 546–48.

————. "Letter from on board steamer 'Dora' to Brother Bachman. June 29, 1892." *The Moravian* 37, no. 34 (1892): 532.

————. "Letter from Kuskokwim Bay. July 3, 1893." *The Moravian* 38, no. 35 (1893): 547.

————. "Letter to Bishop de Schweinitz. August 12, 1885." *The Moravian* 30, no. 45 (1885): 712–13.

————. "Letter to Bishop de Schweinitz from Bethel. August 3, 1887." *The Moravian* 32, no. 42 (1887): 658–59.

————. "Letter to Brother Wolff. November 28, 1887." *The Moravian* 33, no. 24 (1888): 376–77.

————. "Letter to Friends. May 4, 1885." *The Moravian* 30, no. 22 (1885): 340.

————. "Letter to the Provincial Elders' Conference. June 2, 1888." *The Moravian* 33, no. 32 (1888): 497–98.

————. "Letter to Rev. E. de Schweinitz. December 1888." *The Moravian* 34, no. 33 (1889): 520–21.

————. "Letter to Weinland from Bethel. July 26, 1887." *The Moravian* 32, no. 46 (1887): 727–28.

————. "Letters from Bro. Kilbuck." *The Moravian* 35, no. 29 (1890): 449–50.

————. "Letters from the Kuskokwim. January 22, 1897." *The Moravian* 42, no. 21 (1897): 328.

————. "Letters to Bishop E. de Schweinitz. June 17 and June 21, 1885." *The Moravian* 30, no. 31 (1885): 488–89.

————. "Log Book of the 'Swan' of Bethel, Alaska. Extracts. August 6 to August 18, 1896." *The Moravian* 42, no. 36 (1897): 569.

————. "Log Book of the 'Swan' of Bethel, Alaska. Extracts. August 19 to 29, 1896." *The Moravian* 42, no. 38 (1897): 602–603.

————. "Proposed Orphanage and Training School on the Kuskokwim." In *The Proceedings of the Society of the United Brethren for Propagating the Gospel Among the Heathen*. Bethlehem, Pa: S.P.G., 1919.

————. "The Report of Bethel for 1892. June 7, 1892." *The Moravian* 37, no. 33 (1892): 514–16.

————. "Report of John H. Kilbuck, Assistant Superintendent of Schools in the Western District." In *Report of the Work of the Bureau of Education for the Natives of Alaska. 1917–1918*. U.S. Bureau of Education, Dept. of the Interior, Bulletin no. 40. Washington D.C.: G.P.O., 1919.

————. "Report of John H. Kilbuck, Detailed as Assistant Superintendent of the Western District. In *Report of the Work of the Bureau of Education for the Natives of Alaska. 1916–1917*. U.S. Bureau of Education, Dept. of the Interior, Bulletin no. 5. Washington, D.C.: G.P.O., 1918.

————. "The Report of the Missionaries at the Kuskokwim River. June 2, 1888." In *The Proceedings of the Society of the United Brethren for Propagating the Gospel Among the Heathen*. Bethlehem, Pa.: S.P.G., 1888.

————. "Report to the Provincial Elders' Conference. May 29, 1890." *The Moravian* 35, no. 35 (1890): 551–53.

————. "Report to the Provincial Elders' Conference. May 30, 1889." *The Moravian* 34, no. 33 (1889): 519–21.

————. "Second Annual Report of the Mission in Alaska. May 31, 1887." *The Moravian* 33, no. 31 (1887): 486–88.

Kilbuck, John H. and Edith M. Kilbuck. "Semi-Annual Report of Akiak, July, 1921 to January, 1922." In *The Proceedings of the Society of the United Brethren for Propagating the Gospel Among the Heathen*. Bethlehem, Pa.: S.P.G., 1922.

Korchinskii, Iakov. "Iz Putevykh Zametok Pravoslavnago Kvikpakhsko-Kusko-kvimskago Missionera Sviashchennika Ioanna Korchinskago [From the travel notes of the Orthodox missionary priest, Iakov Korchinskii of the Kvikhpak–Kuskokwim Mission, 1896]." *Russian Orthodox American Messenger* 2 (1896): 653–59.

————. "Nekrolog" (Obituary). *Russian Orthodox American Messenger* 3 (1899): 629–30.

Krauss, Michael E. *Native Peoples and Languages of Alaska*. Map. Fairbanks, Alaska: University of Alaska, Alaska Native Language Center, 1975.

Lamb, May Wynne. *Life in Alaska: The Reminiscences of a Kansas Woman, 1916–1919*. Edited by Dorothy Wynne Zimmerman. Lincoln: University of Nebraska Press, 1988.

Lantis, Margaret. "Folk Medicine and Hygiene, Lower Kuskokwim and Nunivak–Nelson Island Area." *Anthropological Papers of the University of Alaska* 8 (1959): 1–75.

————. "The Reindeer Industry in Alaska." *Arctic* 3 (1950): 27–44.

————. "The Religion of the Eskimos." In *Forgotten Religions*. Edited by Vergilius Ferm. Philadelphia: Philosophical Library, 1950.

————. "The Social Culture of the Nunivak Eskimo." *Transactions of the American Philosophical Society* 35 (1946): 153–323.

Lechat, R. "Evangelism and Colonialism." *Eskimo* (New Series) 33 (1976): 3–7.

Lopp, William. Collection. Library, University of Oregon, Eugene, Ore.

Marcus, George E. and Michael Fischer. *Anthropology as Cultural Critique*. Chicago: University of Chicago Press, 1986.

Martin, Calvin. *Keepers of the Game: Indian–Animal Relationships and the Fur Trade*. Berkeley: University of California Press, 1978.

Mather, Elsie. *Cauyarnariuq* [A time for drumming]. Bethel, Alaska: Lower Kuskokwim School District, 1985.

Maunier, René. *The Sociology of Colonies*. London: Routledge and Kegan Paul, 1949.

McCartny, Allen, ed. "The Frozen Family from Utqiagvik Site, Barrow, Alaska. Papers from a Symposium." *Arctic Anthropology* 21 (1984): 1–154.

Michael, Henry, ed. *Lieutenant Zagoskin's Travels in Russian America, 1842–1844*. Arctic Institute of North America, Anthropology of the North: Translations from Russian Sources, no. 7. Toronto: University of Toronto Press, 1967.

Missionaries at Bethel. "Letter to the Rev. E. T. Kluge, President of P.E.C. January 13, 1896." *The Moravian* 41, no. 19 (1896): 293–94.

―――. "Report of Bethel and its Filials for the Year 1896–1897." In *The Proceedings of the Society of the United Brethren for Propagating the Gospel Among the Heathen*. Bethlehem, Pa.: S.P.G., 1897.

―――. "Report of Bethel for the Year 1890 to 1891. June 1, 1891." *The Moravian* 36, no. 32 (1891): 502–504.

―――. "Report of Bethel for the Year 1893–4." In *The Proceedings of the Society of the United Brethren for Propagating the Gospel Among the Heathen*. Bethlehem, Pa.: S.P.G., 1894.

―――. "Report of the Mission at Bethel, 1894–95. June 1895." *The Moravian* 40, no. 39 (1895): 606–607; 40, no. 40 (1895): 623–24.

Moravian Archives, Bethlehem, Pa.

Morrison, Kenneth M. "Discourse and the Accommodation of Values: Toward a Revision of Mission History." *Journal of the American Academy of Religion* 53 (1985): 365–82.

Morrow, Phyllis. "It is Time for Drumming: A Summary of Recent Research on Yup'ik Ceremonialism." In *The Central Yupik Eskimos*, Supplementary issue edited by Ernest S. Burch, Jr. *Études/Inuit/Studies* 8 (1984): 113–40.

Neck, Helper. "Letter from Nanivagnagtlek." *The Moravian Missionary*, November, 1921.

Nelson, Edward W. "A Sledge Journey in the Delta of the Yukon, Northern Alaska." *Proceedings of the Royal Geographical Society*, New Series, 4 (1882): 669–70.

―――. *The Eskimo about Bering Strait. Eighteenth Annual Report of the Bureau of American Ethnology*. 1896–1897. Part 1. Washington, D.C.: G.P.O., 1899. Reprint, Washington, D.C.: Smithsonian Institution Press, 1983.

Orth, Donald J. *Dictionary of Alaska Place Names*. U.S. Geological Survey Professional Paper 567. Washington, D.C.: G.P.O., 1967.

Oswalt, Wendell H. *Alaskan Eskimos*. Scranton, Pa.: Chandler Publishing Co., 1967.

―――. *Bashful No Longer: An Alaskan Eskimo Ethnohistory, 1778–1988*. Norman: University of Oklahoma Press, 1990.

―――. "Ethnicity or Ethnocide: An Alaskan Eskimo Case Study." Manuscript. 1986. University of California, Los Angeles.

―――. "Historical Population in Western Alaska and Migration Theory." *Anthropological Papers of the University of Alaska* 11 (1962–1963): 1–14.

―――. *Historic Settlements Along the Kuskokwim River, Alaska*. Alaska State Library Historical Monograph 7. Juneau, Alaska: Alaska Division of State Libraries and Museums, 1986.

————. *Mission of Change in Alaska: Eskimos and Moravians on the Kuskokwim.* San Marino, Calif.: Huntington Library, 1963.

————. "The Kuskowagamiut." In *This Land Was Theirs.* New York, N.Y.: John Wiley and Sons, 1973.

Petroff, Ivan. *Report on the Population, Industries, and Resources of Alaska, Tenth Census of the United States, Special Report.* Vol. 8. Washington, D.C.: G.P.O., 1884.

Pierce, Richard. "New Light on Ivan Petroff, Historian of Alaska." *Pacific Northwest Quarterly* 59 (1968): 1–10.

Porter, Robert P. *Report on the Population and Resources of Alaska at the Eleventh Census, 1890.* Washington, D.C.: G.P.O., 1893.

Provincial Elders' Conference. Minutes. Records, 1884–1927. Moravian Archives, Bethlehem, Pennsylvania.

Prucha, Francis P. "Two Roads to Conversion: Protestant and Catholic Missionaries in the Pacific Northwest." *Pacific Northwest Quarterly* 79 (1988): 130–37.

Ray, Dorothy Jean. *The Eskimos of Bering Strait, 1650–1898.* Seattle: University of Washington Press, 1975.

Records of the Bureau of Indian Affairs. General Correspondence of the Alaska Division of the Office of Education, 1903–1935. Record Group 75. National Archives. Washington, D.C.

Reed, E. Irene, Osahito Miyaoka, Steven Jacobson, Paschal Afcan, and Michael Krauss. *Yup'ik Eskimo Grammar.* Fairbanks, Alaska: University of Alaska, Alaska Native Language Center, 1977.

Ridington, Robin. "From Hunt Chief to Prophet: Beaver Indian Dreamers and Christianity." *Arctic Anthropology* 24 (1987): 8–18.

Romig, Joseph. Papers. Moravian Archives, Bethlehem, Pa.

Sahlins, Marshall. *Culture and Practical Reason.* Chicago: University of Chicago Press, 1976.

————. *Islands of History.* Chicago: University of Chicago Press, 1985.

————. "Social Science; or The Tragic Western Sense of Human Imperfections." Hillsdale Lecture, University of Wisconsin-Madison, April 30, 1986.

Salamone, Frank A. "Anthropologists and Missionaries: Competition or Reciprocity?" *Human Organization* 36 (1977): 407–12.

Schneider, David M. "Notes Toward a Theory of Culture." In *Meanings in Anthropology,* edited by K. Basso and H. Selby. Albuquerque: University of New Mexico Press, 1976.

Schneider, Jane, and Shirley Lindenbaum. "Frontiers of Christian Evangelism: Essays in Honor of Joyce Riegelhaupt." *American Ethnologist* 14 (1987): 1–8.

Schultze, Augustus. *Grammar & Vocabulary of the Eskimo Language of Northwestern Alaska, Kuskokwim District.* Bethlehem, Pa.: Moravian Publishing Co., 1894.

Schwalbe, Anna B. *Dayspring on the Kuskokwim.* Bethlehem, Pa.: The Moravian, 1951.

Schwarze, William Nathaniel. *History of the Moravian College and Theological Seminary.* Bethlehem, Pa.: Times Publishing Co., 1910.

Scollon, Ronald, and Suzanne B. K. Scollon. *Interethnic Communication.* Fairbanks, Alaska: University of Alaska, Alaska Native Language Center, 1980.

Shaw, Robert D. "The Expansion and Survival of the Norton Tradition on the Yukon-Kuskokwim Delta." *Arctic Anthropology* 19 (1982): 59–73.

Smaby, Beverly Prior. *The Transformation of Moravian Bethlehem: From Communal Mission to Family Economy.* Philadelphia: University of Pennsylvania Press, 1988.

Smith, Barbara S. *Russian Orthodoxy in Alaska.* Anchorage: Alaska Historical Commission, 1980.

Society for Propagating the Gospel, Minutes of the Society of the United Brethren for Propagating the Gospel Among the Heathen. Moravian Archives, Bethlehem, Pa.

Stipe, Claude E. "Anthropologists Versus Missionaries: The Influence of Presuppositions." *Current Anthropology* 21 (1980): 165–79.

Stocker, Rev. Harry E. "The Moravian Church and Its Mission Work." *The Moravian* 66 (1921): 30.

Tanner, Adrian. *Bringing Home Animals: Religious Ideology and Mode of Production of the Mistassini Memorial Cree Hunters.* New York, N.Y.: St. Martin's Press, 1979.

Turner, Victor, and Edward Bruner, eds. *The Anthropology of Experience.* Urbana: University of Illinois Press, 1986.

VanStone, James W. "Some Aspects of Religious Change among Native Inhabitants in West Alaska and Northwest Territories." *Arctic Anthropology* 2 (1964): 21–24.

———. "V. S. Kromchenko's Coastal Explorations in Southwestern Alaska, 1822." *Fieldiana* (Chicago: Field Museum of Natural History) 64 (1973).

Veniaminov, Ioann. "Instructions of Bishop Innocent to Priests Under His Jurisdiction. Reiterated by Bishop Tikhon, 1899. Part Second: Special Directions Concerning Instructions, Public Worship, and Treatment of Natives, etc." (1841) *Russian Orthodox American Messenger* 3, no 20. (1899): 534–43; 3, no. 21 (1899); 564–74.

Wagner, Roy. *The Invention of Culture.* Chicago: University of Chicago Press, 1975.

———. *Symbols That Stand for Themselves.* Chicago: University of Chicago Press, 1986.

Weber, Caroline. "Diary, December 10, 1890." *The Moravian* 36 (1890): 787.

Weber, Ernest L. "A Trip to Kolmokovsky and Beyond. Extracts from Bro. Weber's Diary. July 23, 1889 to June 2, 1890." *The Moravian,* 35 no. 41 (1890): 648.

———. "Diary." *The Moravian* 36, no. 37 (1891): 583.

Weinland, William H. "To Friends, May 19." *The Periodical Accounts Relating to the Missions of the Church of the United Brethren* 33 (1884): 127–28, 131, 169, 204–205, 266.

———. "Letter." *The Little Missionary,* April 1885, 691.

———. "Letter." *The Little Missionary,* June 1885, 694.

———. "Letter." *The Moravian* 30, no. 22 (1885): 344.

———. "Letter from Bethel. March 10, 1886. (Concluded)." *The Moravian* 31, no. 46 (1886): 723–24.

———. "Letter From Bethel. Letter First. January 20, 1887." *The Moravian* 32, no. 33 (1887): 520.

————. "Letter from Bethel. Letter Second. January 20, 1887." *The Moravian* 32, no. 34 (1887): 536–37.

————. "Letter from Bethel. Letter Third. (Part 1 of 2). January 20, 1887." *The Moravian* 32, no. 35 (1887): 552–53.

————. "Letter from Bethel. Letter Third. (Part 2 of 2). January 20, 1887." *The Moravian* 32, no. 36 (1887): 568–69.

————. "Letter from Bethel. Concluding Letter." *The Moravian* 32, no. 44 (1887): 697.

————. "Letter from Bethel to the Provincial Board. May 4, 1885." *The Moravian* 39, no. 20 (1885): 312.

————. "Report of the Missionary Exploration Expedition to Alaska. (Part I). 1884." *The Moravian* 30, no. 1 (1885): 5–6.

————. "Report of the Missionary Exploration Expedition to Alaska. (Part II). 1884." *The Moravian* 30, no. 6 (1885): 88–89.

————. "Report of the Missionary Exploration Expedition to Alaska. (Part III). 1884." *The Moravian* 30, no. 10 (1885): 152–53.

————. "Report of the Missionary Exploration Expedition to Alaska. (Part IV). 1884." *The Moravian* 30, no. 11 (1885): 168–69.

Weyer, Edward M., Jr. *The Eskimos, Their Environment and Folkways.* New Haven, Conn.: Yale University Press, 1932.

Wolfe, Robert. "Alaska's Great Sickness, 1900: An Epidemic of Measles and Influenza in a Virgin Soil Population." *Proceedings of the American Philosophical Society* 126 (1982): 90–121.

Woodbury, Anthony. "Rhetorical Structure in Central Alaskan Yup'ik Eskimo Traditional Narrative." In *Native American Discourse*, edited by Joel Sherzer and Anthony C. Woodbury. Cambridge: Cambridge University Press, 1987.

Zeisberger, David. American Province Baptismal Records for 1789. Moravian Archives, Bethlehem, Pennsylvania.

INDEX

413